Dr Sam Willis is one of the world's leading authorities on the sailing navy. He is an Honorary Fellow at the University of Exeter's Centre for Maritime Historical Studies and a Fellow of the Royal Historical Society. He has consulted widely on maritime affairs for clients including the BBC, Channel 4 and Christie's. He is the author of several books on naval and maritime history including the *Hearts of Oak* trilogy and the highly successful *Fighting Ships* series.

'A must-read account of the life of a man who embodies a forgotten and under valued period in Britain's maritime history.'   Dan Snow

'A superb chronicler of naval warfare . . . Willis has done a tremendous job of reassessing this neglected period in our rich naval history.'
Mail on Sunday

'Willis is a magnificent describer of the realities of fighting ships at sea.'
Sunday Times

'John Benbow is more than a man, and this is more than a biography . . . Willis' book is a notable piece of naval historical writing . . . and is highly recommended.'   *Navy News*

'Fascinating . . . one of the best naval biographies to appear for many years.'
BBC History Magazine

THE
ADMIRAL
BENBOW

Sam Willis

Quercus

First published in Great Britain in 2010 by Quercus

This paperback edition published in 2011 by
Quercus
55 Baker Street
7th Floor, South Block
London
WIU 8EW

A CIP catalogue record for this book is available
from the British Library

ISBN 978 1 84916 037 7

10 9 8 7 6 5 4 3 2 1

Text and plates designed and typeset by Helen Ewing
Printed and bound in Great Britain by Clays Ltd, St Ives plc

THE HEARTS OF OAK TRILOGY

This is the second book of the *Hearts of Oak* trilogy, which explores three of the most iconic and yet largely unexplored stories of the 'Great Age of Sail'. *The Fighting Temeraire*, *The Admiral Benbow* and *The Glorious First of June*, are the biographies of a ship, a man and a battle that will splice together to form a narrative of an era that stretches from the English Civil War of the 1640s to the coming of steam two centuries later. This 'Great Age of Sail' was once written about in heroic terms but many of those legends have since been overlooked. The details of the stories themselves have become confused and the reasons behind the formation of those legends ignored. With more than a century of professional naval history to draw from, together with new access to previously restricted archives, now is the time to look afresh at those stories of heroism from the perspective of the modern historian; now is the time to understand how and why *The Fighting Temeraire*, *The Admiral Benbow* and *The Glorious First of June* became legends.

> Heart of oak are our ships, jolly tars are our men,
> We always are ready; Steady, boys, steady!
> We'll fight and we'll conquer again and again.

> D. GARRICK, *Heart of Oak* (1759)

Acknowledgements

I am heavily indebted to a number of people who have made this book better than it otherwise would have been. Peter Le Fevre and David Davies have been invaluable guides through the bewildering forest of seventeenth-century naval archives and both have been more generous with their knowledge and time than I deserve. Frank Fox has helped enormously with the ships of the period. Chris Donnithorne has introduced me to new sources for Benbow's career. Andrew Little has negotiated some tricky Dutch archives, and Lucy Morris helped dig for the irritatingly elusive Benbow letters. Andrew Hopper, David Smith, Malcolm Wanklyn, Barry Trinder and Rob Cottrell all helped in one way or another with Benbow's early years. Roger Knight, Nicholas Roger and Michael Duffy have all shown interest and support as always. Bill Benbow, a descendant of the Admiral, helped find a poem, and his own research into the Admiral's life proved valuable time and again. Doug McCarthy at the National Maritime Museum was particularly resourceful in my search for Benbow's ships. Henry Kriegstein very kindly allowed me to use an image of one of his beautiful ship models and a portrait of Benbow. Andrew Bond is a talented and generous wordsmith. Thank you to those correspondents who have generously contributed their expertise to correct errors which have come to light since the hardback edition.

Thank you all.

For Tors

'. . . more valuable than the Indies.'*

*From a eulogy on Admiral Benbow by Robert Park, 1704

Come all ye seamen bold, lend an ear, lend an ear
Come all ye seamen bold, lend an ear
'Tis of our Admiral's fame
Brave Benbow by name,
How he fought on the main you shall hear, you shall hear
How he fought on the main you shall hear.

From *The Death of Admiral Benbow* (anonymous, undated)

Contents

List of Illustrations

(National Maritime Museum)

13. Contemporary depiction of the bombardment of Dunkirk, 1695. (The National Archives)

14. Sketch of Admiral John Benbow. (Arnold Kriegstein)

15. Triple portrait of Thomas Phillips, John Benbow, and Sir Ralph Delavall by Thomas Murray c. 1692-3. (National Maritime Museum)

SECTION 2

16. John Evelyn's plan of his house and garden at Sayes Court, c. 1653. (British Library)

17. A contemporary depiction of the dockyard at Chatham, taken from the opposite side of the river Medway c. 1690. (Scala /Heritage Images)

18. A contemporary depiction of the dockyard at Chatham showing the elevation of the officer's houses c. 1690. (British Library)

19. Peter the Great, Tsar of Russia disguised as a common seaman. (Scala/Ann Ronan/Heritage Images)

20. A modern depiction of the First Eddystone Lighthouse by Peter Jackson. (Private Collection/© Look and Learn/ The Bridgeman Art Library)

21. Contemporary depiction of the dockyard at Deptford taken from the opposite side of the Thames c. 1690. (British Library)

22. Contemporary depiction of the dockyard at Deptford showing its 'accomodations and conveniences' c. 1690. (British Library)

23. A view of Greenwich and the queen's House from the South East by Hendrick Danckerts c.1670. (National Maritime Museum)

24. Sir Christopher Wren's proposal for the Greenwich hospital, 1695 (Sir John Soane's Museum)

25. Greenwich hospital along the Thames in Greenwich, England. (Dave Bartruff/CORBIS)

26. Robert Thompson's journal, Cartagena, 1698-9. (The National Archives)

27. Robert Thompson's journal Portobello, 1698-9. (The National Archives)

28. Benbow's Last Fight. (Mary Evans Picture Library)

29. Mutineer's letter to Benbow. (The National Archives)

16. Probably the *Monmouth* by Van de Velde the Younger or Elder. (Museum Boijmans Van Benningen)

17. An unidentified model of a Fourth Rate of the mid-1690s, of the same class as the *Gloucester*, shown as outfitted in the early 1700s. ('Science Museum/SSPL')

18. The *Play Prize* by Van de Velde the Elder, similar to the *Saudadoes Prize*. (National Maritime Museum)

19. Navy Board model of the *Bredah*, 1692. ('Science Museum/SSPL')

APPENDIX IV: BENBOW'S FRUIT TREES

John Evelyn's plan of his oval garden at Sayes Court, *c.* 1653 (British Library)

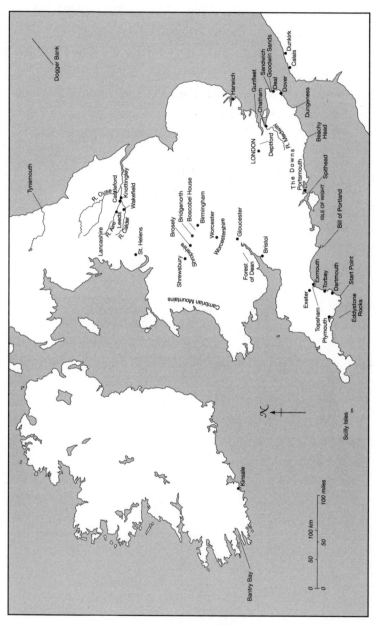

1. Southern England and Southern Ireland

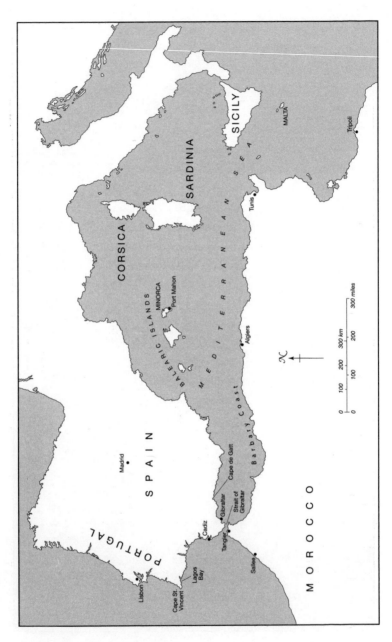

2. Western Mediterranean

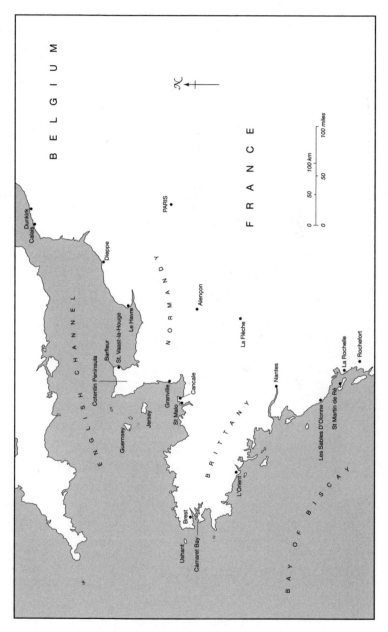

3. North Coast of France and down to La Rochelle

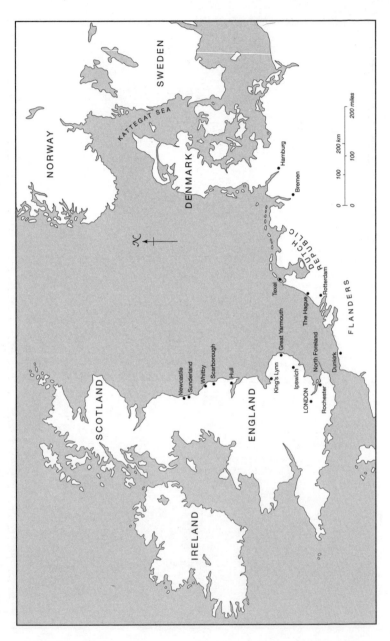

4. Eastern Channel from Dunkirk, North Sea up to Southern Norway

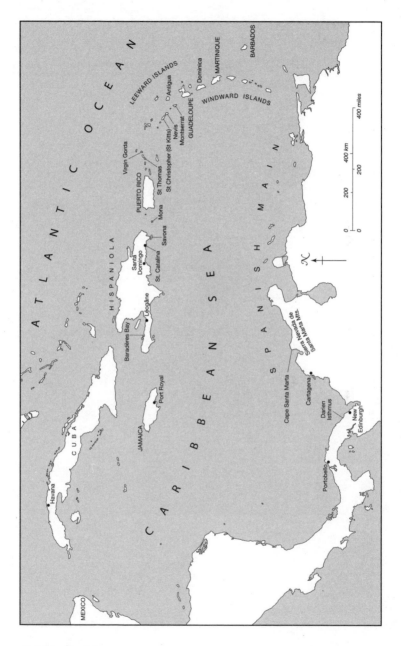

5. The Caribbean

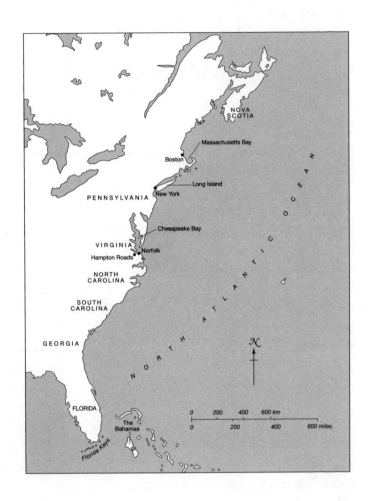

6. Eastern Seabord of America

Introduction:
Benbow's Book

Ask the person sitting next to you if they have heard of Admiral Benbow.

My experience, having done this compulsively for more than a year, is that a surprisingly large number of people, with no conscious interest in maritime or naval history, know the name. Some think it is the name of a pub, others that he was a fictional character. A few will know he was a real admiral and will claim he was the Nelson of his age; some will even recognize his name as the title of a once-famous folk song. Among those who know him to have been a real admiral, some may have heard the story of 'Benbow's Last Fight', a sea battle fought in 1702 off the Spanish Main in which Benbow was abandoned by his captains in the face of the enemy and died of his wounds shortly after. Even for professional naval historians this story raises more questions than it provides answers, and uncertainty surrounds most of his career. His name conjures up maritime glory in a way that other famous naval names do not, simply because it is cloaked in mystery. Nelson is known, and what he did is known, but the same cannot be said for Benbow. His is fame without substance; it is history without meaning.

This combination of awareness and ignorance is intriguing, and it is partially explained by a fictional radio play, screenplay and novel by Ned Sherrin and Caryl Brahms that captured the public imagination in the late 1960s, loosely based on Benbow's life. The novel was a clever spoof: the authors even invented plausible quotes from the diaries of Samuel Pepys and John Evelyn.[1] But Sherrin and Brahms were drawing on an existing awareness of Benbow created by Robert Louis Stevenson's calculated use of the name in *Treasure Island*. The Admiral Benbow is the name of the inn where, in the opening chapters, Jim Hawkins meets Billy Bones, who has Captain Flint's treasure map. This in turn has spawned its own trail of Admiral Benbow pubs that can be found worldwide.

The Admiral Benbow therefore *is* an inn, both in fact and fiction, and he *is* a character of sorts, again in both fact and fiction, but Stevenson did not pluck his subject from historical obscurity. In exactly the same way that Turner chose to immortalize HMS *Temeraire* in his painting *The Fighting 'Temeraire', Tugged to Her Last Berth to Be Broken Up, 1838*, so Stevenson chose the name Benbow: the names were already common currency at the time of painting and writing – Benbow and the *Temeraire* were already famous. In my previous book, *The Fighting Temeraire* (2009), I explained how the *Temeraire* won her fame, and the purpose of this one is to do the same for Benbow.

It is one of the most alluring challenges in naval history. Much of Benbow's fame came from the re-telling of the story of his last fight, but the very subject of Benbow's last fight intrigues. Why, we must ask ourselves, does it matter that it was his last fight? What had he done in his *first* fight, and every fight that followed? The underlying assumption that his last fight mattered at all suggests that he already was famous, that there are two levels or periods of fame: before his last fight and after his last fight. There is perhaps no naval officer better suited to biography. We cannot locate Benbow in history until we understand *his* history; we cannot understand what came last until we know what came first.

This is not as easy as one would hope, however. He died more than a century before the Battle of Trafalgar (1805), and we think he was born around 1650, in the immediate aftermath of the three wars of the English Civil War. Oliver Cromwell then ruled over the broken bones of a country shattered financially, militarily and administratively. During the wars accepted perspectives had shifted. Friends had become enemies, protective walls prisons, churches castles. It is all too easy to see the great naves of English churches as places of spiritual protection, but the Civil War commanders saw them as ready-made strongholds with ready-made watchtowers. Many churches still bear the physical scars of

Civil War conflict, their tough skins pocked with the scars of musket and cannon fire. The perishable flesh vanished, however; and the records of families, births, deaths and marriages were lost. In short, it is very difficult indeed to trace birth dates and locations in the 1650s.

The administrative records of the government, army and navy were also primitive in comparison with the vast bureaucratic machine of the late eighteenth century, and the already basic level of record-keeping was further threatened at times of regime change. The Civil War is one such example, but for Benbow it was just the start of decades of upheaval. When he was nine or ten Oliver Cromwell died and his son took over. Under the leadership of Richard Cromwell, a shadow of his father, the Commonwealth crumbled, and in 1660 Charles II sailed back to England from exile to restore the monarchy. After a lengthy reign Charles died in 1685 and his brother, James, became King. But James's Catholicism presented a threat to the Protestant majority and only three years later England was invaded by a Protestant Dutch prince, William of Orange. William ruled with his wife Mary until her death, and then alone until 1702, when one of James II's daughters, Anne, became Queen. Shortly after that, Benbow fought his last fight and died.

Benbow therefore lived through no fewer than five regime changes as England see-sawed between civil war, military dictatorship, common-wealth and regency, and between Protestant and Catholic monarchs. With such a lack of stability the sources for Benbow's life have suffered, a significant problem further exacerbated by a fire in the Admiralty, fifteen years after his death, in which many of his private papers were destroyed.[2] This has made our understanding of Benbow characteristic of the period in which he lived: it is patchy and unstable. At the same time, however, the instability he endured tells us much about the man. He entered the navy during the reign of Charles II, whom he served with success. Remarkably, that success then continued during each of the next three ideologically and religiously diverse reigns. Perhaps nothing else indicates his professional ability so clearly. Countless others, including such notable professionals as Samuel Pepys, found themselves out of favour at one stage or another. Some, like Pepys, were even con-demned to the Tower of London.

Benbow also lived through a period of extraordinary change in the Royal Navy and the broader maritime world. During his professional career the focus of the navy shifted from East to West; from Holland to France; and from the North Sea to the English Channel and its western approaches, and beyond to the Caribbean. Naval hospitals and naval retirement homes were built for the first time; physicians became regularly employed in the fleet and conducted the first known trials to investigate the effects of life in the service; the coasts began to be scattered with sea-marks and lighthouses; bomb vessels were invented; exploding ships were used for the first time in more than a century; the design of sailing warships improved, stalled and then improved again; inland waterways were cut to join great rivers; dockyards began to change in their location and scope; and operations at sea changed to meet new threats. This was a period of both vast fleet battle and elusive privateering threat; of failed and successful invasion; of aggressive coastal raid and passive blockade; and of merchant, pirate and pirate-hunter. Abroad, colonies succeeded and failed in both the Mediterranean and Caribbean. Benbow had a measure of influence in every one of these issues.

His domestic life is no less intriguing. Consider this: you are in a position of some considerable responsibility at one of His Majesty's dockyards, and a tall stranger with a group of men approaches you and asks you to sub-let your rented house. You agree because the stranger is the Tsar of Russia. You are, however, a little concerned because of the Tsar's unmatched reputation for debauchery and because your house is one of the finest in the land, a regular venue for royal entertainment and owned by none other than John Evelyn, courtier, author and horticulturalist. The garden is one of the finest in the world, with thousands of exceptionally rare species. Three months later the Tsar leaves, having devastated the house and garden through riotous partying. Among the eye-popping damage are three hundred broken window panes, floors ruined with scorch marks, grease and ink, and sixty-five chairs broken or lost. Sixty-five!

Fresh archival research has thrown new light on every aspect of Benbow's career. For example, the muster books of the Royal Navy show us that he did not join the navy aboard Admiral Herbert's flagship the *Rupert* in 1678 as we have suspected for so long, but that he joined the *Rupert* from a smaller ship, the *Phoenix*, and that he had even come there from yet another, unknown ship. Even more significantly, Benbow was not at the Battle of Barfleur in 1692 as historians claim, but was comfortably at home in Deptford. These are but two of many discoveries made in the writing of this book, but they make a very important point about Benbow. Generations of biographers have wanted to fit him into the most significant events of the era, and to link him with the most significant people. For the historian wanting to establish Benbow as the 'Nelson of his age', it was natural to force him into the greatest fleet battle of his lifetime, the Battle of Barfleur, and to start his career with a bang, aboard the *Rupert*, the flagship of the finest commander of the time, Arthur Herbert. That neither of these elements is true does not reduce the value of Benbow as a naval hero. The desire to see him as a precursor of Nelson is an important aspect of the power of his fame. If he was not at Barfleur and did not start his career with Herbert, then the creation of his success and fame becomes even more interesting.

The problem is rendered more complex still by a significant discovery I made several years ago, deep in the shelves of the rare books room of the National Maritime Museum in Greenwich. On a shelf full of volumes from the early and mid-seventeenth century is an extraordinary book about seven inches long and well thumbed, the second edition of a manual of navigation written by Edmund Gunter, Professor of Astronomy at Gresham College, London. Published in 1636, its full title is a perfect example of the laborious verbosity of the seventeenth century: *The description and use of the Sector and Crosse-staffe and other instruments, With a Canon of Artificiall Sines & Tangents to a Radius of 10000,0000 Partes & the use Thereof in Astronomie Navigation and Dialing*. This second edition, '*much enlarged by the Author through the whole worke of his life Time*', includes a '*newe Treatice of Fortification not before Printed*' and was sold by the bookseller James Boller 'at the Signe of the Marigold in Paulls Church Yard'.

Gunter's book is a classic example of an early navigation manual clogged with complex equations and theorems. It was not essential knowledge for the practical seaman, but it was required reading for those interested in the science behind the art of seafaring, and was written by one of the foremost scientists of the age. To own it was to display an interest in, if not necessarily an understanding of, the academic study of navigation, explored through mathematics and geometry. Spherical triangles had to be solved to calculate the azimuth of the sun, which in turn solved problems in Mercator sailing, and trigonometry was also necessary to establish location. The first tables to help mariners with these calculations were published as early as 1594. Not long afterwards Gunter himself invented the Gunter Scale, a straight rule with a slide and engraved with logarithmic scales of numbers and trigonometrical functions. It was still used in 1877, more than 250 years after its invention. The sector and cross-staff referred to in the title are navigational aides and Gunter explained their use in detail.

The importance of Gunter's book and inventions was to make the mathematical solution to navigational problems accessible, while at the same time offering other interesting snippets of information for the mariner, such as the means of measuring time by counting one's pulse or repeating set forms of words. This was over a century before the problem of taking timepieces to sea was solved. Occasionally the book is marked with specific paragraphs, highlighted by a simple pencilled cross in the margin, and there are notes jotted in the margin. What they mean is unclear but their existence suggests that the book did not rest on a shelf for show; it was studied and used.

Nine original copies of the book survive in British institutions, but what makes the copy in Greenwich unique is that its ownership over almost two centuries, from 1636 until 1821, is recorded. To celebrate and further advertise the book's heritage, written on the sides of the pages at the top, centre and foot of the book, and thus visible if it is lying flat on a table, are the three most significant names in that heritage. At the top are the unmistakable six letters that exude the heroism of the Age of Sail and are the very embodiment of naval legend. It simply reads, as a declaration of ownership, 'Nelson'. Impressive enough, but the sense of something really special grows if one flips the book over and looks at the sides of the pages at the bottom. There we find 'Hawke', referring to Edward Hawke, annihilator of the French at the Second Battle of Finisterre in 1747 and the Battle of Quiberon Bay in 1759. And finally, on the long side, is the unmistakable name of Benbow.

Nelson. Hawke. Benbow. All of these names are written in the same hand, with the same coloured ink and apparently with the same nib: they are not the personal signatures of Nelson, Hawke and Benbow made at different times. Inside the front cover, and in the same hand, the full heritage of the book is recorded. This is what it says.

The book was first owned by a John Benbow who, on 5 May 1671, gave it to his son, the future Admiral Benbow, also called John. It was then passed to Captain Thomas Hardy on 30 November 170–. The page has been torn and so the date is unknown, but it would make sense for the book to have been passed on after Benbow's death, in November 1702. Thomas Hardy became Vice-Admiral Thomas Hardy and on 28 March 1717, at the end of his career, he gave it to Rear-Admiral James Mighells. On 4 April 1733 Mighells, now a vice-admiral, passed the book on to a young lieutenant, Edward Hawke. In 1777 Hawke, already six years retired, handed it on to another young lieutenant, this time of the *Lowestoft*, and his name was Horatio Nelson. On 21 October 1805, that famous date in naval history when Nelson destroyed the combined Franco-Spanish fleet at the Battle of Trafalgar and paid for it with his life, the book passed from Nelson to the captain of the *Victory* and his great friend, Thomas Hardy. Perhaps Hardy took it from Nelson's deserted cabin as the Admiral's corpse lay below decks. From Hardy the book passed to Captain Salisbury Pryce Humphreys on 11 June 1813, when Humphreys' seagoing career was already at an end. From Humphreys it passed to its final recorded owner, Edward William Lloyd on 27 July 1821, just eight days after he had been promoted to captain, following an already impressive career. This ancestry is then signed by Lloyd, who also carefully wrote 'Talavera' across the centre of the page, perhaps his then location.

But what should we make of this? Perhaps it is pure fantasy, the product of the fertile mind of the last recorded owner, Captain Edward Lloyd. Perhaps the ancestry of the book was passed down with the book itself, and Edward Lloyd, receiving it on 27 July 1821, recorded it for posterity, personally signing the page as proof of its authenticity. None of it is implausible. The early life of Benbow is so sketchy that there is nothing definitive to say that he didn't have a father called John who was still alive in 1671. Benbow's well-documented interest and ability in navigation would make it a perfectly sensible book for him to have, and, if he did not actually own a copy, it is certain he would have known the work. The links between Hawke and Nelson are also well documented as the two shared a personal friend in William Locker, who studied under Hawke and later became a mentor for Nelson. The dates that the book changed hands also make sense. It changed ownership immediately after the deaths of both Benbow and Nelson, and those who were fortunate enough to survive their naval service bequeathed it later in life or at the end of their career. The names themselves are also interesting as the book was passed between men of extraordinary fame and achievement – Benbow, Hawke and Nelson – and others of more modest success. We do not know how and why the book was passed on, but perhaps it was to men of promise, only some of whom realized that expectation. The mixture of success and failure, of great talent and mediocrity, of great fame alongside anonymity, gives it a clear glow of authenticity.

If its ancestry is authentic, this remarkable little book eloquently locates Benbow in British naval history by making a direct link from Nelson to Benbow via Hawke, each a giant of his own generation. Even if it is *not* an authentic possession of Nelson, Benbow and Hawke, it is still important and interesting. Whoever owned the book believed that a direct link between these great men was possible, plausible and worth celebrating, an opinion shared by many historians since, not least those wishing to locate Benbow at the Battle of Barfleur. In either case it is a significant addition to the Benbow myth and to those that surround Hawke and Nelson. Atmospheric, absorbing and mysterious, it is the very essence of the Benbow legend and it is the inspiration for this book.

Several years later I can say that while some of the Benbow legend is true and some false, far more importantly the legend is only a fraction of the man. His story takes us from the inland navigation of the Severn to the Barbary Coast; from the Glorious Revolution of 1688 to the coastal bombardments of northern France in the 1690s; from privateer hunting in the North Sea to pirate hunting in the Caribbean; from the first Eddystone lighthouse to the first hospital for seamen at Greenwich; and from Chatham and Deptford to Barbados and Jamaica. This book changes the way that we think about Benbow, the Royal Navy and the second half of the seventeenth century, and, in every instance, it takes the reader to unexpected places. It does not begin, for example, in a fully rigged warship rolling gently in green seas off the Spanish Main, but in a cabbage patch outside Shrewsbury Castle.

I.

Benbow's Bloodline

Standing in that cabbage patch was a soldier waiting to die, and his name was John Benbow, a colonel in the army of Charles II that had just been routed at the Battle of Worcester in 1651. It was Charles's last attempt to wrest control of his country from Oliver Cromwell, the man who had created the Commonwealth by executing her king, and Charles's father, Charles I. The Parliamentarian soldiers who captured Benbow were not forgiving, for John Benbow was once one of them, and now he was going to be executed as a traitor.

At the outbreak of the First Civil War, in 1642, Benbow had declared for the Parliamentarians. Immediately given the rank of lieutenant and put in charge of a party of horse, he was ordered to raid Royalist supply lines and soon played a prominent role in two notable campaigns of that first conflict. At the start of the war Charles had established his head-quarters at Shrewsbury, the centre of Royalist loyalty in and around the West Midlands and a town that remained an important symbol of the Royalist cause throughout the wars. In the winter of 1645 Shrewsbury was notably weakened by strong fighting at the nearby city of Chester, where reinforcements had been sent. The Parliamentarians took advantage of Shrewsbury's weakened state and, encouraged from within by citizens or possibly troops disaffected with the Royalist cause, launched an audacious attack in the early hours of a freezing February morning. At 4 a.m. sentries on the Shrewsbury defences noticed men hacking through the palisades. Shortly after, a small group of soldiers, led by John Benbow, crossed the Severn in a specially constructed boat and made their way through the broken palisades. They then scaled the ram-part and crept to St Mary's Water Gate, where the troops were silenced and the gate opened. The Parliamentarian cavalry swept in and took the town within hours. The fall of Shrewsbury is one of only two successful surprise attacks in the entire history of the Civil War, and Benbow played a leading role. He received written commendation from Parliament and was immediately promoted to captain. In 1646 Benbow again fought with distinction, at Beaumaris Castle in Anglesey.[1]

Three years later the strategic situation had radically altered. Charles I had been captured and executed in front of an angry crowd in Whitehall on 30 January 1649. His body, with the head sewn back on, had then been placed under lock and key at St George's Chapel in Windsor, where it could not generate any mob devotion. Within two days the Scottish parliament had proclaimed Charles's son, Charles II, King, but mutual distrust between Charles and the Scots prevented any formal agreement being made for almost fourteen months. On 24 June 1650, however, Charles landed at Garmouth in Scotland, ending his lengthy and wandering exile. After six months of political wrangling he was crowned in Scotland and prepared to take the fight to Cromwell. On 31 July he led an army of twelve thousand Scots into England and they marched solidly for three weeks, heading for the loyal Royalist hinterland of Shropshire and Worcestershire.

Charles had believed, or dared to hope, that his presence on English soil would provide sufficient motivation for those who had supported his father once more to rally to the Royalist cause, but he was badly mistaken. After Charles I's execution Royalists throughout England had been purged. Many had been heavily fined; others forced to give oath that they would not raise arms again against their enemy; some drafted by force into the Parliamentarian ranks, usually to fight abroad. Charles, moreover, now marched at the head of an army of Scots, and for many ex-Royalists this was too much by far. Hitherto the Scots had been the staunchest allies of the Parliamentarians, and many of the Royalists held them accountable for the death of Charles I. At Shrewsbury Charles was met with forceful resistance. Colonel Mackworth, the town's Governor, was summoned to declare for the King, but refused with such breezy confidence and determination that he directed his answer not to the King but to the 'Commander in Chief of the Scotch Forces'.[2] At

Worcester, however, Charles was kindly received and proclaimed King by the Sheriff.

Just as at the beginning of the Civil War, with both armies in the field and recruiting, those of fighting age were forced to make a choice. As one contemporary wrote at the outbreak of the war: 'I find all here full of feares and voyd of hopes. Parents and children, kindred, I and deere friends have the seed of difference and division abundantly sawed in them.'[3] Now, nearly a decade later, the same choice had to be made. For most it was difficult, and for some the answer was not the same as it had been in 1642. Benbow was one of those men. Along with a fellow Parliamentarian officer named Cornet Kinnersly and two of Kinnersly's brothers, Benbow switched sides and marched to Pitchcroft, then a village just north of Worcester, to declare his loyalty to the King. His presence there is recorded in the muster taken on that day.[4] Why he and Kinnersly turned we do not know, but we do know that loyalty in the Civil War was not as rigid as we might suspect. The progress of the wars was at times startlingly swift and the politics and ideology of both parties changed swiftly too. Some swapped allegiances to suit their own interests. Colonel John Morris, the Parliamentarian Governor of Pontefract, let the city fall to the Royalists in 1648, five years after surrendering Liverpool to the Parliamentarians when he was its Royalist Governor.[5] For many the illegal trial and execution of the King was a significant turning point.

Certainly the timing of Benbow's defection from the Parliamentarian ranks suggests disillusionment but it remains a curious and reckless time to have changed. Most established Royalists, however fervent, are known to have been extremely cautious about committing themselves to Charles in 1651 or to any of the intermittent plots in the following years.[6] One other Parliamentarian officer, who is known to have switched sides at exactly this time and about whom we know a little more, was Colonel John Birch. 'Judgement was not his talent' was an inspired contemporary observation on Birch's character. Modern scholars maintain that he was fanatically independent and contemptuous of contemporary opinion.[7]

Benbow therefore was joined by men like Birch and other scattered

Royalists who were willing and able to offer their support to an English king leading an army of Scots. James Stanley, the Earl of Derby, a Royalist who had been based on the Isle of Man, crossed the Irish Sea and raised a small army. Charles proclaimed him 'General of all the countyes of Lancashire, Cheshire, Shropshire, Staffordshire and Worcestershire and the six countyes north of Wales' but the small force he was able to raise was cut to pieces in a skirmish at Wigan, and when Stanley arrived at Worcester he was wounded in the face, arms and shoulders and led no more than thirty horsemen. There were few other names of note at the muster and they were only boosted, in the words of a contemporary pamphlet, 'by some adventurers from London who had been forced to pass through the Parliamentarian army'.[8] Shortly after his arrival at Worcester, Charles had only succeeded in adding perhaps two thousand Royalist Englishmen to his army of twelve thousand Scots, and Cromwell was rapidly descending on the West Midlands at the head of twenty-eight thousand men.

The constables of neighbouring parishes raised men to labour on the defences while the Scots captured and then destroyed all of the significant bridges around the city.[9] Five drapers were commissioned to provide cloth for uniform but there was insufficient time to make them up: the Royalists fought without a uniform, as bedraggled as their cause was bleak, the disunity of their army unmasked.[10] There was open argument between the English and Scottish troops as the tension grew but, of all those men in the Royalist camp preparing to fight, Benbow's future was particularly hazardous. At the start of the Civil War captured turncoats were tried for their lives but few were executed and the majority of all prisoners were simply sent home after swearing not to take up arms again. A particularly unlucky few were transported or 'volunteered' for military service abroad. By the Second Civil War of 1648–9, however, both sides had hardened their stances, particularly after the violent Parliamentary victories at Colchester and Pontefract, and thereafter captured turncoats on both sides were executed.[11]

When Cromwell arrived he set up camp with his main body of soldiers at Red Hill, about a mile south-east of the city. The Royalists took shelter behind the city's walls and dykes, and carefully burned the suburbs right up to the walls so that the Parliamentarians would be forced to approach without cover. That night a strong Royalist force made a sally but the Parliamentarians had been forewarned of the attack by a tailor and they were forced back into the city with significant losses. The traitorous tailor was hanged the next day. Meanwhile, the Parliamentarians kept their position at the top of Red Hill, watching and waiting for the crucial equipment they knew was on its way.

The key to the siege of Worcester were the rivers Severn and Teme, which curled around the city's walls and protected the approaches from south and west. Few armies had any sophisticated engineering equipment that would allow them to cross rivers, even as a temporary measure, so even the narrowest crossings became tactically crucial. The Severn at Worcester is no narrow crossing, however, but a magisterial sweep of waterway that required specialist ferrying equipment to traverse. The river provided the answer as easily as it posed the problem. Despite being so far inland, the river at Worcester is still navigable, and the resourceful Cromwell simply sent a force about twenty miles downstream to Upton and Gloucester, from where they brought a fleet of river boats. On 2 August the fleet arrived and the Parliamentarian forces began to bind them together and strengthen them with extra timber to form a number of makeshift bridges. Charles watched the preparations from the very top of the Cathedral's tower, 170 feet high, from where the panoramic views of the scarred landscape stretched to the horizon at Red Hill. It was a commanding view of a landscape he did not command. The impact on Charles of this location was so profound that the next day he brought his army's leaders to the tower and held a council of war there.

The details of the ensuing battle are hazy as they are so easily overcome by the events that immediately followed the fall of Worcester. At some point in the afternoon, possibly around 3 p.m., Cromwell himself led a large body of men across the temporary bridge over the Severn before leading an assault on Royalist troops in which 'he did exceedingly hazard himself … riding up and down in the midst of the shot and riding himself in person to the enemy's foot offering them quarter'.[12] This was typical of Cromwell. He had demonstrated early on in his career in the army that he was capable of instinctive and decisive acts in the face of extreme danger and by 1645 his ability to inspire loyalty in his men was as absolute as his own loyalty to God.

Shortly before Cromwell crossed the Severn, another strong force had crossed the Teme and engaged the Royalist defenders who had lined the hedgerows stretching right back to the city. Driven back relentlessly by Cromwell's two-pronged assault, the defenders retreated before regrouping for a sudden and violent sally. Yet again, however, they were driven back, but this time with the Parliamentarian troops at their heels, and some of them even in front. The Royalist cannon were seized and turned on their own troops, 'which so wrapt them up with a spirit of terror and confusion, that afterwards, the night being come, we soon gained an Entry and became Masters of the Town'.[13]

The scarcity of eyewitness reports of the final hours of that day at Worcester is the most troubling aspect of the battle. All of that time has been lost to history by those unable or unwilling to write about their experiences. Under the rules and customs of warfare, Worcester had fallen to storm and therefore the population were not protected by the commonly shared principles that governed behaviour in warfare. The Royalist troops knew this as well as the trapped citizens, and panic spread as quickly as the fires that burned the houses. Royalists on horseback trampled their own troops to hasten their escape, and Royalist fought Royalist, each 'readier to cut each others throats than to defend ourselves against the enemy'.[14] Aware the city had fallen, as many inhabitants joined the sack alongside the Parliamentarian troops as had become its victims. 'You cannot hear too bad an account of the inhabitants of Worcester,' wrote Sir Rowland Burkeley, a neighbouring Royalist who had not joined the fight. 'All houses being ransacked top to bottom, the very persons of men and women not expected.'[15] Another compared it to the fall of Constantinople to the Turks, the troops 'giving no quarter to any they found in the Streets'.[16] There is general agreement that there were nearly four thousand dead, and the corpses of both men and horses were piled in the streets. Eventually the dead were carried to the churchyard, the Royal Accounts recording that it was the churchwardens of St Michael's who were charged with the gruesome task of burying the dead and the equally unpleasant task of carrying away 'the litter ... which the Scotts lay upon'. In a further attempt to eradicate all trace of the odorous Scots, the chamberlains paid two shillings 'for ston pitch and rosen to perfume the Hall'.[17]

Almost ten thousand prisoners were taken at Worcester, the majority of them incarcerated in the Cathedral until they could be marched to London. That march was a horrifying experience as most were barefoot and naked. Many Londoners were sympathetic when the bedraggled army appeared.[18] The scale of the victory and the subsequent impact that it had on the Royalist cause is best conceived by studying a brief list of the prisoners. Among those of importance or high social rank were the Duke of Hamilton, the Earls of Rothes, Lauderdale, Carnworth, Kelly, Derby, Cleveland and Shrewsbury; Lords Spyne and Sinclair, Sir J. Packington, Sir C. Cunningham, Sir R. Clare and the King's secretary, R. Fanshawe; six Colonels and nine Lieutenant-Colonels of Horse, thirteen Colonels and eight Lieutenant-Colonels of Foot, six Majors of Horse and thirteen of Foot, thirty-seven Captains of Horse and seventy-two of foot, fifty-five quartermasters of Horse, eighty-nine Lieutenants of Foot, seventy-six Cornets of Horse, ninety-nine Ensigns of Foot, ninety Quartermasters of Foot, thirty of the King's servants, nine Ministers and nine chirurgeons (surgeons). Among the General officers were Major-General Piscotty, Major-General Montgomery, the General of the Ordnance, the Adjutant-General of Foot, the Quartermaster-General, the Marshal-General and the Waggonmaster-General. The Royal Standard, 158 regimental colours, the whole of the artillery, the entire baggage train of both army and King, the King's coach and horses were all taken. The Mayor of Worcester, the Sheriff and all the Aldermen were also arrested.[19]

There was of course one very important person missing from the list of prisoners: King Charles himself. As night fell on 3 September, the twenty-one-year-old Charles, highly distinctive for his height and swarthy complexion, was forced to stop fighting. He had not lacked for bravery, and much like Cromwell had led from the front on a number of occasions, even trying to rouse his cavalry to a final desperate charge. Now he rode to the north while Worcester was sacked and the Scots lay dying. With Charles were a number of his most loyal Generals, including the Earl of Derby, and they rested just beyond Stourbridge, twenty miles or so from Worcester. Exhausted from the fight and flight, Derby advised resting at Boscobel House, a hunting lodge owned by Catholics, equipped with priest holes and surrounded by dense woodland. Derby, moreover, knew its value personally: only eight days earlier he had successfully hidden at Boscobel after his defeat at Wigan. Charles agreed, was hidden in an oak tree and then in a priest hole in the attic, before making his way south, never far from his pursuers and narrowly evading capture on many more occasions than that most famous example at Boscobel. The original oak tree has long since been destroyed, but two possible priest holes still survive, one more convincing than the other. The one linked to Charles is in the attic and is a little over three feet wide and just over four feet high – cramped quarters indeed for a man generally held to have been over six feet tall. Six weeks after his decision to rest at Boscobel, Charles boarded a ship at Shoreham, in Sussex, which took him to Normandy and safety.

The escape of Charles further hardened Parliament's resolve against his captured underlings and it ordered the Council of State to make an example of those taken at Worcester. All officers and every common soldier were court-martialled, and the Governors of Liverpool, Chester, Stafford, Worcester and Shrewsbury were ordered to send all captives to Bristol for transportation.[20] In the end, however, the army simply did not have the resources to punish every captive and most English prisoners were conscripted into the New Model Army and sent to fight in Ireland. Others were simply sent home. Almost eight thousand prisoners, most Scottish, were sent to New England, Bermuda and the West Indies, where they worked as indentured labourers – effectively slaves. Some worked for the rest of their lives mucking out pig houses, sweeping slave quarters or working in the grinding rooms of sugar mills.[21]

Only a handful of high-ranking or otherwise significant prisoners were tried, and Benbow, a man renowned for his local exploits for Parliament in the preceding wars, was one of these. His execution would be a potent symbol of Parliament's triumph and their belief in loyalty. Another man to be tried was the Earl of Derby, who had assisted the

King in his escape and was well known by Parliamentarians for having had a hand in a massacre of Parliamentarians at Bolton in 1644. The court met and resolved that Captain John Benbow was a 'fitt person to bee brought to tryall and made an example of justice'. And so the wheels of Parliamentary justice began to roll. Benbow was to be tried at Chester the following day, charged with high treason against the Commonwealth of England, specifically that he had broken a law that prohibited 'correspondencey' with Charles or any of his party.[22] This was a significant step. The prisoners brought to trial were not being tried for what they had done on the field of battle as soldiers, punishment for which was restricted by accepted rules and customs of behaviour, but as enemies of the State, their offences punishable by death. The wheel had turned full circle. Just as Parliamentarians had not been recognized as lawful combatants at the outbreak of the Civil War, so now were Royalists not protected by the legal custom of military conflict. We do not know much of the detail of the Benbow trial, but we do know that the Earl of Derby was outraged at this legal manoeuvre and couched his defence in exactly those terms, arguing that he should be tried as a soldier and not as a civilian traitor.[23]

When Benbow was eventually brought into the court the prosecution began its case with his defection from Parliamentary forces, 'whereupon he did go from Shrewsbury where he then inhabited, to the said declared traitor and enemy Charles Stuart, and for the carryinge on of his designe and war against the parliament and commonwealth of England'. He was accused, after being granted a commission by Charles, of going around Salop (Shropshire) 'for the raising of horse arms to complete his regiment'. It was claimed he appeared in Newport, Drayton and Bridgenorth, where he had Charles proclaimed King before taking a number of soldiers from the local militia as prisoners back to Worcester. During the battle, it was claimed, he charged the Parliamentary forces before being taken prisoner, and that he did all of this 'contrary to his duty and allegiance, and contrary to several Acts of Parliament'.[24]

Benbow had very little to say in his defence. He admitted that before Charles arrived at Namptwich (Nantwich) he had served the forces of

Parliament; that he had received a commission from the King; and that he had raised a regiment of about thirty horse. He had then marched with Charles to Worcester but denied ever being in Bridgenorth. He also stringently denied taking part in any charge against Parliamentarian troops and further denied any active involvement in the battle before being taken prisoner by Major General Lambert. Otherwise, his defensive stance was purely theoretical: that he never 'knew or overheard before coming to Shrewsbury that the said Charles Stuart and his adherents were ever by Act of Parliament proclaimed traitors'.[25] After a brief speech he was taken away before being brought back once more and given a final opportunity to say anything in his defence. He added nothing and was sentenced to death by shooting, his execution to take place at Shrewsbury, the very place where he had distinguished himself as a Parliamentarian soldier. The man responsible for this ingenious punishment was the same zealot, Colonel Mackworth, who had so stubbornly refused Charles entry to Shrewsbury. The Earl of Derby also pleaded ignorance of the new law declaring association with Charles a treasonable offence and so too were his pleas heard and ignored. The Earl of Derby's death was also symbolic: he was beheaded at Bolton, the site of his massacre of Parliamentarians in 1644.

Shortly before his execution date, Derby escaped down a rope from his window and fled along the banks of the River Dee, where he was quickly recaptured. But Benbow was carried directly to Shrewsbury, where, in a cabbage patch in the castle grounds, he was shot just after 1 p.m. on 15 October 1651 and thus became another in the growing list of Royalist martyrs whose fame was reborn after the restoration of Charles a decade later. He was buried at St Chad's in Shrewsbury and his gravestone is still visible today. While Benbow and Derby were executed, the widow of the tailor who had warned Cromwell's forces of a night attack at Worcester was rewarded with £200 in cash and a further £200 per year: after Worcester loyalty was rewarded as much as disloyalty was punished.[26]

That is the story of Colonel Benbow as far as we know it and there is no reason to doubt the details: his career and fate are well documented. What remains much less clear is how Colonel John Benbow was related, if at all, to the future Admiral John Benbow. He has variously been described as Admiral Benbow's father, his uncle and as no relation at all.

There is no definitive proof for any of these claims, but the assertion that Colonel Benbow was Admiral Benbow's uncle is one of the most interesting because it provides the basis for an apocryphal story which links Admiral Benbow's father directly to the King himself. Colonel John Benbow had a brother named Thomas (or perhaps William), who was also a Colonel in the Royalist army. He too was captured after the Battle of Worcester, but managed to escape and lived out the years of the Commonwealth in Shropshire. When Charles II was restored to the throne in 1660, Thomas Benbow's loyalty was rewarded with a steady if poorly paid job in the Tower of London, working for the Ordnance Office. One day, as preparations were made for another war against the Dutch, the King came to the Tower to inspect the magazines and there he recognized the elderly Benbow. 'My old friend Colonel Benbow!' he cried. 'What do you here?' Benbow explained in suitably loyal tones that he had been given a position that brought in 'fourscore pounds a year, in which I serve your Majesty as cheerfully as if it brought me in four thousand'. 'Alas!' said the King, 'is this all that can be found for an old friend at Worcester? … bring this Gentleman to me tomorrow, and I will provide for him and his family as it becomes me.' Unfortunately for the elderly Benbow, overcome with gratitude and love for his sovereign, he immediately collapsed and died.[27]

There is no written evidence supporting this tale, which came directly from Admiral Benbow's son-in-law, a man named Paul Calton. A valid source, one might assume, but the value of Calton's testimony has been severely attacked.[28] The outlines of the story are not implausible, however. Most well-known Royalist officers were hard-hit by the wars. Either their personal fortunes were spent in raising and maintaining armies or they had been crippled by heavy fines. When Charles II was restored to the throne he set out to reward those who had demonstrated loyalty, and in 1663 he set aside £60,000 for their relief.[29] There are, moreover, striking similarities between the Benbow story and the better-documented fate of another Colonel, John Birch. Like Benbow, Birch had met the King shortly before the Battle of Worcester. When, after his restoration, Charles met Birch again, he rewarded him with a life appointment at the Treasury, even remaining on friendly terms with the Colonel for the rest of his life.[30] It is not inconceivable therefore that something similar happened to the Colonel Benbow who escaped from Worcester.

Admiral Benbow's birth date provides little help in solving his origins as it too is uncertain. The evidence we have comes from two sources. The first and most obvious is his tombstone embedded in the floor of Kingston Parish Church in Jamaica that states that he died in 'the 52 year of his age'. As he died in 1702 this means that he was born in 1651. The second significant piece of evidence concerning his birth date comes from a very curious source: the notebook of John Partridge, an eccentric but very well-known English astrologer, and a contemporary of Benbow. One of Partridge's notebooks is held in the manuscript collection of the British Library. It is well kept and each page is marked with a single square chart, the personal horoscope of an individual that maps the heavens at the moment of their birth. Such a horoscope is known as a nativity.

In the centre of each square a name is entered along with a birth date, and in this case it reads: 'Admiral Benbo natus die 10 March 1652/3'. With some relish Partridge explains why he has been selected for study, as a man of curious fate: 'He died of his wounds at Jamaica in November 1702 being betray'd by a pack of rogues that suffered him to be destroyed and would not come to assist him for which two of them were shot for cowards.'[31]

Leading from the corners of the central 'naming' square are ruled lines, and these in turn are joined together by a larger diamond shape that surrounds the central square. Partridge has inscribed all of these lines with astrological symbols, the purpose of which, as he tells us on the front cover of the notebook, is to allow the astrologer to 'say something of a general judgement thereon'. Unfortunately there are no accompanying notes and we will never know Partridge's conclusions, but one thing is obvious: according to Partridge, the Colonel Benbow who was shot could not have been Admiral Benbow's father; by the time the future Admiral was born, the Colonel had been dead for seventeen months.

Amid all this uncertainty it is important to recognize that the combined stories of the two Colonel Benbows, in which 'both brothers fell martyrs to the royal cause, one in grief, and the other in joy',[32] provide an all too poetic genealogy that must be considered with caution. It is understandable that early historians of Admiral Benbow easily linked the Admiral from Shrewsbury with the famous Benbow brothers of the Civil War, also from Shrewsbury. Each reinforces the other as a tale of loss for the sake of loyalty and honour, characteristics which contemporaries believed to be hereditary and therefore passed down through the Benbow family tree. As the Admiral's earliest biographer wrote:

> He was descended from the ancient and honourable family of the Benbows ... which, though now sunk in point of riches and credit, is still remembered with honour, as it deserves to be, since the misfortune of the family were [sic] not the effects of their follies and vices, but owing to their firmness and fortitude, their attachment to honour in preference to interest, and their unshaken adherence to the good old English principles of loyalty and patriotism.[33]

A good story, maybe, but it remains open to doubt that Benbow was linked in any way with both or either of these men.

For some, however, the specific identity of his relatives is less important than the branch of the sprawling Benbow family tree from which the Royalist brothers came, because that branch of Benbows were wealthy members of the Shropshire landed gentry. There is some mixed evidence in the form of coats of arms to support these claims to his high-born status.[34] It is quite extraordinary that alongside this theory exists an equally potent, equally romantic and equally unsubstantiated theory that argues the exact opposite and dissociates Benbow and his family from any hint of power, money, position or status. This theory maintains that he was the son of a tanner, and one version sees him running away to sea to seek his fortune. It is unclear when this argument was first proposed, but it is referred to indirectly by Benbow's earliest biographer and was then argued in detail by a succession of modern historians.[35] The most recent research, however, leans towards the Admiral being descended from landed gentry.

These, then, are the two radically different theories of Benbow's descent and although it is unlikely that the murky years of the end of the Civil War and the start of Cromwell's Commonwealth will ever produce sufficient documentary proof of his pedigree, the divergent conclusions that have been reached in modern times are important in their own right. The genealogy of Benbow matters not only for the bare facts of his heritage but also for how the Benbow story fitted into a famous contemporary debate about the relative competence of naval officers from different social backgrounds.

That debate was formed in the complex political aftermath of the Restoration. In short, during the Civil War the navy had been purged of officers who were openly loyal to the Royalist cause or even perceived to have a tendency in that direction. They were replaced by officers with a firm and demonstrable dedication to Republicanism and everything that went with it, not least a transparent belief in Puritanism. Most of these men were taken from the merchant marine, although some were promoted from within the navy. As a rule, these men were not of high birth and they were renowned for their knowledge and ability of seamanship. They were hardened salts, and known to contemporaries, because of the oiled canvas of their foul-weather gear, as 'tarpaulins'. The nickname still survives in the truncated form 'tar', as in 'Jolly Jack Tar', and even now conjures up the essence of these men as hard-working, thoroughbred seamen.

When Charles II returned from exile in 1660 he was thus faced with a problem. The State's Navy (as it was known under Cromwell) had conducted itself for the most part with impressive skill and no little success, but now the King was required to purge the navy once more, to guarantee its loyalty just as Cromwell had done before him. Charles's purge was not so extreme as the Parliamentarian one had been, however, not least because in the merchant service the Parliamentarians had enjoyed a far wider base of manpower from which to select their new naval officers than Charles now did. There were few naval officers loyal to Charles with adequate experience and both Charles and his brother James, whom he had appointed as Lord High Admiral, were canny enough to realize that retaining the services of officers who had served under Cromwell, although distasteful, was essential to the future security of England and the prosperity of her trade. In recent years the focus of British foreign policy had been on war with the Dutch. That war, in 1652–4, had been fought entirely at sea and in 1660 there was sufficient tension between England and Holland to indicate that a further war was not out of the question. As a result the majority of the navy's officers were retained but a significant portion of new officers, all of good Royalist heritage and all gentlemen, entered the service.

So in the 1660s and early 1670s there were two distinct groups of officers in the Royal Navy. There was a larger, older and more experienced group, most of them of indeterminate social status, and most of them talented seamen; and there was a smaller, younger group, most of them born into aristocratic, noble or gentry families, and most of them with little experience of the sea. They spoke differently, they wore different clothing, they behaved differently and they performed their duties with different levels of success. Gentlemen officers were the focus of stinging criticism from those close to the navy, not least from Samuel Pepys himself, who, although dedicated to Charles, was consistently and actively hostile to his programme of granting commissions to gentlemen who had little relevant experience compared with established seamen. Richard Gibson, an associate of Pepys, wrote and published a critique of the officer corps in 1690. In it he awarded the gentleman captains 'the honour to bring in Drinking, Gameing, Whoreing, Swearing and all Impiety to the Navy'. 'Before Gentlemen came to Command the Navy,' he continued, 'we were able to fight with all the world at sea.' For others the criticism did not stop there and included every sin imaginable to a good Calvinist conscience: treachery, cowardice, profanity, impiety, wanton cruelty and sodomy.[36]

'Tarpaulins' were not openly criticized in this way, but were lampooned in contemporary poetry, song and theatre for their unworldly appearance, language and honest virtue. A fantastic example survives from a play of 1695 by William Congreve, entitled *Love for Love*. Its hero, Ben, has been at sea long enough to acquire the language of a tarpaulin and he uses it to woo his love: 'If you like me, and I like you, we may chance to swing in a hammock together.'[37] The particular advantage of this debate was that it served as an obvious, but at times quite sophisticated, analogy of Britain's recent troubled past. To criticize the foppish, incompetent gentleman captains was to criticize the new King and his brother the Lord High Admiral; to celebrate the tarpaulins was to celebrate the success of the State's Navy and to revel in the maritime glory that had been won by Britain's honest seamen in the 1650s. In fact this became such a valuable tool for political rhetoric that the debate over the relative abilities of gentleman and tarpaulin officers survived long after the problem had ceased to exist. Recent scholarship has further exploded the notion of a continuing debate by demonstrating that, by the late 1670s, the once-clear division between gentlemen and tarpaulins was rapidly being broken down, that the majority of captains were neither gentlemen nor tarpaulins, but somewhere in between, and it is this new interpretation of the social and professional make-up of the navy that has a direct relevance to the career of Benbow.

Naval command became a particularly attractive field of work after the Restoration. The only wars were maritime wars and so the most effective way of demonstrating one's allegiance to the new King through military service was through service in his navy. Therefore many families with a Royalist tendency, who might otherwise have considered the army, now sent their sons to the navy. At the same time, the majority of those Royalist families had suffered severely in the Civil War through heavy fines or confiscation of their property. But the navy offered the next generation a very real way to revive the fortunes of an established family. A further attraction was that the public nature of the debate between gentlemen and tarpaulins had had a profound effect on Charles and James, leading them to take steps to improve the professional quality of young gentlemen entering the service. They did this by introducing for the first time a formal professional examination for the post of lieutenant, which required the applicant to have had at least three years of sea experience, including a year as a midshipman. The interview that followed was a stiff examination by a number of senior captains. They also introduced the rank of 'volunteer per order', which allowed young gentlemen no older than sixteen to learn seamanship and navigation aboard ship. The result was that, by the time Benbow joined the navy, the former polarity between gentlemen and tarpaulins was already becoming less clear, and within a generation had changed beyond recognition. By 1688 almost all of the rising generation of English sea officers were gentlemen who had entered as volunteers per order.[38] Now, young gentlemen who sought their fortune in the navy could not do so without a significant degree of professional training and examination of their competence. This was, in effect, a 'third way', a dream of a mixture of the good qualities of both gentlemen and tarpaulins.

The importance of this new interpretation of the officer corps of the Restoration navy is that it so neatly fits the broad outlines of the Benbow story as we know it. If, as the evidence seems to suggest, Benbow is somehow related to the executed Royalist Cavalier, then Benbow, son of a ruined gentry family, joined the navy to revive his and his family's fortunes. Benbow's father, perhaps too old to join the navy, could nevertheless pave the way for his son. With exactly this in mind, his father bred him to the sea, apprenticed him to a waterman on the Severn and then presented him with a book of navigation shortly before he joined the navy. He was then so successful in his naval career because he came from a respectable background *and* excelled at seamanship. He was, in essence, exactly what Pepys, Charles and James were looking for: he was the very model of a member of the new professional officer corps. Demonstrably loyal to the King through his family history, young and highly skilled, Benbow represented nothing less than the navy's future. It is certainly a career path that others followed. Consider Sir John Kempthorne, about whom we know a great deal. Son of a Royalist officer and technically a gentleman in that he inherited a coat of arms, his family had lost all of their money in the Civil War. Kempthorne learned his trade on fishing vessels before joining the Levant Company to gain more experience of ocean-going seamanship. Only then did he join the navy, but his rise to Vice-Admiral was as rapid and extraordinary as Benbow's.

If we take the alternative view of the Benbow family tree – that he came from nothing and ran away to sea – then his story is equally significant and equally complimentary towards the Restoration navy under Charles and James's guidance and Pepys's administration. Benbow would thus become one of those famous maritime warriors who rose through the ranks to the very pinnacle of his profession. If we adopt a broad perspective on maritime history, Benbow takes his place alongside Francis Drake, son of a shearman; Christopher Columbus, son of a weaver and cheesemonger; the Turkish Admiral Barbarossa, son of a potter; the Dutch Admiral Michiel De Ruyter, son of a beer porter; and James Cook, son of a labourer. In the context of his contemporary navy, Benbow's name could be added to the greats such as Cloudesley Shovell and John Leake. Shovell started his naval career as a cabin boy and servant, while Leake was the son of a gunner, but both rose to Admiral, were knighted and became Members of Parliament.

In either case, son of a gentleman or son of a tanner, Benbow enjoyed a career that shines a favourable light on the navy in which he served. For either he was a gentleman who became a skilled sailor, or he was a tarpaulin who was allowed to rise through the ranks on competence alone. The fact that either career path was valid was a foundation stone of the officer service that ultimately produced men like Anson, Hawke, Hood, Howe, Duncan and Nelson who dominated the eighteenth century. From varied social backgrounds, each was a thoroughly professional skilled seaman and aggressive fighter, attributes for which they were respected, promoted and rewarded with great success and fame. So, although the detail of Benbow's past remains uncertain, we can say with confidence that he was one of the very first of this new breed of English fighting sailors, a breed that would define British naval success for nearly a quarter of a millennium.

2.

Benbow's Barges

Benbow's childhood and early adolescence were lived during years of tumult in which the foundations were laid for the conflicts that both defined much of his adult life and ultimately caused his death. We simply do not know where he grew up, but it is possible that he spent some time in London until 1665, when he would have been about thirteen.[1] Those thirteen years were among the most extraordinary in the entire history of England. As Charles II lived an extravagant life in exile in France, Cromwell's unique brand of military Puritanism held London in its firm grip, sought to ensure England's safety from invasion and to project the glory of the English Commonwealth beyond English shores through its magnificent new warships. Cromwell's flagship was named the *Naseby* after the battle of June 1645 in which the main army of Charles I was destroyed, and it bore a figurehead of Cromwell himself on horseback, trampling underfoot England, Scotland, Ireland, France, Spain and Holland.

The Commonwealth knew that its Protestant Puritanism was despised by Catholics everywhere and that its regicide was condemned by Protestants and Catholics alike, even by many of those who had fought for Parliament during the Civil War. Aggression born of insecurity; this brashness was reflected in English foreign policy and was epitomized by the Navigation Ordinance of 1651, which effectively banned all foreign merchant navies from trading with England. From then on, goods bound for England, from anywhere in the world, had to be carried and traded by Englishmen on English ships to the profit of English merchants. Thus the Commonwealth sought to protect itself financially but also to provoke on an international scale. The initial aims of the Commonwealth had been met: the English were ruled by a parliament and not by a king, but that war had been won by overwhelming military power and that association of political power and armed force simmered beneath the surface, and at times in open defiance of the democracy that the Commonwealth stood for.

In 1652 this bellicose English foreign policy erupted into war with the Dutch over trading rights. The war, fought entirely at sea, saw more sustained vicious fighting than had ever been seen in northern waters. Again and again the fleets met as the Dutch sought to force large merchant convoys down the English Channel and the English sought to stop them. There were successes on both sides but repeated English victory in battle, alongside an effective maritime blockade, began to badly affect the Dutch desire and ability to fight.

Before the war ended, the English were forced to endure yet another transfer of power when, in 1653, Cromwell took power into his own hands by force, driving the Rump Parliament out of Westminster at musket point in a classic *coup d'état*. Thus the English Civil War, fought to save Englishmen from the tyranny of power resting in the hands of a single man, had led to exactly what it had sought to destroy. In 1653 Cromwell declared himself Lord Protector, a title borrowed from the Duke of Somerset, who had ruled as King during the childhood of Edward VI, Henry VIII's only son. Somerset ended up on the block and Cromwell's fate, though he died of natural causes, was ultimately as sinister.

In 1654 Cromwell concluded the war with the Dutch, despairing at the pointlessness of fighting against a fellow Protestant nation, but he was as much a soldier as he was a religious zealot and the conclusion of the Dutch War simply allowed him to prosecute an aggressive foreign policy against those he felt to be his more natural enemies: Catholics and Muslims. Extended operations against Spain and the Barbary Regency of Tunis followed but on 3 September 1659, seven years to the day after he finally destroyed the Royalist cause at Worcester, Cromwell died. His son Richard succeeded him but it soon became clear that he had inherited none of the savvy that his father had used to keep the powerful factions of Parliament and army in precarious balance. With

Cromwell's death the complex equation of military power and democracy that had defined the Commonwealth became unbalanced and internal order collapsed. He had created a system so tailored to his own personality that without him it could not work. Time and again he had solved complex constitutional problems with temporary measures and threats, and with no sophisticated perception of the challenges of the future.

In London the perceptible loss of leadership immediately led to social disorder. One contemporary witness wrote that 'the city lies under the highest discontents that ever I saw it. Shops are shut up, trade gone, fears and jealousies multiply'; another that 'we are here in great disorder, and expect to be in blood every hour'.[2] The latter comment was made in a letter sent to General Monck, epitome of the changing fortunes of the age. A distinguished Royalist soldier, Monck was captured by the Parliamentarians and condemned to the Tower. There he converted to the Parliamentarian cause and became one of the finest commanders in the Cromwellian army. Next he joined the navy as one of Cromwell's 'Generals at Sea' and served with great distinction in the Dutch War. As the Commonwealth fell apart under Richard Cromwell, Monck took matters into his own hands and staged yet another coup, but this time with the restoration of the King at its heart. He took power himself but, after protracted contact with the exiled Charles, sent a delegation to the Hague to invite him to rule the land that had been denied him.

While much of this would have been beyond the perception of an eight-year-old boy, the celebrations on the London streets after the Restoration of Charles II would certainly have been real enough, with bonfires, the roasting of great rumps of meat and other festivities. These exceptional events apart, the streets of London where Benbow grew up would have remained the same. After Constantinople and Paris, London was the third largest city in the world. The seat of a government and a merchant city only a few miles upstream from the largest naval base in the country, London united everything that was required to make any city great. The result was a sky above the city heavily polluted by the coal-burning dockside industries and the thousands of fires that heated domestic houses; a river flowing with rubbish and industrial waste from the tanners, butchers, soap-boilers, glue-makers and tallow chandlers that lined the docks; and narrow streets pocked with human and animal excrement and rubbish, and blocked by carts, livestock, carriages and pedestrians. This was Benbow's London.

A little over eight months after the Restoration there was another event of great importance, orchestrated and designed for the people of London. On 30 January 1661, the twelfth anniversary of the execution of Charles I, the body of Oliver Cromwell was exhumed from its grave in Westminster Abbey. His body or, as some claim, one purporting to be his,[3] was then hanged for several hours at Tyburn, the location near Marble Arch of all of London's public executions. The man who had been buried as a king in Westminster Abbey, complete with crown, sceptre and orb, was thus hanged like a common London criminal. And still Charles was not done. Cromwell was cut down and beheaded, the divided corpse buried near Tyburn, as was common practice with all those hanged there. But for Cromwell's head a more notable fate awaited: Charles had it placed on a spike outside Westminster, where it remained, rotting and then picked clean of flesh, for nearly a quarter of a century. Eventually it was taken down and, after a curious life deserving a book of its own, was finally reburied in 1960 – 299 years after it was disinterred – at Sidney Sussex College, Cambridge University, where Cromwell had studied.

By 1665 the gloss of the Restoration had worn very thin. London was gripped by the Great Plague that would eventually kill almost a fifth of its population, and war with the Dutch was brewing once again. Press gangs prowled the streets and docks and policed the river. It was an auspicious time for a fourteen-year-old boy to leave London.

The detail of this period of Benbow's youth is flimsy, but there is some suggestion that he was raised in Shropshire, the county of his birth and the stronghold of the Benbow name, where he became a waterman's apprentice on the Severn.[4] There is no documentary proof that he did so, and alternatives have been proposed, but a great deal of circumstantial evidence suggests that he is likely to have followed this career path.

Little is known about the process of placing a boy with a master but it was usually achieved through contacts with parents or relatives. We are certain that bargemen on the Severn did take apprentices, and the river trade commonly made the most of extended family connections.[5] Recent research in Restoration-era probate inventories along the Severn has also revealed that a number of Benbows were involved in the Severn river trade at least from the last quarter of the seventeenth century and through to the mid-eighteenth. A Richard Benbow from Broseley who died in 1673 was a bargemaster who left two vessels in his will, and there were other Benbows active in the water trade at Bridgenorth. A recent (although incomplete) study of the Shrewsbury inventories has not revealed any Benbows,[6] which suggests that the future Admiral may have learned his maritime skills working from the river ports of Broseley or Bridgenorth.

A William Benbow from Bridgenorth, whose probate inventory was made nearly sixty years later, in 1729, had clearly made a success of his business, as it includes two barges and two separate boats, valued together at £50.[7] The inventory is particularly rich and includes two feather beds, curtains, six chairs, twenty pewter dishes and even a clock and case. There is overwhelming evidence that this was not normal for a Severn waterman. Although some made a good living from their trade, most were hard up and few could make a living out of the water trade alone. Richard Benbow from Broseley is a prime example. Although he owned two barges, we know that he made part of his income from cows and sheep and from spinning flax. Other bargemen did the same and on a considerable scale.[8] The apprentices and labourers who worked for the barge owners were always hard-up. In 1724 John Poole a 'labouring waterman' died and his entire possessions consisted of two old lines (probably for hauling boats upriver), one small piece of cloth, an old rope, two barrels and 'a few trifling things not mentioned'. The clothes he was wearing were 'very mean' and the whole lot was valued at £1 18s 6d.[9]

Thus we have in the probate inventories evidence of two extremes of the waterman's trade: the bargemaster who owned the boat and traded for his own profit, and the labourer who helped to load and unload the barge and to haul it upstream. As on other contemporary significant waterways, such as the Thames, Rhône and Loire, in the late seventeenth century there were no towpaths for horses to pull the vessels upstream, and that back-breaking work was done by teams of labourers, usually six strong, who harnessed themselves to the barge with a line running to the top of the mast. They then physically dragged the vessel against the current 'with much strain, force and pains'.[10] One contemporary who saw this work wrote:

> Since the dawn of day, they have wrestled with the impetuous current; and now that it almost overpowers them, how do they exert all their remaining strength, and strain their every nerve? How are they bathed in sweat and rain. Fastened to their lines as horses to the traces, wherein do they differ from the laborious brutes?[11]

The bridge at Bridgeport on the Severn still bears the grooves cut by the ropes passing over the parapet while the barges were pulled underneath.

In the hierarchy between the owner and the labourer were the crew and apprentices, but in all cases they were few, with no barge employing more than three or four people in all. As a result each man was required to be sufficiently capable and physically strong that he would not endanger the lives of the rest of the crew and the safety of the barge itself. Although boys joined the navy from a much younger age, there is no evidence for any bargeman's apprentice or crew getting a position on a barge before the age of fifteen.[12] It is perhaps the most telling indication of the level of competence and individual responsibility required for this challenging trade.

From the comfort of a modern perspective it is all too easy to assume that trade on the inland waterways of the seventeenth century was a placid affair, but in this age before the gentle flow of canals all regimented in their width and depth, the waterman's trade was hazardous in the extreme, particularly on rivers with a large tidal range like the Severn. In effect, the entire Bristol Channel, bounded to the south by the north coast of Devon and Somerset and to the north by the south coast of Wales, acts as a funnel for the Severn: the Bristol Channel itself is the river's estuary, and the full force of the Atlantic tide is channelled up the Severn. This creates one of England's most extraordinary maritime events, the Severn Bore, in which a wave, large enough to surf, is forced upriver by the tide. That tide is so powerful that it can back up fresh water at Diglis Locks in Worcester, a full five hours after high tide at Avonmouth and seventy-eight miles from the sea.

This tide had to be harnessed by the watermen navigating upriver, and for those coming downriver there was a whirlpool at the river's mouth that had to be avoided. Others spoke of 'rockes and perilous deepes, whirling Gulfes and violent streams' between Gloucester and Bristol.[13] Not only did the regular tides affect the river's height, but so too did the weather, and only at certain times of the season was the river navigable in its uppermost reaches. But navigable it was, with detailed knowledge of the local topography of the banks and shallows and the shifting shoals, and of course with the help of oars and poles, which contemporary reports record were used with astonishing dexterity.[14] Because the water level was so critical to the navigation, when it was good, barges worked throughout the night, dramatically increasing the difficulty of navigation for the bargemen. Anyone who has attempted coastal sailing or river navigation at night will know that in starlight, moonlight, mist or pitch darkness the appearance of local landmarks can change radically and that night-time navigation requires an entirely separate set of skills, only attainable through experience. Taken together, these challenges meant that watermen were some of the finest sailors afloat, and those of the powerful Severn more skilled than most. And, crucially for the future career of John Benbow, the short-handedness of the crews ensured that young men were required to assume a degree of responsibility for the vessel's navigation that exceeded anything expected of a young man in the navy.

The boats were known as 'trows', an ancient and highly distinctive vessel with a saucer-shaped hull and D-shaped transom which can be traced back to 1411 (see fig. 1). All were square-rigged on a mainmast and the largest vessels were equipped with a main topmast. Some were even equipped with a second mast at the stern, a lateen-rigged mizzen-mast. The rig of a large trow was thus a mixture of both square and fore-and-aft rig, just like a warship. They were all made without a keel and with a very shallow draft to allow for navigation in dry seasons or in the uppermost reaches of the river, and those that ventured out into the Bristol Channel were equipped with draught-boards to make navigation in an open waterway possible. The largest vessels were as large as eighty tons and perhaps sixty feet long, while their mainmast, capped by a top-mast, towered almost eighty feet in the air.[15] When the river was high it was crowded with vessels making navigation a subtle test of helmsman-ship as much as a test of river knowledge. This was a fine nursery indeed for a man who was to be 'bred to the sea'. It is no coincidence that Benbow went on to be considered one of the finest navigators of his generation and in this respect his career was similar to that of James Cook. Rather like Benbow, as a young boy Cook had cut his teeth in the merchant navy, in his case on the coal barges of the treacherous North Sea coastal trade.

Living an itinerant life, the boatmen suffered as most nomadic communities do from persecution by the permanent communities, who view them as alien. There are very few crimes for which the watermen were not blamed, but drunkenness, theft (usually of food) and sexual promiscuity were high on the list of anyone wishing to criticize them. So one must be a little careful when attempting to understand the life of the watermen, and to take with a pinch of salt the numerous and graphic claims of debauchery and lawlessness that survive. As one contemporary wrote in their defence: 'I know many water-men, and I know them to be like other men, some very honest and some Knaves.' However they behaved, there is good evidence that they were very distinctive, in both their dress and their language: 'they use singular and even quite extraordinary terms, and generally very coarse and dirty ones, and I cannot explain them to you'.[16] Watermen therefore suffered in exactly the same way that mariners everywhere suffered for centuries, their curious garb and language marking them out as different. During his apprenticeship as a waterman Benbow was being eased into the culture of the mariner as surely as he was into the practice.

This early apprenticeship as a waterman does raise one very obvious question concerning Benbow's career. If he had always intended to join the navy, why did he not do so as a boy? There was certainly no shortage of requirement at the time, for in 1666, when we suspect Benbow began his apprenticeship, England was once again at war with the Dutch and needed every available seaman. Seven years later, that is after Benbow had served seven full years of apprenticeship as a waterman and there-fore possessed a great deal of the maritime experience craved by the navy, the third and final Dutch War began. But still he did not join the navy voluntarily and was lucky to miss the presses of Severn watermen that occurred in both the Second and Third Dutch Wars.[17] There is evi-dence of petitions from the Mayor of Bristol requesting that seized watermen be released,[18] and it is perfectly possible that Benbow was one of those men. We can only speculate but the most plausible explanations are that Benbow was not intent on a career in the Royal Navy, but grad-ually came round to it as his maritime experience grew; or that he did intend a naval career but preferred to learn away from the pressures of war. In either case it is unlikely that he was apprenticed as a waterman in order to become a waterman. If, as we suspect, Benbow was being delib-erately 'bred to the sea' by a family who had once enjoyed significant social status, his time as a waterman's apprentice would have been par-ticularly difficult. He may have shared a family name with the bargeman but, in this famously hereditary occupation and close-knit community on the banks of the Severn, the young Benbow would always have been an outsider who enjoyed brighter prospects than those with whom he sailed.

What he knew of those prospects rather depends on *where* Benbow sailed. The Bristol Channel was the great artery of Atlantic trade from which goods left English shores for the Atlantic, Indian Ocean and Pacific, and Bristol was one of England's most important ports for the importation of exotic goods. The great trading ships themselves, how-ever, rarely went beyond Bristol and no vessel of more than thirty tons could get farther up the Severn than Gloucester. Most goods were transshipped at Bristol. Further upstream, it seems rare for vessels to have travelled the full length of the river; bargemen tended to work short sections.[19] Nevertheless, Benbow would have seen the full range of the trade on a river which, as the second most significant in England after the Thames, carried a microcosm of the nation's goods.[20] The Severn was navigable so far inland – almost 120 miles, far longer than any other river in the kingdom – that it also gave access to a vast economic sub-region from south Lancashire to the Forest of Dean, and from Birmingham to Plynlimon in the Cambrian mountains. The only river in England that could be navigated without flushes (a sudden increase in water level), floodgates, locks or sluices, the Severn was the main artery of the West and the Midlands, the pre-industrial heartland of England, and one of the most important rivers in Europe. Exotic foreign consumables went upstream, a trade dominated by wine, sugar, spices, citrus fruit, raisins and tobacco, augmented by a variety of items needed by Midlands industries such as iron, pitch, tar, dyestuffs, fish oils, various types of wood, tin lead and lead shot and exotic animal skins. Downstream came the corn, coal and salt of the Severn valley, alabaster from the West Midlands, cheese, calfskin, bacon, butter, glue, hair, tallow, timber, honey, wool, paper, cotton and linen. But, of all the goods that came downstream, coal was by far the most important. By the mid-1660s, it has been calculated, a hundred thousand tons of coal per year were shipped downstream.[21]

With such a variety of goods passing upstream and downstream, even if Benbow never visited the bustling international metropolis of Bristol, as a waterman he would have been keenly aware of the world beyond the western horizon, from where sailors returned with wild stories and deeply tanned skin, the holds of their ships packed with wonders. If some sources are to be believed, the lure of the exotic was too strong for the young Benbow, who soon left the narrow world of his Severn apprenticeship for the endless horizons of the deep-ocean sailor and headed for the West Indies, where he set up as a privateer.[22]

It was certainly a popular choice for those seeking to make a quick fortune. In 1654 Cromwell's failed 'Western Design', a policy intended to carve out a large West Indian colony failed to take its primary target, Hispaniola (now Haiti and the Dominican Republic), but settled on the return voyage for the capture of the almost deserted island of Jamaica.

This rapidly became a base from which English sailors, issued with a commission from the Governor of Jamaica, legally raided Spanish trade and settlements. The commissions were deliberately broad in concept and allowed the holder 'to attaque, fight with or surprise any vessel of vessels whatsoever belonging to the King of Spain or any of his subjects which you shall meet with ... and also if you finde it prudential to invade any of their lands, colonys, or plantations in America'.[23] The initial success of the privateers, Englishmen boosted by French Huguenots, known as *filibustiers* or freebooters (from the Dutch *vrijbuiten*, meaning to practise piracy), was astonishing. In the sixteen years after the English conquest of Jamaica, English and French privateers sacked eighteen cities, four towns and over thirty-five villages and seized numerous Spanish ships. The privateers' success became famous; hundreds more were attracted to the Caribbean, and the privateers became organized under Admiral Henry Morgan. His skill took the privateers' success and reputation to even higher levels, culminating in the sack of Panama in January 1671 by a fleet of thirty-eight ships. Such experience would have been no obstacle to Benbow's future career – there were a number of famous privateers and even some outright pirates (who attacked trade of any country without a commission), whose success drew their names to the Admiralty and ultimately secured them a commission in the navy[24] – but the idea that he became a privateer is pure speculation. There is in fact little you can say about Benbow's early life that won't be disputed by someone somewhere, but what we do know is that by January 1678 he had joined the navy and was serving on a ship that was destined for the North African coast to hunt the corsairs of Barbary.

3.

Benbow's Barbary Coast

The ship Benbow joined was HMS *Phoenix*, a seven-year-old, 42-gun Fourth Rate, and he was rated as Master's Mate,[1] a petty officer assisting the Master, who was responsible for the vessel's navigation and pilotage. The Master's Mate therefore held a position that was of some significance and required no small degree of professional seamanship. It is highly unlikely that Benbow became a Master's Mate on a Fourth Rate warship straight after being a waterman's apprentice, and so it is probable that a large and significant portion of his early career has been lost to history. It is certain that he had been on another ship before the *Phoenix* as he presented a ship's ticket when he joined, and it is plausible that he had been in the navy for some years before 1678. The earliest evidence from official naval sources for the career of Admiral Cloudesley Shovell, for example, comes from 1672, but we know from the chance survival of private letters that by then he had already been in the navy for nine years, since the age of twelve, and had travelled to the West Indies and the Pacific, and had taken part in the Four Days Battle (1666) and the Battle of Solebay (1672).

On the day Benbow came aboard the *Phoenix* she was anchored in the Downs, an area of sea between Goodwin Sands and Deal on the east coast of Kent, and the only other naval vessels anchored nearby were the *Deptford Ketch*, *Montague* and *Greyhound*.[2] The musters of all of these three ships survive and none records a John Benbow. It is most likely therefore that on that cold day at the end of January 1678 Benbow was rowed out to his new ship from the shores of Kent.

The *Phoenix* was built by Anthony Deane, Master Shipwright at Portsmouth, and generally considered to be the finest shipwright of his age (see Appendix II, p. 330). He was particularly renowned for building fast ships, and the Fourth Rates were designed to be both fast and well armed. They were thus able to both lie in the line of battle and chase corsairs, the two fundamentals of English aggressive naval strategy in the 1670s. The other significant advantage of the Fourth Rates was their relatively shallow draught, which allowed them to go where larger ships could not, and for this reason they were a crucial tool in the projection of English seapower around tidal estuaries and in coastal areas. But the *Phoenix* was unique in one very important way: she was the first English ship to be sheathed in lead to protect her against the growth of weed and barnacles, which always slowed ships down, and against the burrowing shipworm, which weakened their hulls.[3] At first the experiment was deemed a success but it was later discovered that the lead caused the rapid deterioration of the ships' iron fittings through electrolysis, and the experiment was abandoned. The captain of the *Phoenix*, Thomas Roomcoyle, was a veteran of the Dutch Wars and an experienced Mediterranean sailor. We also know from a previous chaplain of his that he was sociable and entertaining, being 'wondrous free, not only of his excellent wine, but also of his owne good and free company among us'.[4]

After four days of shivering in the Downs the *Phoenix* left for Plymouth, where she embarked a company of soldiers and took them to the Channel Islands of Jersey and Guernsey.[5] The voyage was plagued by relentless gales and thick fog but within a fortnight she was back in Spithead, along with a far more impressive ship and the flagship of Vice-Admiral Herbert, the *Rupert*. The *Rupert* was preparing to lead Herbert's squadron to the Mediterranean, where the service was tough, and the little *Phoenix* was going with him.

Herbert had been sent to join Sir John Narbrough, commander-in-chief of the Mediterranean squadron, who had been waging an unsuccessful war against the Barbary regency of Algiers. 'Barbary Pirates' are easily but mistakenly lumped together into an amorphous group, but in practice they consisted of three entirely separate regencies: those of Tripoli, Tunis and Algiers. Originally part of the Ottoman Empire, each regency had successfully claimed its independence and they now ensured their own survival through a mixture of trade and piracy, each having a slightly different economy, leadership, maritime policy and geographical area of operation. The piracy of these three regencies was further augmented by corsairs sailing from the Moroccan Atlantic port of Sallee (modern Salé on the Bou Regreg estuary, opposite the town of Rabat). Sallee was part of the Kingdom of Morocco, an entirely separate entity from the Barbary regencies. Although English ships had at times faced aggression from all three Barbary regencies and the Moroccan corsairs of Sallee, in the late 1670s the navy was focused solely on war with Algiers.

Algiers was the most westward of the three regencies and Algerian pirates cruised the western Mediterranean, using the Strait of Gibraltar as an eel trap in which to catch valuable trade. Nor were they afraid to venture into the Atlantic and even farther afield, and they did so with the knowledge and capability of northern European mariners. Barbary corsairs, it must be emphasized, were not necessarily of Turkish or Moroccan origin. Many were from England, Holland, Provence, Corsica, Sardinia, Genoa, Leghorn, Calabria, Sicily and Malta. It has been estimated that half of the corsair captains were Christian renegades, and that there were almost fifteen thousand renegades eking out a living on the Barbary Coast.[6]

The rapid expansion in the hunting grounds of the Barbary corsairs and the growth of their success in the seventeenth century, were largely due to the influence of renegade mariners from northern Europe seeking their fortune under the protection of the Barbary regencies. They brought with them knowledge of European merchant shipping routes and fighting practices, as well as a detailed understanding of the technology of northern Europe's great sailing ships. Thus the long age of Mediterranean galley warfare was broken open and broadside-armed sailing warships began to prey on European trade alongside the traditional corsair galleys. Equipped with ocean-going ships capable of withstanding Atlantic storms, the Barbary corsairs now broke out from the Mediterranean, raiding as far as Iceland. They were also regular visitors to the English Channel and wreaked havoc on the population of the south-west coasts of England and Ireland. It has been estimated that between 1616 and 1642 some six and a half to seven thousand prisoners were taken by corsairs and sold into slavery. In one single raid in Penzance in 1625 an entire congregation of sixty men, women and children was captured from a church.[7]

The corsairs from Algiers were by far the greatest threat to English trade and English lives. Unlike the Tripoli regency, which was in part driven by legitimate trade, the Algerian economy was driven entirely by maritime plunder and slavery, and, reflecting this, Algiers had the largest navy of all of the corsair ports. Exact numbers are impossible to attain, but it seems that the Algerian navy hovered somewhere around thirty ships for most of the period, the ships ranging from powerful 60-gunners to small lateen-rigged feluccas. It was by any standards a significant force. The ships were very fast and not afraid to hunt in packs. Two ships working together had recently launched a serious and prolonged attack against HMS *Saphir*, which was only saved by the appearance of another English warship. On at least two occasions British merchant ships were attacked by nothing short of a squadron of corsairs, with as many as seven vessels sailing in company.[8]

Whenever a naval ship and a corsair fought, the battle was ferocious. Today it is well known that the corsairs enslaved those they captured, but it is often overlooked that the English reciprocated in kind. Herbert was under explicit orders from the Admiralty to sell as slaves those he captured, and regular shipments of prisoners were sent from the English colony at Tangier, which had its own slave market, to the great slave markets of Genoa, Livorno, Cagliari (in Sardinia), Port Mahon (Minorca), Alicante, Malaga and Cadiz. We even know that in 1679 Herbert sold 243 Turks for the grand profit of 16,862 pieces of eight. At other times he used them to barter for captured Christian slaves.[9] It was the dream of Mulai Ismail, Emperor of Morocco, 'to cruise for you in your English Seas, as you do for us in these'.[10] Sometimes enslavement was a blessed relief: the year before Benbow arrived Narbrough captured an Algerian ship and ordered the entire crew to be drowned, a reprisal for an earlier Algerian atrocity.[11]

Christian renegades serving freely in Barbary ships were treated particularly badly by the English. In 1681 Herbert found an old shipmate of his on a corsair vessel, fighting against his own countrymen. Herbert hung him at the yardarm, 'as I intend to serve all that I can take, that so infamously renounce their religion and serve against their country'.[12] He was not the only English officer to take this blunt approach: Shovell did exactly the same to a captured renegade in the same year.[13] In all of these naval battles, both sides fought not only for the glories of war but to safeguard their freedom and, in some instances, their lives. As a result the fights were brutal and desperate and engagements lasting ten hours or more were common.

Sir John Narbrough had been sent to the Mediterranean in 1676 in an attempt to regain control of the situation, but had achieved little. A great show of force, in which his entire squadron paraded outside the port of Algiers, had little effect. The merchants were offered some limited protection in convoy, but the corsairs were still able to enter and leave their home port with impunity, and there were no English ships cruising the trade routes with the explicit intention of hunting them. The corsairs, moreover, were as bold as ever, if not more so. Violent and tenacious, they enjoyed unequivocal success. In the two years in which Narbrough had been on station, they had captured 123 English merchantmen.[14] Even those corsairs who were unfortunate enough to be caught still took the fight to the colonists. In February 1678 a sloop with a cargo of captured corsairs destined for Cadiz to be sold as slaves was seized by the prisoners, turned back and wrecked off the African coast. Later that year something similar happened to a French ship whose owner had loaded her with Turkish slaves from Tangier, who rose up, cut the throats of the French crew and sailed the vessel back to Morocco.[15]

Thus the situation stood in the war with Algiers, but that was not all that Herbert and his men were to face in the coming months and years. A further problem revolved around the English colony of Tangier, where the Mediterranean squadron was theoretically based. Tangier had been granted to Charles II as part of the dowry for his marriage in 1662 to Catherine of Braganza, daughter of King John IV of Portugal. It was one of two overseas colonies, the other being Bombay, that came as part of that dowry, and, of the two, Charles had the highest hopes for Tangier. He envisaged it as a naval base and merchant trading centre that would reap the wealth of the African interior, the Levant trade and the transatlantic treasure convoys of Spain. These high-minded procla-mations were made in the safety of London, however, and, of the many royal opinions of the value of Tangier, not one demonstrates any percep-tion of the reality of the situation on the ground.[16] In practice the Portuguese were more than happy to be rid of their colony. Lacking any sheltered, deep-water anchorage for a large fleet of sailing ships, Tangier was also surrounded by high hills broken by deep gullies and infested with raiding parties of local Moors, sent by the Emperor of Morocco to ambush foraging parties and otherwise snipe at the colony. One Governor of Tangier, Lord Teviot, had already been killed by the Moors, and he was not to be the last. By 1678 these ambushes had become something altogether different and a vast Moroccan army was assem-bling beyond the city walls to drive the English out of Africa. The governorship of Tangier had always proven to be a poisoned chalice. By 1678 the colony had seen eleven Governors in its sixteen-year life and the relationship between the colonists and the Moors was slowly reach-ing crisis point.

Herbert's Mediterranean strategy was therefore split between two fronts: he was under orders to wage war with the Algerians until they sued for peace, and at the same time he was to provide any assistance he deemed necessary to the increasingly isolated Governor and his garrison in Tangier.[17] All this had to be done with a squadron that was already suffering from a lack of sophisticated naval infrastructure. It was almost constantly short of masts, iron, wood and timber, and the supply of vict-uals for the crew remained such a problem that in times of want captains were frequently forced to help fund the ships' supplies out of their own pocket.[18]

This was the gloomy situation that faced Herbert when he arrived in the Mediterranean, but before that he and his squadron had to get there in one piece. The first problem was navigation, and it was central to Benbow's professional duties. As Master's Mate his job was to assist the Master in the navigation of the ship. Navigation at the time was extremely uncertain. More than eighty years before the clockmaker John Harrison solved the problem of longitude, in the 1670s it was also unclear how to calculate a vessel's leeway. The impact of currents on tides and of tides on currents was imperfectly understood; charts were inaccurate; sea-marks were few; instruments were limited to the sounding lead, cross-staff, quadrant and astrolabe. Most of it was guess-work and the voyage of the *Phoenix* to the Mediterranean is a case in point. Benbow, it must be remembered, is revered by every one of his biographers as a talented navigator, yet within only two days of leaving Plymouth the *Phoenix* was not exactly lost but certainly not where her captain expected her to be. On 10 March, Roomcoyle laconically entered in his log: 'I find that I should be in the latitude of 46:51 by judgement but by good observation this day at noon I find myself to be in the lati-tude of 46:43 which is 8 minutes further southwardly than I was by judgement.' For a navigator in any era, eight minutes is a very large degree of error, but two days later he was back on track, entering, and this time rather smugly, that 'my dead reckoning is very true'. Six days later a ferocious storm forced them to ride downwind under nothing but a mainsail and the entire squadron was split up. Three more days and Roomcoyle was unsure of his location again, having been thrown an entire degree westwards by the previous days' storms. The confusion was ended only when someone aboard 'luckily' spotted the mighty Rock of Lisbon.[19]

The second problem that faced Herbert's squadron was the corsairs themselves, who had been confidently raiding the Atlantic seaboard of Europe for several years. The English fleet was jumpy – several days before the squadron left Spithead, a fleet of unknown ships appeared off the Isle of Wight, a mixture of battleships and fireships. They were soon identified as a friendly Dutch fleet bound for the Strait of Gibraltar, but the immediate response was one of mistrust: aboard the *Phoenix* chests and hammocks were sent down into the hold and the ship 'put … in a fighting posture'. Once their identity was known, however, the English seamen were keen to help when the Dutch Admiral ran aground, and boats from Benbow's ship together with some from the *Rupert* helped her free.[20] Herbert's own squadron was not even a guarantee of protec-tion against the motivated and organized corsairs. The very nature of long-distance sea travel, particularly across notoriously stormy and foggy seas like the Bay of Biscay, all but guaranteed that Herbert's

squadron would become separated at some point and the ships vulnerable to attack in detail, that is to say they could be picked off singly, if
they ran into any corsairs. Which is exactly what happened on the
morning of 20 March 1678.

That morning Herbert's squadron was off Cape St Vincent, the most
westerly tip of Spain around which all vessels bound for the
Mediterranean were forced to sail before entering the Gulf of Cadiz and
then on to the Strait of Gibraltar. Just after 5 a.m. a sailor on the *Phoenix*
saw a strange sail off Lagos Bay and immediately identified her as
Algerian; he estimated her to carry thirty-eight guns and four hundred
men, more than a match for the *Phoenix*. The *Phoenix* was by herself but
she engaged in the hope that the *Rupert* and *Mary* would hear her guns
and come running. Thomas Roomcoyle, the *Phoenix*'s captain, believed
the Turk, as he now saw she was, had mistaken the *Phoenix* for a merchantman because the corsair hoisted his Turk colours and stowed his
spritsail yard fore and aft – a sure sign that he was intending to board.
The Turk then fired a single shot at Roomcoyle, who replied with a full
broadside. Surprised by his mistake, the corsair set every sail he could
and fled. It soon became clear that the corsair vessel was fast, much
faster than the *Phoenix*, and so Roomcoyle, a veteran of the Dutch Wars
and an experienced Mediterranean sailor, cleverly stayed to windward of
her, rather than chasing in a direct line. He waited for the *Rupert* and
Mary, both faster ships and a match for the Algerine, to catch up. It
took a full three hours, but by 10 a.m. the Algerine was trapped between
three English warships and the *Rupert* started to fire her massive guns.
Roomcoyle estimated that two hundred of the enemy were killed by the
Rupert alone.

The fight then continued most of the day and it was not until 4.15
p.m. that a shot from the *Rupert* took down the corsair's main topmast.
The *Rupert* fell on one side of her, the *Phoenix* on the other and the
Mary followed, manoeuvered by her captain across the Algerian's
vulnerable bows. Thus trapped in an arm lock, her captain, a Captain
Hoghomaz, 'A Turk the next man to the King of Algier', surrendered.

At ten that night the *Phoenix* took her shattered prize in tow and they continued their journey to Tangier.[21]

As was typical of fights with the corsairs, this encounter was not one-sided and the engagement was prolonged. Herbert had nineteen men dead and forty-eight wounded, some badly, which was a significant loss only two weeks into their voyage, and before he had even reached his Mediterranean station. One able seaman, John Rose, lost his arm and one account claims that all of the *Rupert*'s officers, right down to the Boatswain's Mate, were killed or wounded.[22] Herbert himself was certainly injured when a bandolier (the cross-shoulder ammunition belt used for reloading muskets), or possibly some loose powder on the quarterdeck, exploded in his face and burned all the clothes off his back. He was immediately blinded and taken ashore at Cadiz, where, according to Roomcoyle, he lay 'very desperately ill and doctors are fearful that he will loose ye sight of his eyes'.[23] Apparently they told him something altogether entirely: he later wrote that his face was 'so spoiled as that yet I have no glimmering of light ... but the chyrurgeon tells me he has great hopes of the recovery of my eyesight'. Perhaps Roomcoyle enjoyed dramatizing events, but within six weeks Herbert had recovered his sight. The crew of the *Mary* also suffered, with ten killed and twenty wounded, but there is no evidence that any were killed or injured on Benbow's ship.[24] By 8 April Herbert could distinguish shapes a little, by the 15th he could open his eyes and by 3 May he was fully recovered.

Even to the very end the corsair did his utmost to frustrate English intentions and the captain ordered all of his ship's arms thrown overboard: if he was going to surrender his ship, he determined to pull all of her teeth first.[25] Not only were her arms jettisoned, but she had been fought until her mainmast and mizzen-mast had gone by the board and the bowsprit and head were both torn off. Once she was captured, it was clear that she mounted thirty-six guns but was actually capable of mounting fifty-six and was therefore one of the largest of the Algerian ships, although, at 450 tons to the *Rupert*'s 832, she was no match for Herbert's flagship. The curious armament interested Roomcoyle, and he learned that she was under-armed to maximize her speed, and the

Algerians believed her to be safe as they never expected to be engaged on two sides at once. Although damaged she turned out to be a fine prize, 118 feet long on her lower gundeck, a fraction under thirty feet broad with a depth of hold of fourteen feet. She was also relatively new and this was only her second voyage. Two hundred and forty Turks and Moors were taken prisoner and, particularly gratifying for the English crews, a hundred Christian captives were released.[26]

On 26 March Herbert's battle-scarred fleet arrived triumphantly at Tangier with their prize in tow, having hopped their way down the coast of Spain from Cadiz before cutting across the Strait to the north coast of Africa and then to Tangier. We are particularly fortunate that only a few years previously the talented artist Wenceslaus Hollar had also arrived at Tangier by ship and had sketched the city.[27] He turned those sketches into detailed engravings and sold them to a curious public, keen to lay their eyes on the new patch of England at the gates of the Mediterranean. As one would expect, the inhabitants made that desert landscape as English as they could, naming parts of the city after locations in London. They even built a bowling green, with which Hollar was particularly impressed (see fig. 3).

Within a month the extant manning problems of the Tangier squadron, together with Herbert's own problems acquired on the voyage south, gave him the opportunity to reward those in his favour, and one of these was Benbow. On 30 April 1678 he was promoted to Master's Mate of Herbert's own flagship, the *Rupert*.[28]

The ship was magnificent (see Appendix II, p. 331). She had been built twelve years previously in Harwich, one of the smallest of the King's dockyards, by the twenty-eight-year-old Anthony Deane, one of the finest of a new generation of talented shipwrights and a personal protégé of Samuel Pepys. A Third Rate ship of the line, armed with sixty-six guns spread over two decks, the *Rupert* was longer and broader than originally planned, a very common occurrence in England during these years as the shipwrights struggled to come to terms with an incessant trend towards larger ships, driven by competition with Louis XIV's new French navy. She was launched in January 1666 at 832 tons, with a gundeck of 144 feet and a beam a fraction over thirty-six feet. Powerful but also fast, she was highly praised by Pepys.[29] With twenty-four twenty-four-pounders on her lowest deck and twenty-four twelve-pounders on her upper deck, with twelve more demi-culverins and four three-pounders bristling from her waist, quarterdeck and forecastle, she was a match for anything she would meet off the Barbary Coast. Not one of the largest ships of the navy, the *Rupert* was still sufficiently prestigious to carry the flag of a squadron commander overseas as the focal point for a British squadron in foreign waters, an unmistakable demonstration of the wealth, splendour and maritime interests of the restored Stuart monarchy. In addition, of course, it bore the name of Prince Rupert, the King's cousin and a man renowned for his courage in battle for the Stuart cause as both soldier and sailor.

However, all of the logs of the *Rupert* for this period have been lost, and we know next to nothing about Herbert's operations against the corsairs from April 1678 to June 1679. The assertion that Herbert blockaded Algiers itself and took a large number of Algerian ships sent out to fight off the blockaders[30] is not borne out by any of his letters or his ships' logs.[31] The only certain facts we have of Benbow's career on the *Rupert* is that he claimed no money for tobacco and so was probably not a smoker, and that he had spent £1 9s on dead men's clothes, the easiest way to augment one's wardrobe.[32]

The exact detail of the operations aside, the most remarkable fact about Benbow's early naval career was that he had one at all. From 1673 to 1688 the navy was on a peacetime footing and the Third Dutch War was officially ended by the Second Treaty of Westminster in 1674. One of the prime reasons for the conclusion of the war was an acute lack of money. Peace with the Dutch did not immediately herald a change in direction of aggressive foreign policy and maritime war with another foe, but a period of consolidation and peace, in which overseas operations were reduced to an absolute minimum and the manning of the navy was reduced accordingly. No one really expected the peace to last, however, and although this was a period of limited naval operations, once the government's finances had stabilized it also became an extraordinary period of naval growth. In 1677 the Admiralty, under its Thirty Ships programme, ordered the building of that number of battleships totalling almost fifty thousand tons of additional seapower, and this focused building plan was nearly complete by 1682. With so much investment in the navy, both in terms of ships and of infrastructure, all enthusiastically supported by the two brothers Charles II and James, Duke of York, there would be a clear opportunity for the aspiring naval officer when English foreign policy once more turned to a war footing with another significant European power. Few doubted that this enemy would be the French, ruled by Louis XIV, the 'Sun King'. In the decade 1666–75 the English had added an impressive forty-five thousand tons of warships to their navy, but to meet the expansionist dreams of the Bourbon monarchy, Louis' naval minister, Colbert, had initiated a programme of naval expansion to match any other in history. In those same years the French navy expanded by 130,000 tons and transformed itself from a decrepit force of eighteen or twenty old and weak ships to a formidable battle fleet of two hundred or more warships.[33]

In the late 1670s, however, the relationship between England and France was not openly hostile, and both nations went through a period of growth and consolidation with an eye open to the future. Louis was determined to usurp the Habsburgs as the dominant European power, something wholly against the grain of English mercantile and national security interests. For the astute young English gentleman with a successful and lucrative naval career in mind, it was essential to position oneself well for the coming naval wars. If the exact detail of the international disputes that would lead to that conflict were still hazy, the reality of the ships in the dockyards was not open to dispute, and ships needed men. Unfortunately for Benbow, this was clear to everyone. After a full generation of naval war with the Dutch, there were plenty of men keen to realize the potential glory and riches of a career in the navy. Competition for places was fierce, and potential officers were forced to endure and negotiate the confused system of patronage and favour that protected the navy like a thicket of hawthorn. Those in a position to grant favours were bombarded by applications from anyone in a position of respectability or power. Courtiers, ministers, MPs and churchmen were those with the most effective formal access to the administrators responsible for manning the navy's ships, but wives, mistresses and servants were also part of an informal network of equal, and frequently greater, potency that ran on emotional blackmail. Thus, while the future Admiral and Knight Sir George Rooke entered the navy in the 1670s owing to the dogged persistence of his father, who was a colonel in the army and who had consistently pestered the Navy Board on behalf of his son, a contemporary of his, Charles O'Brien, obtained his command because his dancing at court impressed a former mistress of the King. Of more particular immediacy to the career of Benbow, William Bagwell, the carpenter on the *Rupert*, owed his place aboard entirely to his wife's illicit liaisons with none other than Samuel Pepys himself. Needless to say, those liaisons had been contrived by the calculating Bagwell for exactly that purpose.[34]

If one was fortunate enough to get a place on a ship, there was still a ladder of preference that had to be negotiated. To put it simply, some ships were better than others, as they would provide more opportunity for personal or professional advancement. In the 1670s, with so few ships actually on active service, to serve in the Mediterranean (as opposed to squadrons in the Channel or its western approaches or on convoy escort to Newfoundland) was the plum appointment for a number of reasons. Firstly, naval officers were allowed to engage in a certain degree of private trade during their voyages. Officially they were allowed to transport gold, silver or jewels for a fee of 1 per cent of the cargo's value. Unofficially, some captains would make use of any extra storage space to load cargoes of any type that they could sell for profit. This trade, although the scale of it became worrying at times, was an important boost to the limited naval salary and it was seen as an expected and, within reason, acceptable perk. Service in the Mediterranean was the easiest means of maximizing the potential of this trade allowance, particularly for those vessels that sailed near the southern Atlantic ports of Spain such as Cadiz, where the homeward-bound silver convoys would first dock. Naval vessels would then be the prime choice for local merchants to transport treasure, usually in the form of silver plate or pieces of eight, throughout Europe.[35]

A further reason why service in the Mediterranean was so attractive was that, in the 1670s, it was the only location where the navy was still conducting hostile operations. In spite of peace being declared with the Dutch and as yet no open warfare breaking out with the French, the Royal Navy was still required to defend English shipping from the ravages of the Barbary corsairs. To serve in the Mediterranean was an opportunity for sailors to make significant money by capturing corsair vessels and claiming them as prizes, and in doing so to gain crucial experience of naval war in a time of peace between the major powers. Nowhere else in the 1670s was it possible to make any significant headway in a naval career by coming to the attention of a captain, or even the squadron commander himself – the man in whom all power over promotion or advancement of any kind was vested. This final point explains why Benbow's appointment to the *Rupert* in the 1670s is so important: he was not on any old ship, but the flagship itself, and within months Herbert would be in sole command of the Mediterranean squadron.

Already experienced at fighting corsairs, he had even survived being shot in the face during an action with a squadron of ten Algerian ships seven years earlier. The bullet remained in his head for some time afterwards.[36] Herbert was also a passionate supporter of talented youth and a man of immense influence in the navy and at court. He was deeply opinionated and keenly aware that the success of his career – both politically and professionally – relied upon surrounding himself with men who were fiercely loyal to him, and to him alone. In battle that loyalty was the glue that knitted the squadrons together. Instructions and orders were still too flimsy to be applied with any guarantees. The only way that a commander could guarantee support in the heat of battle was to surround himself with like-minded individuals, or those who owed him support for past favours. He would respond to that loyalty in kind. It was said of his squadron that 'no man can expect to get anything but those who are his favourites'. Few naval officers took this to the extreme that Herbert did, but in doing so he created a group of men that has been compared favourably with Nelson's more famous 'Band of

Brothers', the group of officers he nurtured in the Mediterranean in the 1790s and who saw their ultimate triumph at Trafalgar in 1805. Pepys himself, who loathed Herbert, had a more cynical view, and referred to them as Herbert's 'creatures'.[37]

In 1678 Benbow was in the best possible location, in the best possible ship and under the best possible commander for any aspiring naval officer. His appointment as Master's Mate to the *Rupert* therefore reveals a great deal about the man that we might not otherwise know. The competition for this place cannot be overestimated. We can be certain that Benbow had a powerful patron working on his behalf and that without question he had already demonstrated a clear ability in ship handling and command. Both of these points add weight to the strongest theories about Benbow's youth: firstly, that he came from a gentry family ruined by the Civil War, but now, with the restoration of the monarchy, he was able to reap the benefit of the system of patronage; and secondly, that he was 'bred to the sea' – that he had been trained as a thoroughbred seaman. He was, in short, both a gentleman and a tarpaulin, and he represented everything that the navy wanted in its officer corps. This approval was then recognized and supported in his appointment as Master's Mate to the *Rupert,* a position that was the envy of many.

Within weeks Narbrough had sailed for home and Herbert had taken over full command of the Mediterranean squadron. Herbert was quick to implement a new strategy against the Algerians. Convoys passing through the Strait of Gibraltar were all given heavy naval protection while Herbert's squadron patrolled in and around the mouth of the Strait, searching for corsairs to engage. It was a much more aggressive strategy than had been attempted before and it immediately began to pay dividends. Narbrough had acknowledged that, as a rule, well-maintained English warships were a match for any corsair vessel except in the flattest of calms, when those with oars enjoyed the advantage.[38] This appears to have been true and in most instances the naval ships were able to outrun their adversaries. The real problem was finding them in the first place. This was not a matter of knowing where to look – that was obvious. In the words of Narbrough himself, they simply cruised in the Strait, 'so that no ships can pass but we see them; it's the only place to annoy the Algerines'.[39] The problem, rather, was dictated by local geography. The Atlantic side of the Strait was, and still is, a nice place to pass through in the summer, but a miserable location to inhabit for any length of time, particularly in the winter. The North African coast is a dead lee shore for most of the year and good-quality, friendly anchorages on that coast were non-existent; furthermore, in the 1670s the Strait was hundreds of miles from any significant naval base with quality naval infrastructure for servicing, repairs or revictualling. The Strait is also plagued by a unique weather pattern that even today fascinates professional forecasters. Part of the problem is that a combination of high temperatures, low rainfall and a lack of large rivers flowing into the Mediterranean means that the water which evaporates from the Mediterranean can only be replaced by the Atlantic, which pours through the Strait at a million cubic metres of water per second, in an attempt to make up the one-metre deficit in sea levels between the western and eastern Mediterranean. On top of this permanent flow lie no fewer than three independent tidal streams that do not run in the same direction at the same time. Meanwhile, the mountainous high ground to both north and south accelerates airflow through the Strait itself, and localized weather systems can form of their own volition in the centre of the Strait. In the summer, the main campaigning season against the corsairs, the confrontation of the cold Atlantic water with the warm Mediterranean air creates banks of dense fog which come and go with the tides, depending on whether warm or cold water is being brought into the Strait. None of this, at least, was particularly alien to the English sailors as there had been a book published on the currents there in 1674, but practice and theory in navigation never lie together, particularly in places like the Strait.

Another part of the problem facing Herbert was dealing with a regular turnover of personnel as men became incapacitated by illness or died. Newcomers were particularly bothered by mosquitoes and 'troubled with a flux' but six months or so later most 'agreed exceedingly well with the temper of the climate'.[40] There is no evidence of any real epidemic for these years, but the poor victuals and weather still took their toll, particularly in the winter. At worst, one naval chaplain was burying sailors at sea almost every other day, two of whom were 'little better than starved to death with cold weather'. One English captain simply said that Tangier 'wasted men'.[41] Necessarily, this squadron's operations were characterized by regular promotions and transfers between ships as vacancies were constantly filled. Thus in June 1679 Benbow was transferred yet again, this time to the Fourth Rate 42-gun *Nonsuch*. But now he served as her Master. It was aboard the *Nonsuch* that Benbow gained most of his experience in the war with the corsairs and the defence of Tangier.

The *Nonsuch* was significantly smaller than the Third Rate 66-gun *Rupert* but similar in size to Benbow's first ship, the *Phoenix*. As suggested by her name, which signifies a model of excellence and perfection, the *Nonsuch* had one characteristic that made her unique. She was built with the grain of *all* of her hull timbers running in the same direction. It was an idea invented by a Dutchman, Laurens Van Heemskerk, who was convinced – or at least he tried to convince others – that building a ship in that way would increase her speed to the extent that she would sail twice as fast as any other. In the early 1670s he was bold enough to approach the Royal Navy, and the idea was eventually presented to the King. The King decided to take the Dutchman at his word, or at least give him the opportunity to prove his claim, and the young shipwright prodigy Anthony Deane, who had built the magnificent *Rupert* and *Resolution*, was instructed to build the *Nonsuch* according to the Dutchman's scheme. Van Heemskerk was given a fraction of the exorbitant £20,000 he asked for (a Fourth Rate itself could be built for around £10,000 at the time) and Deane set to. Everyone agreed that the resulting ship, launched in 1671, was a fine sailer, but that her success was undoubtedly due to the skill of the English shipwright and not to the crackpot renegade Dutchman. Pepys thought the whole episode ridiculous.[42] Nevertheless, she was a fine ship and exactly suited to operations against the corsairs. She was fast and had a significantly shallower draught than Third Rates and so was able to get close inshore and under headlands where corsairs liked to lurk. Ships like the *Nonsuch* (see Appendix II, p. 332) were also designed to hold their own in a line of battle and the largest could even serve as flagships on detached operations.

When Benbow joined her the *Nonsuch*'s captain was none other than George Rooke, destined to be one of the finest Admirals of his generation and already a veteran of the Third Dutch War. He was, moreover, only the first of a series of talented officers who commanded the *Nonsuch* with Benbow as her Master; she appears to have been something of a nursery for naval officers with a promising future.

Her logs kept in Rooke's meticulous hand offer a detailed insight into the war against the corsairs. Their first job was to cruise in the western approaches to the Strait, between capes Trafalgar and Spartell, before returning to Tangier eleven days later. Little happened, though they maintained a visible presence and spoke to several ships of various nationalities that passed by. After a brief stay in Tangier they were back at sea again, this time speaking to some Portuguese warships. They then met up with Herbert aboard the *Rupert* and after a brief bombardment of the town of Asilah, a short distance down the western coast of what is now Morocco, they returned to the southern tip of Spain and repaired the ship's hull at Lagos Bay. Such maintenance was always crucial but it was especially so in this war against fast corsair vessels. The barnacles and weed that grew on the ships' bottoms drastically slowed them down and so they had to be regularly washed and given a fresh coat of tallow, ideally every four months. Once a year they would be properly scraped and tarred.

With no docking facilities anywhere in the Mediterranean the only way to do this was to careen the ships: to heel them over either on land or in the shallows. This always put strains on their hulls for which they were simply not designed. The safest way to do so was with a specially designed vessel equipped with specialist rigging known as a careening hulk. Unfortunately there was no such hulk in the Mediterranean, a source of intense frustration for the Mediterranean captains.[43]

Once clean, the *Nonsuch* cruised again in the same grounds with more success than they had experienced in June, and chased one Algerian a full thirty leagues into the Atlantic before they lost her. On 8 August 1679 Benbow tasted his first success aboard the *Nonsuch* when they forced a corsair ashore and set her alight after a long chase. It was the *Pearl of Algiers*, a good-sized ship of thirty guns.[44]

Thereafter they returned to Gibraltar to water ship. This repeated use of Gibraltar is interesting, as is that of Lagos Bay near Cadiz, where they had careened the ship in June. It is interesting because it is *not* Tangier, nominally the English Mediterranean squadron's home. A full twenty-five miles deeper into the Atlantic than Gibraltar and with none of the natural protection that Gibraltar offers, Tangier was vulnerable to the full force of Atlantic swells. While the weather may frequently be stable off the north coast of Africa, the sea state is often rough as the winds of fierce storms in the Mid-Atlantic force the sea into huge peaks and troughs that travel outwards from the storm like so many ripples from a dropped stone. The only solution, then as now, was to build a mole at Tangier, which is why a mole remains a striking feature of its harbour today, but in the 1670s no such deep tidal-water mole had ever been attempted by an Englishman and its construction was reported regularly in contemporary pamphlets. When it was eventually begun at Tangier it was breached at least thirty times by Atlantic swells. The anchoring ground was also bad and the harbour, being open to the prevailing winds, could trap ships for days at a time. 'There is not security for a boat,' wrote an irritable Herbert.[45] So the English colony of Tangier was almost completely incompatible with its naval strategy and Herbert and his officers were frequently forced to travel all over the Mediterranean to make use of safe harbour facilities such as those at Port Mahon in Minorca. The frequent use of different harbours created its own problems with logistics as none was equipped with English naval storehouses or administrators who could cover the expense of revictualling. In turn this usually led to delay and more often than not officers were forced to spend their own money to solve immediate crises.[46]

Gibraltar was the obvious solution. Close to the Strait and therefore excellent for policing trade and controlling the movements of enemy warships, it was also equipped with a vast and deep natural anchorage, safe from Atlantic swells. Even though it was still a possession of Spain, Herbert nevertheless received permission to use Gibraltar as a base from April 1680, having used it sporadically before, and for the next eighteen months it became his main fleet base. Benbow therefore was one of that group of seamen who witnessed the value of Gibraltar at first hand, long before it became an English naval base and a focal point of English global maritime strategy, which it remains in the present day. One of the greatest advantages, it was soon discovered, was the ability to use Gibraltar effectively as a lookout. 'It lies so conveniently for discovery that at all times, in clear weather,' wrote Herbert, 'we can see ships either to the eastward or westward, before they come within seven miles of the place.'[47] The impact on Herbert and his fellow officers must have been profound, and it is no coincidence that, when Gibraltar was captured from the Spanish in 1704, it was taken by George Rooke and Cloudesley Shovell, two of Herbert's captains who had been with him at Gibraltar in 1680.

By the end of October 1679 the *Nonsuch* was back in action, repeatedly chasing corsair vessels and on the 31st they chased the *White Horse of Algiers* but were forced to watch her sail away when a squall ripped off their fore, main and mizzen topmasts. The entry in the log says rather laconically: 'almost engaged with the *White Horse of Algiers*'.[48]

When Herbert and his men were not out hunting corsairs or repairing at Gibraltar they could enjoy at Tangier all the attractions of a foreign colony. In times of peace witnesses were wont to comment on the wild flowers that grew around the fort and, as one said, 'the hay made there by the garrison is only a wither'd nosegay of Rosemary, Thyme, Marjoram, Pennyroyal, and other sweet-smelling herbs'. Others noted the 'fragrant perfumes of flowers, rare frutes and salads, excellent fayre, meates and wines'. Several officers took houses ashore, exchanging the cramped conditions onboard for 'fine large commodious and well furnished houses', with gardens 'full of sweet Herbs and pleasant trees, especially vines, which running up upon pillars made of stone and Espaliers made of great reeds, all their Walks and Back-sides and Spare-places are covered and shaded with vines, mightily loaden with excellent grapes, of divers sorts sizes and shapes, and some very early ripe'.[49]

As one would expect from a port on the trade routes, there was a lively cosmopolitan mixture of nationalities, with Englishmen, Portuguese, Spaniards, Dutch, Italians and Jews all settled in the colony. The only notable absence was a significant native population. Soldiers and sailors of all ranks did their best to entertain themselves, in predictable fashion, with drink and brothels, but there is evidence that the garrison formed a dramatic company which entertained the busy colonial social scene with a number of plays. The navy, whenever possible, also engaged in their own sort of diversion, usually with a distinctive maritime bent. The naval chaplain Henry Teonge recorded how, while lying idle at Port Mahon, sailors re-created an entire battle between an English and Turkish squadron, using a barge, a longboat and two pinnaces. Inevitably with such spare time on their hands, discipline tended to break down and it is not surprising that in June 1680 Benbow brought Francis Blake, the bosun of the *Nonsuch*, to court martial for disobeying him, drunkenness, neglect of duty and 'lying on shore when commanded on board'. Blake was stripped of his rank and sent home.[50]

For the officers, at least, socializing revolved around food and it is clear that while there is unquestionable evidence of severe and protracted shortage of provisions aboard navy ships and in the garrison, if one had the money almost anything could be acquired. There was some trade with the Moors and some limited hunting was allowed by treaty with the Emperor, but with the maritime trade of Europe on their doorstep, luxuries of every type could be acquired. It is thus the curious nature of service in Tangier that the sailors and the garrison could suffer severely from hunger while the officers aboard one warship on Christmas Day could sit down to

an excellent rice pudding in a greate charger, a speciall piece of Martinmas English beife, and a neat's tounge, and good cabbige, a charger full of excellent fresh fish fryde, a douzen wood-cocks in a pye ... a couple of good henns roasted, 3 sorts of cheese, and last of all, a greate charger full of blew figgs, almonds, a raysings; and wine and punch galore and a douzen of English pippens.[51]

On another festival day the gastronome Teonge gleefully recorded in his diary that they were forced to 'make shift' with 'an excellent salad and eggs, a fillet of veal roasted, a grand dish of mackerel, and a large lobster—so hard is our fare at sea: and all washed down with good Margate ale, March beer, and, last of all, a good bowl of punch'. Teonge actually mentions seventy different types of food in his diary and he sampled twenty-two kinds of drink, ranging from 'rackee' (raki) and 'rubola' to chocolate and lemonade, but generally preferred English ale as 'best of all'. Of the best of times he wrote: 'No life at shoare being comparable to this at sea, where we have good meate, and good drinke, and good divertissements, without the least care and sorrow and trouble.'[52]

For those who could get to them, the fish off Tangier were exceptional and there was 'no place under Heaven perhaps is better furnished with excellent kinds of Fish and great plenty; here are (beside Soles, Gurnets, Mullets, Turbets, Lobsters, Eels, Shrimps, etc. in common with England) Cod-fish, Bonito's, Oldwomen, Porgo's, Salmonetto's, Rock-fish, Star-fish, and many other for which they have no name'. Others praised the quality of the native ducks and it is clear that wine and brandy from France and Spain were imported in vast quantities, and drunkenness was a real problem both ashore and afloat. Colonel Kirke, Governor of Tangier in 1681, claimed more men had been killed by brandy than by the Moors.

For those whose ships were not in port sheltering from the weather, conducting basic maintenance, repairing or revictualling, the hunt for the Algerian corsairs was only set aside when the defence of Tangier became a pressing concern. In March 1680 the storm that had been steadily gathering in the hills beyond the city's wall for two years finally broke as the Moroccan Emperor, the notoriously unstable Mulai Ismail, decided to launch a full assault against the English colony at Tangier, to 'drive the Christians into the sea'.[53]

The situation in Tangier had deteriorated gravely under the careless rule of the Governor, the Earl of Inchiquin. His successor, Sir Palmes Fairborne, who had been Deputy-Governor, wrote:

> I must confess I never saw a place more ruinous than this, noe one thing being in a condition fitt for defence, and what is worse not one spare arme in the stores excepting a few blunderbuss that is come at this time with me. I beseech you to dispatch with all speed at least 1200 ... if we come to a brisk action we shall be in great distress.[54]

To make matters worse, the man who had ordered the assault on Tangier was none other than Mulai Ismail, one of the most bloodthirsty despots in history. The frequent casual murder of his slaves, advisers, soldiers, family and pets is only believable because it is corroborated by so many different and varied sources. His fame, however, came not only from his extraordinary and innovative violence, but also from his success. He had consolidated the disparate and crumbling Moroccan Empire, a task that had required an astute political mind as well as an ability to act with untapped aggression. At the heart of his military power was an army of black slave-soldiers, taken from the African interior and trained for the Emperor's service, and these men formed the core of the force that assaulted the ill-equipped garrison at Tangier. They were led by the Alcaïd Omar of Alcazar.

As the garrison manned the city walls and an unlucky few were sent to the outlying forts to observe their attackers and slow their advance, Herbert assumed the responsibility of protecting Tangier from the seaward. Three hundred sailors manned batteries specially constructed on the mole and he cruised with his ships offshore to drive clear any threatening corsairs. He also fulfilled a crucial role in collecting a force of Spanish cavalry from Spain whose presence would prove decisive in the final battle.[55] Those ships not cruising with Herbert were sent to specific locations up and down the Moroccan coast in an attempt to divert the Moroccans from their siege. The Governor of Tangier warmly thanked Herbert and later claimed that the navy's 'vigilance and care of us is very extraordinary'. The attempted diversions had little effect, however, and the Moorish advance was unstoppable. They first fell on the outlying forts, which were offered no further protection by the main garrison. Once surrounded by the Moroccans, their only option was to fight their way to safety. The occupants of Charles Fort attempted this, but 124 of their 176 died; the Moroccans beheaded their bodies and, as one witness said: 'I think every man had a thousand wounds.' Some men from another fort had made their way to a tiny enclosure overlooking the sea known as Devil's Drop, and though Herbert immediately sent boats to their assistance, only one of the trapped soldiers could swim and the rest were captured. It was a costly show of support from the navy: twenty-two seamen were killed in the boats.[56]

Shortly after, Herbert sent a large body of sailors ashore to hold the line between the south-eastern tip of the town and the outlying Cambridge Fort. One witness commended Herbert's sailors in the highest of terms:

> The heroick Admiral of the Mediterranean, brave Admiral Herbert, increased addition of terrour and multiplied horrour to the Mores by putting ashore 600 seaman, excelling in strength and courage, nothing inferior to the Mores (the most agile people in the world) in agility and activity of body.[57]

Although there is no proof that Benbow was part of that shore party, we are certain that Herbert himself was, and that he took an active part, 'the noble Admiral … always charging on their heads himself'. We also know that he was wounded in the battle.[58] Only the 'best disciplined' men were sent ashore, and they were taken from the *James Galley* and Benbow's ship, the *Nonsuch*. Still, the force totalled six hundred men, boosted by a separate company of Grenadiers commanded by Francis Wheler, captain of the *Nonsuch*. With so many men commandeered from Herbert's squadron and with the *Nonsuch* in the thick of things, it is quite possible that Benbow was one of those sent ashore to fight.

Once landed, some strengthened the garrison troops, others dug and manned entrenchments and still more landed guns to strengthen the defences.[59]

As events unfolded over the coming weeks Benbow is certain to have played a part, for on 27 October every fit man in the navy was required for a classic *ruse de guerre*. The Tangier garrison were ordered to make a bold charge against the Moorish lines while the navy's remaining men were furnished with drums and false colours to give them the appearance of a reserve. Some manned the mole and others the ships' boats beyond the mole to create the impression that an amphibious assault was also planned for the Moors' flank. Fourteen of Herbert's squadron were killed and twenty-two wounded but the diversion was sufficient for the main English assault. Boosted by some two hundred Spanish cavalrymen, it had a greater effect than anyone had hoped and the Moors were routed deep into the surrounding countryside. The siege ended with terrible atrocities performed by the English.[60] Although much of the detail of the events of those final weeks of siege is lost, it is certain that the Royal Navy was crucial to Tangier's survival.[61]

With Tangier secure, temporarily at least, Herbert was able to turn his mind to war with the Algerians and he sent his ships out once more to hunt them down. Shovell had taken over command of the *Nonsuch* from Rooke in July 1680 and after a brief cruise off Sallee in which the *Nonsuch* lost her foremast in a chase, she returned to Gibraltar.[62] In September command of the *Nonsuch* changed hands yet again, this time passing to Francis Wheler. Benbow already knew him well as he had been first lieutenant on the *Rupert* when Benbow served aboard as Master's Mate. Much like Herbert, Rooke and probably Benbow himself, Wheler came from a gentry family with strong Royalist links from the Civil War. There were steady successes throughout the squadron, but nothing of particular note until March 1681, when the *Golden Horse of Algiers*, a large and notorious corsair, was captured in a battle that swiftly snowballed into one of the most significant naval controversies of the seventeenth century, and Benbow was at its heart.

4.

Benbow's Court Martial

The battle with the *Golden Horse of Algiers* and the following controversy is indicative of service in the Mediterranean under Herbert in a number of ways as it reveals frustration and success in equal measure. The *Golden Horse* was one of the Algerians' largest ships. Armed with forty-six guns and manned by 508 Moors supplemented by ninety Christian slaves, she was commanded by Morat Raiz, a renegade Dutchman famous for his corsairing success.[1] A ship so distinctive with a captain so renowned, she was well known to the English fleet and the two forces had already had a number of run-ins. In September 1677 Raiz had fought Captain Thomas Harman in the *Sapphire*, shot down her mizzen-mast and mortally wounded Harman. Three years later she was spotted by Captain Edward Pinn of the *Hampshire* and William Booth of the *Adventure*, but escaped using her sweeps in the calm. So, when she was seen once more from the decks of the *Adventure* in March 1681, a year since their last contact, William Booth had unfinished business with Raiz.[2]

It is quite unusual for a naval controversy because the basic facts of the event are not disputed. On the night of 27 March William Booth in the 32-gun *Adventure* and the fireship *Callabash* sighted and then chased the much larger *Golden Horse*. They engaged in bright moonlight from 2 a.m. until 5 a.m., still perhaps forty-five minutes before sunrise. By then the Algerian's mainmast had fallen but the *Adventure* was so heavily damaged in her masts and rigging that she was forced to heave-to to repair. The loss of the Algerine mainmast 'gave me all the advantage imaginable had I any ropes left,' wrote the frustrated Booth.[3]

The subsequent race to repair, so important in naval engagements in the Age of Sail, was won by the Algerian, and as soon as her mainmast had been fished she ran for safety. After a full two hours of repairs the *Adventure* once more gave chase, and by ten in the morning had hauled the *Golden Horse* back within gunshot range and forced her to engage once more. A full four hours later the firing on the Algerian ship began to falter but, just as the fight appeared to be going in the Englishmen's favour, a strange sail appeared on the horizon and bore down on the shattered ships. With so much interchange of vessels in these pirate waters, neither side was prepared to guess at her identity from her appearance alone: she could be an English, French, Dutch or Spanish ship sailed by corsairs as easily as an authentic naval vessel. In general the flying of false flags was such a well-known ruse that nothing could be taken for granted, though it does seem to have been widely accepted that, once a fight had begun, a captain was under obligation to fly his authentic colours. The appearance of this strange vessel therefore had a significant effect on the fight between the *Golden Horse* and *Adventure* because she was clearly flying Turkish colours: a green ensign probably pointed and decorated with crescents, suns and stars.[4]

Having chased and fought through the night, they were now lying off Cape de Gatt, a renowned Algerian corsair lair, which confirmed in Booth's mind that the stranger was a corsair. His crew all felt the same, 'which gave our men (knowing the great want of shot) a great disheartening for the gowing on'. Also, in the belief that this was a friend coming to save the day, the *Golden Horse*'s gunnery immediately improved. The *Golden Horse* then fired a single shot at the stranger, who replied with two, a conversation in gunfire that apparently confirmed their opinion that the stranger was Algerian.[5]

Aboard the *Adventure*, William Booth took the last option desirable to him, and decided to destroy his prize. He ordered the *Callabash* fireship to make ready for an attack on the disabled *Golden Horse*. The engagement had been so fierce and prolonged, however, that the boats of both English ships were badly damaged. This was important because the ships' boats were essential to a fireboat attack. Once the *Callabash* had been primed and ignited, the crew would then escape in their swift boats back to the safety of the *Adventure*. Nothing could be attempted therefore until the ships' boats were repaired, one of which had seven shot straight through it. As the combustibles were set up on the *Callabash*, however, the approaching stranger changed her colours, and hoisted the English Union flag. She was not a corsair, but none other than HMS *Nonsuch*, captained by Francis Wheler and navigated by John Benbow. Her log reveals that she 'spread Turks colours' at 6 a.m., a full three miles away from the battle, and with the rest of the English squadron still five miles away.[6]

By now the *Golden Horse* was in a terrible state, with 109 killed, 120 more wounded, her mainmast and mizzen-mast shot away, foreyard shot off, foresail lying on deck, spritsail yard unserviceable and six feet of water in her hold. In the face of such carnage the captive Christian crew aboard the *Golden Horse* had risen and taken charge of the vessel and it was handed over to Francis Wheler of the *Nonsuch* without quarrel, while Captain Booth aboard the crippled *Adventure*, who had chased and fought his larger enemy into submission, could only watch.[7]

The presence of the *Nonsuch* had clearly forced the corsair to surrender, and in these instances the prize money was usually shared, but it soon became clear that Wheler had absolutely no intention of sharing his valuable prize with Booth, and that he 'would not grant any pretention to capt Booth only that he had fought him well'.[8] This was not the only source of antagonism between the two. Booth was incensed by Wheler's ploy of flying false colours, as it had led the subdued corsair to renew the engagement with savagery born of the belief that safety was assured, that the engagement had been decided and that their injuries and courage had been rewarded with the unparalleled prize of an English warship. It had allowed Wheler to get close, certainly, but it had also led to the injury and death of more English sailors and the further disablement of one of her majesty's ships. So, when the two English ships sailed into Gibraltar harbour on 1 April, both flying captured Turkish colours, the *Adventure*'s red and the *Nonsuch*'s green, and with the *Golden Horse* in tow,[9] the apparent picture of unity belied deep resentment and division.

Without any doubt Wheler's move was antagonistic. Naval warfare was governed by a complex set of unwritten rules concerning appropriate behaviour in certain situations and Booth's indignant outrage and the navy's immediate support for his case both make it clear that Wheler had transcended not just the rules of engagement, but, far more importantly, the rules of what was deemed as fair. With the possible exception of a thief, sailors resented unfairness more than anything else. By the letter of the law, however, Wheler's position was defensible: the Algerian had in fact surrendered to him. This clash between unwritten rule and behaviour defensible through strict interpretation of the limited written rules was a thorn in the navy's side for almost a century, and it was always very difficult to disentangle such a dispute.

Booth wrote to the Navy Board, who replied with an offer of support. To raise even more support, and in doing so to whip the Mediterranean squadron into a frenzy of faction, Booth had the relevant parts of the Board's letter printed and circulated wherever he entered port. Herbert, meanwhile, steadfastly stood behind his protégé Wheler, in spite of the unjust nature of his actions. Wheler in turn prepared for a stout defence of his prize rights and actually sent the captured ship's colours home to his father so that he could not be forced to hand them over to Booth. Meanwhile, the dispute continued informally between the two vessels and the insults grew personal. To put it simply, the crew of the *Nonsuch* argued that, without them, the *Golden Horse* would never have been taken – the insinuation being that Booth and his crew lacked the courage for the boarding action that would have been necessary to subdue the corsair crew. Herbert unhelpfully claimed that the entire controversy was the fault of the *Adventure*'s crew because they did not board the *Golden Horse* when she lost her mainmast. Herbert, at the same time, incensed by Booth's conduct after the event, in turn wrote to the Navy Board claiming: 'I am told and have by more than one circumstance reason to believe the Gentleman [Booth] is setting up for making faction in the fleet, but I know he hath only malice, but neither merit nor sense enough to bring it about.'[10] That may have been so, but the Navy Board were keenly aware of Herbert's role in exacerbating the situation, or at least in permitting an atmosphere to be created in the Mediterranean squadron where such infighting was conceivable and effective. Pepys believed Herbert himself to be the 'chief disciplinary problem within the navy'.[11]

It was at this stage that Benbow waded into the already convoluted mess. In a clearly animated discussion about the event, he was overheard criticizing Booth in public. Too many witnessed Benbow's indiscretion and a court martial was unavoidable. As always, however, it was presided over by the commander-in-chief (Herbert himself) and the court was made up of others who, like Wheler and Benbow, enjoyed Herbert's patronage. For this reason Benbow undoubtedly got off lightly, as the court managed to find him 'only to have repeated those words after another'. For doing so in public he was fined three months' pay (£12 5s), the money to be used for assisting the *Adventure*'s men wounded in the action, and he was required to ask Captain Booth's pardon in public, 'all the commanders being present, and a boat's crew of each ship's company'.[12] No testament from Benbow's hand survives at all from this troubling and stressful period, but it is interesting to note that at some stage during his service on the *Nonsuch* he had started smoking, as we know that money was docked from his wages for tobacco.[13]

Benbow was not the only sailor of the *Nonsuch* and *Adventure* who was court-martialled and the minutes of the other trials reveal the depth of the antagonism. Sailors from the *Adventure* were understandably incensed because Wheler's action had denied them all a share of the prize money for which they had fought so hard. Thomas Rooke, lieutenant of the *Adventure* and brother of Captain Rooke, who was actually sitting in the court, was dismissed from the navy for 'speaking blasphemously and using unlawful oaths and Curses'. William Jenkins, another member of the *Adventure*'s crew, was flogged for expressing scandalous words about Captain Wheler.[14]

The results of the courts martial were uneven and unsatisfactory, and the dispute continued to bubble over. In 1682 both Wheler and Booth were sent home and Wheler was again ordered to hand over the colours. Once more he refused and was resolved to 'not yield an inch but to dispute my case with the commissioners to the utmost extremity'.[15] The Admiralty responded by stopping his pay. The details of the case exhausted, the argument had become a matter of stubbornness and pride and there it rested until something extraordinary happened. Booth took his complaint direct to the King, who was so swayed by the clear unjustness of the case that he personally ordered Wheler to hand back the colours.

The outcome of the *Golden Horse* affair is indicative of the deep divisions within the navy, one of the defining characteristics of the period and the location. It was said of the Strait fleet that by 1681 it was 'divided into two implacable factions, & the differences between them irreconcilable'.[16] The reasons for that division remain uncertain, although it has been argued strongly that it was to do with Herbert's divisive style of command, the factions being split between those who were in his favoured inner circle, such as Wheler, and those who were not, such as Booth. It is unclear if the *Golden Horse* affair created or simply revealed the existence of that faction to the general public, but in either case, by the time the entire sorry affair had reached a conclusion of sorts, the conflict was deeper and more painful than it had been beforehand, and Benbow had played a significant part in this process. Wittingly or, as the result of the court martial would have us believe, unwittingly, he worsened the dispute with his public insinuations against the character of a fellow officer. Such behaviour was unacceptable and dishonourable, and Benbow would have known that as surely as Booth. It is the action of a man with powerful and like-minded friends, of a man confident that his opinion was safe. Perhaps he was surprised at the vehemence with which he was challenged, but with hindsight it is clear that the courtmartialling of Benbow was the public drawing of battle lines between the two great factions in the Mediterranean squadron.

In spite of this setback, Herbert's tenure as commander-in-chief in the Mediterranean was a success. The naval support was crucial to the survival of Tangier. Herbert's presence guaranteed its safety to seaward; without those English ships the garrison would have been targeted by amphibious corsair raids and her defences would not have coped from a two-pronged attack. Ultimately, however, the maintenance of a colony at Tangier proved too difficult and in 1684 the abandonment of Tangier was ordered, a painful and expensive lesson in colonial failure. As one contemporary wrote:

The old Port *Tangier*, where for good cheer
We never paid extortion;
Which, whilst it stood, was once thought good
To be a Monarch's Portion;
Whilst *English* hearts thy walls possesst,
They scorn'd e're to surrender:
Now to the *Foes* is left, a Nest
For Serpents to engender.[17]

Nevertheless, in its short and troubled life, Tangier had been a foreign naval station of a size and permanence previously unknown in English naval history, and Benbow had played his part in maintaining it. He was one of the pioneers of the overseas naval stations that, in the coming century, would bind the British Empire together through trade protection and the accumulation of wealth, and would provide launching pads for military expeditions to expand the Empire still further. The experience gained at Tangier between 1662 and 1684 was indispensable in this system, if only for the unmistakable way that Tangier had demonstrated its unsuitability as a foreign naval station in comparison with such a shining example as Gibraltar, with its deep, protected harbour and magnificent location.

Not only did Herbert's squadron temporarily save Tangier, but also it won the war against the Algerians. During his command very few English merchantmen were taken while his ships captured or put out of action sixteen Algerian vessels, more than half of the entire Algerian navy.[18] Peace was finally negotiated in 1682, a year after Benbow had been sent home, but he had played his part in creating a reputation for the navy that eventually forced the Pasha to sue for peace, a peace which was to last until 1815 – 133 years. Just as the English government had intended, the navy had demonstrated that England was a more valuable ally than enemy.

Once the peace was signed English ships found themselves free of corsair activity, which now focused purely on the shipping of France, Spain and Holland. Although no peace had been agreed with the

Moroccan port of Sallee, the loss of Tangier as a naval base had no significant effect on the ability of the Royal Navy to protect trade and wage
war against corsairs: it continued to use a variety of Mediterranean ports
as temporary bases for trade protection as it had been doing for over
four years.[19] Merchants throughout northern Europe began to favour
English ships as the security of their passage was relatively guaranteed.
Thus the fortunes of the English merchant marine rose while those of
its enemies were bowed down by the constant attacks of Barbary
corsairs. The significance of this cannot be emphasised enough. As the
wealth of England grew, so she was able to pay for more warships,
which, in turn, could once again guarantee the safety of her merchants.
It was this cycle of protection and reward, a symbiosis between
merchant fleet and navy, which catapulted England to the status of
maritime superpower in the coming years. And, as with the defence of
Tangier against Moorish attack, Benbow and his fellow officers played
their part in achieving this success in the most difficult of conditions.

Thus the young Benbow in one way or another influenced the outcome of these events, but undoubtedly this was a two-way process and it
is worth considering how he himself was changed by his experience. At
the most basic level he had learned a great deal about the pilotage of the
western Mediterranean and North African coast and he had familiar-
ized himself with the tactics and strategy of the Barbary corsairs. He
had seen at first hand how the depredations of trade-raiders could be
halted by systematic protection of trade through a convoy system
boosted by regional squadrons cruising for corsairs. He had allied himself with Herbert's faction within the navy and it is likely that he had
been profoundly influenced by Herbert himself. This period of naval
history is characterized by a total absence of independent and objective
coaching in the methods of command, and young officers simply
learned from the example set them by their patrons. It is no coincidence
that Herbert's gruff style of command rubbed off on the young Benbow.
It is worth emphasizing here that, although Benbow and his patron
were some distance from each other in rank, they were not worlds apart
in background or age, and rank was not the only influence on the
dynamics of social interaction. Herbert was, at the best guess, perhaps

only three years older than Benbow – he was about thirty when he took Benbow to the Mediterranean aboard the *Rupert* and Benbow was twenty-seven. They both came from gentry families devoted to the Royalist cause in the Civil War and they were both thoroughbred seamen – Herbert had joined the navy aged only fifteen.

The two men also seem to have shared some aspects of their characters. Those who had fallen on the wrong side of Herbert were so embittered that they could barely draw the breath to get the insults out, but as insults go they are as good as any in English naval history. As usual it is Pepys who is best able to summon the words he desires, and he says of Herbert: 'of all the worst men living, Herbert is the only man that I do not know to have any one virtue to compound for all his vices'.[20] He has since been described by a modern historian as 'a professional badman'.[21] All agree that in spite of the quality of his family background, Herbert spoke in a rough, plain manner, had a violent temper and was almost obsessively antagonistic. It is quite likely that Herbert in turn picked some of this up from *his* patron: the man Herbert first went to sea with was Sir Robert Holmes, who likewise had a reputation for speaking his mind and irritating others. There are endless examples of Herbert falling out with naval officers, and it should come as no surprise that Benbow, schooled by Herbert, was unable to generate much warmth from some of his officers, a failing which ultimately led to his death.

5.

Benbow's Corsairs' Heads

In late August 1681 the *Nonsuch* returned home despite her captain Francis Wheler's attempts to influence the Admiralty, via his father, to keep her in commission for another year. 'If they are not my Enemy's 'tis not hard to be done,' claimed Wheler.[1] His father was a powerful man with a significant reputation who was Governor of the Leeward Islands and a Member of Parliament, but in practice the economics of peace were less easy to influence: from 1681 there were only a handful of English ships active anywhere in the world.[2] The *Nonsuch*, moreover, had been away from home for over three years and was in need of some serious attention. To make matters worse, the *Golden Horse* affair had served to keep the name of the *Nonsuch* frequently under the noses of the Navy Board, who had been resolute in their condemnation of Wheler's behaviour. With all of these factors conspiring against her, the *Nonsuch* was forced home as an escort to fourteen merchantmen.[3] Her crew saw the Lizard on 31 August 1681 in glorious late-summer sunshine with a steady westerly breeze, an idyllic location in idyllic conditions for any sailor then or now. Start Point off Salcombe soon came into view, then the Isle of Wight, Beachy Head, Dungeness and the Downs, where they anchored. Shortly after she returned home, the *Nonsuch* was laid up and her crew paid off.[4] Wheler himself, perhaps owing to his father's influence, escaped the cull as Herbert transferred him to the *Kingfisher*, which remained in Tangier. Benbow was not so lucky and, with his reputation undoubtedly damaged by his recent court martial, after three years and four months unbroken service in the Mediterranean, he found himself out of favour with the navy, out of the Mediterranean and out of work.

It says a great deal about Benbow's character and his connections that this did not become a full stop to his naval career or indeed to his expectations. He was a skilled mariner with experience in both the merchant navy and the Royal Navy; he knew as well as anyone both the dangers and potential profits of the Mediterranean passage and had first-hand experience of fighting corsairs; he also retained support within Herbert's faction in the Royal Navy, which in 1681 remained the only naval presence in the Mediterranean. Herbert himself was something of an entrepreneur and it is known from his surviving bank accounts that he was willing to loan money to his captains.[5] He was, moreover, just one of many who sought to benefit from the economic revolution that was unmistakable in those years. Recent research has demonstrated that the rate of new investment in commerce was abnormally high from the 1660s. In short, Britain found herself at the centre of a trade in goods destined for new mass markets in Britain and throughout Europe. Before the mid-seventeenth century the majority of British exports had consisted of nothing more than wool. British wool was renowned for its quality and price throughout the world. As the European merchant empires expanded overseas, however, this focus on the wool trade rapidly changed. Exotic colonial goods were imported, and then re-exported to quench an insatiable thirst in Europe, where the population craved tobacco and sugar, the second to such an extent that what had once had been a luxury for the rich had become, by the last quarter of the seventeenth century, 'the solace of all classes'. Between 1630 and 1680 the retail price of sugar halved. There was also a growing demand for the older trades in English-caught fish. Newfoundland cod was particularly prized in Portugal and red herrings in Italy. All of the manufactured requirements for settlement and colonization in the New World that could not be met in the fledgling colonies also had to be imported from England, and thousands of slaves had to be carried overseas to provide the manpower to drive that economy. At the same time, English merchants continued to import from the east spices, silk and calicoes and from Europe fruit, wine and other delicacies. Dyestuffs were always in high demand.[6]

Such was the demand for the shipment of goods within the

Mediterranean that English merchantmen never found themselves short of intra-Mediterranean trade to further balance their voyages and increase their profits. Grain from Sicily and Greece, rice from Egypt and Venice and salt from Sicily were carried all over the Mediterranean.[7] For those wishing to profit from this overseas trade, and particularly the Mediterranean trade, a man like Benbow was exactly what was wanted to maximize the safety of a cargo, and through his Mediterranean contacts to safeguard the expected levels of profit. It is no surprise, then, that in 1681 we do not find Benbow skulking in Shropshire, but serving aboard a merchant ship. One unconfirmed source claims his first ship was called the *Benbow*.[8] If this is correct it is not unlikely that, with his family connections in merchant shipping, he raised funds from within his family, and that the name *Benbow* refers to a group of Benbows, rather than John Benbow alone. It also suggests a measure of pride in the family name, personal confidence and a willingness for self-publicity that are all quite appropriate to what we know about Benbow's perception of himself in later life.

By 1682 Herbert had successfully concluded his peace with the Algerians, but open hostility continued between English ships and the Moorish corsairs of Sallee, and in 1686 Benbow found his merchant idyll shattered by a corsair attack. The story survives because it was told to one of Benbow's earliest biographers by Paul Calton, Benbow's son-in-law, whose testimony historians have had reason to doubt in the past.[9] Unfortunately, as the event happened to a lone trader and history has not been kind to Benbow's correspondence of this era of his life, there are no official logbooks, reports or letters to either corroborate or contradict the story. Nevertheless, a string of scholars have been reluctant to dismiss it out of hand, not least because of the existence of a Moorish skullcap that was passed down through the Benbow family through his sister, Elizabeth. The cap itself was interesting but not remarkable, being made of finely plaited cane and mounted in silver, but crucially it was inscribed: 'The first adventure of Captain John Benbo, and gift to Richard Ridley [a son-in-law], 1687.' One hundred and thirty-eight years later it was still in the possession of Benbow's descendants but has since been lost.[10] The story that explains how this curious skullcap came into Benbow's possession goes something like this.

The frigate *Benbow* was attacked by a large corsair vessel off the Strait of Gibraltar and Benbow stoutly organized her defence. As was usual in this type of attack the corsairs appear to have engaged at a distance before bearing down to the merchantman and preparing to board. Benbow was unable to stop them boarding but, when they did, he and his crew engaged them in hand-to-hand combat of such ferocity that they were forced back to their ship, leaving thirteen of their party behind. At this stage it is unclear if the corsairs left on his deck were alive or dead, injured or unhurt, but Benbow ordered them all to be beheaded, mimicking a well-established tradition of Islamic warfare. Not only that, he then ordered their heads to be preserved in a barrel of pork pickle, thus rendering that part of the corpse 'unclean' in the eyes of Islam. Benbow had a very good reason to preserve the heads. Shortly after the attack he arrived in Cadiz and marched ashore with his servant following, carrying the thirteen heads in a sack. When challenged by customs officials to declare the sack's contents, Benbow refused and was taken directly to the town's magistrates. There he ordered his servant to fling down the sack and reveal its contents, which, rather tongue in cheek, he had claimed were 'salt provisions for his own use'. The whole story was originally told with the air of a practical joke. Benbow, it is assumed – although this is never directly explained – had always intended to take the heads to the magistrates to claim 'head money' for the dead corsairs. Presumably, at some point in the adventure he relieved one of the decapitated corsairs of his skullcap and took it home as a trophy. So impressed were the Cadiz magistrates, we are told, that they immediately wrote to the Spanish King, Charles II, praising the conduct of this courageous and boisterous English merchant. Charles in turn summoned Benbow to court, 'where he was received with great testimonies of respect, and not only dismissed with a handsome present, but his Catholic Majesty also pleased to write a letter in his behalf to King James, who upon the Captain's return gave him a ship which was his introduction to the royal navy'.[II]

We know at least that the last statement in this story is untrue: Benbow had already been in the navy. There is also no supporting evidence of any kind for the rest of the tale but its very existence and association with Benbow is itself historically significant and an important part of the Benbow legend for the elements that it reveals about the perception of English naval heroes. The story originated in the late 1770s, when the historian Campbell was collecting the information for his magnificent *Biographia Britannica*, which included a lengthy entry on Benbow. In those years England was at war with her rebellious colonies in America in what became known as the War of American Independence. The fighting on American soil had to be supported by incessant convoys of troops and supplies transported across the Atlantic, and all protected by the Royal Navy. In turn the navy was targeted by the colonies' maritime allies, the French, and in the early years of the war there was nothing but disappointment for the service. In particular, at the Battle of Ushant in 1778, almost exactly the time when Campbell was writing his book, the English fleet was paralysed by inaction and confusion between Admiral Keppel and his Vice-Admiral, Sir Hugh Palliser. When, four years later, the war was lost and America won its independence, the failure of the Royal Navy was very much to blame. The years in which Campbell's book was written and the immediate aftermath of its publication were therefore a perfect time for nostalgic reflection on previous maritime glory, an age that was perceived as simpler, in which the bravery of naval officers like Benbow was such that it overflowed in its exuberance, as encapsulated by the story of the corsairs' heads. The underlying message, that courage at sea would be rewarded, is also significant, and was an important part of the contemporary appeal of the story at a time when the public was frustrated by naval incompetence and thirsty for maritime success.

The affair of the salted heads, moreover, was not the only tale of contact with corsairs with which Benbow became associated in the 1770s, although it was certainly the one that was retold with the most relish and, one suspects, exaggeration. A year or so later Benbow, it has been claimed, was the owner of a new ship, the *Malaga Merchant*, and in May 1687 she was attacked by corsairs in the mouth of the Strait. All we know about this fight is that the corsairs fired a broadside, followed it up with a volley of small shot and then prepared to board, bracing their spritsail fore and aft. This was always a sure sign that a boarding attempt was being planned. The best way to board one ship from another was not, as one might expect, to do so with the two vessels alongside one another. It was essentially a problem of ship design as vessels of this era were built with exaggerated tumblehome – that is to say their hulls bulged out near the waterline but narrowed at the level of the decks, like a wine glass. The difficulty can be best pictured by placing two wine glasses next to each other, so that they are touching where they bulge out. Although they are touching at the bulge, at the level of the rim – if you imagine this to be the ships' decks – they are still a significant distance apart, certainly too far to jump in the case of the largest vessels. One of the solutions for the aggressor was to attack at right angles, driving the bowsprit onto the decks of the enemy vessel. The bowsprit then could be used as a bridge over which sailors could pass fairly easily from one ship to the other.[12]

The one major drawback of this approach was that the aggressor's intention was obvious: if the spritsail was set, sailors on the defending ship could see clearly the great cloud of canvas hanging below the bowsprit being taken in and stowed by men on the yard itself, before others hauled ropes secured on the forecastle to brace the yard fore-and-aft, in the same orientation as the bowsprit itself. Moreover, all of this took time, allowing a well-drilled crew to prepare for a boarding attempt with men massed at the rails, armed with swords and pikes to keep the attackers at arm's length, and then to fight them with knives and axes in the crush of bodies once they were aboard, when there was little room to swing a cutlass. Merchantmen of this era were all armed, some heavily, and in this period of peace it is likely that many of the sailors aboard had been in the Royal Navy, some with significant experience of engagements with corsairs or even the full-scale fleet battles of the Dutch Wars. Her guns would be loaded and ready and, if there was time, other precautions could be taken. Boarding netting was a common defensive device and occasionally spare yards could be lashed at right angles to the defending ship's hull – almost like the oars of a galley – to keep her attacker at bay. Benbow was sufficiently skilled as a mariner and had enough experience in warfare against the corsairs to know what was coming, and so his men were fully prepared. They gave the corsair 'so warm and steady a reception, that he was quickly glad to sheer off' before Benbow became the aggressor himself and forced the swift corsair to flee.[13]

In both of these tales there are hints of the main constituent elements of the Benbow legend (as opposed to proven characteristics of the man): a natural ability to lead and inspire, an unquenchable hatred of England's enemies, a simmering violence and a dauntless courage. All of these characteristics became the publicly held yardstick against which England's naval officers were compared throughout the decades of maritime dominance to come. Those who matched up to them, like Hawke, Cochrane and Nelson, were publicly celebrated, while those who did not were publicly vilified. The most unfortunate were openly executed in public, a case exemplified by the unfortunate Admiral Byng, who was shot on his own quarterdeck by his own marines in 1757 for 'failing to do his utmost' to engage the enemy during the Battle of Minorca.

The role of tales like these of Benbow and his corsairs is often overlooked in the establishment of a doctrine of expected behaviour against which a sea officer's behaviour would be judged. In these stories we can see the origin of the cult of the naval hero that would ultimately lead to Nelson physically being raised 185 feet above Trafalgar Square in the middle of London. In some respects it does not matter if Benbow did or did not fight off two hordes of Barbary corsairs in the way described above: what matters most is that this is how the public *expected* their naval officers to act. In some respects, when Benbow died he became the first martyr to the cult of the naval hero and his past could be sifted and embellished to create those stories that would illustrate the expected characteristics of the naval hero.

If the corsair stories are apocryphal, albeit useful and interesting in their own way, there *is* certain evidence that Benbow joined the merchant navy in the early 1680s. Ships wishing to trade in the Mediterranean needed to acquire a pass, and ledger books of some of those passes sur-

vive.[14] Thus we know that in June 1683 Benbow was captain of the for-
eign-built ketch *London*. Eighty tons, four guns and eight men, she
sailed on 16 June 1683. There is no date given for her return, so she was
either wrecked, captured or sold by Benbow. Benbow seems to have
stayed out of trouble, however, as in December 1683 he was captain of an
English-built pink named the *Joseph*. Registered in London, she was a
vessel of ninety tons, armed with ten guns and manned by a crew of
eleven. She left on 3 December and returned from her voyage seven
months later.[15] The very day of his return he had another pass signed
and apparently left for the Mediterranean later that day, 17 July 1684. No
date is given for the *Joseph*'s return, but the hardy Benbow was back by
November 1685 in charge of another merchantman, the *Malaga Frigate*,
quite possibly the same vessel as that associated with the second corsair
attack. She was certainly larger than the *Joseph*, being a vessel of 130 tons
and fourteen guns, with a crew of eighteen men. After a seven-month
cruise she was back again in May, and then straight out again for
another seven-month cruise, returning in December 1687. Again she left
immediately for yet another seven-month cruise, this time returning on
22 June 1688. As before, she turned around quickly and left. But she
never came home.[16]

This particular voyage raises one of the most interesting questions
surrounding the history of John Benbow. Where did he go at the end of
June 1688, when the Catholic King James II was tottering under the
weight of intrigue that would very soon deprive him of the crown and
lead to his country being invaded by a Dutch Prince? Where was
Benbow during the Glorious Revolution?

6.

Benbow's Revolution

At some point in the mid-1680s, as Benbow enjoyed his new career as a merchant, he married Martha, a woman we know very little about beyond the fact that she shared her Christian name with Benbow's mother. Soon after the marriage the first child was born and they went on to have seven children, five of whom survived: three boys and two girls. There Benbow's life could have rested, one of thousands of men who lived a relatively dull existence, plying the distant seas to support a growing family at home; but events of great historical and political significance in the late 1680s were changing many peoples' lives, and foremost among those was Benbow's old patron, Admiral Herbert. It was not long before Benbow's past came to call.

After the success of his service in Tangier, Herbert returned to England, where he was already close to both Charles and his brother James. When Charles died in February 1685, with no legitimate son, James became king and Herbert was appointed Master of the Robes in the King's Household. Already he had been Groom of the Bedchamber, possibly from as early as 1681.[1] Both roles carried no more than ceremonial responsibility but they kept Herbert near the King. James also saw to it that Herbert enjoyed a political career by personally nominating him for the Parliamentary seat of Dover. With such powerful royal patronage it is likely that Herbert was elected unopposed. For two years Herbert carried out his various roles at the Admiralty, at court and in Parliament, but in March 1687 the relationship between Admiral and King was fractured suddenly and deeply.

The Catholic James had suffered personally in 1673 from the Test Act, which disqualified Catholics from holding any public office, and he had been forced to resign as Lord High Admiral. Now, as King, he imposed his views of religious tolerance. Privately he sounded out his closest allies to gain their support, but in Herbert he found an unlikely voice of dissent. Herbert refused to back the King, claiming that 'he was a Protestant as he has allwaies professed himself to be'.[2] This is an illuminating response. James was not asking Herbert to become a Catholic, but Herbert clearly thought that, as a Protestant, he could not agree to a law that would allow Catholics to hold public office. It was the characteristic view of the majority of Royal Navy officers in the late 1680s. English sailors after the Restoration, although surprisingly tolerant of other religions they came across on their travels, were violently hostile to the idea of anyone but Protestants serving in the navy.[3] It was a mindset that James badly underestimated, and which Herbert was able to harness in his bold move away from royal protection. Whatever Herbert did next, he knew that he would find some level of protection, if not open support, in the navy. Although he claimed his motive was one of conscience, it may have been caused, or his conscience swayed, by a deep and bitter rivalry with another of James's naval protégés, Admiral Lord Dartmouth.[4] Whatever the case, James's displeasure was immediate and absolute. He sacked Herbert as Admiral and from his ceremonial position as Master of the Robes and refused him leave to work as a naval mercenary for Venice against the Turks. So, in the spring of 1687, Herbert was out of favour and out of work, just as Benbow had been in 1681 and, in terms of his relationship with the Royal Navy, still was in 1687.

In his anger, James missed the political sense of maintaining Herbert's loyalty by keeping him close, but there were others watching events in Britain with a keen eye and Herbert's fall from grace was exactly the opportunity they were looking for. In Holland, the stadtholder William III, a grandson of Charles I and nephew of both Charles II and James II, had been in power for sixteen years, and had been married to James's daughter, Mary, for more than a decade. William knew that James's pro-Catholic policies, even if diluted by his genuinely held beliefs in religious tolerance, provided him with an opportunity to secure the English crown for his wife and to keep

England Protestant. The Dutch, who had been fighting the threat of Catholic expansion for a century, needed to maintain Britain as a Protestant ally, now more than ever before in the face of the Catholic King of France, Louis XIV, with his aggressive expansionist policies and his vast new navy.

So William decided to employ Admiral Herbert. This was not a whimsical decision but one of acute political savvy. William knew that his best chance of seizing the crown and then withstanding James's inevitable backlash was to do so in the guise of a religious saviour, with no bloodshed, to demonstrate that he had 'no other designe but the preservation of the Protestant Religion and the Restoring of the Lawes and Liberties of England'.[5] This in turn would best be achieved by large-scale desertion from the English navy and army to his cause. William knew that Herbert commanded a great deal of respect, and in some cases unquestioned loyalty, from a significant faction within the navy. He therefore sent a secret letter to Herbert by an English defector named Edward Russell, another naval man out of work and out of favour in the late 1680s, asking Herbert to come to Holland.

When Herbert arrived, in the disguise of a common sailor, he brought with him a letter signed by the seven leading conspirators in England,[6] which invited William to intervene in order to save Britain from Catholicism. William welcomed Herbert with every show of respect that had been withdrawn by James. He immediately made Herbert Vice-Admiral of Rotterdam, used him as one of his closest advisers for the coming invasion and within only a few months of the Englishman's arrival had appointed him commander-in-chief of the entire invasion force, to the enragement of senior Dutch naval officers. Thus matters stood in October 1688. Herbert, in an attempt to revive his fortunes, had 'gone to the Dutch service' and a number of English seamen had followed him. The majority, however, even if supportive of William's cause, remained in the Royal Navy, which was subject to explicit, repeated and successful attempts by Herbert and William to spread sedition through letters, pamphlets and agents in the fleet.

We do not know exactly what happened to Benbow in this period, but there is a specific yet unproven tradition that places him in Holland.

Like Herbert, Benbow was a man with ambitions that were unlikely to be realized under the present English regime, so it is conceivable that he joined his patron Herbert in Holland in an attempt to revive his fortunes. This idea seems reasonable, for we do know that it was common for English sailors and petty officers to work in the Dutch navy in times of heavy manning pressure. Some worked for short periods, others for longer periods, while some settled there for good. We also know that some English and Scots sailors did serve in the Dutch navy during the 1688 invasion.[7] As Herbert was his old patron it would make sense for Benbow to join him in an attempt to revive his naval career. However, no documentary research has been carried out by any of Benbow's previous biographers in the one place that matters: Holland. In an attempt to set this right a substantial amount of research was carried out in the archives of the five Dutch admiralties, but still no evidence of Benbow has appeared.[8] Most Dutch crew lists were destroyed by fire in 1844 and none from 1688 is known to exist. Most of the Dutch logs from 1688 were also destroyed in the fire.

The only interesting new material suggests that at least one 'special' British individual (aside from the ever-present British personnel normally in Dutch service) was installed as a navigator aboard one of the Zeeland flagships in the 1688 expedition, though he remains unnamed, presumably for the sake of preserving either security or anonymity. We also know that William III's Dutch secretary, Constantijn Huygens Jr., joined William's ship *Den Briel* and shared the gunroom on the overcrowded ship with Russell and '2 or 3 English pilots'. These men are not named, though another source claims one of them was a Mr Gilbert.[9] Yet another source claims also that Russell came aboard the *Den Briel* 'with the best of all the English pilots they [i.e. he and Herbert] had brought over', though this pilot is again unnamed.[10] It is possible that this man was brought over from one of two pilot boats that led the entire fleet, whose image has survived in a contemporary engraving (see fig. 5). We know that the two pilot boats contained English pilots.[11]

The chaos of the sources from 1688 must therefore remain the single most important factor in deciphering the puzzle, and the invisibility of

Benbow cannot be used to conclude that he was not there, for Herbert and Russell themselves appear only very rarely. Moreover, Benbow's career in the immediate aftermath of the Revolution hints clearly at his involvement.

His patron, Arthur Herbert, was rewarded handsomely by William for his control of the invasion and, after a brief commission in which he was given the responsibility of bringing the Queen over from Holland, he was named Privy Councillor and almost immediately appointed to the head of the new Board of Admiralty and authorized to act on his own authority. He was also appointed Admiral and commander-in-chief of the fleet. With Herbert once more in the ascendancy, Benbow was given a commission in the Royal Navy as a lieutenant on Herbert's new flagship, the *Elizabeth*. He thus made that most significant shift in his naval career from the status of warrant officer to officer. No longer would he be solely responsible for the navigation of a ship but would take a measure of control over her everyday running, and a far greater percentage of any prize money. It was his first real introduction into the navy's upper echelons. His first commission was as a lowly third lieutenant, but within only six years he was recommended to the King for flag rank. It is a promotion of extraordinary speed, and although Benbow may, in his early naval career, have distinguished himself to a certain extent in the Mediterranean and was undoubtedly close to Herbert, neither is sufficient explanation for the speed of his subsequent rise.

Unquestionably the links between Benbow and Herbert had been strengthened between 1681 and 1689, most of which had been spent by Benbow trading in the Mediterranean. With so many men vying for Herbert's approval after the Revolution, Benbow's ascent is extremely unlikely to have occurred if he had remained an anonymous merchant, not involved in the greatest naval operation in living memory. It is also significant that when Benbow was granted his commission he was made third lieutenant of the *Elizabeth*, Herbert's own flagship. We know for certain that her captain, David Mitchell, had served alongside Herbert in the Dutch fleet.[12] Although there is no definite proof, all of the available evidence suggests that the traditional links between Benbow and the

Glorious Revolution are based in fact, and that the silence surrounding his involvement in 1688 is the silence of an unstruck bell.

But what was the role of the pilots in the invasion? Without doubt they played a crucial part in its success, though they did not always cover themselves in glory. The problems facing William were many and complex. His invasion force was more than twice the size of the Armada of 1588, and included four thousand horses and three hundred tons of fodder – enough to feed them for ten days.[13] William needed to secure a safe beachhead, where the troops and equipment could be unloaded and the horses swum ashore. This would necessarily be an extended operation, so the landing point needed to be near a sheltered anchorage with good holding ground. Moreover, before any of this could be attempted, William's cumbersome force, far too large to initiate the invasion in secrecy, would somehow have to either avoid, or fight, the English fleet, which was waiting fully prepared in the Gunfleet anchorage just off the mouth of the Thames. Once these formidable obstacles had been overcome, his army would have to face James's much larger army, now heavily entrenched around London in preparation for its defence.

The one advantage William held, however, was that James was expecting a descent on the east coast. It was the shortest distance from the coast of Holland and as the season advanced into autumn, equinoctial gales were almost guaranteed. A landing on the east coast would expose the cumbersome invasion fleet to the weather for the shortest period of time and would also allow reinforcements easily to be sent from Holland. The east coast, moreover, provided maritime access to London via the Thames estuary and there was known to be strong Orangist support in the north-east of England, which could swiftly be harnessed to swell the numbers of William's army. Finally, there was the power of history to contend with. Only twenty-one years before and well within the bounds of living memory, the Dutch had raided the rivers Thames and Medway and Chatham Dockyard with extraordinary success. Commanded by Michiel de Ruyter, the Dutch fleet destroyed thirteen English warships and captured the *Royal Charles*, the very ship that had brought Charles II back from exile to replace the Stuarts on the throne. At the time James had been Lord High Admiral of England and had personally overseen the re-fortification of the south coast.[14] Those wounds were still fresh. For all of these reasons, James focused his defence around the Thames estuary.

From William and Herbert's perspective, however, there were several key arguments against a landing on the east coast. Firstly and most obviously, it was heavily defended by the English navy, which had also been cunning enough to raise all the buoys, move all the leading lights and even change the arrangement of the lights in Harwich that were visible from the sea.[15] Above all things, however, William was desperate to avoid a naval engagement. Although he had a powerful escorting force of some forty-five warships, if the enemy could break through to the massed Dutch transports they would be easy targets and the potential for catastrophe was chilling. The Dutch could sail to the east coast with any wind in the eastern sector from north to south, but the entire length of the eastern English coastline is a notorious lee shore and if the wind suddenly blew from the east, as it so often did with unpredictability and violence, it would create surf on the beaches which would make a landing impossible.

The solution favoured by Herbert was counter-intuitive to the uninitiated but, to those with maritime knowledge of the English coast, was the safest. He favoured a landing in the south-west. It would require the Dutch fleet to negotiate the narrow entrance to the eastern end of the English Channel and the numerous navigational hazards of the south coast, and would preclude any of the advantages offered by a landing near the Dutch coast, but the south-west had three distinct benefits. Like the north-east, there was strong Orangist support there; there were numerous large, sheltered anchorages of a variety of orientations which would offer shelter from a whole range of wind directions; and crucially, the wind that would drive the Dutch down the Channel would necessarily trap the English fleet, if only for a few hours, in their anchorage at the Gunfleet. This is the plan that was agreed by William and on 20 October the Dutch fleet set sail for the south-west peninsula, but with no specific location in mind.

The hazards of this time of year and the size of the invasion fleet were immediately and painfully demonstrated as the ships were scattered by a savage storm. Many of the vessels were still close enough to the Dutch coast to limp back to shelter, but two later sank at their moorings and a huge number of horses, somewhere between five hundred and a thousand in all, died, suffocated below decks as the sailors were forced to close the hatches to prevent water from pouring into their holds.[16] Only ten days later they were ready to sail again, and this time they were luckier with the weather. They spent the first night drifting in loose formation off the Dutch coast before tightening up to run the Channel the following day. So narrow is the strait there and so large was the Dutch fleet that they were almost immediately spotted by an English scout. But as the easterly wind blew the Dutch down the Channel, so it trapped the English in the Gunfleet as surely as the tide, which had reached its lowest ebb.

As the Dutch ran the wind picked up and the focus shifted from the Dutch captains, who knew their coast so well, to the handful of English pilots, possibly with Benbow among their number, whose responsibility it was to find a suitable landing place. Exmouth was certainly favoured. Exeter was an important civic centre and located up a wide and deep estuary. Transports could not make it to Exeter itself, but it was well served by its port at Topsham, only a few miles downstream, and there was even a large canal which, built in 1563, was England's first artificial waterway and ran up the southern end of the estuary. Exmouth, however, was then guarded by a large and dangerous sandbank that rose proud of the sea. Now hidden, worn flat by centuries of tidal flow, it is still a menace to shipping. It was as they approached this sandbar that the English pilots realized a landing at Exmouth would be impossible as the strengthening easterly wind and preceding storm had created a large swell that now thundered onto the sandbar. Under the pilots' advice the fleet headed farther west, for Torbay or possibly the winding roadstead of Dartmouth. Neither was ideal as the roads from Exeter that skirted south below Dartmoor were notoriously narrow and muddy, too much so for a large army to pass through quickly. The anchorage at Torbay, moreover, although sheltered from the prevailing winds, was a dead lee shore in the easterly gale that drove the Dutch ever farther west. Nevertheless, Exeter was now out of the question and they headed towards Torbay.

That night, however, the leading pilots overshot their mark and the fleet found itself beyond Torbay and heading towards one of the most exposed peninsulas on the entire English coast, Start Point, which juts sharply almost a mile into the Channel. Edward Russell, aboard the *Den Briel*, was incensed with his pilot. But just as Russell and Herbert were starting to think about avoiding shipwreck on Start Point, or contemplating the best landing point on the treacherous south coast of Cornwall beyond Dartmouth, the wind veered to the south-west, the prevailing direction for Devon and Cornwall, and pushed the fleet back to the safety of the now-sheltered Torbay. The transports were herded into the anchorage, where the fine holding ground held them secure and prevented collision while the warships patrolled offshore. Anyone who has swum at Torquay will know how the soft sandy beach rises so gently from the sea that it is possible to wade out an extraordinary distance into the bay. It is, in short, perfectly designed for the landing of horses. The pilots had therefore taken the fleet safely through the treacherous banks that guard the eastern approach to the Channel, had wisely avoided Exeter and brought the fleet into Torbay. But it is often overlooked that a navigational error made by the pilots nearly sent the whole fleet past Start Point and into the unforgiving western approaches to the Channel.

The English fleet, meanwhile, had eventually struggled clear of the Gunfleet but was paralysed by a series of unfortunate events and poor weather before the captains unanimously agreed that they should not, and would not, engage the Dutch fleet. Historians still do not agree over the reasons for this. In the aftermath of the successful invasion it was all too easy for contemporaries to claim that the English fleet had been incapacitated by captains loyal to William. There is little hard evidence of a conspiracy, however, although plenty of evidence suggests sympathy towards the Protestant William, or loyalty towards Admiral Herbert. In either case the landing was successful and William's march on London unopposed. At one stage he stayed at Milton Manor near Oxford and it is still a long-standing, though unproven, tradition that Benbow was part of William's entourage.[17]

James was devastated by the success of the invasion and in particular by the perceived disloyalty of the Royal Navy. The King, it must be remembered, had enjoyed a lengthy and successful naval career and had done a great deal to improve the service, not least by harnessing the innovative technology of the age and introducing into the navy for the very first time a printed signal book. James believed that the navy's loyalty to him would surpass any question of religion, but for a man who had spent so long in the navy and knew the strength of its Protestantism, this is stunningly naive. If that was a curious reaction, James's next decision was even more extraordinary for a man of proven courage in both naval and land battle: he ran away. Yet again a Stuart king had been expelled from his own country. William and Mary were crowned together at Westminster Abbey on 12 February 1689 and the Revolution was complete. For the second time in history England had been successfully invaded by a foreigner named William; and this time it was Prince William III, Holland's Admiral-General, who was King William of England, the third King William and the second William the Conqueror.

7.

Benbow's Battle Fleets

We do not know exactly when Benbow's extraordinary rise through the ranks began, but by 9 June 1689 he was third lieutenant of the *Elizabeth*, Admiral Herbert's flagship (see Appendix II, p. 333).[1] Exactly like his appointment to the *Phoenix*, the first naval ship that we know he served on, Benbow's entry in the *Elizabeth*'s muster is given a ticket number, proof that he had come from another, though unidentifiable, ship. The *Elizabeth* was a Third Rate, and so larger and more prestigious than his previous ship, the *Nonsuch*, and she was armed with seventy guns. Benbow joined her as she was lying at Spithead heavily damaged.

A month previously Herbert had intercepted a French fleet landing troops in Ireland. The Revolution itself may have been a bloodless affair but the aftermath was not so easy. James had fled to France, where Louis XIV strongly supported him in his attempts to regain the crown and reaffirm the Catholic grip on northern Europe, and Ireland was chosen as a bridgehead for an invasion of England. The French fleet Herbert had met on 11 May 1689 was well disciplined and larger than his own, and he was beaten off in what became known as the Battle of Bantry Bay. Fourteen men were killed on the *Elizabeth* and 'severall dismembered'. Now the fleet lay in the safety of Spithead enjoying the 'delightful weather', replacing the masts, mending the rigging, scraping and tallowing the ship's hull. An idyllic scene of naval industry, but the officers were far from relaxed. The French fleet, clearly powerful and capable, was at sea and everyone was jumpy. A fleet of forty merchantmen was mistaken for the French by some ships near the Isle of Wight and they immediately signalled an unequivocal warning by setting their topsails, letting fly their topgallants and firing guns.[2]

Benbow stayed aboard the *Elizabeth* for three months and then in late September he was promoted, not as one might expect from third lieutenant to second lieutenant, or even to first lieutenant of a smaller ship, but to captain, and he was given his own ship, the *York*, an elderly Third Rate of sixty guns which was lying in Torbay.[3] Shortly after, he wrote his first letter to the Navy Board as a captain. It is an unusual letter because he says very little and is rather self-congratulatory and unctuous. 'The lord Torrington [Herbert's new title] has bin plesed to give me order to Comand the said ship,' wrote Benbow, who further pledged, 'I who shall all wayes make it my bisnus to comply with my duty as to your commands.'[4]

A month later and Benbow had moved again, this time to the command of a similarly sized ship, the *Bonaventure*,[5] where he stayed again for a single month. This rapid promotion is itself impressive but nothing better illustrates Benbow's extraordinary ascent to a position of significance in the navy than his probable next move – from the *Bonaventure* to the *Britannia* – on 12 November 1689.[6]

Only eight weeks earlier he had been nothing more than a lieutenant of a Third Rate ship of the line, one of forty-four ships of her class. Now he was the captain of the *Britannia*, a First Rate of 104 guns, one of a class of only eight, and destined to be Torrington's flagship for the summer of 1690 (see Appendix II, p. 335). She was, moreover, the newest of them all, the only First Rate built in the Thirty Ships programme of 1677. So new was she in fact that she had never left her dockyard and since her launch in 1682 had never been beyond the confines of the stretch of the Medway immediately opposite Chatham Dockyard. In those years, moreover, the science of ship design and construction was progressing at such a rate that ships continually exceeded the dimensions of their predecessors and the *Britannia* was no exception: with a keel length of 167 feet 5 inches, a beam of 47 feet 4 inches and a depth in hold of 21 feet, she was so wide and so deep that she wouldn't fit into the dry docks at Portsmouth, Woolwich or Deptford; only three docks in the whole of England – those at Chatham – could accommodate her. With three decks of guns, her lower-deck armament, which consisted of the largest and heaviest guns, weighed more than the entire armament of most Third Rates.[7]

The sheer size of these First Rates had a curious effect on shipbuilding costs: the larger a ship was, the more she cost to build per ton. As a result a First Rate such as the *Britannia* would cost as much as £17 per ton, as opposed to £11 per ton for an average Third Rate. Her cost would be almost £25,000 for the hull and even more, perhaps £35,000, for fitting out. She would consume perhaps 2,400 loads of timber, each load being the timber from a substantial tree, or fifty cubic feet, and at least three hundred loads of planks. A ship like the *Britannia* could easily consume a tenth of the navy's annual budget and a fifth of the dockyard timber in a busy year.[8] Their size made such vessels highly distinctive at sea and surviving images of the *Britannia* clearly demonstrate her intended role as a prestige ship. In particular, the decorations on her bow were sufficiently noteworthy to inspire the famous Dutch artist Willem Van de Velde the Elder to focus on them in detail, whereas the vast majority of his ship portraits are painted from the side or the stern. She was one of the finest of the Royal Navy's ships, built to compete with the fabulous battleships built in France by Louis XIV, though Louis had a class of ships even larger than First Rates, known as the '*premier rang extraordinaire*'. The finest of them all, the *Soleil Royal*, was armed with 112 guns and crewed by twelve hundred men, 420 more than Benbow's *Britannia*.

These huge ships were designed to provide focus points in the line of battle, the backbone being made up of increasingly powerful two-deckers. So, with war looming in 1689, high hopes were pinned on the *Britannia*, those hopes embodied in her name. She represented nothing less than the future of British naval power. For a captain there was no more prestigious appointment in the entire Royal Navy, and it had been handed to Benbow.

For all this prestige, however, there remained some very severe defects with large British ships and the fate of the *Britannia* in the spring of 1690 points to a malaise that beset both the operational capability of the navy and its administrative infrastructure in the 1690s. Benbow should have been associated with the crowning masterpiece of restoration naval architecture, but the *Britannia* turned out to be a debacle. The basic problem was that the largest ships were built too narrow for the weight of armament that they were required to carry by Parliament. The magic figure of a hundred guns had been achieved for the first time forty years previously, in Charles I's three-decked *Sovereign of the Seas*, but it had been achieved at the King's direct request: one hundred guns is far more prestigious than ninety, the number in the original design.[9] Some at the time thought a ship so large was 'beyond the art and wit of man to construct'. Others who admitted it could be built thought it 'very inconvenient, dangerous and unserviceable'. In fact the size of the ship was not a problem – it was the number of guns she was required to carry – and forty years later this was still a significant problem for the navy. The ships were simply not big enough for the armament required to fight against large, heavily armed French men of war in the deep Atlantic. They had been successful ships when required to carry a limited armament for fighting the under-gunned Dutch a generation before, but now they were too short, too narrow and the armament was carried too high. As a result, and this applies to almost all English ships of this period, the ships were tender, which is to say that they heeled too easily. In some instances the design of the ship was so faulty that she could not carry any sail at all, and this is exactly what happened to the *Britannia*.

Since her launch she had been lying in the Medway without her armament and without stores, and she had rotted. By August 1689 she had to be pumped daily and there were some plans afoot to put her in dock. By the end of the summer the full extent of the rot was still unknown. In early September the plans to dock her were still on hold as there was no room until work on the Second Rate *Duchess* had been completed. Because of poor weather and low tides the launch of the *Duchess* and docking of the *Britannia* was then postponed until mid-November and on the 16th Benbow arrived at Chatham to oversee the operation. It was only when she was docked on the 19th 'with as happy a tide as our own hearts could desire' and then inspected under Benbow's supervision that the full extent of the problem appeared. Not only was she rotten, but she was so rotten 'beyond all our expectations' that nothing could be decided until she had received a full survey. Word was sent the length of the Thames to summon carpenters and shipwrights to survey her and decide what to do. It was eventually determined that she was such a mess it would take 150 men six months to put her right. It had become painfully obvious that her crew of exactly 100 were superfluous and that there was no chance of getting her ready for the summer's campaign.[10]

The Commissioners of the Royal Navy were horrified and could not bear to discuss 'the last tearing in pieces of ye *Britannia*'. And William Hewer, the experienced naval administrator and close friend of Samuel Pepys, wrote a double-page letter to the Navy Board, which consisted of a single, furious sentence, expressing his disbelief at how this 'monstrous an imposition on ye worlde' had come to pass with shipwrights, carpenters, shipkeepers and shipbuilders all tasked with an explicit responsibility to oversee her upkeep. The *Britannia* was not commissioned until the following March and even then Russell was highly critical of her performance and recommended that she be girdled. The Navy Board agreed, and an eight-inch-thick girdling was ordered on 3 October 1691. Hewer was quick to point the finger and claimed that the poor design and construction was the result of inexperience on the part of the shipwright. He made it quite clear that she was 'the first ship ever of her weight handled with such freedom by a shipwright and assistant so little conversant with bodies of that magnitude'.[11]

For a man of such promise as Benbow the failure of the *Britannia* did not translate into a stalling of his career and he found himself appointed Master of the new flagship of Arthur Herbert, the *Royal Sovereign* (see Appendix II, p. 336).[12] Yet again it is an interesting move: it was not unusual for a captain to take a role as a master of a large ship, and Master of the flagship was a particularly prestigious position, but Benbow had already been appointed captain of the largest in the navy. It is possible that the *Britannia* had been identified as a future flagship for Torrington with Benbow acting as his captain and that, while Torrington could hoist his flag on the *Royal Sovereign* with ease, the only place available to Benbow aboard her was as Master. Whatever the reason, Benbow found himself once more on the same ship as his old patron and he even decided to give his position a degree of legitimacy by applying to Trinity House for a Master's certificate in March 1690.[13]

The *Royal Sovereign* was another remarkable ship (see Appendix 11, p. 336). Deep down at her most basic structural level, she was the very same ship as Charles I's epoch-defining *Sovereign of the Seas*, which had, by 1689, been rebuilt twice and renamed. The largest of all the First Rates in 1690, she carried her sail well compared with other First Rates, and with her impressive decoration and a fine new lion figurehead she was a satisfactory replacement as a symbol of might for the failed *Britannia*. For much of her career the *Royal Sovereign* was unpopular as a major flagship owing to a rather narrow stern which limited her cabin space; but this deficiency was fully addressed in her rebuilding of 1684–5.

And so Torrington and Benbow found themselves aboard the *Royal Sovereign* in the spring of 1690, getting ready for the coming campaign season. The day Benbow arrived she also took aboard thirty-seven tons of beer. Two days later nineteen more tons were hoisted aboard, and then another twenty-seven. Four hundred and fifteen barrels of powder followed, 11,657 pieces of beef and 12,200 pieces of pork. On 10 April the carriages for the middle and lower gundecks were delivered along with six specialist carriage-makers to fix them in place. The next day the round shot arrived and two small brass guns for the ship's longboat. They were even blessed with two new lanterns, sent specially from Chatham. By 24 April they were ready to sail and, in theory at least, ready for war.[14]

In practice nothing went well. The capstan broke when they tried to weigh anchor, injuring two men. When eventually they set sail the wind backed and forced them to moor again. It was not long before the bowsprit broke, 'being defective in the throat', and the maintopsail split twice, the second time tearing from foot to head. With no spare they had to mend it with a lower studding sail. They then wasted huge quantities of their ammunition and powder in the complex ritual of exchanging gunshot salutes. On 29 May they fired nineteen guns as they were passed by Admiral Delavall and then twenty-one more as it was Restoration Day. The next day they fired thirty-one because Torrington came aboard and then twelve when they met with the Dutch fleet. The salutes were endless – they even fired sixty-six in answer to a Dutch salute the following week.[15]

On 22 June, the real business of war began. England, Holland, the Holy Roman Empire, Spain, Sweden and some Protestant German states had formed a coalition against France and the expansionist policies of the Catholic Louis XIV. The French King's strategy in northern Europe centred on the restoration of the exiled Catholic James II to his English throne, to be achieved by invasion through Ireland or across the Channel, both of which required victory over the Royal Navy. A French squadron had already successfully transported James to Ireland, and William had in turn been landed there by an English squadron. As the two claimants to the English throne prepared to do battle at the River Boyne, Benbow weighed anchor aboard the *Royal Sovereign* and left Spithead for the Channel as 'an express came and told us hee saw the French fleet off of Portland and other expresses confirmed it … about 11 at night wee made ye signal for unmooring'.[16]

The French fleet that had been sighted was seventy-seven men of war strong, with six frigates and twenty fireships, which mounted in total over 4,866 guns.[17] It was commanded by the comte de Tourville, one of the finest commanders of any navy in this period, who, like many French noblemen, had learned his naval warfare in the hard school of the navy of the Knights of Malta, fighting a religious war against the Turks and Barbary corsairs. Tourville was under orders from the Naval Minister, the Marquis de Seignelay, who had outlined a number of goals, both explicit and implied. He was to prevent the English and Dutch squadrons from uniting, ideally by burning the English fleet as it lay at anchor in Spithead. If the fleets met at sea he was to give battle with the intention of destroying the enemy, and he was equipped to launch amphibious raids against English coastal settlements and dock-yards.[18] At its heart, however, the French naval strategy was to use its fleet to wrest control of the narrow seas from the English and Dutch, to leave the path clear for an invasion.

The French were too late in sailing to prevent the English and Dutch from uniting but Torrington's immediate problem was that the reports all suggested that the French fleet was still significantly larger than his own combined fleet. When the two finally met on 5 July these reports seem to have played on his mind because he miscounted the numbers of the enemy, thinking them even more numerous than in reality they were. Nevertheless, Torrington was badly outnumbered in terms of ships (fifty-six to seventy-five) and, as a general rule, each French ship was larger and more heavily armed than her English or Dutch equivalent. To Torrington the solution was obvious: he would wait for the reinforcements that he knew were coming – Killigrew from Spain and Shovell from the Irish Sea. In the meantime Torrington was happy to bide his time, and wrote, 'I shall not think myself very unhappy if I can get rid of them without fighting.'[19] His captains agreed unanimously. Queen Mary, who was acting head of state in her husband's absence, was incensed at this apparent timidity and, closely advised by the Secretary of State the Earl of Nottingham and Admiral Edward Russell, both avowed enemies of Torrington, ordered him to fight. She wrote, 'we chose that you should, upon any advantage of the wind, give battle to the enemy … should you avoid a battle, we must lose more than we can possibly [lose] by one'.[20] The dispatch was sent straight to the fleet cruising off Beachy Head and Torrington summoned his captains for a council of war. The next day they formed themselves into a line of battle and then gradually and reluctantly bore down to the waiting French line.

The English fleet was divided into three squadrons: the van (white), centre (red) and rear (blue). Each squadron was in turn separated into three divisions, each with its own van, centre and rear. The allied fleet was thus formed of nine divisions in three squadrons, and Torrington stood at the heart of it all. The mighty *Royal Sovereign* flew his flag from the centre of the central division of the central squadron. The weather was a perfect English summer's day. High pressure hovered over the English Channel, creating light north-easterly winds over a calm sea: the fighting conditions were ideal for these tender ships. But the immediate tactical situation was far from ideal for the English. The French fleet, in a relatively close line with a significant curve in its centre (see fig. 6), was far longer than the allied line, and unless Torrington was able to stretch his fleet out to match that of the French, he was in danger of being overwhelmed at van or rear and 'doubled', which is to say that the French

fleet would envelop his fleet and engage it on both sides, a tactical catastrophe. Even if his fleet did stretch out with the French, van to van and
rear to rear, Torrington's smaller fleet would be so thinly spread that each
individual ship would be likely to be overwhelmed by two or three oppo-
nents. Nevertheless, in the 1690s there was no real tactical alternative.
The aggressive fleet tactics used by St Vincent, Howe and Nelson were
still not to be realized for over a century.

Torrington, at least, was in the windward position – the wind was
blowing his fleet towards the enemy. Theoretically this would help
him to engage when he wanted, but only if the French were willing to
fight: the wind that blew Torrington towards the French could just as
easily be harnessed to blow the French clear of the allied guns, but with
both fleets under orders to fight, this was unlikely to happen.
Torrington's problem did not lie in forcing an engagement, but in doing
so without opening his inferior force up to the possibility of complete
destruction.

His immediate concern was the rear of his fleet, which was more
badly outnumbered than his van, and so he gradually drifted the ships of
the centre down towards the rear to support them.[21] It was at this stage
that Torrington's plan began to unravel badly. The Dutch squadron,
which consisted of the entire van of Torrington's fleet, began to engage
fiercely, following good Dutch tradition. They did not, however, stretch
themselves right up to the enemy van, but bore down nine or ten ships
behind the van of the French, where they attacked the Admiral, the
marquis de Château-Renault, who sailed in the colossal 110-gun *premier
rang extraordinaire* flagship the *Dauphin Royal*.

It is not clear why the Dutch made such an obvious mistake,
although it is possible that their ships were unable to stretch ahead as
they would have liked without losing formation, as their Vice-Admiral,
Gerard van Callenburgh, was in a notoriously slow ship.[22] Whatever
their motivation, the Dutch found themselves hotly engaged, far more
so than the rear or centre of Torrington's fleet, which was barely within
gunshot range because of the distinctive curve in the French formation.
Soon the leading French ships tacked and brought the Dutch under
fire from both sides. It was difficult enough to engage on a single side of

a ship; to do so on both sides at the same time effectively halved the available manpower to work the ships' armament. While the fire that they received instantly doubled, the damage they could inflict on either opponent instantly halved. The Dutch, inevitably, were swiftly over-powered and the mistake in engaging so far from the French leading ships ultimately cost the Dutch commander, Cornelis Evertsen, his job.[23]

Torrington, meanwhile, now aware of the predicament of the Dutch, had turned his ships northwards once more to come to their support, but as he did so the wind died and his progress slowed. Eventually he succeeded in placing his relatively undamaged ships between the shattered Dutch and the still-hostile French and then, in a stroke of genius, he immediately ordered all of his ships to anchor. They all did so, however, in a very particular way. Usually when a great ship anchored she came to an almost dead stop before doing so, to ease the strain on the anchor cable. The sails were all taken in and the associated frantic activity on deck, not least the huge clouds of white canvas rapidly disappearing, were eminently visible and their purpose intelligible to the trained eye. In battle, therefore, when it was crucial to stay alongside one's enemy, particularly in light winds that made any attempted manoeuvre to regain one's position unlikely to succeed, it was possible to discern an enemy's intention to anchor and react accordingly. Torrington prevented this happening by anchoring without any prepa-ration. He simply let go the anchor and hoped that the cables would hold. Not only did he do it aboard the *Royal Sovereign*, however, but everyone else in his fleet seems to have done it at the same time, which clearly suggests that this was an idea they had discussed beforehand. Its effect was immediate. Unprepared to anchor, a process which could take upwards of twenty minutes, and unable to manoeuvre their damaged ships in the light winds to regain position, the French ships simply drifted to leeward with the tide, leaving the beaten Dutch and outnum-bered English in temporary safety. The English ships limped back to the safety of the Gunfleet and destroyed the damaged ships on the way so that they would not be forced to risk a general engagement to protect them.[24]

The unproven suggestion that Benbow was somehow responsible for 'saving the English fleet'[25] is interesting but almost of no value without considering the specifics. If he was responsible for the idea to anchor the allied fleet suddenly, which, as Master of the fleet flagship and therefore the man responsible for that ship's sailing, is far from improbable, then a good degree of credit must go to him for considering and then executing such a bold and innovative idea. The claim that Benbow 'saved the fleet' might also refer to the return of the fleet from Beachy Head to the Gunfleet, achieved in the lightest of winds, with damaged ships and injured sailors and through a maze of sandbanks. That also is a feat worthy of recognition. The idea, however, that Benbow saved the fleet from the French – rather than from itself – in the aftermath of the battle bears little weight. In the Dutch attack the French had lost none of their ships but as many as seventeen of the twenty-two Dutch vessels had been immobilized and 1,525 Dutch seamen had been killed or wounded. One contemporary estimated that the French fleet at this stage was twice the strength of the Allies.[26] A concerted French attack may have turned into a rout of those allied ships that remained in fighting order. But the French never pursued their beaten enemy as they could. With Torrington's beaten fleet in their grasp and the Channel theirs to command, they simply followed in a leisurely manner, never breaking formation. Quite simply, the English escaped because the French allowed them to.

News of the defeat was met in London and the Hague by uproar. Torrington was immediately cast as a traitor by his enemies, notably by Nottingham and Russell, who had their own hand in the royal order to force him to fight and therefore their own skin to save, and also by Mary, who would have to explain events to her husband upon his return. To make matters worse, and although Mary did not yet know it, William had won a great victory over James at the Battle of the Boyne. He had, in effect, demonstrated the resilience, nous and courage required to defeat the French on land. Torrington, forced to fight in conditions deeply unfavourable, was attacked for failing to do his duty, and in the light of William's victory the defeat did not look good. To many it appeared that he had simply not fought hard enough, so much so that rumours began to circle of his working as a Jacobite agent. His past as a defector to William in the Glorious Revolution now came back to haunt him. Rather than showing his allegiance to William, his service in 1688 was used to demonstrate his willingness to defect – his natural propensity as a turncoat. As soon as he made it ashore he was arrested and put in the Tower, while Mary wrote a humble letter of apology to Holland's States General, which has been described as one of the most humiliating addresses ever delivered to a foreign government.[27] In it she accepted responsibility for the defeat, promised to care for the injured Dutch sailors, repair their ships and punish those responsible.

A Royal Commission was immediately ordered to uncover as many details of the battle as possible while legal preparations were made in London to try Torrington by court martial. The Commission interrogated numerous captains, including Benbow, and the initial findings simply did not match the public hysteria by now surrounding the battle. Benbow deposed that they were in fact 'within half-shot of the enemy for an hour',[28] contrary to the public belief that the *Royal Sovereign* had remained aloof from all the fighting, but his claim is supported by the casualty returns of Torrington's flagship, in which nine seamen were killed and thirty-five wounded. Thomas Mason, the boatswain's mate, had a leg taken off by chainshot and he died from the wound.[29]

Other captains were equally noncommittal, while some thought that Torrington could have done more. In the subsequent trial the naval factors that needed to be considered in judging performance in fleet battle told in Torrington's favour and, much to the horror of his enemies, he was fully acquitted. Curiously, Benbow was not summoned to give evidence (nor indeed was anyone from Torrington's ship), but he gave a written deposition. It has also been pointed out that a large portion of the officers who sat on the court martial were long-term associates of Torrington, though the president of the court, Ralph Delavall, was certainly no friend.[30] It must be considered that those naval men had some professional sympathy for the hand with which Torrington had been dealt, not least the language problems of commanding a fleet one third of which was Dutch. Few English naval officers spoke Dutch and few

Dutch officers English and of course they were used to entirely different signal books, tactics and command methods. Perhaps unsurprisingly, the King, who had been growing increasingly mistrustful of Torrington before the battle, had no such sympathy. After all, the last fleet that lurked in the Gunfleet instead of meeting their foe head on was the very fleet that William had evaded in 1688 before launching his own invasion, unopposed. Torrington never served afloat again.

It was fortunate indeed that nothing ever came of the defeat at Beachy Head. For a considerable time afterwards the French enjoyed uncontested control of the Channel. The quaking Deputy-Lieutenant of Devon wrote to the Navy Board reporting twelve or thirteen French galleys in Torbay, with the rest of the entire fleet only three leagues off, and by 7 August Devonian officials were convinced a descent on Plymouth was planned. English and Dutch shipping in the Channel was terrorized but the French crews were blighted by sickness and all they could manage was a desultory raid on Teignmouth[31]. After only a month at sea they had 2,062 men sick and eighty-nine already dead from disease and now, after the battle, these numbers were bloated with 344 more dead and 811 wounded.[32] They also had insufficient troops to stage a significant landing, and for this reason their naval mastery was never exploited to the full. Their chance was lost, the English fleet given time to recover and Tourville was dismissed for the lost opportunity. He later wryly observed that he had lost his command for not destroying the English fleet while Torrington had been dismissed for not allowing it to be destroyed.[33]

With both countries heavily involved in large naval building pro-grammes, such control of the sea, so difficult to attain, was only ever fleeting. By the end of 1690 eighteen new English ships of the line were on the stocks or had already been launched and, if combined, the Dutch and English fleets could still equal the French.[34] The following summer the allied fleet was at least a hundred strong. So the strategic situation in 1691 was almost identical to that of 1690 in spite of the Battle of Beachy Head. Benbow's situation, however, had slightly altered. Torrington's disgrace had put Benbow in something of a quandary. The man who had been Benbow's patron from his earliest days in the navy was now, once more, out of favour at court, and although Benbow was already starting to make a name for himself in the navy, had already reached the rank of captain and served as Master of a flagship in a fleet battle, he needed a new patron to guide his future career. The man he turned to, or possibly the man who turned to him, was Edward Russell.

Russell was no match for Herbert. His position as commander-in-chief of the fleet had come as a result of treason, revolution and intrigue, and he had none of Herbert's seamanship or command skill and experience. Russell has most recently been condemned as a man who preferred influence to responsibility.[35] He was, however, aware of his faults and was particularly careful to surround himself with thoroughbred seamen. So his sudden alliance with Benbow is not surprising, and reflects the professional esteem in which Benbow was held. Russell also worked very closely with three other talented seamen, all of whom had served in the Mediterranean and were now on the rise: Shovell, Rooke and David Mitchell. With Russell's rise, all four of these men became key advisers in naval affairs.

Benbow moved ships in the spring of 1691 to serve with Russell, who had hoisted his flag aboard the newly altered *Britannia*, and Benbow once again moved from warrant officer to commissioned officer and served as Second Captain, with the specific responsibility of 'strictly charging and commanding all the officers and company belonging to the sd ship to behave themselves jointly and severally in their respective employments'.[36] For once Benbow spent the entire season aboard her, not leaving until early December.

In comparison with the previous year, 1691 was fairly uneventful. The French were consolidating their position in Ireland and under the guidance of the new secretary of the navy, Louis Phélypeaux, the comte de Pontchartrain, the navy was ordered to avoid contact with the English navy but at the same time to attack English trade and protect the French coast against a perceived invasion threat, the confused orders a reflection of Pontchartrain's ignorance. Trained as a lawyer, he frankly admitted he knew nothing whatever of naval affairs. Nonetheless,

Tourville had his instructions and he did his best to follow them. At the start of the summer he spread his fleet wide in the western approaches to the Channel in an attempt to catch a convoy bound to Kinsale. The convoy slipped past, leaving Tourville in a difficult situation. He knew his presence would quickly be reported, which would draw Russell out of the Channel. So, in accordance with his orders, Tourville fled deep into the Atlantic. What followed became known as Tourville's '*campagne du large*' ('campaign of the open sea'), an entire summer spent trying to hide the largest fleet Louis had ever sent to sea, using it as bait to keep the English navy from attacking the French coast.

On board the *Britannia* Russell searched in vain between Ushant, Cape Clear and the Scillies for three full months. The enemy that had been so easy to find and so keen to be found in 1690, had now become a will-o'-the wisp. His crews became sick from a lack of fresh food and a miserable season ended even worse when a violent storm scattered the fleet, sinking the 90-gun *Coronation* with her captain and most of her crew, and the 70-gun *Harwich*. Two more ships had to be salvaged. The only moderate success of the entire summer was a raid on Camaret Bay. Although Tourville had acted with immense skill, the French, and particularly James Stuart, were dissatisfied with the 1691 season. The time had come to invade.[37]

What followed in 1692 was one of the most dramatic naval battles in the Age of Sail, the Battle of Barfleur. By early spring the French had amassed a large invasion army and the necessary transports but the French battle fleet, ordered to sea to wrest control of the Channel from the English and Dutch and therefore pave the way for the invasion, was overwhelmed by a vastly superior allied fleet. Although no ships were actually lost on either side in the battle, the next day the crippled French vessels, driven ashore by their desperate crews, were burned by English seamen in swarms of boats. The French defended their ships to the last. The hand-to-hand and hand-to-horse fighting in the shallows was vicious and the fires so hot that many of the French brass guns melted.[38] Fifteen ships, including the magnificent *Soleil Royal*, the pride of the Louis' navy, were burned. Seventeen hundred French sailors were killed or wounded. Within two years, calamity for the

English at Beachy Head was overturned by triumph at Barfleur.

Every one of Benbow's biographers has attempted, with no support-ing evidence, to locate their hero at this battle. Finally this can be set to rest, however, as a series of letters to the Navy Board written throughout May and June firmly locate Benbow at Deptford Dockyard, and this fact is lent extra weight by his absence from the musters of any of the flagships in Russell's fleet.[39] While we can guess that he would have been enraged at missing the most significant naval battle of his lifetime, it is important to realize that he did not miss the battle because he was sick or unwilling, but because he was doing his job. The extant Benbow legend revolves entirely around his fighting career but his contemporary reputation was far more complex: as well as navigating the largest ships in the navy, Benbow had a desk job.

8.

Benbow's Dockyard

It was as a seaman in the reign of Charles II that Benbow initially established his reputation and it was in that guise that he continued to impress under James II and now in the navy of William III. His professional competence thus endured three changes of regime and his skill as a seaman outgrew the choking weed of political and religious intrigue that prematurely ended so many promising careers in this troubled period. Benbow's career is as remarkable for its endurance as it is for the details of his naval escapades. To concentrate only on those naval operations, however, varied and impressive as they might seem, is only to see Benbow in half the light in which he was viewed by his contemporaries; from this perspective at least half of his professional life remains in shadow. Indeed Benbow's reputation, steady until the 1680s and then increasingly impressive after the Glorious Revolution of 1688, is only partially explained by those exploits. His reputation within the Royal Navy was informed as much by his ability as a manager, administrator and logistical coordinator as it was by his front-line action against the enemy and the navigational skill that made so many of those actions feasible. We must look beyond the ships tossing in a hail of red-hot shot off the Channel coasts, and consider an altogether different but still highly pressured environment: the paradox of corruption and extraordinary achievement that characterized the Royal Dockyards of the 1690s. For it was in that dockyard furnace that much of Benbow's professional reputation was forged.

On 9 November 1689 the Navy Board, having received 'good testimony' of his ability, appointed Benbow as Master Attendant of Chatham Dockyard, the largest dockyard in England.[1] For generations

Chatham had been the most significant of the Royal Dockyards because of its location up the River Medway, a tributary of the Thames. When the enemy had been the Dutch in the 1650s and 1660s this great naval base had provided rapid access to the disputed seas off the south-eastern tip of England while offering unparalleled construction, maintenance and repair facilities. Thus began Benbow's dual naval career. His responsibilities now divided between sea and shore, Benbow would have gained a deep understanding of the infrastructure of the navy to complement his knowledge of its application in war. This was a combination peculiar to the era. In the early 1690s naval operations were mostly seasonal, as they had been for centuries. The exercise of seapower revolved around the operation of large and cumbersome warships restricted in their sailing ability by gunports close to the water, the whipstaff instead of the wheel and an immature rig design. In gales they had little choice but to run before the wind or seek shelter where they could. Even then, the risk of becoming embayed, that is trapped against a shoreline with insufficient room to tack out of danger, was so great that the preference was always to stay clear of shore if a wide and clear anchorage such as Torbay, Spithead, Aix Roads or Brest was unavailable. The overriding strategy of course was to sail only in fine weather, which realistically meant that, at best, the period April to September provided the window for naval operations, and usually the weather restricted that window further still.

Throughout the autumn, winter and into early spring the fleet was kept in the safety of protected anchorages near Royal Dockyards, exemplified by the Medway, where vast open spaces allowed the fleet to ride out the winter, the ships taking turns to be re-fitted in the docks while work on the topsides and rigging continued on those at anchor. The seasonality of the operations posed something of a conundrum to those responsible for manning the navy, for in September or October large numbers of men became surplus to requirements. The obvious response was to employ those men in the dockyards. Sailors were multi-skilled and while it is easy to assume that most of their time at sea was spent keeping the ship clean, setting, furling or reefing sail or helming, in fact an equal proportion of time was spent on the day-to-day maintenance of rig and hull that was necessary for any wooden ship. As a result some of the sailors were highly skilled riggers while most had elementary rigging knowledge, and others were highly skilled carpenters while many were familiar with basic carpentry or ironmongery. They would have known how to protect the ropes by worming, parcelling and serving, each a different technique of preserving rope from damage by wrapping another material around it; they would have known how to set up and remove a mast's standing rigging (the stays that gave each mast its support) and the running rigging (the ropes that worked the sails). All would have been highly skilled at the coordinated brute force needed to set sail and manipulate anchors, masts and yards, abilities which were easily transferable to the dockyard, where large frames had to be moved into place, rudders hung, masts stepped and sails bent. Other sailors were experienced storesmen or victuallers. In short, all of the skills of a ship were required in the dockyard, if sometimes in a different format, and so many sailors of this period had a dual career like Benbow: they sailed in the summer and they worked in the dockyards in the winter. But Benbow is an exception to this rule because of his rank. He was a captain in the navy when he was appointed Master Attendant and although there were many employment opportunities for the common sailor in the dockyards during winter, there were far fewer for the ships' officers, who were forced to find opportunities elsewhere. The most ambitious and well-connected, like Arthur Herbert, went into politics, but the majority were not so fortunate. Most joined the merchant navy, some the army, while others took any work that was on offer. Piracy was always an option, though the less warlike might take to farming.[2]

This duality of shore and seagoing career gradually changed for all sailors throughout the coming century as the requirements of war required squadrons to be at sea year-round and developments in hull and rigging design, together with the infrastructure that allowed crews to remain at sea and healthy for longer, made such annual service possible. Officers, however, frequently retained interests ashore, particularly in politics, and the link between naval officers and Parliament remained strong.[3] But what was rare in the 1690s, and remained rare, was for an active naval officer also to have a job in a dockyard.[4] Certainly the dockyard officers, and particularly the commissioners, were usually naval men, but as a rule they were retired from active service, their job in the dockyard a full-time annual commitment.[5] This made Benbow exceptional, and few active naval officers before or since would have had such a detailed insight into the everyday administrative infrastructure of their navy. This is remarkable as it stands in such contrast to the relationship between ships' officers and dockyard officers in the late eighteenth century, a relationship that was marred by constant mutual mistrust and occasional loathing.[6] The Admiralty even bent the rules to allow Benbow to serve in this way. In 1693 he was granted a deputy to act in his stead while he served at sea. The Clerk of the Cheque explained that 'there is not any officer either in this yard or navy under my cheque, that hath any deputy allowed him, nor was there ever any that I knew of save only captain Benbow'.[7] Benbow's absence necessarily caused the odd administrative problem as contractors and suppliers working with him were forced to find alternative authority to approve their goods.[8]

When Benbow arrived in the winter of 1689 the workforce would nearly have been at its annual peak. War with France was on the horizon and the fleet had not yet left port for their early-season operations. Benbow would have been one of 941 men employed at Chatham that winter, finalizing the arrangements for the coming campaign season.[9] Such a mobilization was something of the Master Attendant's speciality and it can be argued that Benbow arrived at exactly the stage when a skilled Master Attendant was most required. Of all the dockyard officers the Master Attendant's role was the most practical. While others oversaw the collection or distribution of stores, the work on the ships, the allocation of slipway or dry dock or the general running of the yard, one of the primary tasks of the Master Attendant was to take charge of the vessels in and around the slips and docks when they needed to be moved: in the absence of each ship's Master, Benbow became the Master of them all. As full mobilization approached, so activity in and around the dockyard increased, and Benbow was there to ensure that it was conducted safely. Moreover, some of the ships that would have been at Chatham were special, requiring particular care and considerable skill to handle. This was the only dockyard in England with dry docks that could accommodate the largest ships of the fleet. To be appointed Master Attendant at Chatham was to be given responsibility for the welfare of the nation's most prestigious ships as they moved in and out of dock, or were shifted around the anchorage.

The Master Attendant's other responsibilities were varied and in Benbow's case appear to have been adjusted to suit his skills. We know this because a detailed account of the Master Attendant's responsibilities was drawn up by James II in 1660 and survived unchanged, but the letters Benbow wrote to the Navy Board suggest frequent alternative employment. Officially, then, the Master Attendant was of a relatively high rank, being superior to a number of other officers, namely the Master Caulker, Master House Carpenter, Master Joiner, Master Boatbuilder, Master Mastmaker, Master Blockmaker, Master Pumpmaker, Master Ropemaker, Boatswain of the Yard, Purser, Gunner, Carpenter, Cook and Porter. The Master Attendant was of a similar rank to five other senior officers: the Master Shipwright, who was in charge of the work of the yard, the Clerk of the Ropeyard, the Clerk of the Cheque who was responsible for mustering the dockyard workers and ships' companies, the Storekeeper and the Clerk of the Survey, who kept the accounts of the yard's stores. All of these posts were overseen by the Commissioner of the yard, a member of the Navy Board. Once all of these supervisory roles are considered it is clear why historians now consider the Royal Dockyards to be the earliest example of a very large, highly bureaucratized, geographically dispersed industrial organization. No other manufacturing infrastructure in England was comparable until the industrialization of the nineteenth century revolutionized production processes. By the end of the war there were four thousand labourers and artisans alone on the dockyards' payroll.[10]

Large as they were, the Royal Dockyards were only a part of the necessary shipbuilding infrastructure, however. In the 1690s the British shipbuilding programme was so large that private contractors played a crucial part in making the navy the size that it was. Each private yard, however, had none of the scale of the problems that faced the Royal Dockyards. Being privately owned they could easily be supervised by their owners but in the case of the Royal Dockyards such direct super-vision was impossible and the solution to the problem was as yet unknown, although industrial management systems in their recogniz-ably modern form first began to appear in this period.[11] As an officer in a Royal Dockyard, Benbow was part of this management structure, a first-hand witness to both the frustration and success that characterized the dockyards of the time. Undoubtedly limited by corruption at almost every conceivable level, the dockyards, both royal and private, still man-aged to achieve the remarkable feat of building and maintaining a vast fleet of warships, eighty-three strong in 1690 and 113 strong in 1695, dis-placing 152,000 tons.[12]

Within the complex hierarchy of the Royal Dockyards the Master Attendant's official duties as prescribed by James II were a rambling mixture of practical seamanship and dockyard management. He was required to guarantee that the ships riding at anchor were well anchored and that their moorings were kept in good condition; to allocate each day's work to the ships' boatswains and storekeepers; to designate the appropriate quantity of rigging, ground tackle and stores to any ship making ready for sea; to attend the grounding, graving, docking or careening of every ship; to survey any ship recently returned from serv-ice with particular focus on the rigging, ground tackle and stores, and to examine the boatswain's accounts; to bring any ship into her mooring if not equipped with a Master; to monitor the quality of the appointed shipkeepers, 'it having sometimes been too evident that for want of due care herewith, HM ships have been made keepsakes of aged and decrepit men, or else for persons of all callings that have had broken and decayed fortunes'; to encourage boatswains, gunners, pursers and ship-keepers in their duty; to be ready to muster and deploy a watch 'upon any occasion of enemy, accident or fire, storms or other disaster'; to take charge of any ships being moved from their moorings or launched; to monitor the security of the yard and 'allow no strangers to come near the kings ships or unknown people to work on board or doubtful persons to linger about the ships docks storehouses or yards'; and to monitor the quality of the dockyard stores.[13] Although this job description is taken from instructions issued a generation before Benbow worked as Master Attendant, the role did not change and we know that by December 1690 there was still a strong emphasis on both seamanship skill and yard management. The Plymouth Master Attendant was particularly instructed to 'prevent all misapplication or unthrifty expense … prevent the loss of any time in the dispatch of any ship' and to achieve this he was given explicit permission to energize the ships' officers 'by all fitting and reasonable means'. He was to report any particularly badly behaved officers directly to the Navy Board.[14]

The Master Attendant, it is clear, was there primarily for his sea-manship skill and his ability to bring ships safely in and out of dock, and to and from their moorings, but other important aspects of his duties concern the safety of the dockyard, its efficient running and its financial management. All of the other dockyard officers were also given responsibility over the security of the site and its efficiency and so we can see these dual duties forming part of a collective responsibility exercised by every officer. The Master Attendant in particular was expected to think as a businessman and react accordingly. The efficiency of the dockyard was not simply imposed from above but was a very real concern of those involved in its day-to-day running: the dockyard officers formed an integral part of the navy as a business.

One of the first issues that Benbow would have to deal with at Chatham was the fiasco surrounding the attempted commissioning of the *Britannia* in the new year of 1690,[15] but there were no similar alarms for the rest of his employment at Chatham. He did, however, come into close contact with a number of ships he had sailed on in the past and would sail on in the future, not least the mighty *Royal Sovereign*, which was in dock in February 1690 and which Herbert came to inspect personally that month, now that it was clear that the *Sovereign* would be his flagship for the coming campaign in place of the stricken *Britannia*.[16]

We do not know exactly how long Benbow worked at Chatham but it is certain that on 12 January 1690 he asked the Commissioner for permission to travel to London because he had heard that there was an opening for a Master Attendant at Deptford and planned to petition

Admiral Herbert directly for the job.[17] This bold approach clearly worked and by 14 March that year he had been posted to Deptford, where he worked as Master Attendant until he reached flag rank in May 1696, when his increased status and corresponding workload made his dockyard appointment untenable.[18] This change in employment is an important reminder that Benbow was not simply a puppet but a man of personal ambition. He was not randomly appointed to Deptford – he asked for the job.

This shift from Chatham to Deptford is interesting as the initial impression it gives is of a demotion. Founded in 1513, Deptford Dockyard was considerably older than Chatham (1547 is the earliest evidence we have of organized activity on the Medway) but Chatham was undoubtedly larger. At Deptford at low tide, only a foot of water lay between the largest First Rates and the riverbed, and there was restricted space on the river frontage and in the river itself. At Chatham there was an entire fleet anchorage in good, deep water. At Deptford there were 1,370 yards of waterfront; at Chatham 3,500. Deptford had one double dry dock but Chatham had a double dry dock, three single dry docks and a building slip. So Chatham could build six ships simultaneously, Deptford only two. Deptford was enclosed by walls 984 feet long, Chatham by walls of 3,377 feet – more than three times longer. When surveyed in 1698, Chatham was valued at £44,940 4s 5d and Deptford at just over a third of that, £15,7600 15s 2d.[19] Chatham was both a naval base and a dockyard; whereas Deptford, being so far upriver, mostly concerned itself with smaller warships of the Third Rate and below, such as frigates, cruisers, bomb vessels, fireships, machine vessels, landing craft and ships' tenders.

Less eye-catching than the prestige ships, these smaller vessels were the main force behind British naval policy at exactly the time when Benbow worked at Deptford. After the defeat at Barfleur in 1692 the domestic economic situation forced Louis to reconsider his maritime policy and the French switched from great battle fleets designed to wrest control of the Channel from the English and Dutch to a *guerre de course* – a war on trade conducted by privateers. As English maritime policy responded, so the focus of the dockyards necessarily shifted also. Small

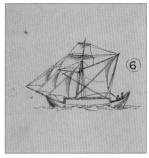

1. Typical trows of the Severn. Note the variety and complexity of the rigs that gave Benbow such a solid grounding in ship handling.

2. An English two-decker engaging a Barbary two-decker, with a galley sinking in the foreground and another Barbary ship in the background. Note the typical Barbary green ensign showing crescents, suns and stars. By Van de Velde the Younger.

3. The bowling green at Whitehall, part of the British colony at Tangier by Wenceslaus Hollar.

4. The Siege of Tangier in 1683. The mole protecting the harbour is clearly visible.

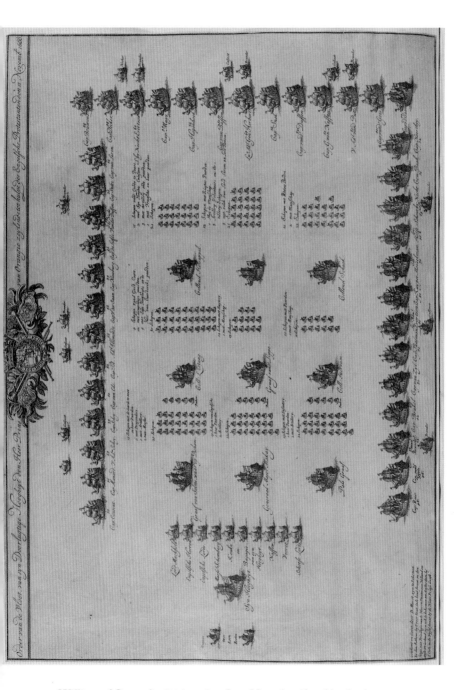

5. William of Orange's 1688 invasion fleet. Note the pilot ships in the van.

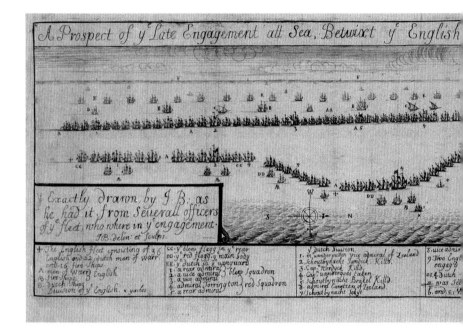

A Prospect of y^e Late Engagement att Sea, Betwixt y^e English

4. The English fleet consisting of 36.
English and 22. dutch men of warr.
and 16. fire-Ships.
A. men of warr } English
B. fire Ships. }
B. dutch Ships } x yachts
Buision of ye English.

cc. ye blew flagg in ye rear
DD. ye red flagg ye main body
EE. ye dutch in ye vanguard
1. a rear admiral } blew Squadron
2. a uice admiral }
3. a uice admiral }
4. admiral Torrington } red Squadron
5. a rear admiral }

ye Dutch Buision.
1. m. undern allen vice admiral of Zeeland
2. Schoutbynacht Janduck. Killd.
3. Cap^n Norduck Kills.
4. Cap^n uandergoes taken.
5. Schoutbynacht Brakel Killd.
6. admiral Euertten, of Zeeland.
7. Schond by nacht Jekyt

8. uice admir
9. Two Engl
engag^d
aa. 4. dutch
a. was see
b. and, c, y^e

7. A bomb vessel by Edward Dummer, 1685. This manuscript is the earliest British intelligence of the bomb vessel. It shows the first design, with the mortars mounted side by side in the waist. The foremast has been struck to allow the mortars to fire.

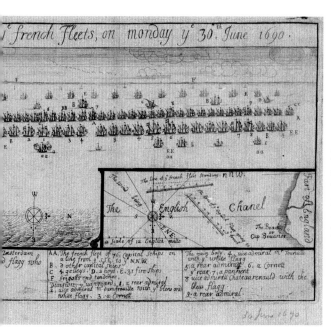

French fleets, on monday y⁰ 30ᵗʰ June 1690.

6. The Battle of Beachy Head, c 1690. Note the distinctive curve in the French line that made it so difficult for Herbert to engage and which masks the numerical advantage of the French fleet.

8. A depiction of Benbow's machine vessel exploded at St Malo. **A** is sand ballast; **B** is ten tons of powder in casks, sealed by a layer of stonework; **C** is a layer of explosives and old metal parts sealed by another layer of stonework; **D** is fifty more powder kegs and various fireworks; **E** is a layer of old cannon and broken iron with the fuse at the very top.

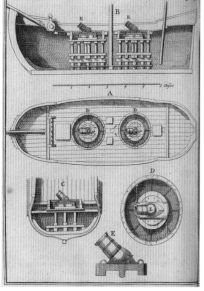

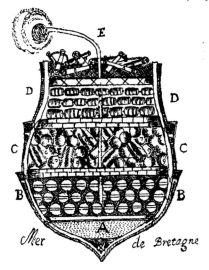

9. The new generation of Bomb vessels showing the mortars on traversable mountings and positioned on the centre line.

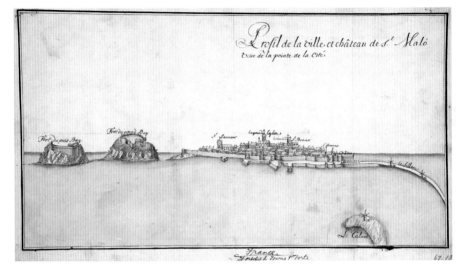

10. View of the town of St Malo, showing its fortifications and prominent churches, both of which were targets for Benbow.

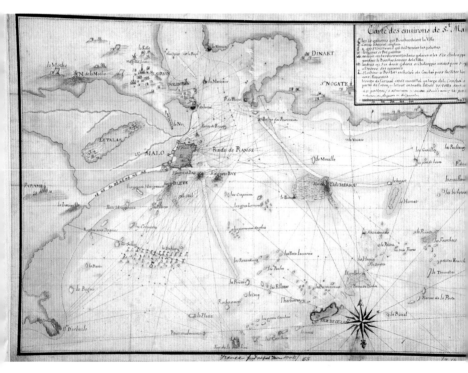

11. Map showing the bombardment of St Malo by the British fleet. It clearly marks the ranges of French batteries and the position of the British fleet at the centre left. Note the numerous rocks and impressive coverage of the French defenders' guns.

12. Contemporary depiction of the bombardment of Dieppe, 1694. The dedication is to the Earl of Romney, Master General of the Ordnance. This was the first operation for the new generation of bomb vessels with traversable mountings and was a major success (see fig. 9).

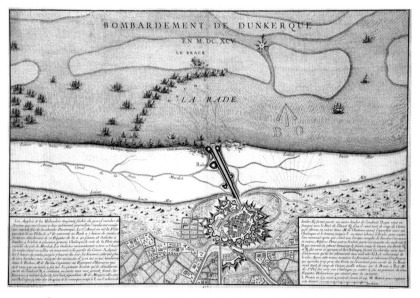

13. Contemporary depiction of the bombardment of Dunkirk, 1695 showing the formidable defences and the path of the British attacks.
Note how the main city remains unscathed.

14. Sketch of Admiral John Benbow, perhaps from later in his life.

15. Triple portrait of Thomas Phillips, John Benbow, and Sir Ralph Delavall by Thomas Murray c. 1692-3. Phillips the military engineer sits to the left with a plan of the fortifications of St Malo; a youthful Benbow is in the centre holding a quadrant, signifying his navigational expertise; Delavall, the Admiral, stands to the right with his hand on the globe and a pair of dividers.

and fast cruisers provided the lumbering merchant convoys with protection from French privateers and they cruised independently on specific stretches of coast to guard against French raids. Bomb vessels, machine vessels, fireships and landing craft were central to a new and aggressive maritime policy against French ports, designed to target privateer bases. Throughout the period 1690–6 Deptford, as a provider of smaller craft, therefore enjoyed a brief resurgence in significance. By the end of the war the growing awareness that squadrons cruising in the western approaches to the Channel were to become central to future maritime policy ensured that Deptford would once again slumber and drift into obscurity as Plymouth rose to prominence and naval warfare burst out of the confines of northern waters, but in the intervening period, when Benbow worked there, Deptford shone the brightest of all the Royal Dockyards.

Deptford, on the south bank of that iconic twisting stretch of the Thames between Greenwich and Rotherhithe opposite the Isle of Dogs, and nearly forty miles from the open sea, was the beating heart of English maritime power. A surprising location maybe, but its very significance was closely linked to that location. Although modern Deptford is part of inner London, in the 1690s the area was not, and there were acres of green fields and lush marsh and meadow interrupted by the occasional private shipyard on the south bank of the Thames between Deptford and the stretch facing the Tower of London.[20] Deptford was also very close to London's commercial docks, just east of the City, and at these docks goods of every kind could be acquired more plentifully and more cheaply in one site than anywhere else in the world. Inevitably highly specialized maritime artisans who could get access to the peculiar materials they needed for their craft settled around Deptford, and it soon became renowned as the best location for the manufacture and repair of compasses, telescopes and other specialist precision equipment. Administrators from the Navy Board could also travel to Deptford with ease from their offices in Crutched Friars in the City, and it is likely that Pepys himself visited monthly. The result of this combination of commercial and managerial factors was that Deptford became the central warehouse for the Royal Navy, as a location that could be directly monitored, that was close to commercial London and yet had sufficient space to receive and then distribute stores on a large scale. Throughout the coming century Deptford remained the location where naval storeships destined for foreign yards were loaded. Indeed it was the only location where some items, such as ships' flags, could be acquired, and was one of only two dockyards, the other being Chatham, where canvas was stored.[21] It enjoyed this reputation from a very early date.

Founded by the ship-loving Henry VIII, Deptford was the closest naval site to Placentia, the magnificent Tudor palace at Greenwich that was his birthplace. The land around Deptford and Greenwich had enjoyed royal connections since the time of Henry V, who had granted some land to his brother, the Duke of Gloucester, in 1427. When Henry VIII ordered a storehouse to be built there in 1513, at 405 feet long it was the largest dockyard storehouse in England and dominated that stretch of the river, associating it for ever with the Royal Navy.

Deptford was also the only dockyard that was blessed with a wet dock – an area capable of berthing a number of large ships protected from the tide by a lock gate – a rare piece of engineering in the 1690s, and the earliest example in England when it was built in the late 1570s.[22] Although much of the motivation for wet docks is now aesthetic – picturesque fishing ports like Padstow in north Cornwall do not become stinking seas of estuarine mud at low tide – the reasoning behind their seventeenth-century origins was purely a matter of practicality. Stores could be loaded and unloaded twenty-four hours a day while the ships remained free of the stresses and strains inevitable in grounding. Those ships not designed to take the ground would be forced to anchor midstream, with stores and workmen being shipped to and from the shore. The wet dock was a magnificent resource but with so many vessels in close proximity and a narrow dock entrance it did require careful management by highly experienced practical seamen such as Benbow.[23]

All of these factors ensured that Deptford Dockyard enjoyed a special reputation, from the time of its foundation to the 1690s but particularly during the period 1692–6, and that significance was reflected in the officers' pay. It may have been smaller, but officers at Deptford were paid higher wages than those at any other dockyard – even Chatham. In fact their wages were almost 50 per cent greater at Deptford, where the Master Attendant received an annual salary of £144 14s 4d, as against £100 at Chatham. The storekeeper at Deptford received a similarly increased sum, although a number of other officers received less than their equivalent at Chatham, notably the Clerk of the Cheque, the Clerk of the Survey and the Master Shipwright, possibly reflecting the relative differences in responsibility between the yards. For the Master Attendant, however, the case is clear: Deptford was by some margin the most lucrative location for a holder of this post, a reflection of the variety of skill required and weight of responsibility shouldered. It is possible that the higher wages were also linked to the slightly different hierarchy at Deptford. As it was very close to London, there was no permanent Commissioner in charge and so much of the responsibility for the running of the yard was passed down the chain to Master Shipwright and Master Attendant.[24]

Benbow's transfer from Chatham to Deptford must therefore be seen as a promotion. His connections, together with his evident ability, had once again furthered his career, with each step moving him both physically and professionally closer to those who made the most significant decisions about the use and maintenance of the Royal Navy. It is no coincidence that, in the years immediately after Benbow's appointment as Master Attendant at Deptford, his name begins to appear in papers of state. This aspect of his career was by no means a frill to his seafaring; the two fed off each other and both were integral to the career path he followed from 1690.

Benbow arrived at Deptford in the spring of that year, the time when the seasonal dockyard workforce went through its most dramatic change. Hundreds of workers and riggers were laid off as the ships prepared for sea and the yards prepared for the reduced workload of summer. But, while Benbow would have been one of many hundreds leaving employment at Chatham, he would have been one of only a handful of men beginning a new period of employment at Deptford. There was no great influx of men at Deptford until December 1690, and by then Benbow had held his position for eight months and would have been well established, aware of the idiosyncrasies of the yard and ready for the intense workload of a winter dockyard. With the same job title as he had had at Chatham, Benbow's work would have focused on the same mix of management and seamanship, but the evidence from Deptford is clear that he was involved in a great deal of other work for the Admiralty, not least in the surveying and valuation of ships to be acquired by the navy and the design of new warships.

When Benbow arrived at Deptford no major ships were being built there; the most recent new ships to have left her dock gates were the Fourth Rates *Assistance* and *St Albans*, three years earlier in 1687. All of this swiftly changed in the new year of 1691, when the painful lessons of the Battle of Beachy Head made it clear that more ships were needed to combat the threat of the French battle fleet. Correspondingly, William asked Parliament to consider granting funds for new ships and it responded quickly, granting £570,000 for twenty-seven ships, seventeen to be Third Rates and ten Fourth Rates. So far so good, but during this period the system of ordering ships between the granting of funds and the laying of their keels in the dockyards was always uncertain. Charles II had taken control of the Thirty Ships building programme of 1677, and he was always keenly interested in the intricate details of ship design. In 1691 William had no such patience or interest. A soldier at heart, he focused on the land wars in Flanders and Ireland. He therefore delegated the responsibility for shipbuilding to the Admiralty Board, who in turn delegated the responsibility to the Navy Board, who then passed it on to the Surveyor of the Navy, who entrusted it to the Master Shipwrights and Master Attendants of the Royal Dockyards.

This desire to pass the buck can be explained in the details of the grant ordered by Parliament. Not only did the politicians grant the money but they also stipulated the size of the ships to be built, and this time they had decided to increase the ships' armament from those that had been ordered in the most recent great shipbuilding programme, back in 1677. Third Rates of seventy guns became Third Rates of eighty guns; Fourth Rates of fifty guns became Fourth Rates of sixty. Yet the implications of the size increase had not been grasped. The Admiralty had been ordered to build 80-gun ships of approximately eleven hundred tons, and 60-gun ships of approximately nine hundred tons, and those who understood ship design soon realized that those weights and armaments were incompatible. Such ships would be badly over-gunned, keep the sea poorly and work themselves loose.

This is the problem Benbow faced in January 1691. He sat down with the Master Shipwright of Deptford, Fisher Harding, and proposed the dimensions of two ships of different sizes, together with a recommendation for their armament, and replied formally to the Navy Board.[25] The Woolwich Master Shipwright, Joseph Lawrence, was not so formal and was evidently cross at the problem he had been given. His proposal came with the important addendum 'as to the third-rate ship which is to carry eighty guns, it's my opinion that (to make her a good man-of-war) she ought to have sixteen inches more breadth than I have given her'.[26] Benbow and Harding's solution was slightly different from Lawrence's. They recommended a ship a full foot shorter and a foot broader to cope with the extra weight of the guns, and their 80-gunner was not eleven hundred tons, as requested by the Admiralty, but slightly larger at 1,135 tons. As it was, the Surveyor of the Navy, Sir John Tippets, considered the drafts from the yard officers and came up with his own design, two feet shorter than Benbow had proposed. All were clearly struggling with the design, but no one had the sufficient authority, courage or clarity of mind to inform the King of the inherent flaw and the building programme went ahead to Tippet's design. Deptford buzzed with activity and built more ships (eight) in this building programme than any other dockyard, royal or private.[27]

Every ship in the entire programme performed badly. Very quickly there were 'mighty doubts'[28] about their ability to withstand the pressures of seafaring and they were all renowned for working themselves loose. The problem was all to do with the extra guns they were forced to carry. With no choice but to cram the guns on forecastle and quarterdeck, the ships were exposed to pressure they were not designed to bear and their keels were forced down at bow and stern. Some attempt was made to solve the problem by joining the quarterdeck and forecastle together, thus forming a complete third deck, but the ships were simply never large enough to carry their armament.

The class of ships built in 1691 were among the poorest ever built by the Royal Navy but it must be made clear that, although Benbow and his colleagues all offered recommendations for the dimensions and armament of the class, their hands were tied by the restrictions imposed upon them. Culpability lay at a higher level, with the Admiralty and Navy Board, who were unwilling to challenge the design paradigm imposed upon them by Parliament. This in turn was largely brought about by the dramatic regime change that followed the Glorious Revolution of 1688. A number of highly skilled, experienced and knowledgeable naval administrators, among them Pepys and the shipwright and architect Sir Anthony Deane, were expelled from office for their perceived allegiance to the old regime. Just as happened after the changes that replaced Charles I with the Commonwealth and then the Commonwealth with Charles II, the regime change between James II and William III had a dramatic impact on the navy's short-term operational and administrative capabilities. With every upheaval experienced men were removed from office; every time those with little knowledge of the sea were charged with maritime affairs; and every time the navy suffered. Benbow and his colleagues were faced not only with the complexities of ship design, which posed difficult problems even without the interference of those who knew little of maritime affairs, but also with the complexities generated by internal political and administrative turmoil.

We can get some sense of the working conditions Benbow would have experienced, as Admiralty orders to all of the dockyards have survived. We know, for example, that smoking was banned at Deptford for fear of fire, which must rank as one of the earliest examples of a workplace smoking ban.[29] The role of the Master Attendant would also have changed as the rules and regulations governing dockyard practice and behaviour themselves changed. Thus he would have been required to enforce a ban that prohibited the selling of alcohol to dockyard workers by porters, who seem to have been keeping 'taverns in their houses ... selling wines, brandy, punch and other potent and intoxicating liquors not fitting to quench workmen's thirst'; to organize random searches of ropemakers for carrying embezzled hemp and workmen for embezzled nails, locks, hinges and lead which they carried out under their coats 'or by other sly conveniences'; to source spare stores from other Royal Dockyards before ordering new; to oversee the dockyard watches, particularly at night, to prevent ships burning, as happened to the *Royal Sovereign* in 1695, or exploding, as happened to the *Exeter* in September 1691. There were countless other minor instructions and underlying most was the desire to save money. As inspector of ships that arrived from service, Benbow would have been involved with monitoring the 'unreasonable practices of altering and re-altering cabins, bulkheads, storerooms, masts, yards and sails, the cutting down of ships, and through their sides unreasonable scuttles' and was required to inform the Admiralty of any 'alteration, destruction or change'.[30] The officers themselves received the occasional dressing-down for employing 'labourers and workmen in their families and on their private affairs', but all was not doom and gloom. There is occasional evidence of corporate support for the workforce. John Maverley, for example, a caulker from Chatham, was granted paternity leave.[31]

The workforce was also clearly part of Benbow's concern. In 1691 he was required to advise on a new messenger for Deptford as the incumbent was elderly and had married and Benbow considered him 'no longer capable of continuing the service'. He recommended a man who had worked there for nineteen years 'and always behaved himself very just to his trust'.[32]

When he was not concerned with dockyard efficiency, Benbow's letters to the Admiralty suggest that he spent most of his time inspecting stores and surveying ships. In his frequent surveys of merchant ships he assessed their ability to carry guns as well as their structural integrity, ultimately advising the Admiralty whether or not they were suitable for conversion into warships. If they were, he advised exactly how that should be done and estimated how long it would take. The *London Merchant*, for example, needed beams shifting, the forecastle bulkhead replaced and new sheathing.[33] He performed exactly the same role for captured ships, together with a survey of their stores. In October 1691, when he surveyed a privateer captured by the *St Albans*, he took her dimensions, noted half a suit of sails in good condition, that she was wholly destitute of anchors, cables and other stores and required a crew of ninety, and estimated the cost of getting her fit for service at the surprisingly exact figure of £629.[34] The detailed level at which he worked is occasionally astonishing. The length and diameter of masts and yards were measured down to tenths of an inch, or 2.54 millimetres.[35] Once these measurements were taken he could then offer his opinion on whether a vessel was over- or under-masted, that is to say whether the height of the masts was correct for the size and design of the vessel.[36] If even one mast was out of proportion, this could have a dire effect on a vessel's sailing qualities. Benbow also surveyed ships for their suitability to act as transports or storeships and he prepared ships of every type, including hospital ships, for service.[37] Not all of this happened at Deptford and Benbow regularly travelled up and down the Thames to perform surveys. In the spring of 1694 his inspections took him to Wapping twice, as well as to Greenwich and Blackwall, and in April he travelled up and down the river in search of suitable ships.[38] Although he surveyed the specifics of stores at Deptford, he also wrote more general letters of advice to the Navy Board. In 1695, for example, he wrote comparing the qualities of different types of canvas, a major concern at the time as English canvas was notoriously poor and Ipswich canvas, in particular, subject to mildew.[39]

In times of pressure all Royal Dockyard employees were required to work Sundays and nights and Benbow would have been no exception.[40] His correspondence with the Navy Board gives the impression of a man of immense industry, with an eye for detail and competence in a number of different fields. Here was a man who could fight but at the same time was interested in making the complicated logistics of naval administration more easily understood and quantified. How many other naval officers of the time could command a coastal bombardment or blockade one week and the next develop a shorthand calculation for costs incurred in preparing ships for overseas service? Benbow could, and his answer was £31 15s per man per month, which would cover all wages, stores, wear and tear.[41]

Unsurprisingly, we know that his presence was greatly valued. In the mobilization for the campaign against the French coast immediately after the Battle of Barfleur, the Navy Board wrote to the Comptroller of the Navy urging him to hasten Benbow back to Deptford as soon as he could be spared, because 'his presence will be mightily wanted'. He was not there because he had already been poached by Portsmouth Dockyard to assist with the repair of the fleet after Barfleur.[42]

As Benbow was valued by others, so he certainly valued himself, a common characteristic in young, competent and aggressive naval captains throughout history. In a letter to the Treasurer of the Navy in July 1693, Benbow carefully pointed out, in what was nothing more than a self-publicizing and self-congratulatory monologue, that:

Ever since my being Master Attendant at Deptford which now is well onwards of Four Years I have given your Office little or no trouble with the Guns & Carriages which our Sixth Rate Frigotts bring up hither with them, & other Stores, when Dockt or hall'd a Shore, which are alwaies taken out and Secured by me and likewise all the Yachts which is a great Ease to your Office, and no small trouble to me, which I hope you will take into Consideration to give me such incouragement, that I may Continue my Care.

I remain: Your Honourable most Humble Servant, Benbow.[43]

From a broader perspective, Benbow's association with the dockyards in this period makes his own reputation vulnerable to the broader reputation of the dockyards, which was a particularly sensitive matter. Embezzlement, corruption and laziness were all rife,[44] but we must be careful not to judge seventeenth-century dockyards according to modern pre-conceived ideas about efficiency and expectation. Corruption and effectiveness were not necessarily mutually exclusive. On the contrary, both are clearly in evidence and that paradox is the most important characteristic of the dockyards of the time. Benbow would certainly have known how the dockyards functioned. The men, who were usually paid less than in private yards, largely determined how hard they chose to work, which, as one modern historian wrote, was 'as much as could be expected'.[45] Work always progressed most smoothly when the men were not interfered with; the zealous enforcement of orders and command had no place in a dockyard. This raises something of a conundrum as the evidence we have of Benbow's professional expectations suggests that these were high, that he was unforgiving and that he had a formidable work ethic, all of which are characteristics that would have made his work in the dockyard frustrating. No evidence survives of disciplinary action taken within the Royal Dockyards and so it remains unclear if Benbow naturally grasped the need for a gentle touch or if he attempted rigid control. In either case the ability to wring out an acceptable level of efficiency from a seventeenth-century dockyard workforce was a unique challenge quite unlike that of working a ship, where word was law and law was strictly enforced. Benbow's career at Chatham and Deptford would therefore have challenged him in new ways, and the scattered evidence we have suggests that he met that challenge well – and that he knew it. Inevitably his dockyard career ended when, in 1696, he was promoted to flag rank. He may have been a valued dockyard officer, but in the end he was considered too good a seaman to stay.

9.

Benbow's Invasion

In many respects the strategic situation presented to the English after Barfleur in 1692 was similar to that obtained by the French after the Battle of Beachy Head two years earlier. In both instances the defeat of the main enemy battle fleet gave immediate and absolute control of the English Channel to the victors. The French, as we have seen, were unable to take advantage of their opportunity and, after a brief period of chest-thumping, returned to France to land their sick and tie themselves in knots over preferred strategy. Strategic indecision combined with logistical and administrative inadequacy had crippled their fleet the moment that they had gained the very advantage their battle fleet had been designed to win. Faced with the exquisite opportunity of control over the sea that they needed to cross, the French were startled into paralysis. In the coming century thousands more Frenchmen would die in exactly the same enterprise, and none of their sovereigns would get any closer to achieving the basic requirements for an invasion of England than Louis XIV did in 1690.

Just two years later and the tables had been turned absolutely. 1691 had come and gone as a damp squib, the skilful French eluding their British pursuers, but by then the English losses at Beachy Head had already been made good. The ships were repaired, they were well manned, and the public debate that loudly condemned Herbert's inaction in the face of the enemy had left his successors little opportunity for prevarication in battle. Resolve, not indecision; aggression, not caution were the avowed and explicit expectations of the Admiral of the Channel fleet. At Barfleur Russell had met those expectations and now the English were faced with the very advantage that *their* battle fleet had been designed to win absolute control of the seas around the British Isles. What would they make of the opportunity?

Historians of the period are often keen to emphasize the security of the English after Barfleur, but at the time there was still great anxiety that the danger of invasion would be renewed within months.[1] The immediate problem was that a significant number of the French fleet had escaped into St Malo. A report from an Englishman who had escaped French captivity claimed there were nineteen ships of the line and two fireships in the harbour.[2] Although this force was easily outnumbered by the English and Dutch allied fleets, if the scattered remains of the French fleet were able to unite and could be augmented by swift shipbuilding, the essence of yet another formidable French navy could be realized in a relatively short time. To defeat this force at St Malo was in many ways to secure the control of the Channel that the English now enjoyed. But the French realized this as keenly as the English, and according to the escapee informant in St Malo, the French had set about 'fortifying every rock' there to defend against an English attack. This was a significant claim, for St Malo's harbour today is as littered with rocks as it was in 1692, and only some of those rocks break the surface. They force approaching ships to navigate intricate courses. Even if a small percentage could be fortified and armed, they would create an impenetrable spider's web of gunfire for any approaching ship. Those areas of sea that were out of range of these fortified rocks were in range of the town walls (see fig. 11).[3] The numerous rocks also provided many different angles and elevations so that no part of the approaches to St Malo could be free from the threat of bombardment by powerful magazines equipped with furnaces for heating shot. Moreover, the harbour itself was protected by two large galleys that patrolled at night.[4] So, if a direct naval attack on St Malo was to be launched, time was of the essence. To minimize casualties and to avoid total disaster, it would have to be launched before the defenders had realized their plans.

The likelihood of such a rapid deployment against St Malo was threatened on many fronts. Firstly and most importantly, it was not the only favoured strategy for the next stage of the war. Admiral Russell himself, although he acknowledged the value of an attack on the remnants of the fleet at St Malo and believed "twill put England pretty well at ease for some time',[5] advised against the scheme, perhaps with the caution of any seaman past or present who knows the dangers of that coastline. Russell favoured direct invasion of France itself, and not from anywhere near St Malo. Others who knew the disadvantages of St Malo proposed attacks on Rochefort or Dunkirk.[6] But Nottingham, the Secretary of State and in William's absence the man solely responsible for the naval war strategy, remained tightly focused on a raid on St Malo and mopping up the remains of the French fleet. For Nottingham, his own man but also the mouthpiece of Queen Mary, the purpose of the Royal Navy was to secure command of the sea by defeating the enemy battle fleet – all of it – and in his mind that had not yet been achieved. Others realized that sufficient damage had been done and control of the sea in reality could not be judged according to such absolute terms. Nottingham insisted on an attack against St Malo even as the true scale of the practical problems of seamanship began to surface. What was required was the advice of a man of unquestionable seamanship skill and experience, so Nottingham and the Admiralty Board turned to Benbow. It is immediately clear from the records that he was respected and his opinions valued.

Russell recommended Benbow to Nottingham as 'a prudent gallant man' and in June Nottingham spoke to Benbow in person. He acclaimed him 'one of the most intelligent seamen we have in England' and shortly after as 'diligent and zealous'.[7] He was subsequently recommended to the Queen to take charge of the small craft in any subsequent attack on the French coast and she wrote to Russell in July approving Benbow for such a command.[8] Benbow advised both Nottingham and Russell on the proposed operation and was actively supportive of an attack. His detailed local knowledge, however, made him careful to add the caveat that any attempt on the French coast near St Malo would need to be made with both land and sea forces acting together, in a two-pronged attack. For the navy to try to achieve anything on its own he considered 'very dangerous' but with land forces '14 or 15,000 strong besides dragoons' who would burn the town first, he believed the operation 'does not doubt of good success'. Nottingham then passed on Benbow's advice to one of William's closest advisers, the Duke of Portland, including Benbow's name, no doubt because it carried weight in naval affairs.[9]

Implicit in Benbow's proposal was the assumption that the land defences were too strong to consider a naval attack on St Malo on its own. From landward St Malo was noticeably weak, not least for the fact that all of its fresh water came from some distance inland. A siege, it was suggested, would bear immediate fruit.[10] With this advice to hand Nottingham ordered Russell to investigate further and immediately met another problem. It was all very well having on your staff people like Benbow who had personal knowledge of the coast, but Russell needed large numbers of pilots to help him take a fleet into St Malo, and for everything that Benbow knew there were certain things that he did not, such as the nature of the anchoring ground off St Malo. Russell's problem was with his pilots, whom he mistrusted. While anchored off Guernsey trying to convince the pilots to take the fleet into St Malo, Russell declared that he was 'extremely apprehensive of their judgements, those few that doe pretend to know any thing being soe very silly that I know not how to trust them'.[11] In essence they were displaying a more extreme version of the mariners' caution which had already shaped Russell's desire to bypass St Malo altogether and Benbow's advice that the French ships could only be taken if the town was taken first: the pilots were so convinced of the folly of the idea that to a man they refused to take the fleet to St Malo.

Not only was St Malo protected by rocks, but they knew that there was a tidal range of forty feet at spring tides and any approach would be impossible without the necessary pilotage marks, which of course the French had removed. The geography of the local coastline was also a major problem. St Malo is at the head of a vast funnel created by the Cotentin Peninsula to the east and the jagged north coast of Brittany to the west. The only wind that was not dangerous for a fleet of ships approaching St Malo was southerly. This, it must be remembered, was a period of cumbersome manoeuvrability for large sailing warships. They were still steered by the awkward whipstaff, not the wheel; most were poor sailers with poor windward performance. This was such a significant factor that Russell himself preferred to keep his fleet in a location where they could outrun a storm in any direction for a full forty-eight hours if there was no safe harbour nearby. For a fleet off St Malo, only six hours to east or west was a vicious lee shore. The pilots still refused to take the English fleet anywhere near, even when bribed with £100, a considerable amount of money. Meanwhile, more reports of the unsuitability of the location came in, including the claim that the quality of the seafloor of St Malo was not good enough for more than forty ships. Other intelligence, gathered by Captain George Mees, suggested that local pilots could take the warships sheltering in St Malo as far as eight miles upriver in case of attack, and that eighteen thousand men had been transferred from La Hougue to defend St Malo from both land and sea attack.[12] Finally it was discovered that the only realistic place to land an army anywhere near St Malo was the wrong side of La Rance to the east, an unfordable river and so fast-flowing that in 1966 it became the first location on earth to generate electricity from tidal power. All of this investigation was conducted in weather 'fitting only for Laplanders to be at sea with' and the grumbling Russell and his captains were gradually edging towards a resolution, finally made on 13 July, that 'it would be infinite hazard for the whole fleet to come before St Malo'.[13]

Nottingham, meanwhile, did not have sufficient time to wait for Russell's final decision before issuing the necessary orders to gather together an assault force and then get them to sea. While Russell was squeezing every unsatisfactory drop of intelligence from the few local pilots he could get to cooperate, back in England shipping for 3,500 men and 380 horses was made ready at Kinsale in Ireland while that for a further four thousand men and fifteen hundred horses was gathered in the Thames, each ship to be as large as possible but with a shallow draught and able to 'take the ground'. Shortly after, an order was sent to Ostend for another fleet of transports which had just taken 4,500 Danes from Ireland to Holland. When these ships finally arrived almost all of their crews were immediately pressed for the navy, greatly endangering the transport fleet itself, which was nearly lost for want of hands.[14]

Simultaneously a fleet of smaller craft consisting of shallops specifically designed for landing operations and well boats was gathered at

Deptford and ordered to sail on 27 June. These would offer crucial support for the warships and transports, act as the landing craft and be indispensable in close warfare on and around the defended rocks in St Malo harbour. The man placed in sole charge of gathering, organizing and sailing this fleet was Benbow. There was a great rush to get them ready and at sea and he was ordered to sail even if they had but two watermen each, and to leave orders for the rest of the crews to follow. After these small craft were readied, Benbow helped to prepare a small fleet of bomb vessels, a craft entirely novel to the Royal Navy, with orders to sail them to Portsmouth.[15]

Once these preparations had been made Benbow was ordered to accompany the Duke of Leinster, one of the highest-ranking officers in William's army, on the expedition itself, aboard HMS *Bredah*, the ship on which Benbow would end his career.[16] While Russell was gathering information that demonstrated as clearly as possible the foolhardiness of an attack on St Malo, Leinster, under direct orders from the Queen, embarked seventeen regiments of foot and two hundred dragoons at Portsmouth and set sail to rendezvous with the fleet.[17] There was at this stage still some flexibility in his orders. Perhaps now realizing the extent of Russell's antipathy towards a St Malo attack, Leinster was given the option of attacking the naval base of Brest itself, or that of Rochefort, or even the massed transport ships at La Hougue and Le Havre that had been destined for Louis' long-planned invasion of England.

On 27 July, at a council of war held aboard the *Bredah*, it was determined that nothing could be done against St Malo and that it was too late in the season to consider taking a fleet of unseaworthy transports and small landing craft into the western approaches to the Channel to then attack Brest or Rochefort. Meanwhile, more orders arrived from the Queen via Nottingham insisting on St Malo as the target. Russell ignored them and simply took the fleet to St Helens, on the east coast of the Isle of Wight, to keep his vulnerable transports, packed with men who were rapidly becoming sick, safe and protected. The impasse was eventually broken by the interruption of the King himself, who needed help with his campaign in Flanders by a diversionary attack on Dunkirk. After a desultory assault by a portion of the invasion fleet, by October they were all home and nothing had been achieved. Even the French ships at St Malo had managed to escape and make it back to the safety of Brest.[18] As the French had been paralysed by their success in 1690, so too were the British in 1692. All of the money, energy and effort spent by Benbow and his colleagues to prepare for an invasion, and all of the lives lost in the battle that had made an attempt on France conceivable, had been wasted in indecision.

An attack on St Malo itself was not an absurd idea, but it had to have been achieved as soon as possible after the defeat at Barfleur, exactly as the burning of the French at La Hougue had been accomplished. As Nottingham wrote: 'half of the number of men a month since would have performed what can be expected from double the number now; for as their fears are greater, so their industry hath not been less...'[19] Delay itself had exacerbated confusion and prolonged debate which had made the task more difficult to conceive, to the point at which it could not be risked. Once that stage had been reached, the Queen and Nottingham's unwillingness to consider (or inability to understand) the practical restrictions of naval warfare ultimately led to a collapse in the relationship between land and sea; between those who gave the orders and those who carried them out. That lack of awareness of the practical maritime factors that necessarily inform naval strategy was exactly what had plagued Louis XIV's war strategy and it went on to become a characteristic feature of French failure right up to and including the Napoleonic wars a century later. In England, however, this is one key feature of naval strategy that changed in the following century. Experienced naval officers determined naval strategy, and the army and navy cooperated to make possible the startling string of successes achieved by British naval warfare in the second half of the eighteenth century.

The English failure in 1692, however, is distinct from that of France in 1690 for one significant reason. As the Queen herself noted: 'All the expence was thrown away, the troops came back as they went, having made us ridiculous to all the world by our great preparation to no purpose.'[20] The point is that the preparation *had* been made, and with great success. The English attempt failed at a very advanced stage. In an astonishingly short period of time after Barfleur a vast invasion force had been gathered at Portsmouth, manned and then sailed to rendezvous with the main fleet. The British weapon was loaded and aimed at France; only indecision at the top had caused it never to be fired. British dockyards, both royal and private, had responded to the excessive burden placed on them at short notice. Landing craft, troop transports, bomb vessels and their escorts were all in place, the ships were manned, armed and victualled. It is an extraordinary achievement, too easily overlooked because of the spectacular failure of the campaign itself, but to have made any campaign possible at such short notice indicates the capability of the British naval infrastructure of the 1690s. It is also significant that in the few sources that survive for this scramble for action, Benbow's name is heard loud and clear. He was a man people turned to when they needed results, a man who could organize, a man who could lead. While Russell and Nottingham both paid the price for the failure of 1692, both being swiftly replaced, the reliable Benbow was well positioned for the next season's campaign and with his reputation enhanced.

10.

Benbow's Nail Bomb

Although the remnants of the French fleet had eventually limped back to Brest in the autumn of 1692, the French naval campaign of 1693 and the following years was dramatically different from those that had gone before. The French were in the middle of a huge programme of naval construction that was not abandoned until 1694, but the country was starving, resources were diverted to the army, overseas trade was collapsing and a terrible grain harvest in 1693 forced Louis and his ministers to explore other means of conducting a naval war in northern waters without using the main battle fleet.[1] The solution was the *guerre de course* – a war directed at British merchantmen, conducted by private seamen with a royal licence to raid enemy shipping and supported by a handful of royal warships. Louis' magnificent fleet, which even after the defeat at Barfleur was on parity with the combined English and Dutch navies, lay unused. No further attempts were made to wrest control of the sea from the English, and the western Mediterranean, which had been nothing less than a French lake since the 1670s, was once again open to foreign influence.

France was ideally suited to a war against British and Dutch trade. To reach London from the west the fat British merchantmen had to run up the Channel, past a series of French ports from which privateers could dart out. Of those ports St Malo quickly rose in status, partly perhaps because of the lack of a commercial hinterland behind the port, unlike the ports of Nantes or Le Havre, which are linked by large rivers to the area of the capital, Paris. The Malouins had no alternative to a living made from the sea and many of the thousands of sailors released from the French navy found their way there. From 1693 Malouin privateers were a constant presence in the Channel and its western approaches, and were seen as far afield as Chile, Peru, China, Arabia, Guinea, the Caribbean and the lucrative Newfoundland cod fisheries.[2]

If the situation in the west of the Channel was dire, that in the east was no better as the French exploited the location of Dunkirk, a port that had been fabled for over a century for its privateering. Located just to the east of the narrowing of the Channel between Dover and Calais, it commands the choke point of trade from the Channel into the North Sea in exactly the same way that Algiers was perfectly positioned to prey on trade forced through the Strait of Gibraltar, a similarity that did not escape contemporaries. Some even called Dunkirk 'the Algiers of the North'.[3] Dunkirk had proved its value repeatedly in the Spanish wars of the 1580s, when it was used as a base for Spanish privateers in their conflict with Holland and England. Blessed also with a rich hinterland, Dunkirk became an object of intense jealousy between maritime powers and it is not surprising that Cromwell saw it as a crucial staging post in both the expansion and the security of the British Commonwealth, capturing it from the French in 1657. The French use of Dunkirk as an effective privateering base in the 1690s was a particularly heavy cross to bear. Only two generations earlier, it had been an English possession before Charles I sold it to Louis XIV in 1662 for 4,654,000 livres, the only such example of territorial alienation in British history. Louis poured money into making Dunkirk secure, entrusting the work to Vauban, the most talented military engineer of his age. By 1688 it was protected behind a formidable network of forts, basins, jetties and canals which Vauban himself called '*le plus beau et le plus grand dessin de fortification du monde*' ('the most beautiful and largest design for fortifications in the world'). It was certainly the most secure of all of France's port-citadels and it became the home of one of France's most successful privateers, Jean Bart, whose statue now marks the centre of the city.[4]

As a rule the French privateers were resourceful, highly skilled and courageous. Many were veterans of the French navy and therefore veterans of fleet battle: this is not one of those periods in naval history like the 1740s when skill was lacking for want of practice, but quite the opposite. Both sides had honed their skills at Bantry Bay (1689), Beachy

Head (1690) and Barfleur (1692). The fogs, tidal races and hidden dangers of the North Sea, Channel and Irish Sea required seamanship and navigation to be of the very highest quality, a reputation that Malouin seamen in particular carried. So good were they that they enjoyed a legal right to man the French flagship and a strong Malouin element was considered essential for any good crew.[5] The nature of their new work required them to be creative in their warfare. Fast ships faked crippling injuries, heavily armed ships pretended to be harmless, convoys were infiltrated under the cover of night. To improve their chances of success, hunters acted in pairs or even squadrons, some six ships strong, and extreme violence was used to discourage defence. This was a time of sheep and wolves.

The English sailors were equally skilled and experienced, if ignorant of some of the local hazards of the French coastline, but when it came to fighting they likewise drew on their experience of fleet battle, and engagements in northern waters in this period are characterized by prolonged violence. Although the French strategy had significantly changed from the lumbering majesty of the three-decked ships of the line, the enemy the Royal Navy was facing was no less of a challenge, if of a different sort.

Some privateers were highly successful. Grossly inflated figures, generalization from port to port and absurd propaganda cluster around statistics in these years, but a recent study has estimated that a reasonable figure for the eight years of war between 1689 and 1697 is that the French took some four thousand British prizes. The effects of this on the French economy is another matter open to some debate but the most important point is that it forced a change in English strategy.[6] It was unclear what form that change would take until, in 1693 off the coast of Smyrna, ninety-two English merchantmen were captured in a single day. The financial severity of the disaster has been compared to that of the Great Fire of London in 1666.[7]

England's immediate response was a clause tacked bizarrely onto the end of the Land Tax Bill of 1694 requiring forty-three naval ships to be available at all times for trade protection. The efficacy of the legislation is somewhat doubtful and it was a formalization of a strategy already two years old, but it signalled a new awareness of the problem and an intent to solve it.[8] In addition, fast cruisers were stationed on stretches of coast regularly threatened by French privateers and it was decided to take direct action against the privateers' bases themselves. Already experienced in trade protection and pirate-hunting from his naval service in the Mediterranean, and with a peculiar sympathy for the merchant marine born of his time as a merchant captain, Benbow became involved in almost every aspect of this war against the privateers. Nothing could have suited him more.

Another feature of the English response is particularly interesting in that its uncompromising violence brought the notion of 'total war' closer than ever before to English naval activity. The campaign 'can be dismissed briefly', wrote one historian of the French navy, 'for they were concerned with ports little used by the navy',[9] but that is exactly why they must *not* be dismissed. In the process of attacking privateering bases, English forces also deliberately burned civilians' homes to the ground. Moreover, some ports were targeted that had no obvious role as a privateers' base but were simply commercial centres. They too were bombed and burned, and the man responsible for all of these actions was Benbow. Some considered this mode of warfare repugnant but Benbow had no such qualms, and he seems to have comfortably made what he believed to be a necessary adjustment to the extant strategic situation. He did this by bringing the actions of the navy closer to warfare practised on land, in which civilians were regularly targeted.

The difficulty that faced Benbow was that the maritime enemy was now elusive. Not only were the privateers' ships fast, but their crews were privately employed. Benbow was not faced with a traditional enemy paid and supported by the enemy crown and who worked state-owned ships, but with one whose allegiance was to personal profit, whose favoured style of warfare was the cunning ruse and who, once ashore, became invisible, melting into the local population. The expected 'rules' of warfare therefore shifted in line with the change in French strategy. There are striking similarities with land warfare of the same period. The regular troops of state-controlled armies fought according to well-established rules and conventions, but these were all immediately dropped when an army was confronted with guerrilla warfare. Some of the worst atrocities seem to have occurred when state-controlled armies and professional soldiers faced amateurs in arms.[10] Something of this kind can be seen at work in Benbow, and it is a significant trait of his character that he was prepared to pursue such an approach to warfare with his customary vigour. He displayed a ruthlessness that cannot be ignored as well as a willingness to embrace new strategic situations. Distasteful as it seemed to many then, Benbow was an English pioneer of this mode of naval warfare.

It is easily overlooked that Benbow was also an English pioneer of the weapons he used to conduct this kind of warfare – the bomb ship and machine vessel. The mortar, a short, wide cannon used to fire explosive or incendiary projectiles over large distances was, by the 1670s, an established feature of the armament of land armies but it had not been swiftly transferred to sea. The French were the first to do so and towards the end of that decade their craft, known as *galiots à bombes*, were used against both Genoa and Algiers. Then, in 1683, one of their craft was closely inspected by an English shipwright and traveller, Edward Dummer, who brought the intelligence back to England.[11] The first English bomb ship, the *Salamander*, was not ordered until 1687 and another soon followed, the *Firedrake*. It is unclear exactly when bomb vessels were first used by the British, but there is some suggestion that one was present at the Battle of Bantry Bay in 1689.[12] By then the basic structural requirements of the craft were clear, but the details and method of their application remained a complete unknown.

To absorb the recoil from the twelve- or thirteen-inch mortars, each weighing as much as four tons, the hulls of the bomb ships were built with massive reinforcing timbers and designed with an unusually large beam to provide a steady platform. Although this design served its purpose, it had unfortunate implications for the vessels' sailing qualities: they were all sluggish, leewardly and difficult to manoeuvre. These problems were exacerbated by problems with the rigging. The earliest designs appear to have placed the mortars in the centre of the ship side by side, firing forward, thus forcing the mainmast to be moved aft from its ideal position (see fig. 7). This helped keep the rigging safe when the mortars were in use but made the vessels unhandy and idiosyncratic in their sailing characteristics. Unfortunately, however, the designs of the mortars themselves ensured that the ships' sailing abilities remained intricately linked with the weapons' performance. The mortars themselves were fixed into position, in terms of both elevation and rotation, so that their aim could only be adjusted by manoeuvring the ship itself. The final significant factor in the bomb ships' operation derives from their construction. They were relatively small for their job and the need to build deep supporting beds for each mortar ensured that there was very little spare room for anything else, not least ammunition, powder, victuals, living accommodation, boatswains' stores or a secondary, defensive armament. The result was that bomb vessels were highly dependent on direct and sustained support from their fleet.

The use of these early bomb ships therefore posed a distinct problem, as they would have to be deployed by, and with, a large squadron of warships. This would have been a problem anywhere in the world but on the hazardous north coast of France the challenge was particularly thorny. The unique geographical features around the Cotentin Peninsula accelerate the wind by up to one force on the Beaufort scale; farther east the straight coastline around Dieppe strengthens the prevailing westerlies; the Dover Strait funnels wind from the Channel into the North Sea and increases wind strength by up to 20 per cent; the summer thunderstorms that gather in the great landmass of France sweep northwards out to sea accompanied by violent squalls; even at the height of summer the coastline can be plagued with fog; the tidal races in and around the ports of Normandy and Brittany can reach six knots, as fast as a large sailing warship under full sail; the port of Granville, just east of St Malo, has the largest tidal range of any port in Europe – a twelve-metre range at spring tides, which can rise by three metres per hour (five centimetres per minute) at the height of the flood; even modern pilot books advise authors in highly engineered modern yachts to keep two miles clear of the coast in fine weather and four miles in poor weather; there is an uneven seabed off Dieppe that leads to particularly rough seas; Calais and Dunkirk are protected by shallow sandbanks and St Malo by a random scattering of sharp rocks. All of these problems were exacerbated by the presence of a fully prepared and heavily armed enemy. A contemporary map shows the coverage of the defenders' guns at St Malo and another the defences around Dunkirk (see figs. 11, 13).

Given all these considerations, that Benbow was prepared to launch himself into a series of raids on the French coast in the winter of 1693 says something of his confidence and determination, of which some of his most powerful contemporaries were all too aware. In August Lord Cornwallis wrote to Nottingham specifically regarding Benbow's response to the debacle of 1692. In his letter he claimed that 'Capt Bembo is discouraged rather by the opinion of the flag officers than the hazard of the enterprise'.[13] If Benbow was not discouraged by the hazard of his new enterprise, he certainly went prepared for it. Nothing better illustrates the challenge that he faced in trying to prevent his ships from wrecking, let alone being able to damage the enemy, than the following list, compiled in August 1693, when he began to gather together a squadron of ten small warships, two fireships, four brigantines, six bomb vessels, forty shallops and three tenders for a raid on St Malo. In addition to the usual mooring and anchoring stores that would have been issued for each ship (six anchors for Fourth Rates[14] and seven cables of 15–16 inches in circumference of the standard length of 120 fathoms), he specifically requested six additional cables of fifteen inches, four cables of thirteen and a half inches and six cables of twelve inches, six spare anchors of twenty-four hundredweight, four of seventeen hundredweight and six of twelve hundredweight. That is, in total, sixteen more anchors weighing 284 hundredweight (14.2 tons) and 1,920 more fathoms of cable – and to that he added almost 200 fathoms of chains.[15]

The second weapon that Benbow pioneered for the Royal Navy in these raids was the machine vessel: an exploding fireship. This was no English invention, having been invented in Antwerp in 1585 by Dutch ordnance officials assisted by a local clockmaker. It was a solution to a specific problem. The Spanish army under the Duke of Parma had besieged Antwerp as part of their attempts to quell the Dutch Revolt, and in doing so had built a remarkable bridge across the River Scheldt at Kalloo to get troops to and from the city. This bridge was one of the finest engineering achievements of the Renaissance and immediately became the key to the capture or survival of Antwerp. In response the Dutch built two machine vessels, their holds jammed with incendiaries in the form of up to seven thousand pounds of gunpowder, grapeshot and scraps of iron, and fitted them with a clockwork device that would ignite the fuse. The two vessels were released in a fleet of fireships and disguised to look identical so that the Spanish would not be able to identify them as a peculiar threat. Accordingly the Spanish manned their bridge with hundreds of soldiers, all making ready to keep the fireships at bay with long poles and buffer rafts. One of the machine vessels grounded on its approach but the other made contact. When it exploded over a thousand Spaniards instantly died and a two-hundred-foot gap was blasted in the bridge. However, the Dutch never followed up on this victory, the bridge was rebuilt and Antwerp eventually fell. Yet the advent of the machine vessel had made a profound psychological mark. It had become a weapon of terror as much as an agent of destruction. It is possible that the idea of a machine vessel was resurrected in 1628 when an English fleet attempted to relieve the besieged Huguenot city of La Rochelle, but we can say with far more certainty that the French built and intended to use explosion vessels in their attack on Algiers in 1680, yet these were never actually used. So, since 1585, no further attempt by any nation had been made to deploy machine vessels, although the impact of their use had clearly been profound enough for the idea to have endured for over a century.[16] And eventually it filtered down to Benbow.

As with the bomb ships, the purpose of the weapon remained clear but the actual tactics of its deployment remained problematic, albeit for slightly different reasons. Machine vessels, like fireships, had to be set on a course and then abandoned by the crew. On the high seas this was not impossible, though immensely difficult, but against a stationary land target the machine vessel would be susceptible to the faster tides of coastal waters and the defenders would, if prescient enough, be able to take precautions to prevent the exploding ship from coming too close by

sinking buffers and poles offshore. Nevertheless, the destructive capability of the machine vessels was obvious and, as the force of an explosion
was likely to be vertical, with the sides of the hull initially containing the
blast, heavy and burning debris could still cause a great deal of damage
over a large circumference, even if the machine vessel was unable to get
on shore or alongside an enemy harbour front. It was with these entirely
untested ideas in mind that in November 1693 Benbow led a fleet to
attack St Malo.

Unlike the proposed assualt in 1692, which had been designed to
mop up the remains of the French battle fleet scattered after Barfleur,
the 1693 raid was designed purely to combat the threat of French privateers. Modern research suggests that the target was well chosen:
although the reputation of the Dunkirk privateers perhaps exceeds that
of the Malouins, we now suspect that the latter were more successful.[17]

Benbow and an army officer called Thomas Philips were summoned by
the Admiralty in September to receive orders 'to go upon a particular
service on the coasts of France'. The following months were taken up
with the necessary preparations and by mid-November the force had
been gathered. On 16 November, a dark winter afternoon, the fleet
arrived after being well supplied with pilots from Guernsey. Their
orders were uncompromisingly clear: 'use your utmost endeavour to
destroy the same by bombarding or setting it on fire, and to burn,
destroy or take such ships as you shall find in the harbour'. Once that
had been achieved they were given the authority 'to bombard any other
port or place to the east of St Malo'. As is suggested by the vagueness of
the summons to Benbow and Philips to present themselves for 'some
particular service', great effort had been made to keep the attack secret
and both of them were explicitly ordered 'not to touch at any place on
the way unless forced by contrary winds'. And if indeed they were thus
forced to stop, they were 'not to suffer any boats to go ashore except for
the necessary carrying on of the service'.[18] In the web of rumour and
intelligence that traversed the Channel via fishing boats, traders and
warships, it may have been difficult to disguise the purpose of such a

distinctive fleet, but with care it would have been possible to disguise the ultimate destination. It is unclear whether they succeeded in keeping it secret but the raid was successful, and far more so than later ones, when it is more certain that the Malouins were prepared.

Benbow's fleet was immediately foxed by the wind and tides around St Malo. Several ships collided with each other and one grounded.[19] But once the initial scares were over, that night they attacked, the bomb vessels hurling their explosive and incendiary charges deep into the town. As the tide ebbed they were forced to warp clear to prevent grounding, but as soon as the flood ran again the bombardment ensued for as long as it could. Meanwhile, Benbow and Philips had been scouting the local geography for suitable targets to attack and it is highly characteristic of these anti-privateer raids that two very different targets were given equal attention. One was a fortified gun emplacement being built on Quince Rock, which commanded the approaches to St Malo; the other was that institution so dangerous to a fleet of warships crammed with heavily armed men – a convent. The fort was demolished and the convent burned.[20] Their appetites perhaps piqued by the success of the first two days, on the third Benbow and Philips ordered the *Vesuvius* fireship to be converted into a machine vessel, to be launched against the town, where it could destroy the houses and churches built so high and close together in the streets running down to the harbour. To Benbow and Philips these were valid targets, the physical and spiritual shelter of Catholic privateers.

They started to prepare what they believed was an appropriate response. It was a 300-ton ship crammed with exploding mortars, 230 incendiary 'carcasses', iron bullets, broken glass, chain shot, loaded pistols and broken iron bars. These all lay on top of a hold packed with twenty thousand pounds of gunpowder which was covered with pitch, sulphur, rosin, straw and faggots. Six large holes were cut in the ship's sides to ensure the fire could breathe (see fig. 8). It was the seventeenth-century maritime equivalent of a nail bomb in a truck, detonated outside a railway station, the target in this instance being a civilian harbour. The French were oblivious to it all. We know that in one house near the harbour people were sitting down to a game of cards. Just after seven the ship began to make her final approach to the harbour, with Philips and Benbow themselves aboard. She then struck a rock within pistol shot of the town, possibly wetting some of the powder, and she could not be shifted. Then she exploded before anyone expected, leaving nine dead or wounded. Benbow himself appears to have escaped and eight more men eventually found their way back to their ships, to the great relief of their shipmates. It is unclear what happened to Philips but he died aboard Benbow's flagship a few days later and it is likely that he was injured in the explosion.[21]

The explosion was 'terrible beyond description' and one witness claimed it could be heard as far as Alençon and La Flèche, seventy and a hundred miles away respectively. Part of the mighty sea wall that surrounded St Malo harbour, still a feature of the place today, was destroyed and a rather dramatic French source claimed that the roofs of three hundred houses were struck off, including the Episcopal manor and the Duke de Chaulne's house, and that all the glass and earthenware for three leagues around was broken while chimney stones fell two leagues away. The capstan of the machine vessel, an iron bollard weighing more than two hundredweight, was launched into the town and easily crushed the Crescent Inn, where it landed. The ship's bell, her 'boiler' (stove) and her yards and chains were all hurled onto roofs and streets throughout the town. The poor card players 'were so terrified that they deserted both game and money'. During the following attacks thirty privateers and an unspecified number of merchant ships and transport vessels were destroyed, sixty cannon were taken from Quince fort and the cathedral was burned to the ground.[22] It is unclear if this last was a deliberate ploy, but for a man who was prepared to burn a convent as part of his war strategy the destruction of such a high-profile and symbolic building would have offered some satisfaction.

There were, however, as many reasons for discontent as for celebration. A witness of the machine-vessel attack who was standing in the deanery garden recorded rather gleefully that 'no life was lost except a cat in a gutter'. Benbow himself reported that the town was set on fire in three or four places, which indicates yet another remarkable escape for the Malouins, as there is evidence that nearly two hundred incendiary carcasses were later removed from the town, all unburned.[23] It is unclear how much of this Benbow was aware of but he was certainly frustrated and as soon as he was ashore he complained to the Admiralty Board about the behaviour of several, unnamed officers. It was the first of many personal visits to the Admiralty he would make throughout the subsequent bombing campaigns.[24]

Benbow was particularly enraged with the captain of the bomb vessel the *Mortar*, Henry Tourville, who, he believed, had not carried his ship close enough inshore. He had him court-martialled but the blame was laid on the captain's pilot, who had refused to take the ship any closer to shore, claiming that she 'would be [so] dry that the enemy might walk round her' and insisting that 'he would not be hanged for any of the King's ships'.[25] Nevertheless, Benbow was prepared to place himself in the very centre of danger and expected as much from his captains. There is also some sense that he had an eye to the future and an ambitious mind, as he claimed he could have captured the town with a force of ten thousand men.[26]

Soon after the St Malo attack the English fleet weighed anchor and returned, their exploits well reported by the press if poorly received in some homes. John Evelyn was particularly horrified as he immediately feared for his own safety, living as he did in the magnificent house of Sayes Court near the naval dockyard of Deptford. 'News of Cap: Benbows exploit & seting fire on St Mallows,' he wrote in his diary:

In manys opinion not well don, for the small damage we did them may infinitely indanger our Coasts, by their numerous Vessels our Rivages lying so much more open to them, & many Gentlemens houses well furnish[ed] &c within so few miles of the Coast: whereas all the French Townes & every small Dorp, [village] is Walled, & so not obnoxious to sudden Incursions, I pray God we do not feele it reveng'd on us in the Summer.[27]

No doubt he was reminded of 1667 and the Dutch raid on the Medway which had forced the jumpy Evelyn to remove all of his valuables from Sayes Court.

Benbow also brought back sixty-two prisoners captured on Quince Rock. The King immediately ordered these to be exchanged for British seamen taken captive by Malouin privateers. For his work at St Malo Benbow received £200, although it is unclear if this was a reward or a repayment of expenses.[28]

The bomb vessels themselves – and it is important to remember that this was the first time they had ever been used by the Royal Navy for such an operation – were clearly inadequate. The *Kitchen* and *Salamander* were equipped with traversable mountings, which allowed the mortars to be trained independently of the ship, but the others were not and proved immensely frustrating. The location of the mortars abreast and amidships was found to be disadvantageous for the effect it had on the location and performance of the rig. It was also discovered that prolonged firing caused the bronze of the mortars to distort.[29]

Benbow was heavily involved in the redesign of these bomb ships. Immediately on his return he was ordered to the Navy Board to suggest alterations and was interviewed by a committee of Ordnance officials swiftly set up to explore design improvements.[30] The result of this consultancy process was an entirely new class of bomb vessel ordered for 1695, and in the interim a number of merchantmen were converted. Ships of the appropriate size were acquired with some difficulty as the owners were very reluctant to give up the opportunity of the excellent freight rates that the French war on trade was creating, but by March 1694 they had ironed out any such problems and the merchantmen were in Deptford undergoing alteration by the Ordnance office and under the careful eye of Benbow.[31] The elevation of the mortars remained fixed at forty-five degrees and did so until 1726, but all of these new ships were fitted with traversable mountings and the mortars were located fore and aft on the centre line (see fig. 9). This meant that they could now fire their armament broadside to their targets, which meant in turn that the ships could be fitted with a proper and permanent foremast and could locate their mainmast in the correct place. They were also given a strong secondary defensive armament of eight six-pounders, four four-pounders and six swivel guns, and they were now designed for a substantial crew of sixty-five men.[32] More improvements were made to other equipment, notably the materials used for fixing carcasses, driving fuses for bombs and preparing quick match, of which fuses were made.[33] All of this was done amid an unprecedented hubbub of excitement and energy. Only three weeks elapsed between the inception and completion of the idea to mount bomb vessels with traversable mountings and daily reports were made to the Admiralty concerning their progress.[34] The return of Benbow's fleet from St Malo was not an end, but a beginning.

II.

Benbow's Bombardments

After the St Malo expedition Benbow was quickly sent out again with a small squadron to intercept the homeward-bound French Baltic convoy, crammed with shipbuilding stores and supplies. The Baltic was the shipbuilding storehouse of Europe where all the great maritime powers sourced much of their raw material, especially hemp, flax, iron and tar, and the beautifully straight pine trees that grew in the Baltic forests and made such superb planks and masts. It was not just that these Baltic resources were of very high quality but that France and England had little or none of their own of these to exploit. So to capture the French Baltic convoy was a valuable proposal in both material and strategic terms as it would cram British dockyard warehouses with the stores they so desperately needed while denying them to her enemy and stunting her shipbuilding programme. Keenly aware of this, the French had commissioned Jean Bart to escort the convoy home.[1]

The pace of the 1693 campaigns continued throughout 1694, with the Royal Navy maintaining a substantial and violent presence on the north coast of France. In early spring Benbow cruised off St Malo and took or drove ashore several vessels and dismantled some small forts.[2] The next major campaign of 1694, by contrast, was a dramatic failure condemned by Jacobite treachery. The King and the navy, their ambition piqued by Benbow's relative success at St Malo and still smarting from the failures of 1692, determined to attack the French naval base of Brest itself with a large amphibious force supported by the newly altered bomb vessels. Unfortunately the French knew about the plans long in advance, possibly having been informed by John Churchill, the Duke of Marlborough, a high-ranking soldier with suspected Jacobite sympathies who had fallen far from royal grace. Betrayed or not, the French were certainly prepared and had even shipped Vauban himself to Brittany to improve the defences around Camaret Bay, the nearest attractive landing place for a large amphibious force, while local militias were drilled to meet an attack. When the English forces landed on the beach a triple line of heavily armed trenches, unseen by the reconnaissance patrols and supported by batteries, devastated the troops. At least five hundred English sailors and soldiers died or were captured.[3]

The fleet limped back to St Helens like a whipped dog and the Admiralty began to formulate a different strategy. Large amphibious operations were put on hold in favour of bombardment raids in the mould of Benbow's attack on St Malo in 1693. This time, however, the net was to be cast wider and several ports, all far smaller than St Malo and all commercial fishing or trading ports with no naval presence, were targeted. The first of those was Dieppe and the unspoken destruction wreaked by Benbow is most elegantly told by the Louis XIV arcades that surround the port today, built to replace everything that the English fleet destroyed. Benbow bombarded Dieppe with such ferocity that the town burned for three days. 'If we had been in the town, and nobody to oppose us, we could not have burnt it better,'[4] wrote John Berkeley, the fleet's Admiral. From the hills that frame Dieppe several troops of horse watched the fleet do its work, and an estimated fifteen hundred shot and shells were fired at the English ships, but with almost no effect. Only five English sailors were killed or wounded.[5] By contrast the eleven hundred bombs and carcasses rained onto the harbour burned half the town within hours, and once again the religious focus of the community was targeted. 'Just as we sailed,' wrote Berkeley, '[we] had the satisfaction to see the Jesuits' steeple tumble.'[6] This religious element, so common a motivation in atrocities committed against civilians in land warfare,[7] was becoming a recurring theme in Benbow's attacks, along with his reputation for uncompromising violence. Once again he sent in a machine vessel crammed with gunpowder topped with iron and glass debris. The fuse appears to have gone out at some stage and a Captain Robert Dunbar made the extraordinarily courageous decision to go back aboard and relight it. But, even then, the ship could not be positioned as intended, and when it finally exploded, it had little effect, only killing those who were near it on shore.[8]

From Dieppe Benbow sailed to Le Havre, a merchant port in the mouth of the Seine principally interested in the Caribbean trade, though with a proven role in raising money to fund privateers.[9] With no pilots and no local knowledge of the treacherous harbour, Admiral Berkeley sent Benbow, accompanied by the Masters from the fleet's First and Second Rates, to sound the approaches. They found sufficient water to launch an attack, though the ships were forced to lie a great distance from the harbour. Nevertheless, as at Dieppe, Le Havre was a commercial town with few defences and few skilled men to man the batteries and was unable to withstand Benbow's assault. It was estimated that a third of the town was burned. Once a fire had been started it looked like the English ships would be forced home for lack of water, but their Dutch allies, who had participated in some of the attacks, issued water to the most needy ships, which allowed the bombardment to continue and prevented the Le Havrians from putting out the fire.[10] The defenders, however, did enjoy a single and remarkable success: they landed a shell directly on the bomb vessel the *Granado* – aptly, her name refers to a simple hand-held bomb used in sea warfare – which exploded violently. The captain survived but he lost two nephews in the blast as well as one of Sir Cloudesley Shovell's lieutenants.[11] Worn out from the attacks at Dieppe and Le Havre, the fleet returned to England, the mortars themselves warped and quite unusable until they could be recast. As soon as he landed at St Helens Benbow was summoned to London to report and he was later reimbursed with £50 he had spent from his own pocket during the campaign.[12]

By August Benbow was back at sea, cruising again off St Malo. In one particularly noteworthy operation he stood in close to the town under French colours to entice a patrol boat to approach. The ruse worked and Benbow made off with the boat and her valuable crew of pilots and intelligence. He also captured nine French ships in this brief but highly successful cruise before returning once more to join the fleet for yet another bombardment.[13] The summer's success against the soft targets of Dieppe and Le Havre had raised confidence to a level where another ambitious target could be contemplated and in September the fleet was pointed at Dunkirk itself, Vauban's defensive jewel that nestled behind shifting sandbanks and miles of impenetrable fortifications, a target so formidable that it generated crackpot schemes from entrepreneurs convinced they could break these defences.[14]

To break these down the English took with them their new machine vessels, in which they had placed a great deal of faith, and Shovell, who commanded the fleet, was in no doubt who he wanted to command the attack itself. He wrote to Sir John Trenchard, Secretary of State and one of the men who effectively ran the war in William's absence:

> If the machines are to produce the effect designed, it is necessary a knowing seaman be appointed either in joint command with the engineer ... or to be with him to advise, and that they have absolute power over the commanders and companies in the machines. I know no man so fit for such an employment as Captain Benbow.[15]

Trenchard concurred, and thus Benbow found himself facing the unique challenges posed by the great fortress of Dunkirk.

The reaction of the Dunkirkers once they had heard of the impending attack was both unhurried and unfussed, a reflection of the confidence they felt behind their great redoubts and the fact that they enjoyed a full three weeks' notice. The Governor had ordered the guns in the town's citadel to be moved to the fort that guarded the approaches to Dunkirk, and it was reported that 'he would not suffer the burgesses to remove their household stuff out of the town, believing it will not be in danger'. To prevent any fireships or machine vessels from getting close enough to do real damage, the Dunkirkers planned to blockade the entrance to the harbour with three or four ships filled with bricks, while the powder in the formidable Rysbank magazine was moved to a safer location. Bart's men of war, meanwhile, were unloaded of their valuable armament and victuals.[16]

Today, just as in 1694, Dunkirk can only be approached at an angle from the west or east; directly offshore and running parallel to the coast is a large sandbank that prevents anyone approaching directly from the north. The sandbanks as they were in 1694 are shown in Fig. 13, along with the defences. Note the channel to the sea, over 1,200 yards long, 100 yards wide and heavily protected at its mouth. The lines running from the forts show the range of the forts' guns. One of the earliest English plans was to approach the city from the western channel, bombard it as the fleet passed and then leave the approaches to Dunkirk via the eastern channel.[17] They would not risk anchoring and would minimize the fleet's exposure to the defenders' guns. From the perspective of self-preservation it was a valid attack, but even those who invented it doubted its effectiveness. Admiral Berkeley himself exclaimed, 'my thoughts have been upon ye business of Dunkirk, which I am sorry to say ye longer I think, ye worse I like it … I think it will be running an extreme hazard with our ships with little or no prospect of success.' It was widely accepted that 'to attempt to destroy the forts and harbours we judge to be wholly impracticable'.[18]

The correspondingly tame design was also influenced in part by the same problem that had haunted the fleet's summer operations for the past two years: they couldn't get any pilots to take even the smallest frigates in, let alone the entire fleet. 'By reason of the dangerous sands not known to them … they say neither rewards nor threats shall induce them to take charge beyond their knowledge.' Shovell's response was to use Benbow to sound the approaches himself. Benbow worked under constant fire from a frigate and the Rysbank magazine but still found a usable narrow. His advice was later instrumental in determining when the attack could take place.[19]

As it was, the weather conditions the next day began well and the fleet went in, but soon the rising sea interfered with the accuracy of the shell fire. At four o'clock several frigates assisted the machine vessels which were sent against the western and eastern forts. All four of the machine vessels were ignited too early, five cables' length (3,600 feet) from their intended targets, which gave the swell and wind every opportunity to push them off course. To make the matter certain, the burning vessels were towed well clear of the defences by raiding parties of Dunkirk seamen in a flotilla of galleys, pinnaces and other small craft, led by Jean Bart himself (see fig. 13).[20]

Chastened by their failed attempt, the fleet returned to the Downs.[21] The Dunkirk raid was a complete shambles and, much like the disaster at Brest at the beginning of the year, had proved that, for all of its new-fangled inventions, the Royal Navy was unable to cause significant damage to a defended and prepared enemy.

Inspired by the relative success of the 1693 attack on St Malo, however, the development of the machine vessels still continued. Since then a Dutchman named Meesters had been working closely with the Navy Board to improve the design. Although many suspected his integrity at the outset, others seem to have been wooed by his promise of glory, hyp-notized by the magical promise of new weaponry. After Dunkirk those who were frustrated by Meesters began to vocalize their disapproval more strongly. Shovell wrote with exasperation: 'I verily believe, and am not singular in my opinion, that theses sink-ships, and machines, were only an invention to swell his accounts ... it is said he had some materi-als on board his smoke-ships, or machines, as barrels of guns &c. which were of no more use that if he had put so many stones there.'[22] It is pos-sible that the 'machines' that Shovell refers to were not the exploding ships themselves, but iron cylinders filled with gunpowder via a spout in the top and ignited with a clockwork flintlock device. These were then packed into the hold of the 'machine' vessels, apparently a significant technical improvement on the improvised debris bombs made by Benbow.

In practice Meesters' inventions were useless. Shortly after the Dunkirk raid he even stole away with his vessels, all of which he had failed to deploy in the attack. If Shovell was exasperated, Berkeley was apoplectic:

I have sent the *Elizabeth* to bring him by fair or foul meanes and shall keep him a prisoner till I receive further orders about him, for I think all his Faults which are egregious are not to be past by, he is afraid to stand the Tryall of his machines, and now his Business is done, with what money he has got, he is for packing off, but I hope to stop him, all his actions & words have been every day nothing but contrariety, and his design, only to Cheat his Majesty and the Nation.[23]

He later added, after a subsequent run-in: 'As for Mr. Meesters, it has been my ill fortune to have to do with him; I foresee [foresaw] it, and did all I could to avoid it, but it was inevitable. My Lord he is certainly near akin to the father of falsehood...'[24]

Meesters was swiftly apprehended, taken back to England and forced to demonstrate his inventions, and all he could do was produce a little smoke. He himself stopped the experiment and 'there was ye end of his Brags & Inventions'.[25] Thereafter machine vessels fell very rapidly from favour and the fashion for exploding vessels begun by Benbow at St Malo had been burned out by Meesters within two years, though the tolerance shown towards him was in many ways commendable as it reflects an institution willing to look to the future by embracing new technology.

The bomb vessel, the other weapon pioneered by Benbow in these years, remained in favour, although it was still at a very early stage in its evolution and contemporaries were continually frustrated by its performance. Benbow was a vocal critic and complained in particular that the mortars were too small 'being mere baubles and will do no service'. 'It is shells of weight and number that must do our business,' he continued, 'else bombarding will be but an insult upon the enemy which I suppose is not the only thing desired.'[26] The new traversable mountings for the guns, activated by a type of ratchet device, failed to work as well as had been hoped and the guns had to be trained using blocks, tackles and spikes, in exactly the same way as ships' cannon. The elevation also remained fixed and the ships themselves, prisoners of their own function, were so heavily constructed to absorb the massive recoil that they

all remained poor sailers, susceptible to exaggerated rolling, poor windward performance and sluggish sailing.[27]

The strategy of coastal bombardment was also retained after the
failure of Dunkirk, if only for a short while. In late September 1694
Benbow was sent to Calais to sound out the approaches to the harbour
and to attempt an attack. Again he was successful and he led the way
through the sandbanks in the *Kitchen* bomb vessel, followed by the rest
of the squadron. Unfortunately the lateness of the season brought poor
weather and they were quickly forced offshore into safer water. Benbow
had successfully demonstrated that Calais could be bombarded, but his
commanding officer, Sir Martin Beckman, was careful to explain that
this could only be done 'when the wind is fair and southerly and at
spring-tides'. He added, 'It is a folly to attempt to do it at other times,
and we should not have done it now, had my advice been followed.'[28]
The troubled relationship between strategists and sailors that had
plagued naval operations since Barfleur persisted.

For all of the breakdowns in communication, Benbow's skill was
clearly appreciated by the navy's senior figures and in September it was
acknowledged financially by granting him the pay of a Rear-Admiral in
retrospect for his work of the previous summer.[29] In all but name this was
also promotion to that rank, but a lack of available flag positions and an
inflexible system of promotion forced him to wait until one was available.
In the interim he was sent straight back into action as soon as the season
allowed, and in early March 1695 he visited Portsmouth 'upon some
secret service'.[30] Shortly after, he led a fleet of eighteen men of war out of
Spithead to cruise for a French convoy of storeships bound from St Malo
to Dunkirk. On the 15th he found them and drove two ashore near Cape
La Hougue. Five more ran ashore in Great Ance Bay and Benbow sent
in boats to cut them out. Under strong fire from land, the ships were
taken off, laden with salt and tobacco. That night Benbow took yet
another ship, laden with wine, and the next day they chased three more.
Panicked by her pursuers, one hit a rock and sank while the other two
fled for the protection of a fort near Cape La Hougue. Unperturbed,
Benbow yet again sent his ships in to cut them out, which he did with
success. Nine days later two Malouin privateers were chased back into

their harbour and Benbow sent armed boats ashore near Granville, where he captured a small fort and its guns. The King was so impressed by Benbow's success that he gave the royal share of the prizes to him and his sailors, an act of generosity that was noticed outside naval circles.[31]

By June Benbow was pestering the Admiralty with 'a project of his own', which was immediately approved.[32] No detail of this has survived but within a month he was once more off the coast of St Malo, this time in the *Northumberland*, having been a key member of the council of war that had settled on St Malo as that year's initial target.[33] The only significant difference from the previous two years was that now he was not the only John Benbow aboard. On 16 June his son John was rated as a volunteer.[34] It was not long before they were split up, however, as the elder Benbow was now entitled to raise a broad pennant; he had effectively been promoted to the rank of Commodore and now, with three years' experience of operations against French coastal ports, he realized that the best way to exercise command of the inshore squadron was on board a galley.[35] For the following operations against St Malo, executed in a similar vein to those of 1693, Benbow therefore moved from the *Northumberland* and orchestrated operations from the twenty-oared *Charles Galley* (see Appendix 11, pp. 339–40).

It is particularly noteworthy that in 1695 there are specific references to the strategy of coastal bombardment having little purpose beyond the vague but common seventeenth-century term 'annoyance'. Central to the events that unfolded was also an awareness of the significance of morale. Benbow was particularly anxious, once the attack had been made at St Malo with some success, that the enemy should not be given 'occasion … to boast, and prevent all the remaining part of the summer service'.[36] But in practice what he feared came true to a certain extent. Sixty English officers and men were killed and wounded in the assault, the *Carcass* and *Thunder* bomb vessels were badly damaged and the crippled *Dreadful* burned where she lay as enemy galleys swarmed towards her. The *Carcass* was lucky she was not destroyed as an enemy shell burst through her deck, but it failed to explode and only one man was killed. Five or possibly six boats were sunk carrying ammunition and stores to and from the bomb vessels and a number of frigates were damaged in the hull. Without question the French were better prepared than they had been in 1693. The defensive firing seems to have been much more effective; the inshore squadron of galleys was augmented by a squadron of ten 'great boats', each armed with large cannon that sniped at the English ships. There also appear to have been fire-fighting gangs working in the town itself, blowing up houses that stood in the path of the fire to prevent it from spreading. Nevertheless, the English squadron had proved effective once more. Berkeley wrote that 'little part of it [is] free from some share of the desolation'. Other sources claimed that half the town was destroyed by the nine hundred bombs and carcasses thrown into the town and that many civilians were forced to flee to the country.[37]

Benbow was specifically named by Berkeley for the quality of his service in positioning the bomb vessels and orchestrating the supply of their ammunition and other necessities. But then they appear to have fallen out for an unknown reason, and Berkeley wrote to the Navy Board on 23 July: 'Benbow is quitting his ship. I cannot imagine the reason; he pretends sickness, but I think that is only feigned.' Two days later he strongly criticized an Admiralty Board proposal that Benbow should lead another attack on Dunkirk. By the end of the week Berkeley had received an Admiralty query concerning his dispute with Benbow. An irate Berkeley replied:

> As to Captain Benbow I know of no difference between him and myself, nor have we had any. He has no small obligation to me but being called in some of the foolish printed papers 'the famous captain Benbow' I suppose has put him a little out of himself and made him play the fool … time will show I have not been in the wrong, unless being too kind to an ungrateful man.[38]

This episode is interesting for the fact that Benbow had again fallen out with a senior naval officer and also for the Admiralty's support for him, the Lords Justices' evident concern over his well-being and the complete absence of any attempt to mollify Berkeley. The Lords

Justices even directly ordered the Admiralty to allow Benbow ashore if his health required it and that 'care be taken not to lose his service during this expedition'.[39] The dispute had still not settled by August and when Berkeley realized that he was personally under censure for calling off the attack on St Malo too early, he tried to shift the blame to Benbow, whom he had ordered 'to stay as long as he thought fit'.[40] Once more the Admiralty Board's response is interesting. Benbow was summoned to them the following day but there was no mention of St Malo or of Berkeley; he was asked his opinion on the war's naval strategy, while he in return asked for more pay, which was granted. Not only was he granted the extra pay but the Admiralty Board had to bend the rules to do so as 'it was not usual to give a commission to one in Captain Benbow's circumstances ... but he should have an order for it, which would be as effectual'. The Lords Justices later wrote to him full of praise, 'very well satisfied with what has been done at St Malo and the part you have had in it. I do not doubt you have had all the success that you could propose at Granville', which was Benbow's next target.[41]

They were right to be so confident. Shortly after the St Malo attack Benbow took a small force eastwards a few miles to attack the unsuspecting and almost defenceless port of Granville. Defended by only two mortars and three guns in improvised batteries that were unable to reach the English ships, the town was razed to the ground. Locals ran carrying what they could while their houses burned behind them. Benbow ordered the bombs to stop firing only when the bronze of the mortars began to melt.[42] It is clear from the Admiralty's response to the dispute between Benbow and Berkeley that this is what it expected from its naval officers in the 1690s: it wanted men who were both willing and able to burn towns, and in Benbow it had discovered the very model of that capability. To keep him sweet the Admiralty paid him a reward of £84 for the season's efforts.[43]

After the operations Benbow was instructed to inspect the bomb ships personally and send those that required an overhaul to Sheerness.[44] 1695 ended in exactly the same pattern as 1694, with a spectacularly unsuccessful attack on Dunkirk followed by a quick raid on

Calais. By the beginning of September, however, there were insufficient ships available to provide protection for yet another bombing raid and that season's campaigns drew to a close. There was only one more bombing campaign that summer and it is a fine example of much of the naval bombardment strategy of 1692–6. It is worth reading the words of Sir Martin Beckman, commander-in-chief of that operation, describing this savage and apparently pointless event, as it reveals a great deal about the culture of naval thought in the 1690s that Benbow's achievements had done so much to foster: capable, proud and yet senseless to the destruction being caused, and seemingly unaware of the limited military value of the attack. This time the target was the town of Les Sables d'Olonne and the strategically insignificant island of St Martin de Ré, both on the west coast of France near La Rochelle. Beckman wrote of the attack on St Martin:

> two ... fires continued with considerable augmentation in the middle and richest place of the town in so much that we all judged that the best part of the town was destroyed by fire and scattered in pieces by the bombs of which the town received 2,230, 260 carcasses included in that number.

The next target was Olonne. Beckman wrote:

> In this time of bombing these towns took fire in fifteen several places ... these towns especially that on the south side consists only of one street, and the houses stand for the most part far scattering, and a good distance from each other. Upon these places I spent 1,996 bombs and carcasses...[45]

Similar pointless raids on Dunkirk and Calais followed in 1696 and 1697 with Benbow involved in both. It is possible he was wounded in the leg during the second attack.[46]

Although the raids themselves stand out in naval history as a dramatic change from the large-scale fleet battles that had characterized the Dutch Wars and the opening years of William's war with France, it is important to acknowledge that there was a lengthy precedent in land warfare for this kind of action against such 'soft' or civilian targets. In the winter of 1688–9 the French themselves had devastated the Palatinate and large parts of Germany by bombardment; in 1689 and 1691 Louis XIV's forces, in their action against the Bishopric of Liège, had burned Malmedy and Stavelot, pillaged Huy and fired heated shot into Liège itself during an unsuccessful siege. These bombing raids are a reminder that in the late seventeenth century civilians did not just live in peace as war raged all around them, but were frequently caught up in the action and were threatened from sea as well as from land. To consider that 'total war' started in the Revolutionary and Napoleonic period, and to claim that warfare of the *ancien régime* was in some sense more 'civilized' than what followed, is badly misguided.[47]

In the seventeenth century there was, nevertheless, mixed opinion about such conduct of war. Of the soldiers, none was more bellicose than Adolphus of Sweden, one of the finest military commanders of his age, who said: 'Neutrality is nothing but rubbish, which the wind raises and carries away. What is neutrality anyway? I do not understand it.'[48] From the evidence of the bombing raids of 1693–6 it is clear that Benbow shared this uncompromising view of warfare, unlike some of his less warlike contemporaries. The English historian and bishop Gilbert Burnet commented that 'these bombardments seemed inhumane' while Edward Russell was clear that 'burning a town or village in my humble opinion is of noe more service to England than an accidentall fire at Knight's Bridge would be a disservice'. The Duke of Shrewsbury, one of the council acting for the King in his absence, wrote to William arguing that 'the designs we have on foot appear so frivolous that it is not very pleasant writing upon them'. Perhaps most damning of all was the eloquent John Evelyn, who considered 'bombing and ruining three paltry towns … an hostility totally adverse to humanity, and especially to Christianity'. It is also significant that the use of fireships, let alone exploding machine vessels, was considered by many underhand and was exempt from the normal rules of naval war: crews of fireships if captured would be shot on sight.[49]

If the coastal raids of 1693–6 are viewed from a narrow perspective, in the words of Herbert Richmond, one of the Royal Navy's earliest and finest historians: 'With great certainty we can say they contributed nothing whatever.'⁵⁰ But from a wider perspective they played their part in helping the navy develop into the formidable fighting force that it would become within two generations. Each individual campaign tested the ability of the dockyards to prepare the vessels and then repair them when they returned, in many cases shot to pieces. Each individual campaign tested the sailors in what was, in terms of seamanship, the harshest possible environment. This was no cruising across great oceans on reliable trade winds for weeks at a time but duty that rapidly improved seamanship skill. None of the bombing raids could be carried out without complex anchor work, warping, drifting and sounding. Everywhere they went their knowledge of the northern French coastline improved; every time they attacked, more men gained experience of coastal bombardment. All the while, moreover, the French navy operated in tiny squadrons that offered no comparison with the actions attempted by the English. While the English were learning, even if through failure, they were at least moving forward, whereas the operational capability of the French navy had stalled.

12.

Benbow's Convoys

On 26 April 1696 Benbow was finally promoted to Rear-Admiral of the Blue, although he had been receiving the pay of a Rear-Admiral for almost six months, and he hoisted his flag in the 70-gun *Suffolk* (see Appendix II, p. 341). This was the start of the final phase of the war, which differed in character to the previous four years of shore bombardment. The difficulties of attacking Dunkirk were central to this. It had been made quite clear that the French ships within the port could not be destroyed by any attack, and so the only other option was to contain them by blockade and to protect trade by convoy and cruising, three distinct types of operation that later became the bedrock of British maritime success. Never so glamorous as cutting-out operations, fleet battle or coastal raids, this was the tedious and largely unrewarding duty that was so easy to resent, and it is not hard to see why.

The problem necessarily revolved around the merchants and their ships. The mercantile response to enforced, that is protected, convoys was mixed. While some greatly appreciated the extra security that the navy could provide, others objected to the inevitable economic repercussions of such a system: rather than trade goods trickling in or out of a country, thus ensuring that the price of a commodity remained stable, the arrival of a convoy flooded that local economy and drove down the price of the imported goods, which reduced the profit that could be made on each voyage. The security of a convoy, moreover, was also rather unpredictable. In theory, by grouping the ships together the merchantmen were harder to discover. In practice all convoys were cumbersome and for safety's sake were forced to use well-known and predictable sailing routes. For transoceanic voyages this meant that the start and end points of a voyage were to a certain extent predictable: privateers did not hunt their prey randomly, but systematically, with the shared knowledge of generations of seafarers who knew the routes, ports, tides and seasons of trade. The harvest times of tobacco and citrus fruits, the seasonal winds in the Indian Ocean and the onset of Baltic ice were all in their own way knowable and had a necessary impact on the timetabling of convoys.

It was also very difficult to get dozens of ships to sail together in anything resembling parity, and this was a particular problem for the relatively swift warships and the lumbering traders. The traders themselves, with the exception of some East Indiamen, were slow in relation to each other as well as to their escorts. The inevitable result was that, in any convoy, there would be stragglers, and stragglers were easy prey to fast privateers. Once an attack had been made the convoy would often scatter and the ships would be no better off than if they had started independently. Even if there was no such threat the likelihood of collision between cumbersome ships that were frequently undermanned and commanded by officers entirely unused to working in company, but now forced to operate in a fleet usually over a hundred strong and sometimes as large as 180,[1] was an added danger that many captains resented being forced to take.

This already troubled framework could then be further threatened if the naval officer or merchant masters were particularly difficult. Consider the case of Benjamin Crow. The event occurred several years after Benbow commanded convoys, but it is a rare surviving example that illustrates the extent of the problem with which naval officers could be faced. Captain Hennington of the *Bristol* was in charge of the convoy, when:

> On the 3rd of August at eight in the morning I perceived the fleet to be very much scattered. Some were as far ahead of me, and some to windward, as I could well see them upon our deck, I making but an easy sail, the better to keep company with the ships that sailed heavy, which at that time were a great way astern; upon which I fired a shott ahead, for those ahead to bring to, but

found they took no notice of it, so continued still my saile, and fired another shott, and as I came up with them they brought to. About noon I was come up with the headmost of them, and fired a shott athwart their forefoot, which they observed. I hailed the *Mary* of Yarmouth, Benjamin Crow master, and bid him bring to, and sent my lieutenant aboard to bring the master to me, with a design to reprimand him for his offence, and to make him pay my gunner for the shott. And the lieutenant brought me for answer that the master refused to do it, and sent me word he had no business with me, and would not go out of his ship. Upon which I sent my lieutenant again to bring him aboard; but when he came, he found the master armed with fire armes; who told him that if he offered to medle with him, [he] would shout [shoot] him.

Hennington was so shocked that he bore down to the *Mary* and shouted across to Crow, demanding to know the reason for his insolence and ordering him, once more, aboard the *Bristol*, threatening to open fire if he resisted. Crow once more refused to come aboard, ordered his men to their battle stations and further added that if Hennington sent anyone else aboard his ship he would shoot him. Hennington had no choice but to back off and leave Crow to his own fate as he sped off ahead of the convoy. This type of behaviour, though not always so extreme, remained a problem for many years.[2]

Against this background, Benbow's role in the protection of English trade between 1695 and 1697 is noteworthy for the respect with which he was treated by merchants. There is no firm evidence that Benbow particularly enjoyed his job but he certainly appears to have been very good at it. On a number of occasions, the Admiralty received petitions specifically requesting that he escort a valuable convoy, and when it received a request for protection he was the first name that sprung to mind.

In September 1695 Benbow was the preferred candidate to escort an East India Company convoy but was already occupied with the bomb vessels. The following year the valuable Hamburg fleet was ready to sail to England with a cargo worth an estimated £400,000 and Benbow was requested by name. He brought them home safely and then provided the same reliable service for the Muscovy fleet and then another from Holland. It must be a strong possibility that Benbow's early experiences as a merchant, together with his history of fighting corsairs and privateers, made him particularly sympathetic to the plight of the merchants. In any case, throughout 1696–7 Benbow was used repeatedly to escort valuable convoys to and from English shores and he did so with great, and acknowledged, success. In September he escorted three East Indiamen home and for his care was given a thousand guineas by the Company.[3]

The only significant example of failure came in May 1697, when Benbow left Portsmouth escorting three outward-bound East Indiamen. They were soon shadowed by some unknown ships and Benbow was forced to go twenty or thirty leagues beyond his orders in an attempt to lose their pursuers. When it became clear that this had failed, Benbow insisted on returning home as ordered, to cruise for the homeward-bound Virginia fleet. The captain of the Indiamen asked for some protection to remain with their fleet but Benbow refused to divide his squadron and sailed for home. Almost immediately two of the Indiamen were taken, amounting to a loss of £70,000, although the *Tavistock*, which was worth the same again, escaped the initial attack. Benbow does not appear to have been censured for his action and he brought home safely the Virginia convoy, which was worth an estimated £200,000 for Customs alone.[4]

One of the characteristics of Benbow's convoy service is his dedication to duty and on one occasion he chose to sail both undermanned and understored to protect an incoming fleet rather than wait for the supplies he so desperately needed. It is possible his desperation in this instance was caused by the knowledge that Bart was out, also hunting for the convoy.[5] His reputation for safe passage was even enough for Benbow to be trusted with the safety of the most valuable object in England, the King himself, and on several occasions in 1697–8 he acted as the King's private cross-Channel ferry, escorting him with a force of eight warships to and from Holland.[6] In terms of his commitment to convoy duty, which so many officers considered a burden, Benbow yet again was a model officer for the Admiralty, which at the time and in subsequent years was repeatedly forced to reprimand or severely punish those officers who neglected their convoys.[7]

When Benbow wasn't escorting convoys his time was occupied blockading Dunkirk with an allied Dutch squadron or hunting the Dunkirk-based privateer Bart as he ravaged English and Dutch shipping in the North Sea and escorted his own valuable convoys safely to France. As has been explained, the approaches to Dunkirk are protected by sandbanks and there are entrances to east and west. It quickly proved impossible to keep a close watch on both entrances at the same time. The coast is plagued by fog that drastically reduces visibility and the southern wind that allowed ships to sail from Dunkirk necessarily kept the blockading ships at bay. Bart, moreover, made excellent use of the 290-foot-high tower of St Eloi to observe the scene.[8] As a result the blockade of Dunkirk proved a very inexact science and little could be done to restrict Bart's movements. In May 1696, for example, Benbow was guarding the eastern channel with three ships, each lying no more than five miles from shore. More ships lay farther out to sea and to the westward, a mile apart but still in touch with the eastern blockading force. But Bart still escaped, leaving to the westward just before dawn and hugging the coast in the hazy weather. No one saw him leave and then, when it became known that he was out, the Dutch squadron refused to follow him, claiming that their orders required them to blockade Dunkirk, and not go chasing off across the North Sea. It required a detailed explanation from Benbow as to how he proposed to chase Bart as well as specific orders issued by the King to get the Dutch to cooperate, but by then the rare opportunity had long since passed and another had failed to materialize. A frustrated Benbow boldly told the Lords Justices that the subsequent capture by Bart of an East India Convoy could have been prevented if only the Dutch had chased with him.[9]

Bart had certainly been successful. Shortly after escaping from Benbow he fell in with a large Dutch convoy between the Dogger Bank and the Texel. He burned the entire Dutch escort and twenty-five merchantmen before escaping from another Dutch squadron and heading north. Benbow then chased Bart all the way to the Baltic and spent two weeks sheltering from the weather in the Kattegat Sea between Denmark and Sweden before making his way to the southern tip of Norway, a long-established haunt of Dunkirk privateers and where, Benbow had received intelligence, Bart had established himself in a fortified camp ashore, defended by fifty guns. Ultimately, however, the weather that kept Bart in his fortified camp forced Benbow home with his ships shattered and leaking from prolonged cruising in foul weather and his men suffering from a lack of water. The Duke of Shrewsbury wrote to appease an anxious Benbow: 'I do not doubt that you have done all that was in your power for the finding out of du Bart, but if you have met with contrary weather it ought not to be imputed to you, and you may be assured I shall be ready to serve you on this or any other occasion.'[10]

It was not until September that Benbow was given another opportunity to get at Bart, but yet again he was disappointed. On 19 September Benbow intercepted a fleet and his leading ships got to within two miles of the enemy before they fled. Later, in a letter to Richard Haddock, he lamented that 'he never shortened one jott of sayle in order to battle'.[11] A few weeks later Benbow was forced to see his nemesis sail once more across the horizon. Even when it grew dark he did not give up hope that his headmost ships might keep in touch with the slowest French throughout the night 'but they neither showed light nor burned false fires' and he gave up the chase on the banks of Flanders. He finished his letter to Haddock: 'I am sure I used my utmost endeavours and diligence to execute my orders, nor has anything but good sailing ships been wanting to compeat 'em.'[12] Four more strangers were chased the following day but they too were swift and Benbow eventually gave up near Calais.

In another letter Benbow complained that 'had our ships been clean we should have given a better account of him, having had six or seven hours fair chase, but the worst of his sailing ships wronged the best of ours'. His own ship, the *Suffolk*, was so leaky that one of her pumps had to be constantly manned, while another ship, the *Russell*, had sprung her main and foremast in the chase.[13] The following year and it was a lack of beer, peas and oatmeal that forced Benbow home in similar circum- stances,[14] and a document from July 1696 reveals that, of his squadron of eleven ships, five had significant problems, from the *Pembroke*, whose gundecks needed caulking, to the *Woolwich* and *Mary Galley* and *Hunter*, whose hulls were either 'unserviceable' or in such disrepair that the pump was continually manned. Only one ship had masts, yards and hull in 'good condition'. By September the entire squadron was desper- ate for anchor cables, twine, tackle, hooks, buoys, grindstones, scrapers, brooms, rope and tar.[15] Ten of the eleven ships were also undermanned, some seriously so. The *Suffolk* herself had only 323 of a full complement of 446, that is only 72 per cent of her crew, and the *Woolwich* laboured under an identical percentage.[16] In August 1696 the *Chatham* was undermanned in one very significant way: her Master had fallen over- board and drowned.[17]

These failures all point to the underlying problem that plagued Benbow's operations in this period. Forced to keep the sea for weeks at a time and with no sophisticated system of rotation to relieve ships for repair, when the opportunity arose Benbow's squadron were in no state to chase Bart, who, blockaded in port, had all the time in the world to make certain that his already fast ships were in excellent condition for their forays. In May 1696 a frustrated Benbow thus reported that priva- teers were seen every day, but that every one of them outsailed his ships.[18] For all his aggressive intent, Benbow never stood a chance at getting at Bart unless some accident happened to the Frenchman's rig- ging or a lucky shot crippled one of his ships. Nothing like that occurred.

So, while Benbow's dedication to his duty of trade protection was unquestionable, he was repeatedly frustrated by the weather, a shortage of water or the breakdown of his ships, itself caused by long service, yet all of these factors remained significant logistical hurdles for a century or more. It must not be forgotten that this war was the very first in which the Royal Navy was faced with the problems of blockading the French coast. The system was still unrefined in the 1690s; it was in fact embryonic and the navy's achievements must be judged in those terms.

Even to get within sight of Bart's fleet once it was clear of the coast was an impressive achievement that demonstrated the good sense of the strategy, and it is certain that the improved convoy system helped to protect trade. There was no repeat of the Smyrna disaster of 1693 and on numerous occasions escorts defended their convoys with considerable courage and skill.[19]Although unable to do anything about it, the contemporary naval administration openly acknowledged the need for speed to revictual and repair. Their immediate response to news that Benbow's squadron had returned in May 1697 was to note the 'necessity there was of hastening them out again for the protection of trade'. All of this seems to have been backed up with an efficient intelligence system that warned of imminent French sorties.[20] It is particularly interesting that Benbow saw not just frustration in these logistical hurdles, but opportunity too. In August 1697 he wrote to the Navy Board asking for six of his ships to be cleaned. He realized that if he met a French squadron in the meantime the French would notice how poorly the Englishmen sailed. If they then met again, with the clean ships now reunited, Benbow reasoned, 'they [the French] will be the bolder to see our squadron ... and if so may find their mistake'.[21] This was no slight advantage: modern research has shown that clean ships could sail up to a knot and a half faster than foul ones.[22] Such cunning was central to English tactics in the 1690s. We also know that the Channel fleet was issued with French flags in July 1696 and it was generally accepted that 'Colours were not to be trusted'.[23]

Another important aspect of Benbow's convoy duties in this final stage of the war against the French was their location. Throughout 1696 he was primarily based in the North Sea, where the English east coast trade, which accounted for at least three-quarters of England's entire coastal trade, was dominated by the colliers and food traders of Newcastle, Sunderland, Whitby, Scarborough, Hull, (King's) Lynn, (Great) Yarmouth, Ipswich and Rochester. The east coast was centred on movement by trade between the Tyne, Tees and the Thames, while Scottish ports maintained strong links with Scandinavia, Hamburg, Bremen and

Rotterdam.[24] There were also valuable herring fisheries off Yarmouth and North Foreland (a headland just off Margate at the mouth of the Thames where the English Channel becomes the North Sea). From December 1696, however, Benbow was based in the western approaches to the Channel, which reflected a fundamental and highly significant shift in English naval strategy. The disaster at Barfleur had made the French all too aware of the logistical problems of allowing a large battle fleet to enter the Channel. Even in the summer the prevailing winds were westerly or south-westerly and there was nowhere safe for a large fleet to ride out a storm. Across the entire north coast of France there is no natural shelter the equivalent of Plymouth Sound, Torbay or Spithead. Nor were there any docking facilities capable of taking a First or Second Rate warship: if the largest and most cumbersome ships became damaged in a battle or a storm, there was nowhere safe to repair them.

The response of the French was another subtle shift in strategy as they began to send ships to windward of the Channel, deep into the Atlantic, where they could prey on English exotic convoys from the Americas and the Caribbean. Merchantmen from even farther afield were also vulnerable as they carefully stayed to windward of Brittany to navigate safely into the entrance to the Channel. To windward of the Channel the French were safe, as they could run to Brittany and the safety of Brest or Camaret Bay in a storm, or even farther down the west coast, to Rochefort or L'Orient. The English response was to meet this threat by sending their own squadrons out into the western approaches. In fact, after 1692 the French only sent a large battle fleet into the Channel on three occasions (1744, 1779 and 1781) and, although they planned to do so once more (1805), all of these were times of over-whelming superiority or attempted surprise. From the winter of 1696 onwards a large part of the naval wars between Britain and France was played out in the western approaches.

From May 1697 this is where Benbow was posted aboard the *Lenox* (see Appendix 11, p. 343), more specifically 'from ten to an hundred leagues W from Scilly', to meet and escort home the valuable Virginia and Barbados fleet and to escort three East Indiamen out of the Channel.[25] By then this was an idea that had been simmering since the earliest example of a squadron being sent into the western approaches in 1650, but by the 1690s it was rapidly becoming the forefront of British naval defence, a changing priority reflected in the massive programme of construction at Plymouth from 1689, where a dockyard was built to service the Western Squadron.[26] Still the navy suffered from manning problems, however, and before his cruise in the spring of 1697 Benbow was particularly anxious about a lack of surgeons.[27] When he finally got to sea the situation was already quite tense as a French squadron of five 50-gunners had attacked a West India fleet, and two English ships had been sunk, three others badly disabled and 120 men killed or wounded. But the cruise was largely uneventful, despite the occasional sighting of privateers, and when Benbow was forced back to port for want of provisions he finally met the incoming fleet, 120 ships strong. He escorted them to Plymouth and then received specific orders to protect them on their journey up to the Downs.[28]

In July Benbow took a small prize and four prisoners off Brest and a few weeks later he took another lone trader full of brandy and wine off Dunkirk.[29] By then the incessant discomfort of blockade duty had caught up with him and he petitioned the Navy Board for time ashore to recover his health. Permission was granted, but by then he had adjudged himself sufficiently improved to stay at sea. In spite of his unrelenting service at sea this is the only evidence we have of Benbow's health failing and it must be taken as evidence of a hardy constitution and iron will. The Admiralty was certainly desperate to keep him there: in August he wrote asking to come in for fresh water but it was sent to him instead and the ships in his squadron that needed repair were all given priority in the dockyards, whose officers were ordered to repair them as swiftly as possible. By September it had been decided to appoint Benbow in command of a winter water guard, a permanent Royal Navy patrol. This was an extraordinarily ambitious proposal for the Bay of Biscay at that time of year, but given his proven ability and endurance it was deemed viable.

Benbow thus saw action in almost every location of naval activity in this war, from Norway to Biscay, from the Gunfleet to Plymouth, and he did so year-round, an entirely novel concept. He played a crucial role in the unglamorous work of trade protection that complemented his pioneering efforts in aggressive operations using bomb ships and machine vessels. If there is an abiding lesson of this war it is that English naval strategy was split into two very distinct parts: one part focused on aggressive action against the enemy, either on land or at sea, the other on trade protection. This dual strategy provided the foundation for British naval supremacy in the coming century, and Benbow had a clear hand in the development of both in the 1690s. As the war came to a close with both sides exhausted, Benbow even helped secure the peace by convoying the King and several French ambassadors to Holland to negotiate peace terms, and he brought back troops from Flanders.[30]

13.

Benbow's Benevolence

As Benbow's career at sea was only one part of his naval career, so was Benbow's work in the Royal Dockyards only one part of his career ashore. The dockyard at Deptford was not the only ancient maritime institution in that suburb of London and Benbow quickly found his path crossing that of the Brethren of Trinity House. Like Deptford Dockyard, Trinity House was established by Henry VIII and in the same year, 1513. It was an independent organization, governed by seamen who had been elected by seamen, and run for the benefit of seamen.

Trinity House had originally been established with a simple, dual purpose in mind: to superintend pilotage on the Thames and maintain an almshouse at Deptford. The London docks, the commercial heart of England, lay nearly forty miles from the open sea, and both the course into the southern North Sea and the route from there to the English Channel were protected by appalling navigational hazards. Dominated by the Goodwin Sands, the route into the Thames, even today and with modern navigational equipment, is treacherous. Sometimes thirty or forty miles from shore sandbanks are uncovered at low tide and tidal races swirl around the shallow estuary. The area of danger stretches from where the Essex coast swings north-east towards Aldeburgh right down to the Kent coast as it swings eastwards towards North Foreland. The banks regularly shift and form channels and cul-de-sacs that offer no way through and no space to turn around. When a ship was embarking on a lengthy voyage or just arriving at her destination were the times at which she was at most risk. So close to shore meant so close to danger; the endless miles of ocean that isolated the deep-ocean sailer also secured her safety. As with all ports, moreover, changing weather and sea conditions could render what was familiar instantly alien and transform confidence to fear. The only way to safeguard the approaches to most ports, and in particular London, was to employ full-time specialist pilots who could read the approaches in fog and rain, at spring tide and neap, and on the darkest of nights. This, essentially, was the service that was provided and safeguarded by, to give Trinity House its full title, the Guild Fraternity, or Brotherhood of the Most Glorious and Undivided Trinity in the Parish of Deptford Strond. This corporation was granted powers to regulate pilotage and in 1604 received the exclusive right to license pilots on the Thames.

All of the members of Trinity House were experienced seamen and membership required competence of the highest order. By 1692, moreover, the Guild was nearly 180 years old and so Benbow was following in some very significant footsteps. Thomas Spertt, master of Henry VIII's magnificent carracks *Mary Rose* and *Henry Grace à Dieu*, was one of the earliest Tudor seamen to make his name in Trinity House. He was followed by John Rut, who led one of the earliest voyages of exploration to the New World. From the same period came John Bartelot, famed at the time for his discovery of a new channel in the Thames. By the 1580s Stephen Borough, who had made a name for himself as a navigator on the first voyage of the Muscovy Company, had become a member and so too his brother, William, who sailed as Vice-Admiral to Francis Drake on the Cadiz expedition of 1587. In that same period Sir John Hawkins, the Treasurer of the Navy, Sir William Wynter, the Surveyor, and William Holstock, the Comptroller, were all members of Trinity House. In the following century Henry Mainwaring, a talented mariner and convicted pirate, went on to become the Master of Trinity House in 1642. Pepys himself held this position twice. Of Benbow's contemporaries, Captain John Hill, elected Master in 1694, was one of the best-known of the owner-masters trading to the Levant, themselves the cream of the merchant service. Rooke, Shovell, the hydrographer Greenville Collins, the secretary to the Admiralty Josiah Burchett, the shipwright Anthony Deane and Jonathan Leake and George Byng, impressive young captains who would go on to have impressive careers, were all members.[1]

The Guild was run by the Brethren of Trinity House, divided into two classes. At the junior level were the Younger Brethren, and at the senior the thirty-one Elder Brethren who governed all Trinity House business, overseen by the Master. On 11 February 1692 Benbow was elected a Younger Brother, the twelve hundred and fifty-second in the institution's history.[2] In itself the appointment is unsurprising, for Benbow was a skilled mariner with proven experience, a renowned pilot and a Deptford resident. He was also a protégé of Arthur Herbert, who had been an Elder Brother of Trinity House for four years. It is more than likely that a certain degree of patronage was involved in Benbow's nomination. If that nomination to the Younger Brethren was not surprising, however, his promotion to the Elder Brethren was quite extraordinary and reminiscent of his rapid rise through the ranks in the aftermath of the Revolution in 1688. Benbow was sworn in as an Elder Brother (the hundred and fifteenth) on 4 May 1692 in place of Captain Thomas Browne, John Evelyn's father-in-law and the Master of Trinity House,who had died. His age at promotion was not unusual; he was probably forty-two or forty-three, and most Younger Brethren became Elder Brethren in their forties or fifties,[3] but two things stand out about his appointment. Firstly it was normal for Younger Brethren to have been in position for several years before nominating themselves for election to the Elder Brethren, and secondly there was usually a ballot recorded in the minutes detailing how the court of Trinity House voted. Neither of these things happened with Benbow. He was elected to the Elder Brethren less than three months after being elected to the Younger Brethren, and his election was secured by a unanimous vote.[4] Benbow was fast-tracked into position.

His election would have formed part of a complex annual celebration at Deptford, the site of the original Trinity House Hall. The day-to-day business was carried out at their offices in Water Lane, near Tower Hill, but each year on Trinity Monday the Younger and Elder Brethren all gathered at Deptford for their annual elections. It was an event of great festivity and we know that for the celebrations of 1661 'two barrills of strong beere' were laid in at Trinity House against Trinity Monday. In the same period the cost of the festivities ran to £120, a figure which caused considerable scandal.⁵ Pepys himself enjoyed the elections on numerous occasions and recorded in his diary that he had 'great entertainment' there, though on one occasion he was riled that, before the election of their Master and his assistants, they read their charter 'like fools, only reading here and there a bit, whereas they ought to do it all, every word…' Thereafter he sat down to a 'very great dinner' and spent the evening talking about the appearance of spirits and the worrying fact that the Devil had recently been spotted in Wiltshire, apparently with a drum. They swiftly moved on to talking about women, and one in particular who worked at the market in Bury who Pepys believed 'the prettiest woman I ever saw'. Pepys eventually made it home with a severe hangover, but a visit from his barber and a spot of violin practice before bed set him right.⁶

We even know what Benbow would have heard during the elections that took place in 1695 because the sermon preached to the Brethren survives. It was all impressively maritime-oriented and began with a well-known maritime quote from Isaiah 43:2: 'When thou passes though the Waters, I will be with thee: and through the Rivers, they shall not overflow thee.' After a ramble through scripture that must have lasted at least an hour, the sermon ended with yet another quote specifically directed at the maritime community. God alone, it was proclaimed, 'can rebuke the storm and still the raging of the Sea. He who is mercifully present in all places, is powerfully present in these Waters…'⁷

The annual celebrations in Deptford were discontinued after the death of the Duke of Wellington, who was Master from 1837 to 1852, and the only evidence of this landscape that survives today is the church of St Nicholas in Deptford, appropriately the patron saint of sailors, built on a site that has been holy since 1183. The stone tower of the church that stands today was constructed in the fifteenth century and would have been a familiar landmark to Benbow, not least during the annual festivities and corresponding sermon delivered in the church. The offices at Water Lane have also now gone, as the Brethren moved in 1796 to a new site on Tower Hill, where the current magnificent home of Trinity House now stands and where they continue to hold their impressive annual celebrations.

In stark contrast to the frivolity of the annual elections the work of the Brethren touched numerous topics of abiding and serious concern to the nation's sailors. In general the records of Trinity House are well preserved but unfortunately the one significant gap in the minutes of the Trinity House court is for the eleven years 1692–1703, when Benbow was an Elder Brother. Nevertheless, the minutes do survive for the first year of his time at Trinity House. Thereafter there are sufficient scattered references to build up a picture of some of the projects that the Brethren of Trinity House were involved in, although it must be borne in mind throughout that this evidence is patchy, and from what we know about the earlier history of Trinity House, their involvement in maritime affairs would have been far greater still than these examples suggest.

The appointment and regulation of Thames pilots took up much of the Brethren's time. To regulate pilotage in the Thames was essentially to oversee the safety of shipping in the busiest river in England, a responsibility they took seriously by ruling with a firm hand. In August 1692 a pilot was found guilty of negligent navigation, was barred from acting as a pilot, stripped of his position at Trinity House *and* imprisoned for three months.[8] The maintenance of high levels of professional skill was not the only concern of Trinity House, however, and that winter it dismissed a pilot for nothing more than insolent behaviour and abusive language, though his skill was never questioned.[9] Such a harsh stance even in a one-off case is even more surprising given the continuous grumbling of fleet commanders in these years over the lack of pilots.[10]

Integral to the supervision of Thames pilotage was Trinity House's responsibility for keeping the Thames accessible to shipping by dredging the channels and generally keeping the river clear. The sand and gravel dredged by the company was then sold as ballast and the profits retained. This was significant indeed as from 1660 Trinity House exercised a complete monopoly of the sale of Thames ballast. The banks of the river were also a particular concern, and in the winter of 1692 the Brethren wrote to the Navy Board about breaches to the river in Long

Reach.[11] If keeping the river deep and constrained was one challenge, keeping it accessible and clear for everyone's use was quite another. In November 1692 they wrote to the Lord Mayor complaining about the damage being done to the river by the large number of ships that lay abreast 'stopping sullage from being carried away'.[12] This was a real concern as all of London's industrial waste and domestic sewage was removed by the Thames. At times this river filth was even more sinister and Trinity House was particularly concerned in the winter of 1692 about the 'annoyance to ye river and passengers thereupon by deadmen driving to and against without care taken by any person to have them taken up and buried as was formerly done'.[13] 1692 was not a year of plague or epidemic though many will have died from the usual outbreaks of smallpox and assorted 'fevers' that were common, and corpses frequently floated down the river. Common as they were, the Brethren of Trinity House took a certain responsibility for this distasteful topic, which, together with their concern over the dispersal of sewage, makes them one of the earliest champions of the London environment.

Trinity House's specific responsibility for the Thames did not extend to the other major waterways of the country but they were always consulted about significant events or proposals that might seriously affect a river's navigation or the use of a particular harbour. In November 1696 there was some detailed correspondence between the Navy Board and Trinity House concerning the suitability of Fowey harbour in Cornwall to shelter naval vessels.[14] In Benbow's time the Brethren were also involved in projects to deepen the silted-up harbours of Dover and Sandwich.[15] In terms of inland waterways, in May 1698 the Elder Brethren were asked for their opinion on a Bill proposing alterations to the Yorkshire rivers the Aire and Calder, which run through Castleford to Leeds and Wakefield respectively. Both rivers run into the much larger Ouse (see map 1), which flows through York itself and then on to the great Humber estuary. The purpose of alterations to the Aire was to make it navigable as far as Leeds, and to make the Calder, a tributary of the Aire, navigable from Castleford to Wakefield. The great cloth centres of Wakefield and Leeds would thus be linked to the Ouse and thence to the sea. Trinity House was extremely cautious about any alterations to rivers that might affect the navigation of the Ouse itself in case that great artery was deprived of the water necessary to make it navigable. The solution was to build tidal locks and dams at Knottingly.[16] This type of consultancy could have held a particular interest for Benbow because of the likelihood of his early experience working on barges on the Severn.

Trinity House was also responsible for the small but growing number of lighthouses around the coast that made money by collecting dues from passing shipping. Some were owned by the Guild and others privately but all entrepreneurs wishing to construct a light first had to gain a patent from Trinity House to build, and then they paid an annuity to use the light, sometimes sharing the profits with the Guild. With no regulation the quality of the light, cast by fires or candles, was often poor and its maintenance not always reliable. In the 1660s, for example, the owner of the lights at North and South Foreland economized with fuel for the fires, which then burned so low that several ships became endangered and others had no choice but to heave-to until dawn broke.[17]

The way lights were used then was not the same as it is today: nowadays it is safe to assume that known lights are both lit and visible, neither of which could be assumed in the late seventeenth century. This unreliability in turn directly affected the way that some viewed the helpfulness of lights. Mariners, it was believed by some, would 'neglect their arte and truste to an uncertain light'.[18] This initial caution was starting to be peeled away by the 1690s, when Benbow became involved with Trinity House, and that decade saw a noticeable shift in the attitude towards navigational aids of all sorts, and the construction, maintenance and regulation of lighthouses began to take up increasingly more of the Brethren's time.

In the spring of 1692, for example, Lord Villiers offered to sell his lighthouse at Tinmouth (now Tynemouth at North Shields, near Newcastle) to Trinity House for £6,000, which he had worked out at twenty years' income of £300, raised from passing shipping. The

Brethren were keen to purchase the light but were also shrewd business-men and negotiated over the price for a full seven months. They first determined in a meeting at which Benbow was present that they were prepared to pay £3,210, worked out at £214 for fifteen years, but would first offer Lord Villiers less. Villiers then said he would accept nothing less than £3,500 but the confident Brethren stood their ground and found 'no reason to give more than they had already bid unless some-thing towards ye charge of passing the patent'. In effect this meant that they refused to pay any more for the light but offered Villiers the con-cession that they would pay for the administrative costs of the sale, a negotiating point that would be used today in business transfers. The Brethren were then forced to withstand another round of aggressive bargaining with Villiers in October but eventually the transaction was resolved at a meeting in December with Benbow in attendance: they eventually bought the light for half of the original price.[19]

Not all lighthouse projects were met with such enthusiasm and as always the Brethren seemed careful to consider each case with great care. A proposal for a lighthouse on the Dagger and Shield was considered that summer but rejected, 'judged useless'.[20] The court was also that year occupied with a light in the Downs, confusingly known as Scilly Light. The Brethren ordered a fresh coat of white paint for the tower and fuel for the light to last the rest of the summer and winter. They were also concerned with the wages of the collector, a Captain John Fox, who had been granted by the Guild a commission of 4d for every £1 in fees he col-lected, less than 2 per cent.[21] As well as poorly rewarded, his was also a difficult job. Soon after Benbow joined the court the Brethren settled a dispute between Fox and the master of a 300-ton flyboat, the *Seven Provinces*. The only vessels exempt from paying the light dues were war-ships and so the *Severn Provinces* had to pay. Her captain, however, had other ideas and offered the honest Fox a bribe of two guineas. 'The Captain is a knave,' wrote Fox, who then went on to recount with no small degree of pride another of his exploits in which he sniffed out an armed Danish merchantman which was pretending to be a warship to avoid paying. 'I found it not to be so,' wrote the glowing Fox, '...for which reason he paid me.'[22]

The final lighthouse for which we have direct evidence of Benbow's involvement is the Eddystone light, which guards the approaches to the Channel, a full nine miles south of Plymouth on semi-submerged granite rocks pounded by Atlantic swells. The current light is the fourth to have stood there, but in 1692 the first had yet to be built and Benbow and the Brethren were involved only in the proposals. It was four years before building work started, but in June 1692 the proposals for the light were passed and the letter patent from the Queen granting Trinity House the right to receive duty from the proposed Eddystone light was read.[23] The lighthouse on that dangerous rock was still only a dream, but Benbow and his contemporaries were courageous enough to believe it possible. No other offshore lighthouse had ever been built; no one had attempted to build on isolated sea-swept rock. Everything would have to be shipped there from Plymouth; nothing could be done at high tide; and there was nowhere safe to unload the building materials. During every stage in its construction the tower would have to be strong enough to withstand thirty-foot waves and gale-force winds. The Brethren had the vision and drive to make it a reality; it was just a matter of finding the right man to build it.

The man chosen was Walter Whitfield and in 1692 he was granted a patent to build a light. He was not the right man and construction never even began. Four years later and they had their man, an eccentric engineer from Essex named Henry Winstanley, who had personally suffered from the Eddystone Rocks when they wrecked the merchantman he part owned. His plan was to anchor a granite and timber construction to the rocks with iron piles and straps. Twelve months into the project, in the very summer that Benbow was patrolling the western approaches and no doubt monitoring Winstanley's progress, a French privateer destroyed the foundations and kidnapped Winstanley, taking him back to Paris. Louis XIV was enraged and in the apocryphal tale, immediately released Winstanley, claiming that 'France is at war with England, not with humanity'. Winstanley went back to work and completed the lighthouse in 1698, a fantastic construction of granite and wood bound together with iron hoops (see fig. 20). It guarded those rocks for five years, in which no ships were sunk, before being destroyed in the great storm of 1703. Winstanley himself was there that night and he died along with his tower. Nevertheless, its value had been demonstrated and no time was lost in building a new one. When that was destroyed in 1755, another tower was built, and when that became unstable in 1877 yet another was built – the tower we see today. Significant as this is to our lives now, it is important to be aware how much more significant this was in all but the most recent past. Before the rise of mass-market air travel in the 1960s and 1970s, the only way to approach England from abroad was by sea. So, for two and a half centuries, the first evidence of the English state that anyone would have seen if approaching from the west would have been the Eddystone lighthouse. That iconic structure, which together with its predecessors has saved thousands of lives, has its origin in 1692, in the court of the Elder Brethren of Trinity House, in the vision of Benbow and his contemporaries.

Closely linked to the issues surrounding lighthouses were those of the sea-marks – buoys or other markers that served in one way or another as aids to navigation. Because of the nature of coastal navigation these were necessarily varied. Buoys or poles marked rocks, sandbanks and channels, while conveniently located houses, trees and church spires served as highly sensitive leading marks for vessels approaching or leaving harbours and anchorages. The Brethren therefore found themselves engaged in some interesting cases of architectural and environmental conservation underpinned by the everyday maintenance of buoys, poles and beacons. Such sea-marks had always been crucial to coastal navigation but, much like the explosion in the number of lighthouses that occurred around 1700, there was also a dramatic increase in the number of sea-marks positioned and maintained by Trinity House. They varied from the most basic buoys – pieces of timber six or eight feet square secured by a stout iron chain – to poles as much as thirty feet high driven into the seabed. Some were equipped with lanterns.[24] The Elder Brethren themselves periodically inspected the placing of the buoys in the Thames, some of which were broken in collision or became no longer necessary as the sandbanks shifted. At times of invasion scare the Brethren were also responsible for taking up buoys and sea-marks to fox enemy pilots.[25] With such a vested interest in pilotage and navigational aides, Trinity House was an interested party in the process of those courts martial that concerned shipwreck or damage through pilotage error or the failure of navigational aides, and corresponded regularly with the Navy Board.[26]

For an institution of such apparent benevolence, Trinity House's reputation in the 1690s was not quite as shiny as one might expect. In the early years of the seventeenth century the Brethren had acquired quite a reputation for not fulfilling their role with any zeal or much care and they became a regular target for pamphleteers.[27] To a certain extent, however, this is only to be expected from a seventeenth-century institution. Public interest was always tempered, and usually heavily influenced by, private interest, and that applied as much to the Brethren of Trinity House as to the Royal Navy and even Parliament. Nonetheless, the evidence points to progress being made in this period towards an institution that accepted responsibility for the safety of all mariners around English coasts, and made them safer than they ever had been before.

The work of Trinity House so far discussed was for the benefit of all mariners approaching or leaving English shores, and therefore for the benefit of the nation. Increasingly, however, Trinity House came to be used as an informal sounding board for both the government and navy. Its nautical expertise thus provided a very important balance to the Admiralty Board, which, after the 1688 Revolution and regime change, had become dominated by landsmen and politicians. In the absence of experienced seamen close to the government to advise on naval policy and maritime law, Trinity House began in the 1690s to play an important maritime consultancy role that further raised its profile as well as those of its individual members.

In the aftermath of Barfleur, for example, the Royal Navy gave some thought to recovering the significant number of anchors and anchor cables lost on the coast near Cape Barfleur. The navy particularly wanted to know whether the ground there was of sand or rock, and if the anchors had been let go on the ebb or flood tide. Four months later, after a lengthy period of consultation, the Brethren responded that any attempt to recover the anchors would be 'of such difficulty and uncertainty that they dare not advise'.[28] When it came to the devilish problem of manning, the government was also quick to turn to Trinity House. The problem was essentially twofold: of quality and quantity. On the question of quality, the Brethren retained some influence in the navy throughout the period as they were granted the sole authority to examine the navy's masters from 1661 and after the failure of command at the Battle of Beachy Head in 1690 it became more involved in the thorny issue of command competence. In 1691 Russell, Nottingham and the Admiralty concocted a plan to bring fresh blood into the navy from the merchant service. In December the Brethren were asked to provide a list of 'all the tarpaulin commanders that have used the sea these thirty years: it being design'd to imploy some of them in our fleet'. The list was duly delivered, studied and still survives as a valuable document that demonstrates in no uncertain terms Nottingham's policy to promote good-quality officers irrespective of background. Some officers were rapidly dismissed, like poor old William Harman, who was condemned for eternity as 'dull', while others were given nothing less than a mini-biography. Thomas Coale, for example, was 'challenged per an inferior officer under his command. Defended in a 5th rate the whole collier fleet against privateers. Promoted per order of Council. Had £50 reward from Turky company.'[29]

A year later and the Brethren were asked by Parliament to consider two bills 'for the better furnishing their Majesties ships with seamen',[30] and thus became involved in the second manning problem: quantity. In the winter of 1689–90 twenty-two thousand men were on the navy's books, the summer following it was thirty-three thousand, and still they were short.[31] The Brethrens' opinions on both bills are as revealing of their interests as their experience: Trinity House was as much a representative of the seamen as an advisory body. Thus the proposal that masters and owners of all ships, large and small, 'pay £5 for each 50 Ton or send an Able Seaman into their majesties service' was rejected as 'a grievous and unreasonable imposition', while the second, which was the far less intrusive policy of creating a register of seamen, was met with 'no material objection and were on the contrary of the opinion that it would go a great way towards answering the end thereby intended'.[32] In spite of Trinity House's support, the register scheme, which was unlike anything that had previously been attempted in England, never got off the ground until 1696, and only then in a weakened form. Unlike the manning system in France, in which all coastal inhabitants were subject to compulsory naval service one year in three, the English scheme of 1696 was voluntary and it was never backed financially by a destitute, if enthusiastic, government. The men who volunteered, instead of being rewarded by various financial privileges, were treated exactly the same as before and none of them received the £2 annual retainer that was integral to the scheme.[33] The system, so favoured by Trinity House, swiftly collapsed, as much for the political reluctance of a government to be seen to enforce registration on its seamen as for its inability to meet its financial commitments.

The Brethren's role as maritime consultants to the government in this period also stretched to ship design. As has been discussed, the design of warships was referred to the master shipwrights of the Royal Dockyards but there was no such focal point for the merchant marine, where ships were built in a vast array of private yards and slips throughout the country. That did not mean, however, that merchant shipbuilders were beyond regulation, and in 1694 the Brethren were consulted with regard to the Shipbuilding Act. What the government was particularly concerned about here was the size of English merchant ships. Given the constant threat from privateers in the mid-1690s, it was determined to force merchant shipbuilders to make their ships defensible. Thus the question was posed to Trinity House: what made a defensible merchant ship? Benbow would have been in his element. From his experience hunting privateers and corsairs in the Channel and the Mediterranean, together with his own experience of merchant vessels and of being attacked, his opinion would have been central to the Brethren's debate. They finally reported that all merchant ships should be of three decks, built with a forecastle, quarterdeck and roundhouse; that there should be at least six feet between each deck; that their hawsers should be between decks; that they should have no fewer than ten gunports on each side and carry in total no fewer than thirty-two guns of which eighteen were to be between decks; and that they should carry no fewer than seventy men. The Brethren concluded by emphasizing the need for height and size. 'Ships of two decks and half,' wrote the Brethren to Parliament, 'are not defensible ships.'[34]

All of the interests of Trinity House so far discussed had a direct bearing on the active, or operational, side of the English maritime world, but what makes Trinity House stand out so clearly now, as it did in the past, is the equal weight of interest that the Brethren invested in the sea of dependants that British maritime policy left in its wake. It is too often forgotten that generations of naval warfare not only brought security and wealth to England but also created an entire social underclass unable to sustain itself. This was the world of sailors too old to work but destitute after a lifetime of service; a world of sailors blinded or limbless from fighting or crippled by disease; a world of widows and orphans; a world of desperation. Trinity House took up the cause of these lost souls.

Charity has been central to Trinity House since its inception. From 1590 sailors had to pay a portion of their wages into something known as the Chatham Chest, a fund designed to help sick and wounded seamen. Although many of the payments never materialized as the Chest was an obvious target for corrupt administrators, it was, in theory at least, there to pay £6 13s 4d a year for life to a man who had lost a leg or an arm, £13 6s 8d for both legs and £15 for both arms, if the unfortunate sailor was unable to earn a livelihood. He also received £5 for a permanently disabled arm and £4 for loss of an eye.[35] It essentially worked like permanent health insurance.

Impressive as this was, a sailor's dependants – wife, children and parents – all suffered as he became too old to work, was injured or died. Trinity House stepped into this breach, the money provided from a fund similar to the Chatham Chest, into which sailors paid a fraction of their wages. This is the earliest known example of what we would call an occupational pension scheme. So far so good, but Trinity House's active engagement in that service, together with its ability to help, took a boost in the 1690s. In 1695 the income was significantly increased when an act was passed which ensured that both Trinity House and the Chatham Chest received a portion of prize money. Between them they received a full eighth of the prize, which was to be spent from the Chest on sick and wounded seamen and by the Brethren of Trinity House for the relief of widows, children and parents of those who had died in naval service.[36]

If the purse allowed, the Brethren did not limit themselves to naval men alone but distributed funds more widely to the poor. They also built almshouses, usually after the receipt of a generous legacy such as that of 1680, when Captain Richard Maples left the corporation £1,300, enough to build a block of almshouses at Deptford for twenty-four widows.[37] Soon after Benbow joined the Elder Brethren a small surplus of money allowed the backrooms of some of those almshouses to be converted into two more self-contained units, and through subsequent grants this block eventually extended to thirty-eight blocks, containing fifty-six separate apartments and large gardens.[38] Benbow would also have been involved in the securing of land at Mile End that had been bequeathed by a Captain Mudd in October 1692, and the development on it of almshouses. Within three years they had been built and they survived until 1941, when they were bombed.[39] 'To my own mind,' wrote one traveller contemplating the Trinity House almshouses in the nineteenth century, 'these monuments of benevolence, which stand so thickly all around London, are fairer than the most magnificent King's palace'.[40]

The Brethren were also used as a type of independent assessor to examine those who sought relief from other charitable funds; sought licences to beg; were raising money to ransom captives in the three Barbary regencies or elsewhere, or were repaying those who had already put up the ransom; or those who had lost everything in other maritime-related disasters, not least of which was shipwreck.[41] In the 1690s the Brethren enjoyed links with Christ's Hospital, an equally ancient charitable institution, founded in 1552 as a school for destitute children. Originally in Newgate, in the City of London, but now in Horsham, West Sussex, the school sent pupils with an interest in learning navigation to Trinity House for examination.[42] This role of the Brethren as independent assessor and examiner stretched to legal matters where they settled disputes between seamen out of court.[43]

With such an active interest in the well-being of sailors and their dependants, it was natural for the Brethren to be consulted in the summer of 1692 about the possibility of converting the unfinished royal palace at Greenwich or the derelict Carisbrooke Castle on the Isle of Wight into a hospital for sick or wounded seamen. They were so enthusiastic that they immediately approved both locations and even recommended another at Plymouth. They were also anxious to include sailors from the merchant navy as potential beneficiaries of the hospitals, and suggested that they pay 4d per month out of their wages towards the hospital, as opposed to the 6d proposed for navy men, a reflection of the greater risk that was run in operating a warship. Experienced seamen every one, the Brethren were particularly supportive of the idea that disabled seamen could live out their years surrounded by fellow sailors and friends forged in the service.[44] It was thus through his work at Trinity House that Benbow became involved in one of the most significant philanthropic projects of the age: the construction of a magnificent hospital for seamen in Greenwich, London.

14.

Benbow's Hospital

The Royal Hospital at Chelsea, a home for veteran soldiers who had been 'broken by age and war', had been established for more than a decade before William and Mary turned their minds to the fate of elderly and disabled sailors. The initiator of the scheme, it is often said, was the Queen herself, who was so horrified at the fate of the wounded and crippled seamen after Barfleur that she pressured her husband into building a hospital for them. We now know, however, that by then a variety of hospital schemes had already been proposed, and that Mary's enthusiasm was part of a decades-long history of sporadic interest in such a project. John Evelyn had presented detailed plans for a hospital at Chatham in 1666 but nothing had come of it and in 1689 after the victory at Bantry Bay Herbert had similarly proposed a home for crippled sailors that was also overlooked. Even Mary's support in 1692 had little impact and it was not until her death in 1694 that the idea of a seaman's hospital in Greenwich received the requisite royal interest and support in both emotional and financial terms to get it off the ground. William committed himself to the scheme as much as a memorial to his beloved wife as a necessary gift for the nation's seamen.

They certainly needed it. Life at sea in the seventeenth century was fraught with danger and beset by the common problems of overcrowding in cramped conditions surrounded by water. The gundecks were always stuffy and damp and either too hot or too cold. But one's thoughts are automatically drawn towards the carnage of battle, where falling masts crushed bones, canon shot dismembered and disembowelled, iron-hard rigging severed limbs and foot-long splinters cut flesh and blinded. The injuries suffered by John Heylen and Samuel

Giles in the mid-1660s sum up that horror: Heylen had his 'back broke and belly burst', while Giles was hit in the mouth and leg by splinters that ripped out most of his teeth and 'tore and dislocated' the toes of his left foot.[1] To this must be added the everyday accidents of working on slippery decks or aloft in swaying rigging, with raw fingers struggling to grip frozen canvas. Sailors were also very good at falling down hatchways and giving themselves hernias. Simply being near large quantities of explosives was also a problem: on 30 April 1692 the surgeon's mate of the *Deptford* was relieving himself in the heads when a bow chaser, which had been loaded to celebrate the Queen's birthday, accidentally went off and instantly killed him.[2]

Cleanliness, particularly of clothing, remained a concern and in 1679 seaman Francis Forrest was said to have been 'eaten to death with lice'.[3] Those who frequented brothels were susceptible to various venereal diseases that could cause in their mildest forms discomfort, and in their most extreme forms heart disease, paralysis, insanity, blindness, deafness, bone and joint pains and even death. Those who abstained from the pleasures of the body were nevertheless susceptible to the illnesses that all mariners could be exposed to – notably scurvy, typhus and yellow fever, this last recently emerged in the 1690s – all of which struck in hot climates. Hitherto, military planners had no concept of how to deal with such invisible threats. When Captain Robert Wilmot took twenty ships to Jamaica in 1695 more than three-fifths of his men died of yellow fever, including Wilmot himself.[4] Throughout the war of 1689–97 against the French, every expedition sent to the West Indies was forced home because of disease and one contemporary estimated that, for every man who died in battle, four died from other causes.[5] Even so, scurvy and yellow fever remained significant problems for over a century and the best way to achieve a perspective on medicine and health at sea in the 1690s is to consider that this was still fifty years *before* George Anson's circumnavigation of 1740–4, in which fourteen hundred of his squadron of nineteen hundred died of disease and starvation.

All English ships from Sixth Rates upwards had a surgeon, so the vast majority of active English sailors had immediate access to a man with some medical knowledge. The surgeons, although required to produce a certificate of competency after examination at Surgeons' Hall, were of mixed ability, however, and none had anything more than rudimentary training. While some undoubtedly performed impressive procedures with minimal equipment in poor conditions, others were hopeless. A contemporary seaman, Edward Barlow, complained that his diagnosis and treatment consisted of no more than enquiries about 'when he was at stool, and how he feels himself, and how he has slept', followed by a quick administration of some medicine at the point of a knife 'which doeth him as much good as a blow upon the pate with a stick'. A quote from a contemporary medical pamphleteer addressing a ship's surgeon sums up the problem: 'When I speak of *Abdomen* 'tis possible the young Surgeon ... may not know what I mean.'[6]

Above all, the distinguishing factor of this period is that most medical science was focused on cure, not prevention, and even those cures were rudimentary. A ship beset by fever would swiftly find itself, and its entire crew, scrubbed with vinegar.[7] The navy thus provided an exceptional commercial opportunity which some surgeons were all too ready to exploit. One named Cockburn invented a 'cure' for dysentery that he sold at fifty shillings per pound with every ship in the navy, taking four pounds. Doubts about its effectiveness soon followed but Cockburn was not to be beaten and next he invented a cure for the flux. Somehow he convinced Cloudesley Shovell of its merits, and Shovell personally insisted that all hospital ships in the fleet should carry his remedy in their stores.[8] 1691 marked a major breakthrough as, for the first time, physicians, rather than surgeons, were appointed to the fleet. At first there were only two, but by 1702 one was appointed to every squadron, home and abroad.

These problems were common to all navies, however, and the Royal Navy, at least, was several steps ahead of the others in providing care for its sick and wounded, and in the 1690s, just when Benbow's career was taking off, there appears to have been a new focus on the problem. Other navies had surgeons of course, but the Royal Navy had an infrastructure that allowed men to be treated away from their ships. Hospital ships, a common site in English waters from the reign of James I (1603–25), were embedded with most large fleets.[9] Converted merchantmen, their roomy holds were equipped with more medical supplies and more food than was standard and they were staffed with a naval surgeon supported by four surgeon's mates and three more assistants. Women were frequently employed as nurses aboard the hospital ships, although the apparently impeccable male staff of one ship resented their presence, the women being 'continually drunk as often as opportunity would permit – and then very mutinous'.[10] If the injured sailor was near English shores and could be taken ashore there was also an infrastructure in place for shore-based convalescence. Two of the largest London hospitals, St Bart's and St Thomas's, had been required to take a quota of naval men from 1646 and were paid two shillings a week for each man. In wartime they even had beds reserved for seamen, which were used in times of heavy demand such as in the aftermath of Barfleur.[11]

A network of coastal lodging houses run by landladies paid by the Admiralty also provided temporary shelter for the injured or sick, albeit for only a month. Impressive as this sounds, and it certainly was impressive when compared with the French system where such care was non-existent, those who ran the London hospitals resented the Admiralty's imposition of the naval men. The system of lodging houses was very difficult to regulate because the landladies were in it as much for profit as they were, if at all, for their charitable inclinations. Most boarding houses were squalid even by seventeenth-century standards and men turned out from their lodgings or the London hospitals gathered in groups, in London around Tower Hill, 'till there wer Maggotts in their wounds'.[12] Others who were well enough simply used their freedom ashore to run.

This was the situation that faced Dr Lower, the man appointed by the Navy Board in 1690 to survey issues of sailors' health, and shortly after he made his critical report he was ordered to consider a naval hospital for seamen. He originally suggested six possible locations: Carisbrooke Castle on the Isle of Wight, Dover Castle, Liverpool, Plymouth, Chatham and Greenwich. The options were whittled down to Carisbrooke and Greenwich before the Brethren of Trinity House were asked their opinion of the two locations, and the Queen had already identified the Brethren as a suitable body to act as trustees, being 'capable to take a grant of the inheritance'. After numerous delays and financial and legal setbacks, by the autumn of 1694 the project was under way with a royal grant of £2,000 per year to provide a home for injured sailors, shelter for their widows and education for their children. The work was focused on Greenwich, which ultimately would soak up all of the energy for the naval hospital movement, as the intended hospital at Carisbrooke was never even begun nor was another that was intended for the site of the old Savoy Palace in London.[13]

Nevertheless, there was to be no shirking at Greenwich and even now the records exude a profound sense of men gathering together for the benefit of all. Once the King's financial commitment had been confirmed in principle, although it failed to appear for several months, an appeal for voluntary contributions was sent out, and John Evelyn was appointed Treasurer of the fund. Evelyn himself, keen to help where he could, never took a penny of the salary he was due as treasurer.[14] By 1695 £8,000 had been raised. A grand committee of notable men was established who would give their time and expertise to oversee the details of the project for free. Benbow, for two years now one of the Elder Brethren of Trinity House, was asked to be a member of the Grand Committee alongside such notable men as Sir Isaac Newton and Christopher Wren, the greatest architect of his age, who even offered his services for free. The achievement of grandeur was a central part of the architectural brief at Greenwich; in Mary's words it was to be a 'fixt intention for magnificence', and together these men united their energy to produce what has since been described as the 'apotheosis of secular glory'.[15]

As the project's architect, Wren sat with Benbow on the Grand Committee, but they would have had more in common than their involvement with the hospital. Most obviously, both came from families who had enjoyed strong Royalist ties in the Civil War, and both had successfully negotiated the constitutional, political and religious upheaval of the change from Charles II to his brother James II and then the Revolution of 1688, with their reputations enhanced. Few men with even moderate public profiles were so fortunate. Wren, moreover, is now famed for his architectural work, particularly as the designer of St Paul's Cathedral in London, but his fame in the 1690s rested as much on his interest in mathematics, astronomy and navigation as it did on his architectural ability. In fact much of what we now take for granted as Wren's work, such as the fifty churches he rebuilt in the centre of London after the Great Fire of 1666, including St Paul's, and Greenwich itself, were in his lifetime building sites hidden by scaffolding and camouflaged by swarms of workmen, mud, timber and stone, their future magnificence a figment of Wren's powerful imagination.

Twenty years older than Benbow, Wren had demonstrated his precocious talent at an early age and by his late teens had designed an air pump he called a 'pneumatic engine', the design for which was later perfected by Robert Boyle; a pasteboard star calendar; a *sciotericon* to plot equal hours from a sundial; a device for writing in the dark; a recording weather clock; and a pasteboard calculator for the orbit of the moon. John Evelyn described him as a 'miracle of a youth'.[16] His research came to centre on mathematics and astronomy and his formulation of the inverse-square law for the force governing the motion of the planets led Sir Isaac Newton to proclaim him 'one of the foremost geometers of this age'. By 1655, when Benbow was only six, Wren had helped build an eighty-foot telescope specifically designed for studying the face of the moon.

While the physical evidence for Wren's career as an architect is too numerous to mention, there is little similar evidence for this early period of his life, though the sundial on the Codrington Library at All Souls College, Oxford, designed and positioned by him, is a magnificent example. Wren's association with Oxford University is also significant as he taught navigation there for several years. His other nautical interests included inventions to aid fishing, underwater construction and submarine navigation.

The leap from inventor and mathematician to architect is actually not as curious as it sounds at first, as architecture was seen as both a branch of applied mathematics and a gentlemanly activity, and in 1669 Wren was appointed Surveyor of the King's Works. By the time he came to work on the designs for Greenwich, he had been at the very top of his profession for a quarter of a century, if not quite at the peak of his ability for all that time. Nevertheless, scholars tend to agree that by 1694 Wren's few idiosyncrasies as an architect had been ironed out and he was approaching a level of skill that combined exceptional artistic vision with engineering proficiency. It is fortunate that the Greenwich project came to Wren so late in his career as it would test all of his natural ability and experience.

The site was the ancient Tudor royal palace of Placentia, which had been knocked down by Charles II. The intended replacement, designed by John Webb, had never properly got going, and by the 1690s work had only just been completed on one half of the design and it was now used as a powder store. The other significant extant feature to the Greenwich landscape was Inigo Jones's Queen's House, England's first truly classical building, an important personal possession of English Queens in the seventeenth century and the home of the widowed Henrietta Maria when she returned to England with her son, Charles II, in 1660 (see fig. 23). Unlike Placentia, which had been built on the riverbank, the Queen's House was sited some distance away, towards Greenwich Park. It had been built directly over the main road that bisected the royal site at Placentia and the Royal Park. It was a glorified bridge that allowed royal parties to cross from palace to park without enduring the squalor of the public road. Nevertheless, it was given an impressive frontage looking down towards the river, and when the King granted the palace site as the location of the hospital he insisted that the view from the Queen's House remained unobstructed, and a strip of ground the width of the house, 115 feet, running right down to the river, remained Crown property, as it does today.

The challenge Wren faced was somehow to unite half an unfinished palace designed by someone else with a small private residence built to an outdated design and scale. It is not surprising that one of his earliest solutions was to build the hospital somewhere else, but given the financial restrictions of the project and its charitable status this was never feasible.[17] The very advantage of the site was that one vast accommodation block already existed in the guise of Charles II's unfinished palace, and so Wren was forced to be ingenious. We know from earlier plans that what he really wanted to do was use the King Charles block as one half of a design, to be mirrored by a matching block and then united by a cross-wing with a vast central dome, but this would have blocked the view from the Queen's House, a point which Wren soon discovered to be non-negotiable (see fig. 24). His solution, so simple, so effective and so distinctive, was to see the hospital as part of the broader landscape and extant heritage of the site, and to incorporate the Queen's House into the design rather than trying to avoid it or somehow mask it. He thus left his design for the hospital open at the centre, rather than closed by a cross-wing, the opening to be framed by two small domes, rather than closed off by a single large one. The result is an extraordinary exercise in perspective, similar to that which was achieved by Louis XIV at Versailles. In the view from the river, the eye is drawn ever closer from the magnificent central courtyard, past the domes, and on to the Queen's House, as if it was always supposed to be there. But at no stage is there any attempt to match what was there before; Wren's design was uncompromisingly modern yet allowed what had gone before to retain its own identity – a very modern design philosophy (see fig. 25).

Not everyone agreed with Wren's achievement and the author Samuel Johnson was perhaps the most famous critic, considering it 'too magnificent for a place of charity'. Another made the crushing point: 'The money which is thus thrown away as it were on building and outward ornament had better have been spared towards making a more ample supply of Provisions and necessaries, and that more beef and worse beds would give greater contentment to these wretches.'[18]

But these are isolated voices in the historical record. Wren himself knew that the construction of a hospital for seamen in that location, on the banks of the busiest river in the world, was as much a political statement as a functioning hospital. 'Architecture has its political Use,' wrote Wren, '…publick Buildings being the Ornament of a Country; it establishes a Nation, draws People and Commerce, makes the People love their native Country, which Passion is the Original of all great Actions in a Commonwealth.'[19]

From this perspective Greenwich was a monument to those who had died as much as a hospital for those who had not, and what better gift from a king than to elevate the needy to the status of kings with their very own palace? For a Dutch king now ruling a country that had, in living memory, roused itself in civil war and executed its ruler, such benevolence was required as much as it was celebrated. From the restoration onwards, no King of England could take from his people without tacit acknowledgement of their sacrifice. There is also an element of kingly rivalry here. Louis XIV had closely followed Charles II's Chelsea Hospital with one of his own in 1670, the vast Les Invalides in the heart of Paris, which today ranks as one of the most magnificent buildings in that city. Much like William, Louis is said to have taken a close personal interest in its construction, visiting regularly, often in disguise, and always with '*un nouveau plaisir*' ('a fresh pleasure').[20]

As Wren and William were occupied with these high-minded concerns, Benbow's role as a member of the Grand Committee, and also of the revenue sub-committee, was at the day-to-day level of administration.[21] Thus he had to make decisions about contracts and expenses, about which we know a great deal because a complete contract book for the Greenwich project survives. We know that their primary concerns were to dig the foundations and remove the rubble. Daniel Foe, a London brickmaker, was then contracted to supply half a million bricks and deliver them to Greenwich wharf. Men were employed to lay the bricks and cut mouldings, ornaments and arches, while specialist masons were brought in for quoins, cornices, door mouldings and window jambs. And so the project crept forward. The requirements for each wing were all slightly different but the variety of work required remained constant, from leadworkers making the guttering to carpenters laying the floors of yellow deal, ironmongers making hinges and glaziers making windows. Only after Benbow's death did they become concerned with the quantity and quality of the candles required to light the hospital, and who would make the 460 hats and 1,250 pairs of stockings needed for the residents.[22]

As a member of the revenue sub-committee Benbow was particularly concerned with the project's finances. Although their minutes do not survive we do know a little about the financing of the construction. The King's annual endowment of £2,000 and the limited pockets of

Evelyn's charitable fund helped to get the project off the ground, but the finance committee was forced numerous times to pressure the Treasury to squeeze out the King's money. To this income was added a tax of 6d per month on sailor's wages that in the initial stages of the project some sailors were required to pay in addition to the tax for the Chatham Chest.[23] Thereafter it was all brought into a single levy that would pay for disabled seamen, for the widows of such of them as might be 'slain, killed, or drowned in the Sea-Service', and for such of their children as were 'not of Ability to maintain or provide comfortably for themselves'.[24] The income from prize money already assigned to the Chest was now used to build and run the hospital, together with income generated from fines at courts martial. Thus in June 1697 the unfortunate Captain Riddall, whose pink the *Hind* was taken off Folkestone by French privateers, was found solely responsible for the loss and was ordered to forfeit three months' wages to Greenwich Hospital. Two years later Lieutenant Thomas Man of the *Bideford* was found guilty of beating his bosun and fined £50 for the use of the hospital. That winter the bosun of the *Griffin* forfeited a month's pay to the hospital for selling 'unserviceable' stores.[25]

The fines seemed fair but not everyone was happy about the extra tax for the hospital, particularly the men at the dockyard in Kinsale, and those responsible for collecting the tax from merchant seamen in Bristol.[26] From a much wider perspective, objection to this duty became the foundation of a far deeper anger in English colonies over their 'right' to be taxed only by their own assemblies. In the second half of the eighteenth century this eventually erupted after the imposition on the American Colonies of the Stamp Act of 1765, and that anger played a significant role in the outbreak of the American Revolution. This part of the story is well known, but it is too often overlooked that, by 1765, the colonial resentment over excise issues already had a long history, which had begun seventy years before with the tax for Greenwich Hospital.[27]

Meanwhile, the financing of the hospital was causing enough immediate problems of its own. Despite the numerous schemes to pay for the project, by November 1696 it had cost £5,000 but had received only £800, and within three years of work beginning it was already

£9,000 in debt, a figure that had jumped to £19,000 by 1702. Attendance at the revenue sub-committee meetings, at which Benbow should have been present, started to suffer as the task became increasingly difficult.[28] In fact the project was so beyond its means that it was not until 1735 that it reached any sense of financial stability and that was only because the rents from the Earl of Derwenter's estates were granted exclusively to the hospital, and that was still a full twenty years after he had been found guilty of supporting the Jacobite rising of 1715 and been beheaded for treason. The main drain on the resources was not just the acquisition of building materials and labour but the cost of securing the land. The revenue sub-committee soon discovered that the land the King had granted was neither sufficient for the project nor was it empty. They had to ask the King for more land, negotiate with the East India Company and pay to remove some sitting tenants. A certain Mr Stag, who was living quite happily on the ground that was going to be occupied by the new hospital, had to be removed. He was offered £150 (a little over Benbow's annual wage at Deptford) for his small house, but the stout Mr Stag hung on for another tenner before selling up. Six months later, when he was finally paid, he demanded, and received, interest. The word seems to have gone round that digging in was worthwhile and within a year the residents who still had not been cleared off were demanding 'extravagant' prices.[29] If the meetings of the various committees raised difficult issues, the members certainly did not stint in providing for their own comfort. Rooms in Charles II's glamorous building were fitted out with two tables and twenty-four Russian leather chairs, and at one meeting of the fabric committee they ordered four ribs of beef, a leg of mutton, six chickens, two loaves of bread and ten half-casks of wine.[30]

It is important to realize that the buildings now at Greenwich are notably different from those that Benbow would have known. As a member of the Grand Committee he would certainly have seen and approved Wren's plans, and the foundations of all the buildings were laid by 1701, but the actual construction of the King William block was not even begun until 1698, and the base block of Queen Anne Court not until 1700. The first dome was completed in 1704 – that is two years after Benbow's death – and only then were the colonnades started. The Greenwich domes themselves, smaller but so similar to St Paul's, actually pre-date it, and so Benbow would not even have been able to use the great Cathedral as a guide. Now one of the principal attractions of the site, the magnificent Painted Hall was not even begun until 1708. In fact the only part of Wren's design that might have been completed before Benbow's death in 1702 was King William Court, but that date itself is uncertain and there is nothing to suggest that Benbow would have seen it even if it was finished.[31]

It is also too easy to concentrate on the aesthetics of the building, as so many architectural and maritime historians have done, without pausing to consider life for the men inside, which was of course central to the design. Perhaps most importantly, it never became a hospital as we under-stand the term: it was not used for treating wounded sailors, but as a residence for those 'who by reason of age, wounds, or other disabilities, shall be incapable of further service at sea and be unable to maintain themselves'. The first true naval hospital as we might understand it was Haslar at Gosport, Portsmouth, not opened for another half a century, and until that time the immediate shore-based treatment of sailors remained a serious problem.[32]

In comparison to the details of Greenwich's construction only glimpses survive of the curious day-to-day existence of the residents. Hundreds of institutionalized men kept together necessarily needed rule and regulations and a few of those have survived in records at Greenwich and Paris. At Les Invalides blind soldiers were forced to mess together, to prevent sighted men cheating them of their victuals. We know that at Greenwich swearing and blasphemy were punished by the loss of one day's diet, while lying, defilement or defacement caused the offender to be exposed in the hall with a broom and shovel tied to him for the duration of three meals. A pensioner caught frequenting whorehouses would be forced onto a diet of bread and water for a week, which was rather lenient when compared with the French: in Paris a pensioner caught bringing 'naughty women' into the hospital would be tied back to back with his chosen lady and placed for several hours on a wooden horse in full view of all passers-by.[33] All of these problems were new to members of Greenwich's Grand Committee, and Benbow was never part of that process: the first batch of pensioners was admitted in 1705, fully three years after Benbow's death. His experience of Greenwich, not unlike ours today, would have been cleansed of the complexity of its operation as a hospital.

For us even the detail of the architecture is slightly different from what Benbow would have known from Wren's plans. Wren's personal assistant from 1696 had been Nicholas Hawksmoor, a man who in time would establish his own formidable reputation as an architect, and Wren allowed him a great deal of leeway at Greenwich in the early years of design and construction. In fact King William Court and Queen Anne Court are now in their entirety attributed to Hawksmoor and not Wren.[34] From 1698 Hawksmoor was appointed Clerk of the Works at Greenwich and from 1710 Wren stopped attending the meeting of the building committee altogether. Another of his protégés and the future architect of Blenheim, John Vanbrugh, also became heavily involved in the design and construction of Greenwich, along with his great contemporary and the future Surveyor of the Works at Greenwich, James Stuart.[35]

Most obviously, however, the difference between our modern experience of Greenwich and Benbow's perception of it is that it is no longer the site of a hospital for seamen. In 1869 the old sailors were moved out and it became a college for training naval officers. That too ended in 1998, when, as part of the incumbent Conservative Party's programme of privatization, the site was handed over to estate agents instructed to receive commercial tenders for its use. It is now a university campus. As the buildings have survived the test of time, the benevolent motivation behind their construction has steadily slipped away. One visitor in the nineteenth century wrote: 'the great and noble Naval hospital, now inhabited by nearly two thousand honest veterans – they will never, be sure, be turned out of this, their stately home, until England hath lost her pride in her sailors'.[36] Indeed. But it did not have to be this way: on the other side of London, Wren's Chelsea Hospital for army pensioners is still going strong, adapting to modern challenges and opportunities, not least the much-celebrated acceptance of female residents.

When considering Greenwich today there is a particular burden on us to remember both its original intention and those who had the strength to make it happen. It is not just a monument to Wren's genius, to the commitment of the nation's sailors or to William's munificence, but is testament to that generation of men who took it upon themselves to do something about the callous abandonment of England's naval veterans, and to pursue that cause in their own time and through severe financial and logistical restraint until it was realized. Benbow was one of those men; he was part of that process. Invisible as it is today, the buildings at Greenwich bear his fingerprint.

This side to Benbow's character is all the more important now that we know he was capable of burning cathedrals, convents and exploding 300-ton bombs full of shrapnel in civilian harbours. His earliest biographer was certain that he cared deeply for his own sailors and that 'he was constantly their patron, which made him much beloved by them'.[37] Another contemporary was careful to note that his death would be particularly sorely felt in the parish of St Mary's, Shrewsbury, which 'will miss his annual Benevolence'.[38] He contributed ten shillings towards the church's bells in 1694 and in June 1698 the beneficiaries were sufficiently grateful to him to stage a banquet in his honour which was aflow with booze. The accounts read: 'Paid for to treat Admiral Benbow, half a dozen of sack, and half-a-dozen of sherry, 24s; a dozen–and-a-half of claret, 30s – £2 14s 06.'[39] Otherwise we know nothing of this side to his character beyond the fact that he insisted on including a hospital ship in the squadron he took to the West Indies in 1701 and during the same tour he actually built a hospital in Jamaica.[40] It is important to bear in mind that the patchy nature of the sources from this period skews our understanding of Benbow towards the combative side of his personality, when in reality much of his time was spent away from the enemy; to most men most of the time he was more Mr Jekyll than Mr Hyde, and he had a hand in the realization of one of the most significant charitable achievements in English history. As one contemporary wrote shortly after Greenwich was completed in all its splendour: 'There is nothing which reflects greater honour upon human nature than those Institutions which owe their rise to motives of benevolence.'[41]

15.

Benbow's House

It is ironic that more famous naval officers' homes have survived than have their ships: it is far easier today to see where these men spent a fraction of their time than it is to see where their careers evolved. And yet, for so many, these homes were the motivation for personal risk and a memory cherished in the darkest of nights in their cramped, cold ships. To visit those houses that survive today, and to appreciate their comfort and beauty, is to walk through a homesick sailor's dream, centuries old. Some of these houses have lost all connection with the sea, while others revel in their naval heritage. For a rare few the naval link is fleeting and all the more rewarding for those who know where to look. Consider Chippenham Park in Cambridgeshire, once the home of Benbow's great contemporary Admiral Russell. Somewhere on the estate are the remains of a grove of trees planted by Russell in his fleet's formation to commemorate the Battle of Barfleur of 1692. While we now see bare branches, impressive as they are, Russell saw masts, heard guns, smelt victory.

Luckily and thankfully Chippenham still survives, is beautifully kept, and is open to the public. So too are Hatchlands Park in Surrey, Edward Boscawen's home; Shugborough Hall in Staffordshire, George Anson's home; Melford Hall in Suffolk, Hyde Parker's home; and most extraordinary of all, for its 700-year survival, Buckland Abbey in Devon, Francis Drake's home. Elsewhere are houses which were occasionally visited or permanently occupied by naval heroes and which are now still in private hands. There are many in London that are known and there will be hundreds more that are unknown. We know, for example, that Horatio Nelson lived at both 147 and 103 New Bond Street in 1797 and

1798 respectively; that James Cook lived at 88 Mile End in the East End; that Thomas Cochrane lived in the glorious surroundings of the Outer Circle in Regent's Park, in a house that was later occupied by one of his direct naval descendants, David Beatty. From Beatty's era we know that John Jellicoe lived at 25 Draycott Place, near Sloane Square, and that Jackie Fisher lived at Queen Anne's Gate, just off St James's Park. Elsewhere in England there are scattered townhouses, such as Admiral Hawke's home in Green Street, Sunbury-on-Thames, and, as magnificent as any townhouse in all of England, Admiral Richard Howe's home in Bath, at 71 Pulteney Street, near the beautiful Pulteney Bridge. Other houses remain in private hands but have changed function: the Catholic Presbytery in Morpeth, Northumberland, was once the home of Cuthbert Collingwood.

For obvious reasons, the further we go back in time the less likely the houses are to survive, and, from Benbow's era, unless the houses were particularly notable or on Crown property, there is unlikely to be any record of them at all. In the particular and peculiar case of Benbow, however, we are blessed. None of his houses has survived, but because he worked in the Royal Dockyards, plans and other records exist of the dockyard officers' houses and, most wonderful of all, shortly after Benbow was promoted to flag rank in 1696 he moved into Sayes Court in Deptford. One of the most notable houses in England, Sayes Court was also endowed with a garden of extraordinary rarity and beauty. It was a site of regular royal entertainment, and for the previous forty-one years had been the home of the courtier, diarist and friend of Pepys, John Evelyn. So, although the sources are limited, we know a good deal more about Benbow's houses than we might of any other naval officer of his period.

The first secure evidence comes from his time as Master Attendant at Chatham. Chatham Dockyard is one of the most remarkable survivals of the Age of Sail. It played an important role in shipbuilding deep into the twentieth century, specializing in the construction of submarines throughout both world wars, and so it is all the more impressive that her sail loft, mast house, wheelwright's shop and officer's quarters, to name but a few of her historic buildings, have survived. The entirety of that landscape, however, postdates Benbow's period: the earliest surviving building, the Commissioner's house (now known as Medway House), dates from 1703 – twelve years after Benbow worked there and a year after his death. The imposing terrace of officers' houses now visible at Chatham was built a generation later, in 1722. Although it is possible to form some impression of Chatham as a dockyard, to get a detailed impression of its layout and architecture in the 1690s we must look in the shadows of the buildings for the masked footprints of vanished construction, and at the fabulous plans of the dockyard that have survived.

From these we know that the Master Attendant at Chatham had his own house overlooking the great double dock that cut deep into the foreshore. To his immediate left was the Master Builder's house and to the right the much larger residence, almost twice as big, of the Commissioner. Houses for the yard's other main officers stretched in either direction, giving the impression of a large block similar in footprint to that which remains today. The surviving coastal view of the yard confirms this and depicts a large central clock tower in the centre of that block (see fig. 18). Between Benbow's house and the shore was a collection of workshops and other small industrial structures, including saw pits, the boat pitch house, the Porter's woodshed and the Joiner's shop. In the other direction, away from the river but still close to Benbow's house, were the officers' stables. To the rear of the dockyard, gently sloping meadow and pasture lead up to thick woodland, a landscape radically different from that which can be seen today. The Master Attendant's house was brick, large in relation to many of the other officers' houses, and was supplemented by a timber summer house, privy, chicken coop and woodhouse (see fig. 18). It is unknown if Benbow used his house as an office when on site, his family perhaps renting a property in Chatham, or if Benbow, Martha and the five children all squeezed in together.

If Chatham is the most startling dockyard to survive from the Age of Sail, Deptford must be the most disappointing loss. There is now no sense at all that it was one of the most significant yards in the world, but once again the surviving plans indicate how the yard was laid out and give some impression of the officers' houses. Benbow's immediate impression of Deptford would have been that it was much smaller than Chatham, the waterfront being a little over a third of the size. There were also fewer officers' houses at Deptford, seven to Chatham's ten, and generally less in the way of facilities. At Chatham, for example, there was a teamer's house and yard for horses and carriages and the Commissioner even had his own stables. So close to London, Deptford did not even have a Commissioner's house, so the Master Attendant's would have been one of the highest-status dwellings on site. Otherwise there were striking similarities to life at Chatham. Benbow's house once again was very close to the large double dock, where he would have spent much of his working time, and again appears to have been close to a clock tower. At both Chatham and Deptford time, authority and discipline went hand in hand. Time cost the King money, and the officers were there to ensure efficient, economic work as much as they were there to oversee its quality. At Deptford Benbow lived next door to the storekeeper and alongside the Smith's shop, whose furnace would have provided welcome warmth on winter watches. A short walk away was the hexagonal wet dock and beyond that again the mast dock, where timber was soaked to retain its sap. In contrast to Chatham, however, we are certain that Benbow lived on site with his family.[1] The house itself was significantly more impressive than that at Chatham. He now had a lovely garden, back parlour and even a banqueting house in the garden (see fig. 22).

The officers' quarters at the dockyards provided the naval administrators with yet another problem. In 1692 the Surveyor of the Navy realized that he was almost entirely ignorant of the condition of officers' houses both externally and internally. This was a serious problem because the officers tended to 'deface them in an extraordinary manner, and carry away furnace clocks, lead, locks, hinges, chimneypieces, hearths and other things belonging to their Majestys'.[2] To prevent this it became standard practice to survey the officers' accommodation, noting down what was privately owned and what belonged to the Crown. Regular checks were then carried out and accounts drawn up quarterly, the resident paying for any alterations or repairs necessary. The officers themselves were also prepared to flex their muscles if the houses were not up to scratch. When Martha Benbow moved out of the house at Deptford and William Wright, the new Master Attendant, moved in, he complained that two of the rooms were not 'wainscotted', as they were in all of the other officers' houses.[3]

By the mid-1690s Benbow's sustained success in the Channel War had begun to generate considerable wealth in prize money and when he was promoted to flag rank in 1696, his status and wealth took another leap forward. The added responsibilities of his new rank led him to stop work as Master Attendant at Deptford but, clearly fond of the place, he decided to make a home in the town. His attention naturally fell on the only significant construction in Deptford that was not part of the dock-yard: Sayes Court, a magnificent and by now very ancient manor house, and the home of John Evelyn. Benbow took a lease on the house in June 1696 for three years, which would turn out to be three of the most bizarre years in the long and already impressive history of that house. To appreciate fully the impact of those years on Sayes Court, it is first necessary to look in some detail at the house itself.

The land around Deptford Dockyard had been important baronial territory since the death of William the Conqueror in 1087, and a little over a century later it first became associated with the powerful De Say family under the reign of Richard I, the Lionheart. They were so close to the King that Geoffrey de Say was one of the barons who took the ransom to the German Emperor Henry VI to secure the release of Richard in 1193. The link with the Crown remained and there is some suggestion that Margaret of Anjou stayed at Sayes Court shortly after her marriage to Henry VI in 1445.[4]

A little over two centuries later the manor house still existed and John Evelyn, royalist courtier, author and horticulturalist, came back to England from exile in France where he had lived out the Civil War. He moved into Sayes Court, which by then had become the ancestral home of Evelyn's wife, Mary Brown. The house was on three storeys with Elizabethan gables and came with land that rambled over two hundred acres of the Deptford waterfront. It was old, out of fashion, dark, damp and in most places quite ruined by the ravages of civil war. Sayes Court, wrote Evelyn, 'was very much suffering, for want of some friend, to rescue it out of the power of the Usurpers'.[5] Evelyn then dedicated himself to its restoration until, forty-four years later, he leased it to Benbow after a lifetime of work by a man who cared deeply about architecture, garden design and horticulture. He grumbled in his diary about the cost, calling it 'ye ruind house', and at a particularly low point declared that 'better I had don to have puld all doune at first',[6] but it was the emotional and professional investment in its restoration that mattered the most to Evelyn.

It is ironic that nowadays Evelyn is considered famous for his diaries, which he never planned to be published, when, at the time, his fame rested on the twenty books he wrote during his life. As an author he was both prolific and wide-ranging and although he has, since the publication of his diaries, been dismissed as an amateur generalist, his latest biographers have cast his contribution to seventeenth-century culture in a far more favourable light.[7] To garden historians, however, there is no doubt about Evelyn's place in history both in terms of the books on horticulture that he wrote and of what he achieved at Sayes Court. His unpublished work *Elysium Britannicum* is now considered one of the most important books on gardening written in the seventeenth century. While Evelyn quickly replaced all the windows at Sayes Court, installing modern 'canted' or oriel windows of twelve lights, some of double height; transformed the south, east and west elevations; built a magnificent skylight to light the stairs; rebuilt the kitchen; built a new chapel, 'buttry', study, cellars, outhouses, walls for the estate, still houses and an orangerie;[8] the particular cultural value of Sayes Court as a property lay outside, in the garden. When Evelyn let it to Benbow, he did so 'with Conditions to keepe the garden & C'.[9] This was no small commitment.

Evelyn's garden had been carefully constructed around a thoughtful philosophy. 'What is in generall to be sayd,' he wrote of the 'plotting' of a garden:

is, that it would be so contrived and set out, as that Art, though it contend with nature, yet might it by no means justle it out. At no hand therefore let our Workman [enforce] his plot to any particular phantsy, but, contrive rather how to apply to it the best shape that will agree with the nature of the place; and studdy how even the most imperfect figure may by the Mysteries of Arte and Fantsy, receive the most graceful ornaments.[10]

Thinking this way, Evelyn was an important precursor to the better-known landscape gardeners of the eighteenth century. He was also deeply committed to introducing new species into his garden.

Plans for his original 1653 design survive (see fig. 16), and show a garden complete with island planted with raspberries and mulberry trees surrounded by a moat stocked with carp, swans and ducks (no. 103). The focal point of the estate was a lush oval garden (no. 36) that we now know was modelled on a famous contemporary Parisian garden, from where many of the plants were sourced. The island was linked to a banqueting house by the Long Walk – 526 feet long and twenty-one feet wide (no. 43). There was even a carp pond fed by the Thames at every high tide (no. 30) and a bowling green (no. 26). An area Evelyn referred to as the 'grove' was planted with more than five hundred trees of oak, ash, elm, service, beech and chestnut, with thickets of birch, hazel and 'Thorne, wild fruites, greenes, &c.'. The grove was crossed by eight walks leading to a central point planted with bays and a small circular walk was edged with laurel (no. 50). Off the walks were other paths like 'Spiders Clawes leading to the Cabinetts of Aliternies [*Rhamnus alaternus L.*], and a great French walnutt [*Juglans regia L.*] at every one'. To the east of the grove and separated from it by a lilac hedge lay the kitchen garden with thirty-eight beds for pot herbs as well as plots for melons and two larger beds for peas and beans (no. 94). The coachway was lined with elms and a double avenue of limes planted only four and half yards apart (no. 121) and his orchard had no fewer than three hundred trees in it, with sixty-five apple trees of twenty-two varieties, forty-eight pears of twenty-nine varieties, 134 cherries of twenty varieties as well as gooseberries, currants and roses (no. 118). The pride of his garden, however, was his mighty holly hedge, seven feet high, three feet thick, and at its most mature, four hundred feet long (no. 42 in this image, when it was immature). He had his own nursery (no. 65) and particularly delighted in the rarest of plants. We know, for example, that he imported cedar seeds from their only natural habitat on the globe, Mount Libanus in Lebanon, a tree celebrated then for its rarity rather than beauty. No domestic cedar seeds were available in England for another forty years and none reached the continent until 1734 at the earliest.[11] The very first cedar ever planted in France can still be seen at the Jardin des Plantes in Paris.

None of this was achieved without loss. Most plants were raised from seed and others, though two years old, were lost to hot weather or 'unpropitious winds'. Evelyn lost between four hundred and a thousand plants in his oval garden to winds when he first planted it out. Others were stolen. He once lost 'at least forty of my very best and they have all been carried to Gr[eenwich] parke'.[12]

Responding to such losses, changing fashions and the availability of new plants, Evelyn redesigned his garden from time to time, and by the time Benbow moved in, the Parisian oval garden had been replaced by a semi-circular bowling green surrounded by fruit trees, each individually numbered and lettered on Evelyn's plan (see Appendix IV). His prize holly hedge still remained, now extending the full width of the bowling green. Gooseberries, currants and strawberries were planted between every tree. His cherry and pear varieties were chosen to give fruit throughout the summer, and Evelyn noted the characteristics of every tree's fruit: when they had to be picked and if they had to be stored to mature and ripen for fullest flavour. His collection was so large and varied that some of the varieties don't even survive at Brogdale, in Kent, the site of the National Fruit Collection, one of the world's largest collections of fruit and an internationally recognized genetic resource for fruit trees.

Sayes Court was also one of perhaps three places in the entire country with a glass beehive (no. 64). Straw hives were common everywhere and bees were farmed for their honey, but the concept of a glass beehive, which allowed the viewer to watch the bees at work, was completely new and so powerful that it drew the King to Sayes Court to witness it, which he did 'with much satisfaction'. He went on to discuss honey with

Evelyn at a period perhaps twenty years before anyone realized that honey came from the pollen in flowers and fifty years before it was explained fully in print for the first time. Evelyn himself thought that honey came from the air.[13]

Evelyn, it must be remembered, had made all of this out of nothing. When he had arrived his garden had been 'all one pasture field to the very garden of the house'. At Sayes Court, he had realized his philosophy of gardening, which was to create a 'delicious place' called 'Paradise', a garden which 'of all terrestrial enjoyments [was] the most resembling Heaven'. His guests, some of the most influential people in the land, adored its splendour and it later became the site where the poet Abraham Cowley, a great friend of Evelyn, wrote his famous Latin poem on trees.[14]

Beyond Sayes Court's idyll, the dockyard scrambled up to the garden walls on one side, while on the other the 'deep ford' of the Ravensbourne creek that gave Deptford its name poured its heart into the Thames. Only a little distance upstream the river swiftly became 'a pretty brook of pure water and deep holes under trees, and babbling shallows, running between high banks, where the primroses, in March and April, lie in thousands'. Even two centuries after Benbow's time it was still a popular spot for fishing, bird's-nesting in spring, picking wild roses in summer and gathering nuts, sloes and blackberries in winter. The contrast with the river front could not have been more stark. As one author who knew Deptford in its maritime prime wrote, 'The whole town makes its living by the sea. No one speaks or thinks of anything but the sea and the things which are concerned with the sea.'[15] The river was packed with traders from the East and West Indies, Holland and Africa, Arabia and the Baltic, and with English coastal traders. There were East Indiamen, brigs, brigantines, schooners, yachts, sloops, galliots, tenders, colliers, hoys, barges, smacks, herring-busses, or hog-boats, all there as well as First Rate battleships, frigates, sloops-of-war, cutters, fireships, 'and every kind of vessel employed to beat off the enemies of our country'. From these ships came every kind of sailor, 'the phlegmatic Hollander, never without his pipe; the mild Norwegian; the fiery Spaniard, ready with his dagger; the fierce Italian equally ready with his knife; the treacherous Greek; and the Frenchman'. All day long 'and never ending save on Sunday', these men heard 'the sound of hammer and of saw, the whistling of the bosuns and foremen, the rolling of casks, the ringing of bells and all the noise which accompanies the building and the fitting of ships, and smell perpetually the tar and the pitch (which some love better than the smell of roses and of violets)'.[16]

For Benbow, Sayes Court presented the perfect mixture of luxury and elegance, deeply embedded in a maritime lifestyle. Its location next to Deptford Dockyard recalled a juxtaposition with which he was familiar and safe, in effect being the landlocked equivalent of a luxurious flag officer's cabin on a working, noisy warship. Such a meeting of two worlds was never going to sit well with Evelyn, however. Evelyn was deeply interested in behaviour and manners, and had even written a book upon it in 1659, *A Character of England*. He was also against any sort of noisy disruption, describing the new fast coaches of the 1690s as 'hell carts'. He loathed decadence of any kind.[17] Perhaps unsurprisingly, Evelyn soon found the salty Benbow insufficiently refined for Sayes Court and noted in his diary with distaste that he had 'the mortification of seeing every day much of my former labours and expense there impairing for want of a more polite tenant'.[18] If Evelyn thought Benbow was trouble, however, he was in for the shock of his life. In January 1698 a foreign visitor arrived in England with royal blood, a taste for luxurious accommodation, a deep interest in maritime affairs and an unmatched reputation for debauchery. That man was Peter the Great, Tsar of Russia, and he was coming to stay.

There has perhaps never been a more unwelcome guest in all of history. We know Evelyn as a careful, thoughtful, austere, conservative, timid man devoted to his home and family. The young Tsar of Russia, by contrast, was a human storm from an alien culture: an asteroid to Evelyn's flower. Modern biographers of Peter list among his favourite hobbies pulling teeth and performing autopsies. Drunkenness was the rule; at parties or receptions it was enforced if the participant was unwilling, the victim being made to drink vast quantities of brandy until he – or she –

collapsed. Peter himself, renowned for his iron constitution, was often left seriously ill after such parties. In one instance he was in bed for six days. Modern biographers claim that some of his guests died from drink. As he was a dedicated fan of obscene pageantry, these bouts, if on days of national or religious celebration, could be preceded by processions of dwarfs, freaks and jesters. At the wedding of Peter's own jester the happy couple were followed by the highest dignitaries in the land, riding oxen, donkeys, pigs and large dogs, and were dressed either magnificently or in sacking, cat skins or mouse-skin gloves. His own Christmas celebrations one year were preceded by a 'cavalry' of twenty-four dwarfs. Later in life he started collecting such natural curiosities, and encouraged towns to sell their 'freaks' to the state. Among the haul was an eight-legged lamb, a three-legged baby, a two-headed baby, a baby with its eyes under its nose and ears below its neck, Siamese twins joined at the chest and, a little less plausibly, a baby with a fish's tail, a baby with two heads, four arms and three legs and two dogs born to a sixty-year-old virgin. It is important to add that a taste for the bizarre was a feature of the age and that collecting was onsidered a gentlemanly pursuit, but perhaps nothing sums up Peter more than his response to this initial collection – it was not as good as he had hoped.[19]

As if this was not enough, his other favourite hobby was making or igniting fireworks. In Russia he had enjoyed regular mock battles and took particular pleasure in designing firework displays. Shortly before coming to England he personally planned a spectacular show that began with a fifty-six-gun salute before moving on to flames tracing out the name 'Romodanovsky' and then the image of Hercules mastering a lion. All the while Peter let off rocket after rocket, each weighing as much as five pounds. One poor nobleman was struck on the head by one and died instantly. The battles Peter played at were also violent, with imitation bombs made from earthenware pots that could easily maim. He himself was badly burned in one such war game and in another one of his favourite Generals, the Scottish mercenary Patrick Gordon, was forced to bed for a week to recover.[20]

Peter had come to England as part of a grand tour of Europe, a tour imagined by the Tsar himself, who was ashamed at the relative lack of education, science and culture that characterized Russia when compared with France, England and Holland. Necessarily his decision to westernize himself and his country translated into even more bizarre behaviour – in this case the enforced shaving of his entire court so that they looked more like westerners. Anyone who refused would have his ears boxed by a jester.[21] Above all, however, Peter wanted a navy and he wanted Russia to become a naval power. From childhood he had been fascinated by the sea and his visit as a youth to Archangel, the only Atlantic Russian port, convinced him to drive his nation towards westernization, backed by naval strength. Before he could do so, however, he needed to study western shipbuilding and science, and that was the core purpose of his European tour. Perhaps surprisingly to our way of thinking, most were willing to accept Peter's mission and to offer all the help that they could.

Of all the European monarchs who met Peter on this tour, England's King William III was the most committed to help. He allowed Peter access to the Royal Dockyards, the Royal Mint and the gun foundries; he was allowed to talk to whomever he wished, particularly the shipwrights, who 'shew'd him their Draughts, and the Method of laying down by Proportion any Ship or Vessel, of what Body soever required, with the Rules for moulding and building a Ship, according as laid down in such Draught'. He was allowed to take notes and hire whomever he wanted to build his navy. Keen to travel, experience and learn, Peter nevertheless valued his privacy and, for all his excesses, loathed being a spectacle. So Sayes Court was the ideal location for him. He was near the river, where he could sail (and repeatedly crash) the beautiful yachts provided for his amusement by William, and he could easily access the dockyard – but that did not stop him making a hole in the garden wall to make his access even easier. He was also out of the worst of the public eye and the few trips he made out in public, such as going to the theatre or visiting the Ashmolean Museum in Oxford, were usually followed by a hasty retreat if recognized.[22]

William's desire to help Peter centred on his awareness of Russia as a growing military power and of the potential commercial opportunities in Russia, particularly for the importation of British tobacco to serve the newly discovered Russian tobacco market. He was also aware of the Russian control of vast areas of the Baltic that had prime natural resources for shipbuilding alien to the British Isles. It is likely that Benbow was aware of the bigger picture but he was certainly aware of the King's need to find a suitable residence for Peter, who had found his initial residence in Norfolk Street not to his liking. When Peter approached Benbow in person and requested the use of his house, Benbow 'Freely Consented' and sub-let it to the Tsar and his entourage. Peter was clearly delighted and William re-furnished the house and paid for 'all he has'. Benbow, still legally responsible for the upkeep and maintenance of Sayes Court and its garden, had just let the fox into the chicken coop.[23]

What actually happened behind the wall of Sayes Court over the following three months remains a tantalizing mystery with only two clear exceptions, both of them expectedly strange. We know that a female giant came to Deptford to be seen by Peter, and when 'she stretched out her arm and without bending down the Decurion [Peter] walked under her arm'.[24] This was some achievement, bearing in mind that Peter was six feet seven inches tall. We know too that a man named Moses Stringer was summoned to Sayes Court for two reasons. Most obviously, he was a chemist and among Peter's many interests was a love for scientific experiment. It has also been suggested that Stringer was somehow related to Benbow by marriage.[25] Perhaps this got Stringer the break that he needed and soon enough Peter sent for him to 'shew him some of the Choicest Secrets and Experiments known in England'. Stringer duly turned up and proposed twenty-four experiments that demonstrated how certain metals and minerals could be separated and refined, while others explored geometry, medicine and philosophy. Peter was then allowed to chose which ones he wanted to see. The first he chose was 'to Melt Four Metals, with a destroying Mineral together: the Gold, Silver, Copper, and Iron, with Antimony, into one Lump, then to dissolve them all, and then to separate each Metal distinct again, without destroying any one of them'. Stringer duly made 'some Lead out of its Ore, and Silver out of that Lead, and called the Gold from the rest of the Metals mixt'. Then, 'being transported into a merry Vein', he offered to make the Tsar an artificial gem of any colour the Tsar chose to name to set in the gold. And he promised to do all of this with an old broom staff and a piece of flint. Peter was delighted and Stringer set to work. We don't know what colour the flinty and broomy 'gem' was, but we do know that it was hard enough to cut glass.[26] As is clear with anything surrounding Stringer's career, some of it is doubtful and most is extraordinary, but there is little doubt that the fiery experiments were all carried out at Sayes Court, given Peter's interest and the subsequent scale of the damage there. The only other evidence we have of Peter's entourage comes from the pen of one of Evelyn's servants who had stayed behind to serve Benbow and now served the Tsar. It is inadvertently eloquent and sums up much of what went on. He wrote to his old master: 'There is a house full of people, and right nasty.'[27]

Much of Peter's stay in England has been lost to us. There are only fifty-two entries in his semi-official journal for those 105 days, and they tell us next to nothing of his social escapades. The few episodes that have survived have been exaggerated and distorted by generations of story-telling, embellishment and anecdote. In the case of Sayes Court, however, we are blessed with solid facts by one of those quirks of fate that shines a piercing light deep into the gloom of history. We may not know exactly what the Tsar got up to and when, but deep in the records of the Admiralty lies a minutely detailed survey of the house made in the immediate aftermath of Peter's hurricane. When Benbow moved back in, he was faced with such an unexpected and shocking scale of destruction that he immediately wrote to the Admiralty and begged for compensation. 'Your Petitioner,' he wrote:

> ...did some time since take the House of John Evelyn Esquire, call'd Sayes Court at Deptford, and is bound by Agreement to keep the same (together with the Gardens), &c., in Good and sufficient Order and Repair. And to leave them in the same at the Expiration of his Terme: And so it is (may it pleas your Honours), that his Czarish Majestie coming to your Petitioner about Three

Months agoe, did request the use of his House, during the time of his stay in England, as also the Furniture in it, as it stood. Hee freely consented thereto, and immediately removed his family out of it and gave him possession. Soposing it might be a pleasure to his good Master the King, and that he would have used his house, Goods, and Gardens otherwise than he finds he hath: which are in so bad a condition that he can scarcely describe it to your Honours; besides much of the furniture broke, lost and destroy'd.

Benbow went on to ask the Admiralty to survey the damages and recompense him for the loss. The Admiralty reacted quickly and it reacted well. Not only did it agree to send a man to survey the damages, it sent none other than Sir Christopher Wren himself, accompanied by the King's gardener and a member of the King's Wardrobe. Their discoveries are worth quoting in full:[28]

• •

May 9th 1698
Account of damages done to the building and Fences by the Tsar of Muscovy and his Retinue at Sayes Court in Deptford

	£	s.	d.
For 150 yards of Painting at	7	10	0
For 244 yards of Whiting in the House	2	0	8
For 300 squares in the Windows	0	15	0
For 20 Quarries	0	1	8
For 3 Brass Locks	2	8	0
For 9 more that's dammag'd	2	5	0
For Keys wanting to all the said Locks	1	0	0
For 90 foot of Dutch Tyles to repaire in Chimneys	1	10	0
For 100 foot of Flemish Tyle paving to repaire	1	5	0
For 90 foot of Purbeck paving to repaire in ye Kitchen	1	10	0
For mending the Stoves there	0	10	0
For plaining the Dressers	0	10	0
For repairing an oven dammaged	0	10	0

	£	s.	d.
All the floores dammag'd by Grease and Inck	2	0	0
For 2 new Deale Dores	1	4	0
For a new Flore to a Bagg House	0	10	0
For repairing 300 foot of flint and Pebble paving	1	0	0
For 240 foot running of Posts and Pales of Firr	60	0	0
For 170 foot running of Post and Railes of Oake	17	0	0
For new pollishing 4 marble foot paces and a marble table	1	4	0
For 3 wheelbarrows broke and Lost	1	0	0
Measured by William Dickenson Clarke.	107	7	0

An Inventory of Admirall Benbow's Goods that is Lost, Broake, and damage done to them while the Czar of Muscovy Lodged theire, is valued as followeth:

	£	s.	d.
The Bedchamber hung with blew paragon and a blew paragon bed			
lined with a Buff colloured silke all much stained and spoyled	4	10	00
A Japan Cornish Broake	00	10	00
An Indian silke quilted counterpaine Blankets and Bedding			
much stained and dirted	02	10	00
A dressing table lined with silke broake and spoyled	01	00	00
A Wallnuttree table and stands broake	00	15	00
A brass harth, a pair of tongs, fend iron, fier showell broake			
and some parte lost	01	00	00
A field Bedstead broake to pieces, with a crimson paragon furniture			
lined with a striped Persian silke, much tore and spoyled	02	00	00
(In the Clossett)			
Foure pieces of thread damaske hangings much soyled	00	10	00
(The Greate Roome)			
One pair of Large bras hand irons broake	00	05	00
(The next Roome)			
Hung with tapestry to be cleaned	01	00	00
(Next Roome)			
A stained calico Bed lined with white calico, the curtains tore in			
pieces, and a large indian quilt tore in severall places	03	10	00

Fourteen hollands matted bottome chares all broke and spoyled	02	10	00
Twelve back chairs covered with druggett much dirtyed	01	00	00
(Next Roome)			
A sad colloured Camblett Bed much tore and spoyled	02	00	00
An ordnary stained calico quilt tore and burned in several places	00	10	00
A black wainscot table and stands broke and spoyled	00	10	00
A pair brass hand irons, fier showell and tongues broke	00	07	06
(The Next Roome)			
Two beds, one of Druggett, the other Green Searge, much tore and soyled	02	10	00
An old chest of Drawers, fier showell tongues, and hand irons broake and spoyled	00	10	00
(Next Roome)			
A blew striped calamanco Bed lined with a striped India stuff, embroidered, verey much dirtied and spoyled and the cornishes broake	03	00	00
Twelve back chares covered with blew paragon, much dirted	11	00	06
Three old hollands matted chares broake	00	07	00
A Wallnuttree chest of Drawers and a Wainscott table much spoyled and broke	00	15	00
Six white thread damaske window curtaines tore and spoyled	01	10	00
A warmeing pann broake and burned to pieces	00	05	00
(Below staires)			
A Japan table, two chares and a couch all broke and spoyled	01	10	00
Seaven caine chaires broke and lost	01	00	00
Elleaven green plush cushions stained and one lost	01	00	00
One large pair of brass hand irons, one pair of tongs, fier showell, one grate broake and spoyled	00	15	00
Two inlayed tables damnyfied	00	10	00
One large Turkey Carpett dirtied	00	05	00
Five Leather Chares lost	01	00	00
Three ordnary wickered bottom chares and four green Searge chares broke and lost	00	17	06
Two fether Beds and two Bolsters Lost	08	00	00
Three paires of new doune pillows lost	03	00	00

Eight Fether beds, eight bolsters, twelve pair of blankets very much dirtied and spoyled	03	15	00
One iron stove grate broke to pieces	00	15	00
Three paire of three breadths fine new Holland sheets	07	10	00
Three armed and five back wooden cained chares broake to pieces	01	00	00
Twenty fine pictures very much tore, and the Frames all broake	10	00	00
Severall Fine Draughts and other Designs Relating to the Sea Lost, valued By the Admirall att	50	00	00
In all	127	2	6
St. Genua Table broake and spoyled, valued att	006	00	00
Jos. SEWELL, May 9th 1698.	133	02	06

Some observations made upon the gardens and plantations which belong to the honourable John Evelin, Esq., att his House of Sayes Court in Deptford, in the county of Kent.

During the time the Zar of Muscovie inhabited the said house, several disorders have been committed in the gardens and plantations, which are observed to be under two heads; one is what can be repaired again, and the other what cannot be repaired.

1. All the grass worke is out of order, and broke into holes by their leaping and shewing tricks upon it.
2. The bowling green is in the same condition.
3. All that ground which used to be cultivated for eatable plants is all overgroune with weeds, and is not manured nor cultivated, by reason the Zar would not suffer any men to worke when the season offered.
4. The wall fruite and stander fruite trees are unpruned and unnailed.
5. The hedges nor wilderness are not cutt as they ought to be.
6. The gravel walks are all broke into holes and our of order.

Great damages are done to the trees and plants, which cannot be repaired, as the breaking the branches of the wall fruite trees, spoiling two or three of the finest phillersas, breaking severall holleys and other fine plants.

Wren then made a personal report to the Admiralty and summarized the damage to the house as £107 7s, and to the garden £55. The damage to Benbow's goods, including what he was owed in rent came to £158 2s 6d, and so the total cost of Peter's stay came to an astonishing £350 9s 6d, nearly two and a half times Benbow's annual salary as Master Attendant at Deptford.[29]

As well as informing us of the scale of the damage, this list is valuable because it allows us a brief glimpse inside a seventeenth-century Admiral's house. History is usually blind to the interior of most houses from this period, and yet we know that Benbow's bedroom was lavishly furnished with 'blew paragon' (a costly eastern fabric, similar to velvet) and buff-coloured silk. His taste for the exotic is clear from his Indian-silk quilted counterpane, crimson 'paragon' and striped Persian silk. He would have enjoyed the beautiful glow and dappled colour of the walnut table in his bedroom and an open fire provided warmth, the fire equipped with high-quality brass equipment. He also had a 'field bed-stead', presumably some kind of folding bed that he could take with him to sea and on campaign. Elsewhere in the house there were tapestries, another Indian quilt and at least thirty-eight chairs for entertaining with at least eleven green plush cushions. He had fine Holland sheets for the beds and a large Turkish carpet. On the walls hung twenty framed paintings and he had a separate collection of maritime drawings.

The impression this gives is of a man who had collected on his travels, who revelled in luxuriously coloured, patterned, cosy furnishings and who enjoyed collecting art. This knowledge is unique among all naval officers of the seventeenth century and most of the eighteenth.

Understandably, Evelyn was as distraught as Benbow and travelled to Deptford on 9 June 'to view how miserably the Tzar of Moscovy had left my house'.[30] When he discovered the scale of the damage he erupted in a characteristic way, by praising his holly hedge, one of the few plants to have survived Peter's ravages. 'Is there under the heaven,' wrote Evelyn:

a more glorious and refreshing object of the kind than an impregnable hedge of about 400 feet in length, nine feet high and five in diameter, which I can still show in my ruined gardens at Sayes Court (thanks to the Tzar of Muscovy) at any time of the year, glittering with its armed and variegated leaves, the taller standards at ordinary distance, blushing with their natural coral? It mocks the rudest assaults of the weather, beasts or hedge-breakers.

He ended his rant with 'Et illum nemo [me] impune lacessit' ('no one provokes me with impunity'), a slightly elongated version of the motto of the Order of the Thistle, a chivalric order that had been revived by the King as recently as 1687, and in the presence of Evelyn.[31]

Nothing further was ever heard of the incident, which could so easily have been used as an excuse to sever diplomatic relations. On the contrary, William was happy to forgive Peter his behaviour in return for the new relations forged with Russia, which had led, among many other things, to an English monopoly on tobacco importation to Russia. The effect of Peter's behaviour is particularly ironic. He was there because he wished to transform the reputation of his country from being backward to a nation that could rival any in arts, science and warfare, but his behaviour confirmed the contemporary perception of an ill-bred Muscovite. But, for all of the damage caused, some lessons were learned and Peter went on to build some of the most beautiful cities in the world, equipped with some of the finest gardens. Later in life he took particular delight in the impressive gardens at Peterhof and the Summer Palace in St Petersburg.[32] Peter's peculiar stay in England has been celebrated by historians ever since as one of the most interesting and important episodes in the whole history of Anglo-Russian relations.

Neither Benbow nor Evelyn ever returned to Sayes Court to live, though Evelyn occasionally visited when he was nearby. In the 1850s it became an emigration depot and, a generation later, lay desolate and miserable, partly enclosed in the King's Yard and partly given over to weeds and puddles. By 1945 a single mulberry tree survived from Evelyn's garden, but that, it seems, has now gone.[33] The only evidence that anything occurred to link Evelyn, Benbow and Peter the Great survives in the street names of Deptford; there is an Evelyn Street, a

Czar Street, a Sayes Court Street and a Benbow Street, all within a few hundred yards of each other. But nothing suggests that overlooked, run-down Deptford once had an unrivalled maritime past.

16.

Benbow's Caribbean

Benbow's tenancy of Sayes Court was the most overt demonstration that his personal and professional circumstances had dramatically changed since his promotion to flag rank, but his change in status carried with it more than financial reward. The balancing factor was increased responsibility that challenged Benbow in new ways. One of these was the need to achieve the subtle mixture of authority and justice expected from a flag officer sitting on courts martial, and we can form a good impression of the issues that concerned him as a naval judge because most of the court-martial records survive.

One of the first trials Benbow sat on was that of the officers of the *Seaford* and *Bonaventure* for their apparently poor conduct in action with the French in May 1697. Every man was acquitted after the weak state of both ships was explained. He also had to adjudge responsibility for the loss of an escorted merchantmen whose captain had chosen not to sail under his allotted naval convoy, and the guilt of a captain who had deliberately run ashore his ship, the *Newport*. Customarily the court accepted extenuating circumstances, usually relating to damage received by the ship in question. Occasionally, however, the judges were exacting. HMS *Portsmouth* was lost to the French in October 1696 when she was missing both topmasts, was ill-manned and was surrounded by four Frenchmen. Her officers surrendered before any attempt at boarding was made, and this was deemed unacceptable by the court, which ordered the captain and entire crew to be deprived of their pay.[1]

The want of men that plagued the Royal Navy throughout the Channel War posed a serious problem for Benbow and his fellow judges. Desertion was a capital offence but executing sailors would only make the underlying problem worse. So in cases of desertion they were very careful to listen to both sides of the story, and were quick to acquit if an adequate excuse was given. Seaman Timothy Marshall, for example, was initially condemned to death for desertion but was granted mercy on the seemingly flimsy grounds that he was only making a brief trip to London and planned to return thereafter.[2] In a similar case two seamen were simply judged to have been in harbour without leave, a crime which could easily have been condemned as desertion in a different location and at a different time.[3] In clear-cut cases of desertion Benbow's court still came up with an ingenious solution. In March 1699, when William Storey, George Denke and Benjamin Amberly deserted, all from HMS *Gloucester*, they were each at first condemned 'to be hang'd by the neck, till they are Dead, Dead, Dead'. But to the navy losing three seamen was simply unacceptable, and so the court forced the men to roll a dice to determine which of them would die. The unlucky man was George Denke. The others were paraded around the fleet in neck halters but the entire crew petitioned Benbow to write to the Admiralty to plead for Denke's life, which he duly did, although the records do not indicate if he met with success.[4] Other men were beaten with the cat o' nine tails for desertion and, in an isolated case of a man who deserted without proffering repentance or an excuse of any kind, claiming that 'he did not care to goe as a man of Warr', the sailor was hanged with no mercy.[5]

Otherwise embezzlement of ships' stores was a frequent concern, a surgeon who was found guilty of repeated drunkenness was dismissed from the service and a man found guilty of getting gunpowder wet was beaten.[6] Mutinous behaviour and excessive violence were also crimes Benbow was forced to negotiate, occasionally with some ingenuity. In June 1702 Commander Francis Gregory was found guilty of beating a sailor and had his wages confiscated. The sailor, who lost the sight of one eye because of the attack, was found culpable of provoking his captain, but it was felt that his loss of sight was appropriate punishment.[7] In the single court martial that Benbow sat on concerning sodomy, a seaman of the *Greenwich* was found guilty of abusing the ship's boy and was promptly hanged. This refusal to tolerate sexual crime was the norm. When, in February 1699, a sailor from the *Defiance* was found

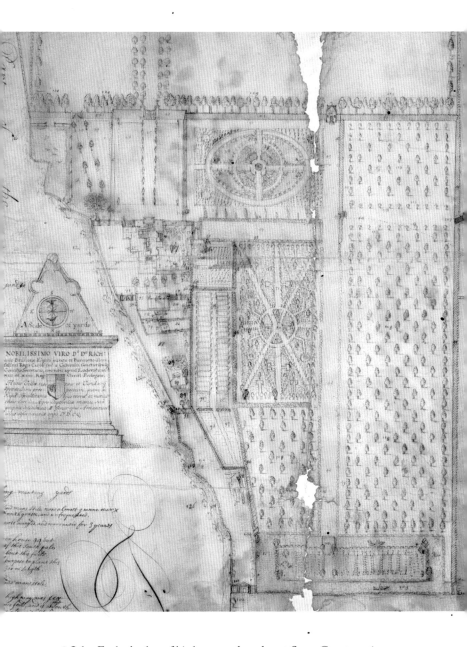

16. John Evelyn's plan of his house and garden at Sayes Court, *c.* 1653.

17. A view of the Royal Dockyard at Chatham, taken from the opposite side of the river Medway c.1690.

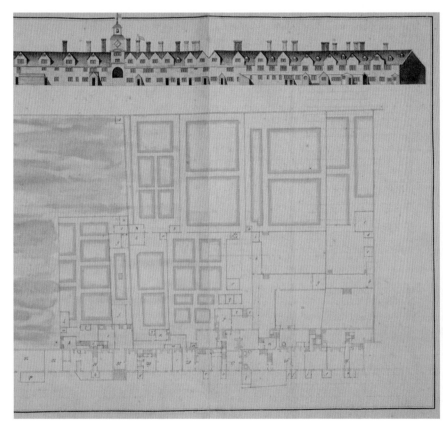

18. A view of the Royal Dockyard at Chatham showing the elevation of the officer's houses. Benbow's house was no.25, on the right-hand end.

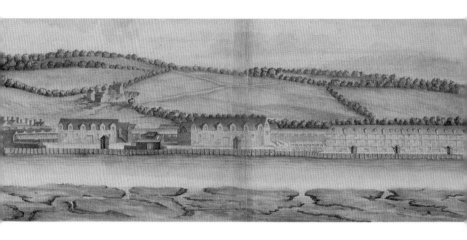

19. Peter the Great disguised as a common seaman.

20. A modern depiction of the First Eddystone Lighthouse.

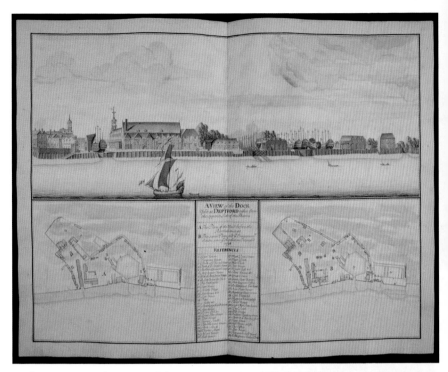

21. Contemporary depiction of the dockyard at Deptford taken from the opposite side of the Thames.

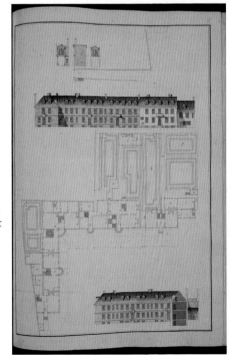

22. Contemporary depiction of the dockyard at Deptford showing the officers' accommodation. Benbow's House is the magnificent white one on the right hand end. *a* is the back parlour; *b* the kitchen; *c* the wash house; *d* the banqueting house; *e* the wood-house; *f* and *g* are privies, right down the end of the garden; *h* is the Doctor's garden; *i* the Clerk of the Survey's garden and *j* is his banqueting house. Benbow's garden is probably the unlabelled space below the Doctor's garden.

23. A view of Greenwich and the Queen's House from the South East. Note the single block of Webb's unfinished palace and how the Queen's House straddles the main road.

24. Sir Christopher Wren's first proposal for Greenwich hospital in which the view to the Queen's House is blocked by a central dome.

25. Greenwich hospital. Wren's smaller domes now frame the Queen's House in dramatic perspective.

26. Robert Thompson's journal, Cartagena.

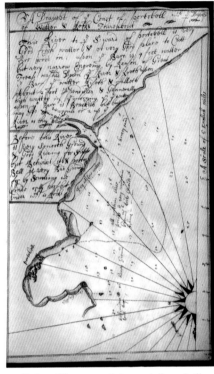

27. Robert Thompson's journal, Portobello.

28. One of numerous depictions of Benbow's Last Fight produced as his fame grew in the 19th century.

OPPOSITE: 29. The original mutineer's letter to Benbow.

At a Consultation held on board her Ma:ts Ship Breda the 24 August 1702 off of Cartagena on the Maine Continent of America, it is the opinion of us, who's names are undermention'd, Viz:t

First — Of the great want of men, in Number; Quality and the Weakness of those they have.

2:ly — The Generall want of Ammunition of most Sorts.

3:ly — Each Ships Masts, Yards, Sailes, Rigging and Guns being all in a great measure disabled

4:ly — The Winds are so small and variable that the ships cannot be Governed by any Strength each Ship has.

5:thly — Having experienced the Enemyes force in Six dayes Battle following. The Squadron consisting of Five Men of Warr and a Fireship under the Command of Mouns:r Du Cass, their Equipage consisting in Gunns from Sixty to Eighty & having a great Numbe[r] of Seamen and Soldiers on board for the Service of Spaine.

For which reasons abovemention'd Wee think it not fitt to Engage the Enemye at this time; butt to keep them Company this night and observe their motion, and if a fair oppertunity shall happen (of Wind and Weather) once more to trye our Strength with them.

Richard Kirkby
Wm: Constable
John Constable
Tho: Hoyt
Coop Wade
Tho: Hudson

30. Portrait of Benbow by Sir Godfrey Kneller, 1701.

guilty of sodomizing a turkey, both the man and the turkey were hanged together from the yard arm.[8]

In all of these verdicts we see the navy enforcing its regulations with a certain degree of humanity and understanding, as well as isolated cases of absolute enforcement. Such flexibility was required of naval flag officers forced to balance the need for regulation with an appreciation of the wide variety of situations in which naval officers found themselves throughout the world. Without such flexibility the system would have been unworkable and inhumane and the flag officers provided a sort of cartilage between the word of the law and the unforgiving reality of naval operations. Over time, naval rules and regulations expanded and became more detailed, but flag officers continued to play this important role as manning issues, foreign service, weather and the presence of the enemy forced men into unforeseen circumstances and unexpected behaviour. Nevertheless, the efficacy of courts martial of the 1690s is open to serious doubt. We know for certain that naval officers manipulated the system to their own advantage and that many punishments were simply never carried out. Ostensibly a means to regulate the navy, courts martial were too intricately linked with the courts' vested interests to work as effectively as they might.[9]

Benbow's improved status also made him one of the most valuable people to know in terms of patronage: he had at last achieved the position that Herbert had once provided for him. When a man called Charles Adderley was desperate to get his brother into the navy he commended himself on his 'good fortune' at getting him well recommended to Benbow, who took him under his wing.[10]

These responsibilities were peripheral to his career, however, which in 1698 took a dramatic turn. One of the most powerful lessons of the Nine Years' War of 1688–97 between Britain and France was that the Caribbean was going to become central to any future wars involving France and Spain. The income generated by the sugar and tobacco plantations of the New World was simply too significant to be ignored; it was the purse that would fund future wars. Another powerful lesson was that the imperial ambition of Louis XIV had not been quenched, and many considered the Treaty of Ryswick, which ended the Nine Years' War, to be at best a delaying tactic and at worse a sham. The final ingredient to the diplomatic and strategic situation in 1698 was that Charles II of Spain, owner of most of Italy, southern Holland and a huge colonial empire, was childless and almost permanently unwell because of generations of Habsburg interbreeding. With a clear French claim to the Spanish throne, Louis was itching to unite the French and Spanish empires, and the English were determined to stop him.

The government's response was insightful. Aware that the Caribbean would be an important part of any future war with France or Spain, and that the English position could only be maintained by force and not through diplomacy and negotiation, it decided to send a man to the Caribbean on a fact-finding and intelligence mission to test the tenor of support among the Spanish colonies, to examine defences of all nations and to improve navigational knowledge of key areas. This was all to be done as subtly as possible and the publicized aim of the expedition was to be something entirely different though plausible: the suppression of piracy.[11] The man they chose to lead the mission was Benbow.

As Benbow began to get his squadron ready, he started to lose patience with the Admiralty, his evident irritation perhaps the result of his raised status. In a direct letter to the Navy Board he wrote: 'I made my request to you some time since, that His Majesty's ship *Gloucester* [Benbow's new flagship] ought be furnished with a main sail and topsail ... which was granted as also other stores...' As a reminder this would easily have served, and the majority of such letters from flag officers to the Board are similarly brief, but Benbow goes on, ending: 'I desire you'll supply the same without giving me further trouble.'[12] There is no evidence of the Admiralty response but this is an extraordinarily rude letter, and a rare example of a lack of respect for his superiors and a startling contrast with the first letter Benbow wrote to the Navy Board – that fawning declaration of loyalty already discussed.[13] It is, moreover, only the first of a series of hot-blooded outbursts that characterize Benbow's treatment of others after his promotion to flag rank. It is unclear if this was caused by a natural streak of intolerance now only maturing, if it had always been there but is hidden to us by a lack of evidence, if his promotion had gone to his head, or if it was the result of honest frustration at the slowness and incompetence of the great naval machine.

There is certainly evidence that Benbow felt frustration with the Admiralty in general and in particular about ship design and the logistics of getting a squadron ready for overseas. The preceding spring he had written an enormously complex letter to the Navy Board in which he took the commissioners to task over numerous issues and asked them to do something about these. In each case he explained the problem and suggested a solution, some of which were accepted by the Board, who were clearly taken aback by his forthright tone. To one of his proposals they simply said, 'it being a new proposition we know not what to say to it'. He was very concerned about the transport of water and wanted to try storing it in lead-lined cisterns, rather than the traditional casks. This was a radical idea many years ahead of its time, but Benbow was allowed to try it on one ship. He was also allowed to secure the foot of the masts on 'one or two' ships with copper to see if that improved their strength and performance. He was also allowed to 'worm' the shrouds – that is to protect the rope shrouds with their own casing of wound twine – a practice common in the rest of the Age of Sail but not yet widespread by the 1690s. He was also allowed to equip each and every ship of his squadron with a spare main and topmast, something else that was not standard practice.[14] It is the letter of a man simply bursting with new ideas as well as the energy to see them through and, perhaps more than any other letter written by Benbow, reveals him as a key player in the improvement of the service in the late seventeenth century.

Before Benbow ever reached the West Indies he was required to perform one final special service for the Admiralty in his role as experienced convoy escort, and this time his charge was particularly special. As is so often the case in British naval history, a period of peace encouraged the government to use the power and reach of the navy to assist in expeditions that had the national interest at heart. It is no coincidence, for example, that James

Cook's first two voyages to the Southern Ocean (the southern Pacific and Antarctic oceans) occurred between 1768 and 1771 and between 1772 and 1775, in those long periods of peace between the Seven Years' War of 1755–62 and the War of American Independence of 1775–83. Constantine Phipps's Arctic expedition of 1773 was also made in this period.

These later peacetime scientific voyages share a common ancestor, and that is the expedition made in 1698 by the astronomer Edmond Halley, the discoverer of Halley's comet. For the very first time a scientist was sent in a naval ship for the sole purpose of taking scientific readings. Halley was instructed, in particular, to explore and record the phenomenon of magnetic variation that plagued every mariner's compass. Many believed at the time, Halley included, that magnetic variation could be used in some way to solve the single most trying navigational problem of the time: the inability to measure longitude. And yet there were no accurate measurements of magnetic variation from either the east coast of South America or the west coast of Africa, both of which Halley was ordered to explore.[15] He was also required to record accurately the names and location of any land that he came across, and to look for the fabled southern continent, the *terra incognita*, which was not discovered by an Englishman until Cook mapped New South Wales in 1770.

So precious was the expedition deemed to be that Benbow's entire West Indian squadron was instructed to escort Halley past the threatening corsair shore of West Africa that Benbow knew so well.[16] As the two men were of a similar age, it is likely that Benbow would already have known Halley, who was likewise a colleague of Sir Christopher Wren and Samuel Pepys. The ship Halley took with him, the pink *Paramour*, was specifically built at Deptford for the expedition during the time when Benbow was Master Attendant. We also know that Halley had come into regular and close contact with Peter the Great during his stay at Sayes Court and that some of Halley's foremost interests lay in navigation, tides and cartography. He had also invented a new type of log to measure the speed of ships, and improved the Davis quadrant and the azimuth compass, all of which were subjects close to Benbow's heart.[17] Much like Benbow, Halley also seems to have had the knack of pleasing every monarch he served under, or at least of remaining inconspicuous; he was favoured by Charles II,

James II, William and Mary and later Queen Anne. Given the convoluted nature of court politics in this troubled era, this was no mean feat, and it places both Benbow and Halley in rare company.

Halley was very keen to have Benbow serve as his escort and he wrote a rather pleading letter to the Admiralty claiming that Benbow had 'promised to take care of us' and asking for an official recommendation from the Admiralty, together with the necessary alteration to Benbow's orders. 'This is the last favour I have to begg,' he wrote, 'and I humbly hope it will not be refused...'[18] Halley's wishes were granted and, having been delayed several weeks by bad weather and the poor condition of the *Paramour*, Benbow, with Halley in company, eventually left England on 29 November 1698 and sailed directly for Madeira. There were no incidents on the voyage and within hours of arriving, Benbow weighed anchor for the West Indies, leaving Halley alone to head south.

In mid-January Benbow arrived in Barbados, where the westerly trade winds had so carefully delivered him. Benbow was already experienced at working overseas, but the Caribbean provided an altogether different challenge. One of the major issues was the distance from English shores and the relative infrequency of new arrivals. Service in the Gibraltar Strait, by contrast, had the advantage of being close to Cadiz, one of the busiest of all European ports, and thousands of tons of international fishing passed regularly through the Strait. From Gibraltar it took only a few short weeks to sail directly back to England, and a network of naval presence, fishing vessels and traders, made communication with the Admiralty in London simple by comparison with the Caribbean. The sheer distance involved increased the responsibility carried by the flag officers. They were unable to check the whim of their masters and were given much broader powers than flag officers at home. Throughout the Channel War, for example, Benbow had been summoned repeatedly to report to the Admiralty in person, where issues were discussed and opinions sought. None of that was possible in the Caribbean, as there was no permanent naval presence. The lack of supervision also meant that Governors of the colonies were granted extraordinarily wide-ranging powers. Understandably, this led to clashes when high-ranking army and naval officers suddenly appeared, exercising their authority over colonial Governors who were quite unused to anyone interfering in their own little kingdoms.[19]

The sense that one gets of the Caribbean in the late 1690s is of an unregulated mess. So easy were the pickings that many of the lawful Caribbean privateers of the previous war had taken to unlawful piracy. Uncharted islands were beyond any naval gaze, while the wealthiest of the world's merchant ships, carrying silver, gold, emeralds, slaves, tobacco and sugar travelled on predictable routes to catch the trade winds at predictable times of year. For those who were supposed to provide a measure of security, internal dispute consumed their time: the one glaring characteristic of colonial correspondence in this period is complaint. Those who had colonized the plantations were wealthy entrepreneurs, and those who were willing to act as Governors or colonial administrators saw opportunity in their post. Everyone in the Caribbean, with the exception of the poor slaves forced to work the plantations, was on the make, and Benbow was no different. Within weeks of arriving and comfortably out of the Admiralty gaze, he awarded his son, who had sailed out with his squadron as nothing more than a volunteer, an officer's commission. The young John Benbow, at the whim of his father, therefore became first lieutenant of the 24-gun *Maidstone*, with status sufficient to allow him to bring aboard his own servant.[20]

Almost immediately Benbow Snr. started irritating the local Governors. One of his first acts was to divide his squadron between those who would go with him on an intelligence-gathering mission to the Spanish Main, and the *Falmouth* and *Lynn*, who would sail straight for the British colony at Jamaica. Their arrival at Jamaica immediately sent Governor Beeston, a tricky and irritable man at the best of times, straight to his desk to write the first of numerous poisonous letters to the Navy Board concerning Benbow. 'These ships would have done more service had they had orders to cruise after pirates than to lie herein port, where there are no orders for them, and get their men sick by idleness and drinking,' wrote Beeston. 'The sailors tell me they know not why they were sent hither, so till the Rear Admiral arrives I am wholly in the dark about them.' Benbow, meanwhile, the Governor carefully informed the Admiralty, had gone to the Spanish Main.[21] Beeston believed there was an ulterior motive at play here, and he was correct, though it was not what he suspected. Unaware of Benbow's secret orders to gather intelligence, the cynical Beeston regarded his trip to the West Indies to be motivated by the fragrance of Spanish treasure.

Over the coming months the two men's relationship deteriorated. The healthy campaigning season of the Caribbean ran from December until May and by mid-August Benbow's ships were suffering appallingly from sickness, so much so that he was forced to press men in Jamaica. Beeston sprung to his island's defence. His letters to the Admiralty are crammed with more vitriol aimed at Benbow. The colonies themselves were fragile and, in a similar way to modern Caribbean tourism, each individual island or settlement needed to lure as many people as possible to its shores to boost its economy and give it the best chance to profit or at least survive. Before Benbow arrived, Jamaica had enjoyed a reputation as a free port, where sailors could relax in the knowledge that they would not be forced into the King's service. But Benbow changed all of this by plundering the local maritime population for service on his ships. The Governor's concern was divided between the wives and families of those who had been pressed and the well-being of the colony itself. Such action would drive would-be settlers, or would-be spenders, elsewhere in the Caribbean.

Of particular worry to the administrators of Jamaica was the latest newcomer to the Caribbean colonial system, the colony of Darien, founded by the Scots that same year. With so many ports to chose from and so little naval presence anywhere else, those in Jamaica knew that pressing men 'will frighten away all our seamen and ordinary people … any place else where they think they can be easy'.[22] Benbow at least acknowledged, in a letter to the Navy Board, the stir he had caused, but he did so with no hint of regret and with the full confidence that the safety of a warship was a higher priority than the Governor's hurt feelings. 'We have hardly men to secure her,' emphasized Benbow of his flagship. In another he claimed that 'necessity has no law'.[23]

Benbow was just as irritated by Beeston as Beeston was by him, and summed up the Jamaican Governor in such an outburst of hate that his already suspect grammar completely collapsed. 'There is nothing but cunning and deceit acted from the highest to the lowest, and in general hates anything that serves the King, but gives all ye encouragement that can be to all villany in the world,' he wrote after he had requisitioned a local sloop to assist with piloting and the transfer of stores. She became so useful that Benbow was forced to have her careened but Beeston refused to pay for the careening or the hire of the vessel, a cost estimated at £40 per month.[24] Benbow's letter was written on the same day that he informed the Navy Board that he had been forced to press men; by the time he sat down to write the letter concerning the sloop he had obviously enjoyed a run-in with the incensed Beeston, who had then refused to give him any money for the sloop.

Benbow's reliance on Beeston for money is interesting. Funding naval operations so far from home in locations with their own unique economies was immensely difficult, and the solution was a system of credit. Cash was almost useless for the quantity of spending that Benbow required. So he was granted separate lines of credit in different locations: £2,000 at Jamaica, £3,000 at Barbados, £500 at the Leeward Islands, £500 at Virginia and £2,000 at New York.[25] All of that credit, however, was administered through the office of the colonial Governor, and if they fell out there was little that Benbow could do. He started the voyage with nothing more than £500 in cash.[26]

With the bridges of civilized behaviour irrevocably shattered, the two continued to peck at each other until Benbow finally left the Caribbean, but not before a broader question of 'authority' had been raised. Benbow reacted to Beeston's refusal to pay for the sloop by refusing him any influence in maritime affairs. In Beeston's words:

> as soon as he arrived he took the ships from me and told me I had nothing to do with them when he was here … The Rear Admiral also told me that whilst he was here I had nothing to do with anything that moved on the water, not even in the harbour, nor could send out any vessel nor grant any commissions, and that if I did he would take away their colours and hinder them.[27]

In another letter the Governor complained that Benbow 'exercises his authority as if there was no other here'.[28] An objective observer noted: 'They have got in such a notion of the authority of the Admiralty that they slight and despise all other.'[29] Benbow certainly took seriously his threat of controlling the seas. At one stage, when divers under Beeston's orders recovered 150 jars of oil from a wreck, Benbow promptly confiscated them, a valuable prize indeed.[30] In a similarly staged operation, when Beeston determined to raise his profile and purse by capturing the infamous pirate Captain Kidd on his own initiative, Benbow merely sent a boat after the vessel sent by the Governor, with orders to take the ship and Kidd from them by force if they were successful. No confrontation ever occurred, however, as the elusive Kidd had once more slipped the net, but on the return of Beeston's ship, Benbow's captain threatened to take her colours away if they were not immediately taken down, which they were.[31] Thus Benbow's presence ruffled more feathers and seems to have created something of a mini-civil war between the Royal Navy and the Governor. Beeston was certain that Benbow's presence had served no good at all, and had in fact 'ruined all trade and the place'.[32]

If that is difficult to prove, the Caribbean tour had certainly ruined Benbow's squadron. 'This country confounds ships and stores as well as men,' he grumbled to the Navy Board.[33] His flagship, the *Gloucester*, was in a particularly bad way. Benbow was forced to careen her twice in successive failed attempts to stop a leak that kept the pump going constantly. With no dockyard facilities anywhere in the Caribbean he had no choice but to make near-constant temporary repairs to keep her afloat, but conceded that 'as fast as one leak is stopped another breaks out'. After one attempt to careen her she still had eight feet of water in the hold and made four feet of water per watch, which led Benbow to compose another brusque letter to the Navy Board, revelling in their incompetence and his skill. It is a letter that reeks of ego. 'I believe the King has not a better ship of her dimention,' he wrote, before slyly adding, 'nor one that was ever sent on Forraigne voyage fitted in such a manner'. He went on to say with no little black humour that the leaks were so bad that the men were now too worried about drowning to be worried about dying from sickness, and he finished with a spot of advice for the Board, recommending none other than himself as the best man to oversee the construction of a ship bound for foreign service. In the meantime he graciously promised to use 'all the Care and Genious' he could to keep her afloat.[34]

Our understanding of Benbow's intelligence-gathering mission to the West Indies of 1698–9 is blessed. Because of the nature of the mission, Benbow specifically ordered his Master, Robert Thompson, to keep a highly detailed and illustrated journal of everywhere they went during the voyage, a document entirely separate from the usual Master's log, which also survives.[35] So precious was the information that it was obviously well cared for on its return and it is still in magnificent condition, though it has never been studied by any of Benbow's biographers.

This immaculately kept journal, written in a steady and clear hand illustrates with bird's-eye views, harbours and passages, and sea-level views of approaches to islands with distance and bearing carefully noted alongside observations of longitude, latitude, variation in currents and tides, the location of sandbanks and the quality of holding ground. In every instance the size or appearance of islands is compared with islands or views from the British Isles with which the reader would be familiar. Thus an island near Barbados was 'about ye largeness of ye island of Wight but not altogether so high but a smooth frutefull island'. Another stretch of coast was compared to 'ye west coast of England' and a headland of Hispaniola 'a very long and very low point like Dungeness' and yet another 'like the bill of Portland', and off the Florida Keys they came across some sandy hills 'that showeth something like the seven cliffs by Beachy Head'.

The harbours that Benbow was most interested in, because he knew the least about them, were covered in extraordinary detail. Unsurprisingly, those in Spanish possession were given the greatest attention, not least Portobello, where he sounded the entire harbour, made observations on the tidal rise and submerged hazards, identified an excellent location for getting fresh water and explained how ships' boats could access it up a nearby river and even identified a location where a warship could anchor while she waited. Cartagena received a similar detailed investigation (see figs. 26, 27). At times the painful slowness of the expedition's progress is all too clear: in unknown waters they were forced to stop suddenly when, off the coast of Darien and plagued by lethal currents, they realized they were in only five feet of water, above sharp coral.

They also recorded the distance between locations in and around Jamaica to get a sense of how quickly a maritime force could be moved around that island, and they plotted courses for specific legs of those voyages: 'from plumb pointe to yallouw pointe', for example, 'ye course is E by S dist 5 leagues'. They were even careful to mark the location of an alligator pond for the unwary sailor searching the Jamaican shoreline for water or wood. Notable rocks received their fair share of attention: as well as descriptions ('a small white rock above water like a ship under sail') there were directions on how to avoid them and on which side to pass. Everywhere they took detailed observations of compass variations and they talked to anyone they could for intelligence or navigational information: local hunters, Indians and turtle catchers were all questioned. It is a deeply impressive manual of colonial intelligence, bursting with the unspoken motivation behind its creation: conquest and expansion.[36]

This voyage began in mid-January 1699, when they headed for the Spanish Main from Barbados via Guadeloupe, Antigua, Montserrat and Nevis. They reached the Spanish Main at Cape Santa Marta, the very location of Benbow's last fight three years later. Once in touch with the coast they cruised westwards, investigating the Spanish colonies as they went. Benbow was singularly unimpressed by these and saw in their weakness an opportunity to strike. He wrote in his official report, clearly aware that he was overstepping his role:

I humbly conceive that this kingdom of Peru[37] might be conquered in less than six months after forces arrive tis now in our power and to let slip this opportunity we may repent when too late. I humbly beg pardon for giving my frank opinion in this matter, nor am I fond of broken bones, but justly to serve my country...[38]

The first significant location where they stopped was Cartagena, where they went with a mission 'to huff them out of some of our vessels they have taken from us without any reason'. There were even reports that the Spanish had 'use[d] the men worse than prisoners if we had war'. After plenty of huffing, the physical presence of his warship backed up with numerous threats, Benbow succeeded in getting the ships released and left, though frustrated that 'we have no liberty to make them sensible of their indignities'.[39] While there, however, Benbow had been careful to gather as much intelligence as he could and he learned some very interesting things. The Spaniards were all desperate to know of the current health of their king and all seem to have been disappointed when Benbow assured them that he had recovered from his latest illness. The Spaniards, feeling increasingly vulnerable as more European powers sought colonies, and as larger squadrons of battleships began to patrol the islands more often, favoured French assistance. Louis, they knew, for all of his faults and ambition, had a powerful navy, and for the colonists of the new world that spelt security and wealth. According to Benbow the Spanish in Cartagena were all so pro-French that all Louis had to do was 'send a serjeant to declare for him, [and] they would surrender all to that power'. Benbow believed that this would surely lead to French control of the entire Kingdom of Mexico, and if that happened, Benbow's vision became apocalyptic indeed: 'they will be not only masters of America, but of all the habitable part of christendome, for in these parts are the sinews of war, and whatever potent prince has them, will command everything'.[40]

At Cartagena Benbow made contact with some Scots from their new colony on the Darien isthmus, and therein lay more troubling news. New Caledonia had been founded by the Scots on the east coast of Central America in 1698, and almost immediately had run into severe trouble. The site was ill-chosen, the settlers ill-equipped and William, from the moment he had heard of the Scottish intention to found a colony, had been determined to frustrate the scheme. An even greater obstacle was a complete failure to organize credit for the colonists. Not only did they have few supplies, but also they had no access to any money to buy more. Another major error was that they had chosen to found their colony on land already claimed by the Spanish. In a place where friends were essential, the few Scots who were not immediately struck down by disease in their damp colony were alienated and ostracized. Levels of desperation rose within weeks of their arrival, and the *Dolphin* was sent on a trading expedition to raise capital. She ran aground off Cartagena, her crew were immediately captured and enslaved and her trade goods confiscated.[41]

The Spanish at this stage had also begun to mobilize to drive the Scots from Darien and there had been at least one skirmish on land. The archives of the Darien colony suggest that Benbow actually met at least one member of the colony, Captain Maghie of the *Maidstone*, receiving him very civilly. But, pressed by Maghie to help him achieve the release of the imprisoned Scots, Benbow refused, claiming that he saw no reason to 'ruffle the Spaniards' feathers'. Maghie then made the unproven assertion that Benbow's desire to keep the Spaniards on his side was because he was in the process of selling them a cargo of Negro slaves. No other sources mention Benbow's involvement in slaving, although there is some scattered evidence that naval officers did become involved. Coming as this did from the pen of a Scot, however, it is likely to be anti-English propaganda.[42]

With both the English and Spanish turned against them, and through their own poor preparation, the Darien settlers were doomed. The next time Benbow came across members of the colony, in July 1696, they were in even sorrier shape. Conditions had become so bad on the isthmus, and they were under such constant threat from the Spanish, that the few surviving colonists had agreed to abandon the settlement. The *St Andrew* was the only Scottish ship to make it to Jamaica carrying its cargo of dying men from their jungle hell. Her captain, the resolute Colin Campbell, begged Benbow and Beeston for help, if only for the muscle power to move their ship to a safer anchorage, but received none.

Nor were they given any provisions; in fact the only charity offered was a place on Benbow's depleted crew for those who could take it.[43]

From Cartagena Benbow sailed to another Spanish stronghold, Portobello. As at Cartagena, English ships and sailors were being held at Portobello, though Benbow's visit was not so successful. He conducted a lengthy dialogue with the Spanish Governor, who refused to hand over any of the seized Englishmen and 'answered him very ruffly',[44] believing that the interests of the Scots and English were 'inseparable'. Benbow did his best to explain that this was not the case. But it was not until the *Maidstone* arrived from England off Portobello some weeks after Benbow's arrival, her captain carrying an official proclamation regarding England's stance towards the Scottish colony at Darien, that the Spanish relaxed their position. It was unequivocal and read in part:

> do not presume, or any pretence whatsoever, to hold any correspondence with the said Scots, nor to give them any assistance of arms, ammunition, provisions, or any other necessities whatsoever, either by themselves or any other for them, or by any of their vessels, or of the English nation, as they will answer the contempt of His Majesty's command, at their utmost peril.[45]

This proclamation improved the Spaniards' attitude towards Benbow to such an extent that they started to look to him for protection, fearing an assault from the Scots. When Benbow was finally forced to leave Portobello for Jamaica because of the leaky state of his ship, the *Gloucester*, and the need to hunt turtle to replenish food stocks, he left behind a small squadron of ships to maintain a presence and sent the *Maidstone* to cruise off the Darien isthmus to keep a close eye on the Scots.[46] However, he did not return to Jamaica empty-handed, as he had used his time well to study the defences of the city and the approaches to the harbour. He then used Jamaica as a base from which to explore the islands of the north Caribbean, visiting Hispaniola, St Catalina, Savona (now known as

Saona), Mona, Puerto Rico, St Thomas, Virgin Gorda, Nevis and St Christopher's, and while he was doing this he began to focus on the other significant part of his orders: he started to hunt for pirates.

Of all the pirates who haunted the Caribbean and the Indian Ocean, in 1699 none was more famous and more wanted than Captain William Kidd. What made Kidd stand out was that his piracy had caused a great deal of political embarrassment and it is this cocktail of politics and piracy that ensures his reputation endures today as one of the era's most successful pirates, a reputation that is entirely unjust.[47] History is littered with examples of more successful and more violent pirates than Kidd, and yet in the summer of 1699 he became the focus of a manhunt on an extraordinary scale, in which Benbow played a part.

Kidd's political crime was that he had turned on his masters. A naval officer, equipped, manned and armed at the King's expense to fight piracy in the Indian Ocean, Kidd had turned pirate himself and made the problems of piracy and international diplomacy even worse. Very unusually, Kidd's letter of marque giving him the legal right to attack pirate craft was personally signed by the King himself, so William could not fail to be implicated in his crimes. When rumours filtered back to England that Kidd had turned pirate there was uproar. Kidd had failed to attack any pirate craft in the Indian Ocean and was even known to have socialized with pirates in well-known pirate harbours. He had raided a convoy of pilgrims making their way back to India from Mecca. He had then attacked a number of small trading craft before capturing off Cochin the Armenian *Quedah Merchant*, laden with riches. He had also killed a member of his crew, bashing him about the head with an iron-hooped bucket. These are the facts of which we are certain, but it is also clear that Kidd's reputation went before him as a particularly bloodthirsty pirate, and Benbow was quite happy to spread the rumour. In early 1700 he passed on a story that Kidd 'was so wicked as to murder all the Moors he took in the ships he made prize of, in cold blood; and that he murdered several English and Dutch among 'em; only there were ten or twelve young Moorish boys he saved, intending to make slaves of 'em'. One of those boys apparently found his way to Jamaica, which is where the story came from.[48]

Such rumours had followed Kidd to the Caribbean. Born in Scotland, Kidd grew up in New York and had served as a privateer in the Caribbean in the previous war there, so he knew the region well; he knew its hiding places and he knew its markets. It was also a stepping stone to a return to New York, to make contact with Richard Coote, Earl of Bellemont, English MP, Governor of New York and one of Kidd's original backers. Kidd, it seemed, trapped in a web of events that some have claimed were beyond his control, thought he could talk his way to safety. In reality, however, his crimes and the political climate in England made any association with him political suicide. The Whigs, who had backed his privateering enterprise, were under constant and vicious attacks from the Tories, who now wielded Kidd's crimes like a mace against their enemies. In November 1698 English authorities throughout the New World were ordered to find Kidd and bring him home. The orders were given to Benbow, who carried them to the Caribbean. Once there he sent the Governor of every American colony a letter urging him to

> take particular care for apprehending the said Kidd and his accomplices wherever he shall arrive … as likewise to secure his ships and all the effects therein, it being Their Excellencies' intention that right be done to those who have been injured and robbed by the said Kidd, and he and his associates be prosecuted with the utmost rigour of the law.[49]

Benbow knew that he had no chance of capturing anyone in the leaky *Gloucester* and so transferred to the *Saudadoes Prize*, a 36-gun Fifth Rate, captured from the French in 1692 (see Appendix II, p. 347). One of his first stops was the Danish island of St Thomas in the Virgin Islands, a port renowned for its relaxed attitude towards harbouring pirates and selling their goods. Kidd had indeed been there and offered the Governor a bribe of forty-five thousand pieces of eight for protection, but it had been refused. Benbow himself had little more luck. As soon as he arrived he demanded to know why there was a Danish flag flying over the smaller Crab Island, an English possession. The Governor was 'extremely astonished' at Benbow's objection, for the island, as far as he was concerned, was Danish. Benbow then demanded the release of some wanted men but, for all his words, failed to force the Dane to hand over or concede anything. An irate Benbow claimed that 'the people of this island are very insolent, and are ready to commit all the villainy in the world when [they] have opportunity'. Once again, however, Benbow used his time at St Thomas wisely to report on the approaches and the harbour, which he found 'very commodious for ships, and water enough for any ship, and would be of great use to our English nation in case of a war in these parts, and may be made very easy secure, which is now only a receptacle for thieves'.[50]

From St Thomas, Kidd went to the little-known island of Mona in the channel between Puerto Rico and Hispaniola, where he had supplies delivered and started to sell his loot. Meanwhile, increasingly fanciful rumours circled as to his location and the size of his treasure. Some thought he had gone to Darien, which was more than plausible because Kidd was Scottish, and others claimed he had the astronomical sum of more than £400,000 worth of treasure aboard his ship.[51] Benbow, meanwhile, was cruising continually, but with little success, and in the spring he received orders to head home via the east coast of America to continue his cruise against piracy. Kidd had also headed north, and now appeared off Long Island, having spent a little time at Boston meeting old allies and unloading some of his treasure. But there the net finally closed. Bellemont, to whom Kidd had effectively entrusted his own safety, had him arrested and sent to England.

With Kidd in captivity a major effort was made to recover his treasure, as rumours of secret caches electrified the eastern seaboard of America and the Caribbean. Kidd, in fact, of all the pirates in history, is almost solely responsible for the myth of buried treasure, a myth which keeps treasure hunters occupied even today. If that is all nonsense, we do know that some of his treasure was recovered. Kidd seems to have spent much of his time off the coast of Boston feathering his nest in case things went wrong, distributing wealth in various forms among a number of people. Bellemont lost no time in retracing Kidd's footsteps and even found some gold dust and ingots between two feather beds in the house in which Kidd was arrested.[52] All in all, 1,111 ounces of gold, 2,353 ounces of silver, forty-one bales of goods, some bags of silver pieces and various jewels were discovered scattered between New York, Boston and the West Indies. Although an impressive cache, valued at £14,000, it was only a fraction of the £40,000 of which Kidd himself had bragged and the £400,000-plus that others had claimed was captured in the Indian Ocean, rumours which have kept him famous.[53] Some, and possibly all, of this treasure was delivered to Benbow for safekeeping as the *Gloucester* lay in Massachusetts Bay on 1 June 1700.[54] This is the full inventory:[55]

• •

	Gold Ounces	Silver Ounces
In Captain Wm Kidd's Box		
One Bag qt. 57 Silver Bars		357
One Bag qt. 79 Bars and Ps Silver		442 ½
One Bag qt. 74 Bars Silver,		421

One enameled Silver Box gilt, in which are Four Diamonds set in Gold Lockets. One Diamond loose, one large Diamond set in a Gold Ring.

Found in Mr. Duncan Campbell's House. Kidd and his wife were lodging in Campbell's house at the time of his arrest.

	Gold Ounces	Silver Ounces
No. 1. One Bag qt. Gold	58 ½	
No. 2. One Bag qt.,	94	
No. 3. One Handkerchief qt.,	50	
No. 4. One bag qt.,	103	
No. 5. One Bag qt,.	38 ½	
No. 6. One Bag Quantity,	19 ¼	
No. 7. One Bag qt,.		203

Also, 20 Dollars, one Half and one Quarter Ps. Of Eight, Nine English Crowns, One small Bar of Silver, One small Lump of Silver, a small Chain, a small Bottle, a Coral Necklace, one Piece white and one Piece of chequered Silk.

In Captain Williams Kidd's Chest.
Two Silver Basons, Two Silver Candle-sticks, One Silver Porringer, and some Things of Silver, Quantity, 82

Rubies small and great, 67; Green Stones, Two;
One large Loadstone.

Landed from on board the Sloop Antonio, Captain William Kidd, late commander.
57 Bags of Sugar.
38 Bales of Merchanture.

Received of Mr. Duncan Campbell
Three Bales of Merchandize, whereof One he had opened, being much damnified by Water, qt.
85 Pieces of Silk, Rumalls, and Bengalls.
60 Pieces of Callicoes and Muslins.

Received the 17th Instant of Mr. John Gardner

No. 1. One Bag of Dust Gold, qt.,	60 ¾	
No. 2. One Bag coined Gold,	11	
And in it Silver, qt.,		124
No. 3. One Parcel Dust Gold, qt.,	24 ¼	
No. 4. One Bag, qt. 3 Silver Rings, sundry precious Stones,	4 ⁷⁄₈ Oz.	

On Bag unpolished Stones, qt. 12 ½ Ounces.
One Ps of Crystal and Bever Stone, Two Cornelian Rings, Two small agats, Two Amethysts, all in the same Bag.

No. 5. One Bag Silver Buttons, and a Lamp, qt.,		29
No. 6. One Bag broken Silver, qt.,		173 ½
No. 7. One Bag Gold Bars, qt.,	353 ¼	
No. 8. One Bag Gold Bars, qt.,	238 ½	
No. 9. One Bag Dust Gold, qt.,	59 ½	
No. 10. One Bag Silver Bars, qt.,		212
No. 11. One Bag Silver Bars, qt.		309

The whole of the Gold above mentioned is 1111 Ounces Troy Weight. The Silver is 2353 Ounces.
The Jewels or precious stones, weighed, are 17 Ounces, ¾ of an Ounce; and 69 Stones by Tale.
The Sugar is contained in 57 Bags.
The Merchandize is contained in 41 Bales.
The Canvas is 17 Pieces.

• •

Kidd and his treasure were then taken with thirty-two other prisoners back to England in HMS *Advice*, a frigate which had been sent over for that sole purpose, after it had been decided that Benbow had too much on his plate to cope with Kidd as well.[56] Benbow transported nine more captured pirates back to England in the *Gloucester*, a mixture of Henry Avery's crew and Kidd's.[57] Avery, like Kidd, was much wanted because he too was a navy man turned pirate, though Avery, as first mate, had been forced to lead a mutiny to take over his vessel, the *Charles*. A very successful pirating career in the Indian Ocean culminated in his capture of the *Ganj-i-Sawai*, a treasure ship belonging to the Mughal Emperor of India. Much like Kidd, Avery then took his crew to the West Indies, where they sold the loot and went their separate ways. Six other members of Avery's crew had been captured and condemned, and five of them were hanged in October 1696. The men Benbow took back in the *Gloucester* were the only other members of Avery's crew captured and Avery himself was never heard of again. It has been suggested that he settled in Bideford in Devon and died there in poverty, having been cheated of his money by Bristol merchants.[58]

We know a little of the men Benbow took back with him. Among their number was James Brown, the Governor of Pennsylvania's son-in-law and a shipmate of Kidd; David Evans, Avery's man, who had already been tried – and acquitted – of piracy at the Old Bailey; Terlagh Sulivan, who claimed he was forced aboard Avery's pirate ship, was poor, hard-working and had a wife and three small children. The Governor of Boston, perhaps taken in by these stories but more likely corrupt, believed them all innocent.[59] Five other sailors, Nicholas Churchill, James How, John Eldridge, Robert Hikman and Derby Mullings, were all Kidd's men. The last man was Robert Bradenham, Kidd's surgeon, 'the obstinatest and most hardened of 'em all'. Shortly after his return, however, Bradenham broke, became a star Admiralty witness in the prosecution against Kidd and received a royal pardon.[60]

When Benbow arrived at St Helens in the Isle of Wight he was given special orders to sail round to the Thames, where he could deliver the prisoners to the Admiralty's own prison at Marshalsea with greater security. Churchill, Eldridge and Mullings were all tried alongside Kidd, all found guilty, all sentenced to be hanged and, unsurprisingly for the time, all ultimately walked free.[61] Kidd's trial was held in London in May 1701 and it was one of the most extraordinary of the time. At the end of proceedings conducted as a political show trial under intense public scrutiny, Kidd was condemned. Even his execution was abnormal: Kidd's rope snapped and he had to be hanged twice. His body was then hung in chains at execution dock in Wapping on the Thames. Benbow was in and around London at the time of the trial and although he had failed to capture Kidd himself, he would have been delighted at one consequence of his capture: Kidd's personal effects were condemned and sold, and the new monarch, Queen Anne, agreed to donate the entire purse to the running of the newly opened Greenwich Hospital.[62]

Benbow reported on his Caribbean espionage immediately on his return to London, a report which focused (as his orders had required) more on issues of intelligence and the characteristics of the Caribbean as a theatre of war than on the suppression of piracy. The defences of Jamaica, he argued, were inadequate. He had discovered a mile-wide channel, formed, he believed, by the devastating earthquake of 1692, which now gave access directly to the harbour out of range of any of the port's extant defences. The channel was also oriented in exactly the right way to allow ships to sail in and out of the harbour with ease by harnessing the consistent and predictable trade winds of the Caribbean. Benbow recommended that three new forts be built to protect the harbour and a separate fort built in the large bay to the west of Port Royal known as Old Harbour. He was particularly concerned about the east side of the island, being the closest to Hispaniola and the most open, as well as the vulnerability of the few and narrow mountain passes across the centre of the island. He also advised every parish to have its own fortification, supplied with water, as a place for safe retreat for the entire community, 'negroes etc.', while warning that the entire island could raise no more than two thousand white men to fight.[63] The Leeward Islands were particularly vulnerable as they were entirely undefended apart from St Christopher's Island (St Kitts), where there was a single fort and one company of foot soldiers. Benbow had learned that the French, who occupied the other half of St Christopher's, had many more soldiers already there.[64] Barbados was less of a concern as it was naturally fortified by rocks on the leeward side and a number of defences on the windward, augmented by a trench seven feet broad and five feet deep in front of a breastwork six feet high and three feet broad that ran the entire length of the windward coast.[65]

In general Benbow was worried that most of the Caribbean settlements were open to coastal raiding as much as they were to full-scale invasion, and he lamented in particular that none of the local inhabitants seemed to have any awareness of their potential danger, so much so that they were 'not willing to receive those who will protect them'. He concluded rather stridently that 'their own safety must be forced upon them' and believed that, if the islands were fortified as he suggested, and each island equipped with sufficient troops, any attempted invasion could be met. 'But whenever that fails,' he wrote, 'all must.'[66]

Benbow, in short, was horrified at the vulnerability of English interests in the New World. He also explained that he had found no evidence of French attempts to interfere in any way with the Spanish treasure convoys, but he did make it clear that it would become the first target if war broke out, and further explained that the ability to capture or protect the *flota* – the annual treasure fleet that carried the extraordinary wealth of the New World back to Spain – would turn on naval mastery of certain choke points in the Caribbean.[67] This report, together with his earlier letters discussing the potential loyalty of the Spanish settlements, won Benbow more plaudits than his constant rowing with Beeston had lost him friends, and the King granted him an augmentation of arms on his return.[68]

Historians have been far too quick to dismiss Benbow's Caribbean achievement. He was unable to secure the release of English prisoners from Portobello or of wanted pirates from St Thomas, but his very presence in the area had immediately calmed the French, who had been sniffing around for somewhere to found a new colony of their own, and they rapidly adopted less threatening language.[69] He had also spent several months navigating a squadron around unknown and potentially hostile waters. In seamanship terms alone this is an astonishing achievement, but it is important to realize that his whole purpose there was *because* the Royal Navy had no detailed knowledge of those waters. Although the Caribbean had already been 'discovered', discovery was a lengthy, ongoing and multi-layered process, and by the 1690s a very important part of the exploration and discovery of the Caribbean was still incomplete. A Captain Long had been sent to continue the process of exploring for riches in uncolonized areas,[70] but it was still impossible to use and protect the Caribbean in the way that the English government wanted to without detailed knowledge of its hydrography and geography, and Benbow provided it with that. His role was instrumental in the 'opening' of these seas to naval warfare and to British success there, which in the future so often led to British success in war.

The April after his return, Benbow was promoted to Rear-Admiral of the Red and then promoted again in July to Vice-Admiral of the Blue, flying his flag in the *Bredah* (see Appendix ii, p. 348). It was his last command and he would shortly be sent back to the Caribbean on his last tour, where he would fight his last fight.

17.

Benbow's Last Fight

Charles II died on 1 November 1700, the sixth and last Habsburg King of Spain, and he named as his sole heir the duc D'Anjou, the sixteen-year-old grandson of Louis XIV King of France. But in spite of Charles's will there was more than one claimant to the Spanish throne and the succession was contested. England, Portugal and Holland all chose to support the claim of the Holy Roman Emperor, Leopold I. Before war broke out there was a period of diplomatic jostling. Armies were raised Europe-wide while William III nurtured the support he needed in both England and Holland to declare war on France. With Benbow's frank warnings of the vulnerability of the West Indies still ringing in its ears, the Admiralty quickly sent him back to protect English colonies and to prevent the Spanish treasure convoy from falling into French hands.

Based at the Downs, Benbow spent the end of 1700 and the early part of 1701 preparing his fleet for Caribbean service, but now his letters to the Navy Board rang with authority. As he had experienced at first hand the ravages of tropical sickness, a disproportionate quantity of his correspondence concerned health. Bedding, surgeons and timber to make cradles for the sick were all requested.[1] The Admiralty was equally concerned and Benbow was ordered to conduct a number of medical trials in the first naval therapeutic trial on record. By a curious coincidence or perhaps the result of a network of like-minded individuals, the man whose medicines were to be tested was none other than Moses Stringer, the scientist who had entertained Peter the Great so well in Sayes Court. Stringer had since concocted the elixir *Febrifugium Montis* and the more sober-sounding *Salt of Lemons*, the first a cure for fevers and calentures (a specific type of delirium), the second a cure for scurvy and used to turn the elixir into a powder. The surgeons of every ship and Benbow himself were all ordered to observe carefully the effect of the remedies and report to the Navy Board.[2] Unfortunately no evidence of the findings has been discovered, though Stringer was only too keen to sing their praises from the rooftops. In a published tract he claimed the elixir cured, among many hundreds of other ailments, nothing less than the plague, the pestilence, all malignant fevers, snakebites, 'and all inveterate deadly poisons whatever', deafness, smallpox, ringworm and miscarriage. The Royal Navy was specifically mentioned as a happy customer.[3]

To provide some measure of spiritual relief to the unwell, or to those anxious over the rigours of service in the West Indies, Benbow also took with him six thousand copies of a new tract preaching moral and religious guidance, roughly enough for one for every two seamen in his squadron. Written by the prolific moral reformer Josiah Woodward and published by the newly formed Society for Promoting Christian Knowledge (SPCK), the tract was entitled *The Seaman's Monitor* and proclaimed itself a source of 'Advice to Sea-faring Men, With Reference to their Behaviour Before, In, and After their Voyage, a Kind Caution to Prophane Swearers and an Earnest Persuasive to the Serious Observation of the Lord's Day'. The rather optimistic Woodward hoped to make 'each of Her Majesty's Ships of War ... so regularly and peaceably ordered, that it may appear to be a Sanctuary of Devotion, a School of good Discipline, and a Nursery of virtuous and valiant men...'[4] He preached of the wickedness of alcohol, gambling and loose women – everything, in other words, that sailors loved. Nonetheless, this tract was favoured by Benbow as much as it was by Rooke, Shovell, Vice-Admiral Thomas Hopson, Commissioner of the Admiralty and future Admiral George Churchill, and John Cutts, soldier, diplomat and MP. It is likely that these pioneering officers and the SPCK faced a considerable challenge in attempting to reform English seamen, most of whom were notoriously irreligious, although minutes of SPCK meetings from the time make it clear that sailors were more willing to listen (to anything, one suspects) if they were first given a little tobacco.[5]

Benbow's letters were also coloured by his experience of what happened to his ships when submerged in warm, wormy waters and exposed to the brutal squalls of the Caribbean. When a new ship was proposed to accompany him, he insisted that she be equipped with her own careening gear and a lead-lined water cistern, and he further insisted that every ship in the squadron be given two spare pump chains. Six weeks later and with their departure growing ever closer, Benbow became angry that his pumps had still not arrived. Again, drawing on his new knowledge of warfare in the West Indies, not least the difficulty of hiring craft while there, he ordered a sixteen-oared boat to take with him, 'believing she may be of great use in the West Indies'.[6] He also took sufficient canvas for a hundred tents to protect his men from the sun and rain when ashore and £10,000 worth of credit to be drawn from the colonies, a full £2,000 more than his last voyage.[7]

Benbow was initially sent out with Rooke's Channel squadron, which had been patrolling the western approaches and monitoring French activity in Brest. Spies in Paris, meanwhile, were regularly drip-feeding the English government with information concerning the French plans overseas.[8] Benbow was then sent to the Western Islands (the Azores), where he was to cruise for the homeward-bound *flota*. If he discovered it he was first to inform the Spanish commander that he had orders to carry it to an unnamed 'port of safety'. If, as one might suspect, the Spanish commander was unwilling simply to hand over his vast treasure convoy politely to Benbow, Benbow was then empowered 'either by fair means or by force' to seize the entire convoy. If this had to be done, Benbow was under orders from the Navy Board, which was terrified of embezzlement, to immediately seize the ships' inventories and then seal up the hatches. But if none of this happened at all, the Admiralty wanted its intentions to be forgotten as surely as the *flota* itself was never seen, and any other vessel that saw Benbow's fleet was to be captured to prevent the secret from getting out.[9] The *flota* never materialized and Benbow, secret safe, was eventually forced to the Caribbean when his beer ran out in the second week of October.

By now the rumours of war were setting the Atlantic world alight.

Benbow knew that the Portuguese settlements in the Azores expected war and the colonies in the New World were growing increasingly nervous. For all their bluster in the previous few years of peace, with war on the horizon a naval presence was badly wanted. For more than a month British forces at Jamaica had been expecting Benbow daily. 'Pray God that he may come,' wrote one captain and Governor Beeston penned a particularly fretful letter to the Admiralty ringing with fear of French assaults. At the same time the defences of Jamaica, presumably in response to Benbow's survey the previous year, had been put in better order, with a new citadel being constructed and entrenchments dug at the once vulnerable site of Old Harbour, and at the town of St Jago. Meanwhile, the French on both sides of the Atlantic were in great fear of Benbow; they knew he was at sea but had no idea where he had gone or why.[10]

War had still not broken out, however, and Benbow's new orders, those to capture the *flota* now conveniently forgotten, were non-aggressive but different from those of the previous year, for he was now specifically required to assess and encourage Spanish loyalty to the Austrian claim to the Spanish throne. Any chink of light was to be exploited, and he was empowered to offer the Spanish as much assistance and protection as the Royal Navy could offer if they supported Leopold's claim. Even if the Spanish colonies decided to split entirely from Spain, Benbow was still encouraged to nurture their friendship through mutual trade agreements. If the French got in the way at any stage, he was ordered to use any means at his disposal of 'annoying them, till they shall be reduced to a better temper'.[11] The last time Benbow was ordered to 'annoy' the French, don't forget, he burned a convent, exploded a 300-ton nail bomb in a civilian harbour and rejoiced at the destruction of Catholic Churches. No wonder the French were worried about where he had gone.

Benbow arrived in Barbados in mid-November and then travelled to Jamaica via Martinique to inspect the French preparations for war, on to Dominica for wood and water, where they found kindly natives, and then on to Nevis. All this time the Governor of Nevis was beside himself with worry, being well informed that Benbow had arrived at Barbados but still with no idea of where he had gone since.[12] A month after making land at Barbados, Benbow's squadron – two Third Rates, eight Fourth Rates, one bomb ship and two troop transports – arrived at Jamaica amid more rumours that the *flota* had still not sailed, but that a French fleet was waiting at Havana to escort it. There were also rumours that the Spanish were unwilling to trust the French, which proved to be well founded. In fact the first French fleet sent to escort the *flota* had been forced to return empty-handed and had not even been allowed to buy victuals from the Spanish. Now a new emissary from France, this time led by the marquis de Château Renault, was on its way again to negotiate the release of the treasure into French custody.[13]

War, meanwhile, had still not been declared although Benbow, chomping at the bit, was doing his best to start one of his own: he provoked a diplomatic incident by capturing a French merchantman, the *Hermione de Nantes*. The enraged Governor of Martinique claimed in a letter that her cargo and been 'seized and robbed' and her captain attacked, a clear breach of the Treaty of Ryswick. 'I await instructions from France,' he ended, 'but if your ships of war continue these acts of violence, I shall not hesitate to make reprisals…' Benbow explained that she had been seized to disguise his presence, and as a further defence he added that she was clearly English-built but had no papers adequately explaining how she had come into French ownership. If the first excuse was justifiable, the second was a long shot and, after initially denying any knowledge of the incident, the Barbados authorities eventually apologized and returned her to the French.[14]

Going out of his way to annoy the French, Benbow was equally conscious of his duty to woo the Spaniards and he wrote lengthy letters to the Governor of Havana and the Viceroy of Mexico in which he offered a robust English perspective on the European war:

> The King of England tells me that he has lent the great fleet of England to the Emperor to transport his son the Archduke of Austria with 40,000 men into Spain, where he is confident he will be received as lawful King without any bloodshed or opposition being well assured that nineteen parts of twenty in Spain languish with impatience for the happy opportunity, having already had a taster of the French yoke.

Unashamedly, he continued:

> As success in Europe is certain I am ordered to offer my ships and
> men to help such of the Governors of the Spanish Indies as are
> early in their service for the Austrian King ... I will say no more
> except that so long as there is a ship or man in my master's Indies
> they will be used to help so just a cause.

He carried on in the same vein before firmly concluding that the
English and Spanish, divided as they were by religious, mercantile and
dynastic interests, 'shall be good friends'.[15] Well aware of the poor hand
he had been dealt, however, he wrote a simultaneous letter to the Navy
Board making it clear that success in Europe was a necessary precondi-
tion to peace in the West Indies, as the Spanish there 'will be very
cautious to declare without a certainty'.[16] The reality of the situation in
Europe was nothing like as hopeful as Benbow had led the Spanish to
believe; an attack on Cadiz, envisaged as the powerful opening gambit
of the war, ended in drunken farce with English soldiers desecrating
churches and turning every Spaniard they met against them.[17]

Meanwhile, the problems of waging war in the tropics were beginning to take their toll on Benbow's squadron and threaten his ability to
wage any kind of war at all. On Christmas Eve 1701, 250 men were sick
ashore with scurvy and flux, which Dr Cockbourn's medicine, a more
established remedy than Stringer's, 'will not answer'.[18] This is perhaps
unsurprising, as what little we know about Cockbourn's medicine tells
us that he favoured powdered crabs' eyes to treat influenza and whole
powdered toad for asthma.[19] Four months later six hundred men were
dead of disease and Benbow himself was ill and wanted to go home, the
second of only two known examples of his professional gaze losing
focus.[20] Some of his ships were now seriously undermanned. His flagship, the *Bredah*, could muster 344 of 370 (92 per cent), the *Falmouth* 159
of 197 (80 per cent), the *Kingston* 221 of 278 (79 per cent), the *Gloucester*
218 of 278 (78 per cent), the *Defiance* 229 of 312 (73 per cent), the
Experiment 81 of 115 (70 per cent), the *Greenwich* 166 of 238 (69 per cent),
the *Seahorse* 55 of 95 (57 per cent) and, worst of all, the *Bristol*, 101 of 197,

a shocking 51 per cent. Any attempt to press men was met by deliberate political and physical obstruction from the Jamaican authorities, and his sailors were even shot at and some wounded.[21]

Unwilling simply to rage against this obstruction (and rage he did), Benbow helped the manning situation by doing something that he already had a bit of experience of: he built a hospital. In the West Indies, getting his sick men better was clearly the only workable solution to this problem. With no dedicated naval hospital, sailors were forced to recuperate in lodging houses in Port Royal, which Benbow believed was even worse for their health. Not only was it expensive but the men suffered relapses caused by excessive boozing. This became such a problem that Benbow actually re-embarked all of his sick into his ships while the hospital was being built.[22] The hospital was certainly a good idea but it was badly let down by its location. The priority, it seems, was that the hospital should be anywhere apart from Port Royal, which one contemporary eloquently described as

the dunghill of the universe, the refuse of the whole creation, the clipping of the elements, a shapeless pile of rubbish confusedly jumbled into the emblem of chaos … it is the nursery of Heavens Judgement, where the malignant seeds of all pestilence were first gathered and scattered to punish mankind … the town is the receptacle of vagabonds, the sanctuary of bankrupts, and a closestool for the purges of our prisons. As sickly as a hospital, as dangerous as the plague, as hot as hell, and as wicked as the devil.[23]

Another succinctly called it as 'the Sodom of the New World' and claimed that its population consisted of 'pirates, cutthroats, whores and some of the vilest persons in the whole of the world…'[24]

Unfortunately Benbow's hospital site was next to a mosquito breeding swamp, a 'morass of standing stinking water',[25] and everyone there, from patients and guards to doctors, contracted yellow fever, regardless of their other ailments. None of this was yet known to Benbow, however, least of all that mosquitoes carried disease, and when his hospital was finished in January 1702 he would have been delighted.

As the months ticked by, Benbow and the Jamaican authorities carried on squabbling, as they had the previous year, usually over men or money and despite specific orders sent by an exasperated Admiralty to avoid 'unnecessary disputes'.[26] Meanwhile, the shadow of war grew so close that Benbow started to become anxious about merchantmen leaving the New World with cargoes that would prove useful to him in a war.[27] By June he had heard of the death of William III and the succession of Anne, James II's Protestant daughter, and Benbow conducted appropriate ceremonies for the officers to swear allegiance to their new sovereign.[28]

A little over a week later he heard the news he had been craving for nine months: England and France were at war. He had missed the last *flota*, which had eventually sailed in April (and right into the hands of Rooke at Vigo), but he was now ordered to target the next treasure convoy and in the interim to seize or destroy any French warships or merchantmen he came across.[29] This was no small challenge. Because of the delicate relationship between France and Spain, with Louis doing everything he could to demonstrate his support for Spain, the French battle fleets sent to the West Indies were vast; far larger than necessary and as much a political statement of goodwill to Louis' mistrustful Spanish allies as a functional requirement.[30] They were also all fresh: they sailed from France, spent a short time in the Caribbean and then returned to Europe. Benbow's force, by contrast, was relatively small, weakened by sickness, stricken by poor canvas and had already been in the Caribbean for eight months.[31] He would have to be very lucky indeed to find himself in a situation where he could press any advantage and inflict a defeat of any description on the French. Even before they joined battle, the odds were not stacked in Benbow's favour. As he began to stretch his muscles and prepare for war, his cruisers heard that a large fleet under Rear-Admiral Jean du Casse was bearing down on the Caribbean, laden with troops to garrison ports on the Spanish Main and carrying a new Governor for Mexico who was enthusiastic about the Franco-Spanish alliance. Benbow's immediate challenge was to prevent du Casse from reaching the Spanish Main. To help him, reinforcements had been sent out under Rear-Admiral Whetstone.

Benbow's first aggressive action of this war is typical of his operational history. He sailed to Hispaniola, where he bombarded Léogâne, took a 30-gun ship and three merchantmen, sunk a fourth and burned a fifth. The ship that was burned was only burned as a last resort. She had been run aground and Benbow sent in a boat directly under the guns of a fort to get her out, but she was stuck fast and he had no choice but to destroy her. Benbow then continued to patrol around Hispaniola and in a spot known to him as Cue harbour, possibly Baradères Bay, he took great delight in taunting the inhabitants. With neither the men nor the equipment for a serious assault, Benbow still cruised with his squadron from one end of the long beach to the other, and was shadowed all the way by the locals, who were terrified that he was going to land.[32] As soon as he heard that du Casse had been spotted en route to Santo Domingo, however, Benbow headed south fast. The fight was on.

At that moment du Casse was in no state to fight anyone. Aboard his flagship was Cartagena's new Governor with his wife and her entire entourage of duennas and maids of honour, all of whom required their own separate cabin.[33] With Benbow hurtling south with seven ships of the line mounting nearly four hundred guns, du Casse was lucky that he got to Porto Rico safely, where he split his squadron and sent two ships on with the Governor. The rest of his squadron, four ships of around sixty guns, one 30-gunner and a troop transport, he took to Cartagena as escorts for the single and heavily crowded troop transport. Benbow caught them off Cape Santa Marta, a port 160 kilometres north-east of Cartagena that lies in the dramatic shelter of the Sierra Nevada de Santa Marta mountains. Only forty-two kilometres from the coast they rise some 5,700 metres above sea level. With such a high backdrop, Cape Santa Marta was an excellent landfall for anyone voyaging south from the Caribbean to the Spanish Main. This was no random rendezvous, but a well-planned interception by a man who knew the local geography.[34]

Almost immediately things started to go wrong. The French were to windward – that is, in the direction *from* which the wind was blowing.

To get at them Benbow would have to sail into the wind, which on the finest seventeenth-century warships was extremely difficult, but was almost impossible on those that had been in the Caribbean for ten months and were in poor condition relative to the new French arrivals. The next problem was that the winds were very light, which made progress painfully slow; in fact Benbow's fleet sailed at roughly two knots – two miles *per hour* – during the first two days of the engagement. In any case Benbow's first priority was one of defence. In the presence of the enemy he needed to form his cruising squadron into a united and unified line, that is grouped together at a uniform distance from one another, that could defend itself if attacked. This took several hours, hours well spent by the French to increase their distance from their pursuers and also to form their own line. Nothing about this first contact was electrifying or in any way surprising; it was all ponderous and predictable.

But if this stage of the battle was dull, the next stage would prove very interesting. As a general rule, in seventeenth-century fleet actions no one really knew what was going to happen. It was well established that the way to engage an enemy line of battle was to sail alongside it until the two lines were roughly parallel, and then to engage all at once, in a sort of formal exchange of fire, but the one clear lesson of naval warfare of the period was that this never happened. Some ships withheld fire until they were close, others fired when a long way off; some ships chose to board, others to engage in a gunnery duel; some captains understood their Admirals' intentions, others did not; wind and sea conditions and varying quantities of battle damage made things unpredictable and unworkable. The finest plans and the best intentions usually went awry. Unlike naval warfare in the late eighteenth century, when gunpowder was more efficient and guns more effective, not least with the introduction of the hugely powerful short-range gun the carronade, seventeenth-century fleet warfare was usually a trial of stamina and perseverance. The ability to withstand enemy fire and cope with damage was as important as the ability to inflict it. To adopt boxing terms, these were battles usually won on points decisions rather than by knockout. The previous two significant fleet battles, Beachy Head (1690) and Barfleur (1692), shared all of these characteristics. The French fleet may have been destroyed at Barfleur, but only because they were driven ashore and English fireships could get at them to effect their destruction: in the battle itself no French ships were taken. Skill, passion and ability on both sides were usually similar. No one was willing to give up their ship easily, so these giants of the sea tended to pound each other into a temporary truce, take a rest and then pound some more. It is also all too easy to lose perspective of chronology in the Age of Sail, but it is important to note that those two fleet battles were no recent event but ten and twelve years in the past respectively. And since Barfleur there had been no other fleet battles, so there had been no practice. Most of the men in both fleets would have been at neither battle; few indeed would have been at both and survived. For most this would have been an entirely new experience, or new enough for them to have to learn again, and there was no time to learn. The crisis was now; it was unfolding in front of their eyes.

When Benbow's fleet eventually formed into line the French were four miles away, still to windward and still travelling at two knots. Even if there was a difference in speed of half a knot between the fleets, they would still not meet for eight hours. The only thing to do was maintain formation, try to keep the French in sight and hope for a shift of wind that would blow the English ships down on the French on the very edge of a fresh breeze while the French lay becalmed, watching their fortunes unravel. This, remarkably, is exactly what happened and Benbow, towards the front of his line, soon found himself coming up with the rearmost ships of the enemy. But not all of his squadron had made such good ground, and several ships were still as much as four miles astern.

Benbow wanted to withhold fire until he had stretched his line the full length of the enemy and was within point-blank range, but such an ideal was simply impractical. It had been difficult enough to get any of the enemy ships within any useful range, and inevitably, with poorly experienced men trembling from nervous exhaustion, both sides began to exchange fire almost as soon as they could. This was not what

Benbow wanted but now he had to adapt. It was obvious that his rearmost ships, even if they were doing their utmost to come into battle, were still as much as two hours away, while the rearmost French ships were clearly prepared to defend themselves fiercely. If he was not careful Benbow would soon find himself the target. This possible turn of events was thrown into sharper focus when one of the English ships, the *Defiance* under Captain Richard Kirkby, simply stopped firing and drifted away to leeward. Without the support of one of the largest and closest ships, Benbow could do very little and both sides drifted apart, the French still trying their hardest to escape from the English foxes snapping at their heels. At no stage in this preliminary skirmish or throughout the next five days of action did the French ever want to stand and fight. If it was not apparent already, Benbow was going to have to force an unwilling enemy to battle, an extremely difficult scenario in warfare under sail for a man with slow ships. The peculiar behaviour of the *Defiance* in the first exchanges also made Benbow aware that he would have to force some of his own men to fight, another enormous challenge. From that moment on, Benbow's last fight was fought on two fronts.

The solution, Benbow reasoned, was to lead the line himself so that 'our people for shame would not fail to follow a good example'.[35] He therefore reissued the line of battle with his flagship at the very front and sent out verbal orders throughout the squadron that they were all to keep up with him during the night and then bear away – to attack the French – when he did so in the morning. But Benbow was badly disappointed and the following day turned out in much the same way as the first day, and the pattern repeated itself for the rest of the week. Winds backed, teasing the English with a brief advantage before veering and taking it away; light winds suddenly but briefly rose to a hurricane, and one violent burst was even described as a tornado.[36] Whenever any action was forced between English and French ships, it was only between the two, or occasionally three, leading English ships and the rearmost two or three French, and whenever a French ship was in danger of being cut off, the French Admiral swept down the line to her assistance, forcing the English ships clear to avoid being outnumbered and cut off themselves. At every stage the French fighting retreat was as valiant and well executed as the English attack was botched. The leading ships of the English fleet never received the help they needed and expected from the rest of their fleet, and were unable to force any kind of meaningful engagement that would stop the French in their slow but steady escape to Cartagena. One French ship, the captured English galley the *Ann*, was severely damaged, but so too was an English ship, the *Ruby*, which was ordered back to Jamaica. And then, in the early morning of the seventh day, Benbow's leg was fractured by a chain shot.

If Benbow's example had failed to inspire some of his captains to fight, then his injury gave them the excuse they needed not to. Shortly after receiving his wound the stricken Benbow was taken down to the surgeon of the *Bredah* on the orlop deck, while ordering the fight to continue. He was then visited by Captain Kirkby of the *Defiance*, the ship that had so curiously stopped fighting during the very first engagement and had failed to engage as Benbow had wished ever since. Kirkby expressed his regret to see the Admiral wounded but went on to claim that it was neither 'requisite nor convenient' to continue the fight. Benbow made no response, refused to shake Kirkby's hand, and insisted that the rest of the captains offer their opinions on how to proceed. They all met first and agreed to sign the following letter, which still survives in the original (see fig. 29).[37]

> At a consultation held on board HMS *Bredah*, Aug 24, 1702, off
> of Carthagena on the Maine Continent of America, it is the
> opinion of us whose names are undermentioned, vizt.
> First- of the great want of men in number, quality and the weak-
> ness of those they have.
> 2nd, The generall want of ammunition of most sorts.
> 3rd, Each ship's masts, yards, sailes, rigging and guns being all in
> a great measure disabled.
> 4th, the winds are small and variable that the shipps cannot be
> govern'd by any strength each ship has.

5th, having experienced the enemyes force in six dayes battle following, the Squadron consisting of five men-of-war and a fire-ship, under the command of Mons Du Cass, their equipage consisting in guns from 60 to 80, and having a great number of seamen and soldiers on board for the service of Spain. For which reasons above-mentioned, wee think it not fitt to engage the enemy at this time, but to keep them company this night, and observe their motion, and if a fairer opportunity shall happen (of wind and weather) once more to trye our strength with them.

R. Kirkby
Sam Vincent
John Constable
Chris Fogg
Cooper Wade
Thos Hudson.

In the preceding days several of these men had failed to fight their ships as Benbow expected but this was something else entirely: a collective refusal to follow a commander's orders. Regardless of whether or not the details of their argument were correct, this was mutiny, and worst of all, it was mutiny in the presence of the enemy. Not all of Benbow's officers were of the same mind, however, and Lieutenant Robert Thompson stood up to them: 'Gentlemen, have you ever seen or heard of such a sight before or read of the like in history?' Then, turning directly to one of the captains, Cooper Wade, he said, 'Is not this a shame?' He went on to tell Kirkby that they were like Flemings in the proverb who 'stay seven years for a fair wind and when it came are not ready for it'. Unfortunately for Thompson, as he himself recorded, 'At this saying Captain Kirkby looked earnestly at me and laughed.'[38]

We don't know what Benbow's immediate response was but he did write a measured reply to the letter, addressing each point in turn.

1. For want of men, I am well assur'd there was not eight men kill'd in all the ships besides the *Bredah*.

2. The want of ammunition was only a pretence, for they had enough.

3. That of their masts and yards to be disabled is false, for every ship's masts and yards stood very well, and in a much better condition than the enemy's.

4. They say that the winds are small and variable, that our shipps can not be govern'd which is erroneous, for all that time there was a fresh gale of wind, and such an opportunity wee have not had in six dayes, wee being then along their side, and to windward of them, that a fairer opportunity could never happen'd to engage.

5. They say that they have experienced the enemy's force in six dayes battle; the *Bredah*, *Ruby* and *Falmouth* indeed has in some measure, but the rest would not or durst not come up. They tell you that the French Squadron consisted in five men-of-war and a fire-shipp from 60 to 80 guns, which is likewise false, for those were but four men-of-war from 60 to 70 guns, and one of those was disabled so much that their Commadore [sic] was obliged to tow her, and as to their numbers of seamen and soldiers, I believe, we pretty well thinn'd them.

These are the reasons they give for not engaging the French, which are all a vision false and coawardize, which I doe aver.

    J. Benbow.[39]

For all of his desire, however, Benbow knew he was in no state to carry on the fight, and his captains had all refused. The squadron headed home to Jamaica. As soon as they arrived Benbow had his unruly captains imprisoned in their own ships and his rage began to be expressed in ink. 'I never met with the like misfortunes in all my life,' he wrote to the Navy Board.[40] According to Benbow the English colonists were equally appalled. 'The people in these parts are extremely incensed against them,' he wrote to Nottingham, 'having never heard or met with anything so base.'[41] For Benbow and most historians ever since the case was clear-cut. With a rare opportunity to engage the French to advantage, he had led an attack that was doomed to failure by the recalcitrance of his fellow officers. He had risked life and sacrificed limb while others were content to watch from a distance. He had been abandoned, stabbed in the back; he had been sacrificed on the altar of cowardice.

The famous letter reportedly sent to Benbow from du Casse which ended 'As for those treacherous captains that deserted you hang them up, for, by God, they deserve it. Yours du Casse' is most likely apocryphal nonsense,[42] but the carefully preserved testimonies of the hastily convened court martial bear out the rude facts and paint the disgraced captains as drunken incompetents in their best light and in their worst as monsters. Kirkby hid and dodged behind the mizzen-mast when there was any firing and gave no encouragement to his men; he even refused them victuals, the crew already having gone days without meat, calling them 'dog and rogue' as they stood by their guns;[43] he threatened to run a boatswain through with his sword when he encouraged Kirkby to open fire; Wade was 'somewhat mellow or otherwise in drink' and happily ordered his gunners to fire though well out of range of the enemy; and aboard the *Greenwich* an old foretopsail, 'fit for nothing but to be cast it's so thin that if it had shivered in the wind it would have blown out of the bolt rope', was bent as soon as the French were sighted. One witness was convinced this was done on purpose, that it 'looks more like a design than a chasing sail'.[44]

The written testimonies that continue in this vein are repetitive and almost endless, filling 233 bound folios, eighty-three of which are copies. Unsurprisingly, the court found two of the captains, Kirkby and Wade, guilty of not keeping the line, failing to support their admiral, cowardice, neglect of duty, mutiny and for the 'ill signed paper and consultation ... which obliged the Admiral ... to give over the chase and fight'. They were sentenced to death by firing squad and executed within days of their arrival in Plymouth, the first port at which their ship touched land.

They were shot on the forecastle of the *Bristol* on 16 April 1703 in Plymouth Sound in the presence of several captains, commissioned officers and numerous other spectators. Kirkby behaved himself throughout his imprisonment and died well, refusing to wear a blindfold, although the friend who described his death was careful to overlook Kirkby's well-known character flaws: earlier in his career he had been court-martialled for embezzlement, plunder, cruelty and oppression, was known to be bitter at being passed over for promotion on numerous occasions and already had a reputation as a coward. Wade, by contrast, was notably 'timorous and of a low spirit' the night before his execution.[45] Afterwards Kirkby's body was placed in his coffin, it 'being by him'. The men were buried in Plymouth Church and all but forgotten until the coffins were rediscovered by chance in 1816 when the pulpit was moved.[46]

Fogg and Vincent, the two captains who had supported Benbow in the fight yet still signed the letter refusing to continue, were dismissed from service but then reinstated after Benbow spoke up for them.[47] Captain John Constable of the *Windsor* was found guilty of breach of orders and drunkenness and ordered to be cashiered, though he was later pardoned. The Admiralty had acquired du Casse's account of the fight by January 1702,[48] and Benbow was reassured by the government that his own behaviour would in no way meet censure. Nottingham wrote to tell him that the Queen was 'extremely well pleased with your conduct and much offended with the baseness of those officers who deserted and betrayed you',[49] a reassurance that he never actually received because, on 4 November 1702, unaware that he had been promoted to Vice-Admiral of the White, and with his wounded leg unhealed, Benbow died after a piece of bone was removed from the wound. He was buried in St Andrew's Church in Kingston, Jamaica, and it was four months before the news of his death reached England.[50]

That, then, is the story of Benbow's last fight, the detail of which has endured in various forms for more than three centuries as an unrivalled tale of cowardice in the face of the enemy, cowardice that caused the death of one of England's finest Admirals. It is a tale that remains significant because of its villains as much as its hero. If one considers

Nelson as the ultimate example of courage, tenacity, ferocity and dedication to duty in the Age of Sail, the value of this Benbow story lies as much in the role of his captains as anti-Nelsons as it does in casting a shadow of Nelson himself onto Benbow. It is as much an example of how *not* to behave in the face of the enemy as it is of how to behave. Because of the story's value in illustrating this broad theme, however, the detail of the battle and its aftermath has rather been overlooked and inconvenient truths ignored. Both the reputations of Benbow as a precursor of Nelson, and of his captains as cowardice personified, have been bloated. Nothing is as black and white as it seems. Moreover, focusing purely on the detail of what happened on that day has caused some of the most interesting aspects of the fight and its position in English and naval history to be consistently disregarded. The fight is a phenomenon not just for what happened but for the fact that its fame has endured, and it is important to realize that the two are not necessarily linked as we might expect. To unravel this complex story we need to give serious thought to two questions, the first of which concerns our understanding of the battle itself and the second the means by which the battle became famous.

Historians of naval warfare are blessed in that records of the Admiralty's courts martial survive in the National Archives. In complex trials such as this, huge quantities of oral and written testimony were taken and more often than not the minutes of the day-to-day proceedings of the trials survive. This allows us a wonderful insight into the mechanics of sailing warfare – not only are we told what happened, but we are told why, and usually from numerous perspectives. Gunners and common seamen gave evidence alongside lieutenants, cooks, captains and admirals. There are, however, several problems with these high-profile cases. They were high profile because a great deal of national interest was attached to them; these trials had political currency and as such they were vulnerable to partisanship. The most famous example of this tendency is the trial of Richard Lestock after the Battle of Toulon (1744). Rather like Benbow's captains, Lestock had failed to support his Admiral, Thomas Matthews, as he engaged a combined Franco-Spanish fleet. Lestock dreamed up every excuse in the book, hid behind the detail of the Fighting Instructions, and was acquitted. For years this case was accepted as being proof of the unworkability of the command system in the navy, when in reality it was proof of a miscarriage of justice.

The trial of Benbow's captains calls for a similar analysis. In the 1690s courts martial were notoriously corrupt, with officers frequently, and wrongly, finding in their own favour.[51] To understand exactly what the minutes are telling us, and of course what they are *not* telling us, requires a level of objectivity that it is rarely afforded to the trial. Unlike the trials after Toulon, however, in which evidence was heard fairly but poorly interpreted, the main issue with the trial of Benbow's captains concerns how the court was actually run, and the man responsible for that was Benbow himself.

From this perspective the most striking aspect of the trial is the almost total absence of any minutes covering the cross-examination of witnesses and, even more seriously, the relative absence of any defence. One after another, testimonies against the captains were read or heard and nothing was allowed to be offered in return. Kirkby in particular was anxious that evidence was heard from his Master and one of his midshipmen, and when finally he was granted permission for his witnesses to come forward, the court broke for a two-hour, and probably boozy, lunch. When they came back and the witnesses were heard they were met by raucous shouting from Benbow that Kirkby lied. 'A trick, a trick,' echoed the President, Rear-Admiral William Whetstone.[52] Liars they may have been, but we do not know for certain, nor are we able to consider their testimony from the comfort of our desks, as it was never actually heard.

In a lengthy diatribe written shortly after the trial, Kirkby also claimed that Benbow had 'made use of his power to terrify some of the officers of the squadron and encourage others with hopes of preferment to form their affidavits to his desire'. He also claimed that he had been brought to trial by 'surprise', that is, that he had been given no time or facility to prepare his defence after a full six weeks of confinement. Nor had the influential and well-connected Kirkby been allowed to write home to any of his powerful Tory patrons. The Judge Advocate appointed by Benbow was a civilian and knew nothing of the ways of the Royal Navy, though this was not altogether unusual.[53] In short, Kirkby concluded, 'Benbow's presence and influence in the Court carried everything as he would have it.' Kirkby even claimed that Benbow had tried (and failed) to get legal permission for an immediate execution.[54]

If Benbow could play dirty tricks, so too could Kirkby. There is strong evidence in particular that he forced his Master to alter his journal,[55] and when a copy of the journal was actually presented to the court, large sections of the text had been put in square brackets. Those sections all give a favourable impression of Kirkby's behaviour, not least a lengthy paragraph that details the damage received by the *Defiance*. According to these new passages, possibly falsely entered, they had been engaged so closely and so hotly that the French had

> damnified our masts and yards viz. mizzen yards shot hanging [in] the splinters, the fore yard in the larboard ditto ½ way through, the main topmast under the main cap one third through, the forepart of the mainmast through the head in the wake of the rigging … the rigging viz. shot the main jeers and block, the main parrel to two parts the one of them stranded, the larboard main-topsail sheet, maintopmast stay, main lifts, main buntlines, maintop bowlines, tow backstays of the maintopmast, two pair of main shrouds at the head of the mast, both foretopsail bowlines, both foretopsail runners, the starboard brace of the foretopsail, two main topmast shrouds, two foretopmast backstays and several ropes more of our running rigging.[56]

Exactly what we are to make of this is unclear. None of it is particularly surprising given what we know about courts martial of the era, but what is interesting is Benbow's clear desire to have his captains punished, and quickly. Kirkby thought he had come across sufficient intelligence to suggest that Benbow was doing this to defend himself, that Benbow 'did not think himself safe from the question at home while I lived'. He even believed that Benbow's anxiety hastened his death.[57]

The sheer weight of evidence from the battle suggests that Benbow was permanently in the thick of the action, but Kirkby's point is important. Benbow would have known that someone would have to take the blame for the failed attack. He had been present at the Battle of Beachy Head in 1690, where the combined Anglo-Dutch fleet had failed to engage the French properly and upon his return Torrington, the Admiral of the allied fleet, swiftly found himself in the Tower. There was little suggestion that Torrington's captains were to blame, though the evidence could easily have been used to point in that direction. Now that Benbow found himself in a similar situation, he acted quickly. Entirely just in his actions though he may have felt, the rapid and apparently corrupt trial of his captains must be considered in the context of his consciously deflecting attention from himself as much as the more obvious context of his punishing them, through his influence on the court, for disobedience and mutiny.

The minutes of the trial also raise other issues that are important to our perception of the fight. As we already know, *all* of the English ships were undermanned, and the crews of those that had been in action were further debilitated by injury or death. The winds were light and variable, not just between squadrons but within each squadron. On the first day, for example, just as the English and French squadrons were divided by a full four miles, so was there a full four miles between Benbow's van and rear. So it was just as possible for Benbow's leading ships to enjoy a gale and his rearmost to be becalmed as it was for the English fleet to enjoy a gale and the French lie becalmed. That stretch of water is directly in the lee of the Sierra Nevada de Santa Marta mountains. In a part of the world that is always susceptible to isolated breezes, bizarre lulls and fierce, brief squalls, the mountains blocking and channelling the wind made the situation even worse. Because of the variety in ship design, hull condition and manning, none of the ships would have sailed at exactly the same speed in exactly the same conditions as any other. Uniformity of performance simply did not exist.

The engagement also took place over a full week, in which damage had to be repaired when the ships were not engaged. Opportunity for sleep would have been very small indeed, and with the constant likelihood of further action, exhaustion would have taken its toll. Even basic decisions would have become taxing but Benbow's captains were faced with the infuriating complexities of line warfare. For them the question was not necessarily 'Shall I attack the enemy?', as we might expect from the comfort of a broad perspective, but was intricately linked to the way that the line of battle worked. The line drew its security from the close links between each ship, like a chain. Each captain's responsibility lay as much in following the example of the ship directly ahead as it did in following the commander's orders. If the line was broken, then the line became vulnerable. In practice, however, not only was that cohesion extremely difficult to achieve, but it raised some confusing questions: what do you do if the ship directly ahead of you is crippled and is failing to keep the line? How do you act if the ship directly ahead of you is not crippled but is failing to keep her position in relation to the ship in front of *her*? Is your priority to maintain the line or to follow your Admiral's orders? What do you do if you are damaged? Do you do your best to muddle through, thereby endangering the cohesion of the line, or do you remove yourself from the line to repair? The question that particularly vexed Kirkby, as later came out in a defence published after his death, was how he should behave when his Admiral, at the head of the line, had stopped to engage the rearmost of the enemy. Kirkby believed he was required to maintain the line until the Admiral had moved on and made room for the ships following.[58] The answer to every one of these questions, moreover, depended both on circumstance and the personal preference of your commander. There was no widely accepted correct answer, but there were an awful lot of wrong ones.

To make matters worse, there was no method of two-way communication. A commander could make limited, clumsy signals over a limited distance and these could be augmented by oral instructions as and when possible, but a captain had no facility to ask a question. Thus Constable of the *Windsor* and Kirkby had no recourse when Benbow fired two guns and Constable and his first lieutenant thought it meant to sail up with the Admiral whereas Kirkby thought that it meant to keep the line.[59] All of this made it very difficult indeed to regain any sense of unity or combined purpose once something had happened, deliberate or otherwise, to endanger the cohesion of the line, and it is no exaggeration to say that Benbow's captains may have had no idea at all what was expected of them in the specific circumstances in which they found themselves. It is highly significant that one of them, Constable, was not found guilty of cowardice or breach of orders, but of ignorance: he simply didn't know what to do. A full four days into the fight he actually received coaching about how to behave when in line. Wade of the *Greenwich* also claimed ignorance, or at least confusion: 'he swore by god he did not understand those verbal orders and did believe that he ought not to follow them without a written order, the Master being of the same opinion'.[60]

If one considers the immense rate at which officers died on Caribbean duty, this is hardly surprising: Stephen Elliot of the *Scarborough* died in December 1701; John Leader of the *Kingston* died in January 1702; Benbow's Rear-Admiral and second in command, Henry Martin, died in February; and in March 1702 Captain John Viall of the *Pendennis* died. All of these men would have had to have been replaced by lower-ranking officers without the experience of command, and many of them, in turn, had been promoted prematurely. In the same month that Viall died, Benbow also lost his third lieutenant and a month later Lieutenant Bara of the *Defiance* died. By mid-April he had lost six hundred men and two hundred were sick ashore. The Caribbean, in short, fostered and encouraged inexperience and incompetence.

Finally, of course, the French, led by the wily and experienced du Casse, did not want to fight. Du Casse was an ex-privateer and slaver with years of Caribbean experience. He knew as well as anybody the tricks to escape a pursuer and the tricks Benbow would use to catch him. Benbow was furious of the French 'using all the shifts possibly they could to evade fighting (and when so, 'tis a very hard matter to join battle)' and historians have been correct to praise du Casse's skill.[61] With all of these factors buzzing around the fight the apparently black and white case of cowardice versus bravery quickly unravels and it becomes much easier to have some sympathy for Benbow's captains.

The second issue with our perception of the fight concerns its fame and the way it has been projected. At the heart of the problem is the question of rarity. It is easy to assume that the story of the fight has survived because it was exceptional – but that so-called exceptionalism needs to be considered very carefully. Most importantly, Benbow's last fight was *not* a unique example of cowardice, incompetence or misbehaviour in the face of the enemy, either in the immediate context of William III's or Anne's navies or even in the broader context of the Age of Sail. His captains' cowardice is but part of the story; by no means is it the sole reason that the story has endured. In fact by 1702 concerns over the ability of the Royal Navy to perform in the face of the enemy had reached something of a crisis point. There had been no significant naval victory for a decade, since Barfleur. Rather, there had been a series of disasters, not least that of the Smyrna convoy of 1693. In fact since the Glorious Revolution in 1688, numerous officers had been censured by Parliament for failing to do their duty in face of the enemy. Among their number were Killigrew in 1690, Delavall, Shovell and Killigrew in 1693, Carmarthen in 1695 and, most recently, in 1702, Sir John Munden, who had failed to engage a French squadron that had sailed past him into Corunna and then failed to engage them there. It is interesting that one of Benbow's captains lamented that this would be 'another parliament business'.[62]

Nor was Benbow's last fight a rare example of failure in fleet command. Benbow was simply unable to get his captains to do what he wished, but, because of the problems already explained, such failure was endemic; it was the norm. Over a century later, and in the competent hands of Nelson, widely considered one of the finest fleet commanders to have lived and one who used his genius to achieve a synthesis of personality and command system, several officers still behaved poorly at Trafalgar.[63] Certainly a factor here was wartime experience. Benbow's last fight was the *first* battle of the War of the Austrian Succession, and throughout the entire century, with the single exception of the Glorious First of June in 1794, the very first battle of the Revolutionary Wars with France, every opening battle of every war was a disaster for the Royal Navy, usually because of command failure.[64] Linked to this factor is Benbow's own experience of command. He may have been used to commanding fleets, but he had never before commanded a fleet in a fleet battle; amphibious operations, bombing raids and blockades, yes, but not fleet battle. In terms of fleet command this was not his last fight so much as his first. To be good at it was a skill that some acquired naturally, but even those lucky few benefited from experience. There was no teaching and no structured training system under which Benbow would have been prepared for this responsibility; to *expect* him to be any good at it would be wildly unfair.

Nor was Benbow's last fight a rare example of incompetence or cowardice in the Caribbean. Quite to the contrary, Benbow himself felt that the threat of illness and the likelihood of death, combined with the lure of immense wealth, attracted the very worst officers to Caribbean duty. Benbow later placed some of the blame on the Admiralty itself for not taking more care over officers chosen for Caribbean service. He wrote: 'it is what I always feared for the Captain that comes these voyages are reckoned as lost [i.e. will die from disease] so it may be thought anything may serve in these parts'. He went on to urge the Navy Board to send good men to match the French, 'for I find the French will defend their ships to the very last extremity'.[65] Long before the fight he had even raised the concern that undermanned ships on Caribbean service would give his officers 'room to excuse themselves why they did not perform'.[66] When first ordered to the Caribbean Benbow also made the interesting statement that 'he knew no difference of climates. For his part, he thought no officer had a right to choose his station, and he himself should be, at all times, ready to go to any part of the world His Majesty thought proper.'[67] At the same time it is significant that one of the most notorious mutinies of the period, that of the *Speedwell*, also happened in West Indian waters. On a number of levels, therefore, Benbow's fight was not a single example of failure amid a host of successes, but a failure amid failures. And Benbow himself expected it.

So in what way *was* Benbow's fight exceptional and why did it become famous? This question needs to be answered in three separate chronological contexts. The first is: why did Benbow's last fight matter to his contemporaries?

In terms of naval competence, Benbow's fight mattered for the exact opposite reason to what is so often assumed. It did not matter because it was a rare example of incompetence but because it was yet *another* example of incompetence. The efficiency of the Royal Navy had become a political football for a squabbling coalition government. Only in March, King William had died and been succeeded by Anne, his sister-in-law. One of Anne's first acts concerning the management of the navy was to replace the Lord High Admiral, the Earl of Pembroke, with her husband, Prince George of Denmark. A man interested in naval affairs but inexperienced in the complex machinations of contemporary politics, he became an easy target for opposition criticism.[68] From the moment of his appointment, naval affairs became subject to intense political focus. There was inevitably a rigid partisan divide over the popularity of a naval strategy, favoured by the Tories, as opposed to one that favoured continental land war, supported by the Whigs.[69] Indeed one can sense from contemporary correspondence that political vultures were gathering around the navy and they were very quick to act. Benbow's fight, although only a matter of months after the accession of Queen Anne, was not even the first attempt to condemn a naval act in that period and Sir John Munden had felt the full force of the opposition. Sent to intercept a French convoy carrying troops to the Caribbean, Munden failed to catch them before they darted into Corunna. Immediately it became blown out of all proportion and Munden was forced to explain himself at formal court martial. Fortunately reason prevailed, at least for a bit, and Munden was acquitted. The new Queen, however, now waded in, examined the minutes of the trial herself, declared Munden had not done his duty, and ordered her husband to discharge Munden. He never served again. A rather laconic Munden declared:

> It is an easy matter for any standers-by to say, after a design has miscarried, that, if you had been on this place instead of that, you had infallibly succeeded … But if it be considered that the sea is a wide place, and that we did not miss the enemy above an hour and a half's time, I hope my enemies will be persuaded to have another opinion of me.[70]

Central to both the Munden and Benbow cases was the interference of the new monarch, and it is important to recognize that Benbow's last fight was exceptional for the severity of the verdict – none of the other officers investigated for cowardice or incompetence between 1688 and 1702 had been executed – and the absence of a royal pardon. In most cases where the death penalty was handed down, reprieves were given, if only at the very last moment, with the noose around the convict's neck or guns pointed at his head.[71] And even the most vociferous of pamphleteers raging against the navy's incompetence suggested that commanders who refused to fight should lose two fingers and be sold into slavery, and hanged only if they ever returned to England. In reality even the most serious incidents rarely led to a conviction of a senior officer.[72] That commissioned officers would be both found guilty and then executed immediately was simply unthinkable. But Anne had clearly had enough, and to demonstrate her resilience and desire to force the navy into better shape, Kirkby and Wade became the fall guys. A strong queen was needed and she was quite prepared to make strong decisions.

The second reason that Benbow's last fight became famous is because it involved Benbow, who was already box-office material for his well-publicized exploits on the northern coast of France in 1693–5. We know that even then one contemporary newspaper called him the 'famous' Benbow'.[73] The story of his last fight became even more newsworthy when Benbow died, thus completing the perfect shape of the narrative. Now it was so easy to interpret it in black and white: on the one hand you had the cowardly captains, and on the other the very essence of selfless duty. As one biographer later wrote, Benbow possessed

That kind of virtue which is of greatest use to society; I mean sincere, active, and well-conducted public spirit. This it was, that distinguished the gentleman of whom I am now to speak [Benbow]. And that in an age when public spirit was not only out of fashion, but out of countenance; when a man who professed to love his country, if known to have sense, was thought to be a hypocrite; and, if not known to have it, a fool. Mr Benbow was neither.[74]

Another wrote: 'His very exit will veil the deeds of Ancient Heroes, as the sun the stars when upon the meridian',[75] and one more composed the heroic ditty:

Benbow, whom wounds animate to fame,
whose great soul triumphed o'er his shatter'd frame.[76]

He even became the subject of a prayer: 'If I lose a leg or suffer other deadly wound, help me to fight as Benbow fought; let me not flinch, let me not faint; help me to hold my head erect, bloody but still unbowed.'[77]

This polarized perception of the main characters – Benbow as good, Kirkby and Wade as bad – added more fuel to the political fire, for it bolstered the case of those who sought to take attention away from the inherent weakness of naval infrastructure, weaknesses that had left Benbow in charge of poor, inexperienced officers in undermanned, slow ships. For them the disaster could never be one of logistics, but only of base treachery, a motivation sung to the rafters by the pamphleteers.[78]

The value of the fight as a political tool was therefore enhanced by Benbow's extant fame but it was boosted even more by developments in the press that had a marked impact on the enduring fame of the fight. Two very important related facts about Benbow's last fight and the subsequent trials are often overlooked. It was the first naval trial *ever* to be published. Previously, the types of trials that made it to press concerned high treason, famous murderers or particularly notable examples of witchcraft.[79] The publication of Benbow's trial also occurred only five months after the first regular English-language newspaper, the *Daily Courant*, first appeared.

In the early 1700s the British press was experiencing nothing short of a revolution. In 1695 the Printing Act introduced by Charles II in 1692, designed 'to prevent the frequent Abuses in printing seditious, treasonable, and unlicensed Books and Pamphlets, and for regulating of Printing and Printing Presses',[80] was not renewed. Printing was no longer restricted and controlled; after 1695 anyone anywhere could set up a printing press and issue publications without being required to obtain permission. Within a single month of the Act's expiry, seven new news titles appeared in London. These newspapers became hugely successful in the burgeoning coffee-house and club culture of literate, middle-class London and their success quickly became self-perpetuating: being well informed became a mark of status. Naval interest was always high in contemporary newspapers. They were mostly read by the upper and middle classes: those with financial interest in overseas trade either as investors or as merchants, and by sea officers. The newspapers were the only easy way to stay abreast of most foreign issues, particularly land and sea campaigns. In fact, because of the difficulty of overland communication within England itself, foreign news was simply easier to come by and therefore dominated the papers.

The journalists wrote to entertain as much as to inform. They created controversy where there was none and they thrived on personal and political confrontation. Samuel Johnson, a journalist himself, described a journalist as 'a man without virtue who writes at home for his own profit. To these compositions is required neither genius nor Knowledge, neither industry nor sprightliness, but shame and indifference to truth are absolutely necessary.'[81] What journalists desired were stories that included foreign affairs, patriotism, heroism, cowardice, law-breaking, politics, religion, personal enmity and, if possible, execution. The ideal story, moreover, would run and run, so provocative would it be. In short, the naval controversies that became famous were those that ticked most, or all, of these boxes. Clearly defined schism among naval officers was perfect fuel for contemporary journalists who were keen to sniff out treachery and treason at critical moments in wars. Oversimplifying these stories for the page made them more attractive to read and therefore easier to sell.

In some respects, therefore, the trial became famous simply because it *could* become famous; it became famous because it was published. This was the first time in history that fame as we know it, the fame that is generated by the media and for the media, became possible. Subsequent generations then came to know the Benbow story because it had been immortalized in print in 1703 and was then reprinted a number of times. With Benbow's perspective of events in print, so it also became necessary for Kirkby's supporters to present their case, and in 1705 an explanation and defence of Kirkby's actions was published, probably by his sister.[82] Three years later the name John Benbow was in the press once more, this time because Benbow's son had survived a shipwreck, and spent four years living off sweet potatoes as a castaway in Madagascar before being rescued by a passing Dutch merchantman. To put it bluntly, at this early stage Benbow's fame endured because his name, as well as his fight, were familiar. This aspect of the Benbow controversy is mirrored by the other famous naval controversies: all of their trials were published, along with the inevitable welter of warring pamphlets that fed on the carrion of those trials.

The fame of Benbow's last fight never died, however, and that is what makes it so remarkable. In the immediate aftermath of the disastrous Battle of Toulon, in which Lestock had not supported Admiral Matthews, a case with so many apparent similarities with Benbow's last fight, the trial was reprinted by Kirkby and Wade, complete with a copy of the Fighting Instructions and Articles of War as a sort of intellectual puzzle for the general public: read this and you decide! An edited version of the trial was then printed as footnotes in his first major biography, published in 1778–9 following the disastrous Battle of Ushant (1778). Then, in the immediate aftermath of the Battle of Trafalgar (1805), interest in Benbow was roused again, this time in attempts to draw direct comparisons between Benbow and Nelson, as each had died both for his duty and his country. This is when Benbow began to be known as the 'Nelson of his time', most publicly in John Thomas's carving of the Benbow monument in St Mary's Church, Shrewsbury, in 1843. With the public's unquenchable thirst for naval heroes, he appeared in Burney's *Naval Heroes of Great Britain* (1806) and Leith's *Lives of the most eminent British naval heroes* (1809), and then received his own dedicated essay in the widely circulated *Gentleman's Magazine* of 1819. The minutes of his court martial had also been reprinted in 1808 in a miscellaneous collection of 'scarce, curious and entertaining pamphlets and tracts'. Benbow's last fight now sat alongside ghost stories, travel accounts and swashbuckling tales of impostors.[83]

Thirty years later, with interest in the history of the sailing navy once again piqued by the advent of steam, the very era in which Turner painted his *Fighting 'Temeraire'*, Benbow was once again revived, first in the theatre with a three-act drama called *Admiral Benbow* which opened on 16 April 1838, and then in published works like Cunningham's *Lives of Eminent Englishmen* (1840), Edgar's *Sea Kings and Naval Heroes* (1861) and Campbell's *Fifty Two Stories of the British Navy* (1896). His court martial was published again in 1843. Popular songs concerning Benbow's fate continued to appear, and none better than the well-composed *Admiral Benbow*, which began:

> So come all you brave fellows, wherever you've been,
> Let us drink a good health to the King and the Queen,
> And another good health to the girls that we know,
> And a third in remembrance of great Admiral Benbow.

In these years public interest in naval history also blossomed, encouraged by the pioneers of professional naval history, John Knox Laughton and Alfred Thayer Mahan. Both produced important works, not least Mahan's *The Influence of Seapower upon History 1660–1783* (1890), which became a publishing phenomenon, and Laughton was in great part responsible for the Royal Naval Exhibition of 1891, which two million people attended over five months.[84] By then the name of Benbow had been worshipped in the Royal Navy to the extent that when, in 1813, a 74-gun Third Rate was launched at Rotherhithe she was named HMS *Benbow*. Her huge figurehead is now preserved at Portsmouth Dockyard. A steam battleship followed in 1888 and another in 1913 which fought at Jutland. The name was preserved, appropriately, for the naval base in Trinidad until 1947, and was used for a Wrens' station in Ireland during the Second World War. We also know that as early as the 1770s sailors of the lower deck had become 'remarkably fond of claiming Benbow as their own' as a gutsy sailor of unquestionable commitment to duty, and as one of the men in the annals of naval history who 'were sailors, rose by being sailors, and were proud of being sailors much more than of their flags'.[85] As his anonymous biographer writing in the *Naval Chronicle* put it in 1808: 'from the admiral to the cabin-boy, the name of Benbow is so familiar to every individual in the navy, and his memory is so often mentioned with respect and admiration, that no excuse can be requisite for presenting a condensed narrative of his life and actions'.[86]

But it was just at the end of this period that one of the most important ingredients to Benbow's fame was added to the already impressive jigsaw. A thirty-year-old author named Robert Louis Stevenson, while holidaying with members of his family at Braemar in the Highlands, came across Lloyd, his stepson, who was, in his own words:

> busy with a box of paints. I happened to be tinting a map of an island I had drawn. Stevenson came in as I was finishing it, and with his affectionate interest in everything I was doing, leaned over my shoulder, and was soon elaborating the map and naming it. I shall never forget the thrill of Skeleton Island, Spyglass Hill, nor the heart-stirring climax of the three red crosses! And the greater climax still when he wrote down the words 'Treasure Island' at the top right-hand corner! And he seemed to know so much about it too —— the pirates, the buried treasure, the man who had been marooned on the island … 'Oh, for a story about it,' I exclaimed, in a heaven of enchantment …[87]

Within three days Stevenson had written the first three chapters and the story was serialized in 1881–2 in the magazine *Young Folks* under the title *The Sea Cook*. A year later it was published for the first time as a novel entitled *Treasure Island*, to become a publishing phenomenon and one of the most frequently dramatized of all novels. Part of the allure lies in the alliterative and beguiling beauty of the characters' names: Jim Hawkins, Billy Bones, Blind Pew, Black Dog, Captain Flint and, of course, Long John Silver. Ever a man with an ear for a name, Stevenson began the book in a pub whose name was carefully chosen to reek of maritime legend. He called it The Admiral Benbow.

Thereafter an endless host of mini-biographies and essays were published throughout the early twentieth century, far too many to name each here.[88] Novels were even published using Benbow's name to conjure up a bygone era, such as Kingston's *Roger Willoughby, or the Times of*

Benbow (1900) and Herbert's *Humphrey Bold, A Story of the Time of Benbow* (1909), while in 1967 Ned Sherrin and Caryl Brahms co-authored *Benbow Was His Name*, a novel loosely based on the Benbow story and inspired by a similar work that they had written for BBC television, itself inspired by a work they had written for BBC radio. And, once the book was finished, they wrote a stage play and film.

Much of this fitted very neatly into the First World War genre of *Boy's Own* adventure stories and a heightened contemporary interest in naval history and historic ships, but the acceleration of interest in the years immediately after the publication of *Treasure Island* is unmistakable. In some ways Benbow's fame has endured simply because of a chance resurrection by a little-known Scottish author, and his fame grew as Stevenson's did. This is not entirely unusual. Consider Admiral Byng. Byng was shot on his own quarterdeck like a diseased dog for failing to do his utmost to engage the enemy in 1756, a remarkable event that enjoyed its own moment of glory in the contemporary press. There it would have remained, however, until the French writer Voltaire became involved. So astonished was he at Byng's fate that he wrote, in his celebrated satire *Candide* (1759): '*Dans ce pays-ci, il est bon de tuer de temps en temps un amiral pour encourager les autres*' ('In this country it is good to kill an admiral from time to time, to encourage the others'). '*Pour encourager les autres*' has become famous in its own right as a beautiful and effortlessly succinct phrase that encapsulates the contemporary approach to crime and punishment. It was even used as the title for a collection of essays celebrating the tercentenary of Voltaire's birth in 1994.[89] Since then it has become something of a general-knowledge cliché in crosswords and pub quizzes. Byng's fame has, to a large extent, simply piggy-backed on Voltaire's skill as a wordsmith, rather as Benbow is linked to Stevenson and HMS *Temeraire* to Turner.

Benbow and Byng's fame makes the point very clearly that the most famous examples of eighteenth-century naval controversy have endured for myriad reasons, some connected, some not, and very few of these have anything to do with what actually happened at the time. Ironically, more people will associate the name of Benbow with Blind Pew, Billy Bones and Jim Hawkins than with his great naval contemporaries

Rooke, Russell, Herbert, Shovell and Bart or the notorious privateer René Duguay-Trouin. For this reason Benbow's fame must be carefully read like a palimpsest: there are layers upon layers of fame, acquired for different reasons and at different times, and each layer is important in its own right. Hopefully this book will now become the start of another layer and will enthuse other scholars to continue the hunt for Benbow. Our understanding of him will never be complete, but in among the encrusted myths, the real Benbow, or perhaps the shadow of him, can be glimpsed as he flits between the moonlit squalls.

Epilogue:
Benbow's Celebrity

So come all you brave fellows, wheresoever you have been,
Let us drink a good health to our King and our Queen,
And another good health to the girls that we know,
And a third in remembrance of brave Admiral Benbow.[1]

Anyone embarking on an investigation of Benbow's life stumbles almost immediately on the apocryphal and dramatic stories that have become attached to him, many of which this book has exposed as groundless and in every sense inadequate testimony for confident biography. There is no evidence that he was linked to an executed turncoat who fought in the Civil War; that his father met and was personally thanked by Charles II; that he decapitated several Barbary corsairs and gave the salted heads to Spanish customs officials in a sack; or that he was taken to the Spanish Court because of this heroic deed. Nor is there any evidence that, as captain of a merchantman, he fought off another corsair attack, or that he took part in the greatest fleet battle of his lifetime, Barfleur.

These stories are all part of the rich, Technicolor tapestry of the Benbow legend. Once his fame had peaked, his past was destined to be exploded (and invented), and what survives are sharp, colourful shards of history embedded in our national biography. Incomplete but significant in its own way, each inflicts scars on history more permanent than one would expect or hope. To replace these squalid apocrypha, this book has uncovered an extraordinary life of a breadth, scope and variety that had never been suspected of Benbow or, indeed of any other naval officer in this period. That life is infinitely more interesting, rewarding and important than his early biographies suggested. It has transformed Benbow from a caricature to a rounded individual who was a major player in the development of the Royal Navy and the world in the late seventeenth century.

Benbow probably worked on England's inland waterways; he was a merchant, trading between England and the Mediterranean; he hunted and fought corsairs in the Mediterranean, privateers in the Channel and North Sea and pirates in the Caribbean; he fought in fleet battles and imposed both close and distant blockades; he took part in amphibious raids and coastal bombardment and was the first Englishman to command a coastal bombardment; he sailed in one of the earliest examples of the Western Squadron; he was involved in the preparations for at least one major invasion (1692) and may have taken part in another (1688); he transformed our knowledge of the hydrography of northern France and the Caribbean and he was involved in ship design, construction, repair and logistics, and there is clear evidence that he was an innovator in these fields. He certainly held ingenuity highly as a professional virtue.[2] He was also a very skilled navigator as well as a naval administrator and adviser on naval strategy; he helped build hospitals and dispense charity; and he was involved in the development of lighthouses, sea-marks and other navigational aides.

This breadth of experience probably makes Benbow unique and it makes one of the most easily overlooked aspects of his life one of the most important. After he died, his widow, Martha, petitioned the Admiralty for assistance. She had lost a husband who had served the navy well. She and her five children were now dependent on the very charity Benbow had spent so much of his time developing. She received an annual income, in perpetuity, of £200.[3] This was the navy at its very best, an institution forged by those who paid as much attention to its administration and its dependants as they did to its fighting capacity.

There is certainly good evidence to suggest that Benbow's industriousness, experience and skill were valued. Herbert, Rooke, Shovell, Berkeley, Halley and the East India Company all specifically asked for him to serve with or for them,[4] and it is clear that time and again the Admiralty turned to Benbow and no other when new responsibilities appeared. The mid-1690s are a fine example. In the aftermath of Barfleur, Benbow was ordered to help design bomb vessels, inspect suitable ships for conversion, oversee their construction, prepare them for campaigns, sail them to the enemy coast, lead them in battle, survey them after battle, supervise their return and help redesign them. When a change in strategy dictated that blockade and convoy were required to blunt the French privateers, the Admiralty turned to Benbow. When a new strategy of patrolling the Channel's western approaches was mooted, the Admiralty turned to Benbow. When the novel idea of a 'winter water guard' was proposed for those same seas, the Admiralty turned to Benbow. When it became clear that the Caribbean would be a new theatre of war and the navy needed both a powerful presence and a skilled navigator to survey enemy harbours and unknown passages, the Admiralty turned to Benbow. When war was expected to erupt and the Admiralty needed someone to intercept the Spanish *flota*, it turned to Benbow. Finally, when someone was needed to protect English colonies in the Caribbean, the Admiralty turned to Benbow.

It is a *curriculum vitae* that oozes professional competence, a perception shared by those who penned contemporary obituaries. 'O unfortunate people,' wrote one of the earliest commentators after Benbow's death, 'to lose a man more valuable than the Indies.'[5] Another claimed, in a ringing endorsement of the skill Benbow bought to his various interests, that he had 'a probity that was never questioned, and a knowledge of men and things, which always procured him credit in whatever station he appeared'.[6] Yet another biographer claimed: 'He was never wanting in his own example, spending his whole time in his duty.'[7] The evidence is strong that Benbow was highly valued. Time and again he was questioned, listened to, respected and rewarded. The great irony of his life is that he is famed for his last fight, which is one of the least interesting aspects of his career and the episode that shows him in the worst light.

Any biographer must also be aware that the net he casts to catch his subject is as much a device to ensnare as it is a collection of holes tied together with string. The fire in 1717 that destroyed so many of Benbow's letters to the Admiralty has badly affected our perception of him, but even for such a dedicated sailor as he was, his professional life was only part of the man and, while we do know some extraordinary facts about his home life, such as the colour of his bed linen and the fruit trees in his garden, we know nothing at all about his relationship with his wife or children. Any assessment of the professional life is necessarily clouded by our blindness of the private. Much of the detail surrounding his career also comes from official records such as paybooks or logs and so much of it all seems so definite. But this can never have been the case. What we are still missing is the cloud of uncertainty that surrounds anyone's life – the alternatives, missed chances or accidents; the indecision, luck or intent. In fact the only stage of Benbow's career at which we know *why* something happened was his promotion from Master Attendant at Chatham to Master Attendant at Deptford – because we know that he asked for the job. But what of his promotion from Master's Mate to Master, from Master to Lieutenant, from Lieutenant to Captain, or from Captain to flag rank? How much of this was chosen for him? How much did he make happen?

Nor do we know how Benbow was perceived by others close to him. There is no record of anyone being particularly close to him and there is certainly no correspondence between him and his friends. Perhaps he had none and was wholeheartedly dedicated to his career. It would not be surprising, given the intensity of his work. One writer testified to his sobriety, a rare trait indeed for the seventeenth century.[8] For all of the information uncovered, we are still lacking a vivid sense of the person and any attempt to recreate that would be nothing more than meaningless assertion. But we do know something very important about Benbow: he was proud, possibly to the point of arrogance but, above all, he was deeply secure in his own professional competence. And here is the point that is central to the whole story.

Benbow had high expectations of himself and much was expected of him at the time. Just before news of the disaster of his last fight reached England, a rumour had spread that his service in the Caribbean had reaped enormous success: that he had taken and destroyed all the French Leeward Islands except Martinique.[9] Nothing could have been further from the truth: by then he had done little more than annoy the

Governor of Jamaica and gather intelligence. And what of his last fight? Here the question of expectation is more complicated than many suspect. It is widely accepted now, as it was then, that Benbow's captains did not do as their admiral, or anyone else, expected. But what of Benbow? It is easy to say that he acted well, but he did so as a captain and not as a fleet commander. As a fleet commander Benbow was expected to lead his fleet into battle and to win. That he failed to do. But at no stage was he censured. His failure was attributed to the cowardice of his officers and not to his ability as a commander. Very few fleet commanders in history have been so fortunate.

If viewed as a product of his time, however, this result is not surprising. The true importance of the debacle of Benbow's last fight is that it throws into sharp relief both how far the Royal Navy had come and how far it had to go. He was fighting on the far side of the world, but without the tools needed to do so successfully. The infrastructure that would allow fleet commanders to gain the loyalty of their subordinates was simply not in place. The navy had yet to learn that reward was a more potent motivation than punishment and that punishment itself never had a place in an uncertain and corrupt legal system. Nor was there a tradition to build upon of sustained victory, or a concept of professional camaraderie. The notion of duty in the face of the enemy, apparently so strong in Benbow, was simply not shared in the way that it was later in the century. Even at the great victories of the mid to late eighteenth century, the two battles of Finisterre (1747) and those of Quiberon Bay (1759), the Glorious First of June (1794) and Trafalgar (1805), that sense of duty was neither service-wide nor reliable, but it was far more potent than it had been in 1702. The end of the seventeenth century was a time when 'work that needed to be done was done, but not expeditiously' and when 'authority was accepted and, indeed asserted, but not completely'.[10]

The final point must relate to our own expectations of Benbow and his captains. Not only did Benbow have no experience of fleet command, but his fleet had no desire to be commanded. His ships were weak and he faced a highly skilled enemy. He cannot be expected to have defeated du Casse. At a far more fundamental level, however, there is much that we can appreciate about the Benbow story today, and we can do so in exactly the same way that his contemporaries did and generations have done since. Difficult and quarrelsome he may have been, but Benbow was undoubtedly brave and dedicated to his duty and as such he *deserved* better. He deserved support from those who could give it, and he deserved help when he needed it most. Therein lies the broad appeal of the Benbow story. It is not one of the navy, or of the complexities of command, signalling, flags and expectation, but of simple human justice. That is where the mass appeal of his story lies; that is why it was publicized as never before; and that is why Benbow became the first true English naval hero. His heroism *is* intricately linked to the aggressive fighting spirit that was shared by Edward Hawke in the 1740s and 1750s and Horatio Nelson in the 1790s and 1800s. In those narrow terms, the direct ancestry claimed by that extraordinary book in the National Maritime Museum that started this story, a book perhaps once owned by Benbow, is valid even if its authenticity is unproven. Now we know, however, that there was so much more to Benbow than his desire to fight. That was only one part of his character, only one part of how he was perceived in the past, and it must remain only one part of how we remember him in the future. A contemporary author claimed that Benbow 'deserved a better fate',[11] meaning explicitly that he deserved better support in his last fight. It is a statement that is equally relevant to how we remember him now. Ever since his death his fate has been sealed: he has been for ever linked to that sorry Battle of Cape Santa Marta. It is time for that to change – he deserves better.

Benbow's Chronology

1642
August. Outbreak of English Civil War
Colonel John Benbow, possibly Admiral John Benbow's father or uncle, declares for Parliament.

1647
August. Cromwell seizes power in London with Charles I captive.

1649
30 January. Charles I executed.

1651
Colonel John Benbow swaps sides and declares for the Royalists.
3 September. Charles II defeated at Worcester and escapes abroad.
15 October. Colonel John Benbow executed as a traitor at Shrewsbury Castle.

c. **1652**
John Benbow, the future Admiral, is born.

1652–4
First Dutch War.

1658
3 September. Oliver Cromwell dies and his son, Richard, takes power.

1660
28 May. Charles II leaves exile and is restored to the throne.

1662

Charles II marries Catherine of Braganza and receives the colonies of Tangier and Bombay as part of her dowry.

c. 1665

Benbow possibly moves to Shropshire to work as a bargeman on the Severn.

1665–7

Second Dutch War

1672–4

Third Dutch War

1676

Sir John Narborough sent to the Mediterranean to wage war against Barbary Pirates.

1677

The Admiralty launches its Thirty Ships building programme.

1678

27 January. Benbow joins HMS *Phoenix* from another, unknown, British warship as Master's Mate and sails for Tangier with Herbert.
Spring. A Moroccan army masses at Tangier.
30 April. Benbow promoted to Master's Mate of Herbert's flagship *Rupert*.

1679

15 June. Benbow promoted to Master of HMS *Nonsuch*.

1680

March. Mulai Ismail launches full assault on Tangier.
27 October. Moorish army routed at Tangier by English and Spanish cavalry charge.

1681

27–28 March. Corsair the *Golden Horse of Algiers* is captured.

Benbow Court Martialled.
August. HMS *Nonsuch* sent home. Benbow paid off.

1682
Peace secured with Algiers that would last until 1833.

1683
16 June. Benbow sails on merchant voyage to Mediterranean as captain of ketch *London*.
3 December. Benbow sails on merchant voyage to Mediterranean as captain of pink *Joseph*.

1684
6 February. Tangier abandoned by English forces.
17 July. Benbow sails on merchant voyage to Mediterranean as captain of pink *Joseph*.

1685
6 February. Charles II dies. James Stuart crowned James II of England and VII of Scotland.
13 November. Benbow sails on merchant voyage to Mediterranean as captain of *Malaga Frigate*.

1686
May. Benbow returns with the *Malaga Frigate* and leaves immediately for another Mediterranean voyage.
Benbow possibly attacked by Corsairs and possibly decapitates thirteen corsairs and presents the heads in a sack to Cadiz magistrates.

1687
May. Benbow possibly fights off another Corsair attack.
5 December. Benbow returns on *Malaga Frigate* and leaves immediately for another cruise.

1688
22 June. Benbow returns on *Malaga Frigate* and leaves immediately. He does not return.

25 September. France declares war on the League of Augsburg. The Nine Years' War begins.

18 October. Dutch invasion fleet sails but is beaten back by bad weather.

1 November. Dutch invasion fleet sails again. William lands in Torbay.

1689

12 February. William and Mary crowned King and Queen of England.

11 May. Herbert beaten off at the Battle of Bantry Bay. There is no evidence of Benbow's involvement but it is not out of the question as, in June, he joins the *Elizabeth* from another, unknown ship.

8 June. Benbow rated Third Lieutenant of the Third Rate HMS *Elizabeth*, Herbert's flagship. He has come from another, unknown British warship.

20 September. Benbow promoted to Captain of the Third Rate HMS *York*, an extraordinary jump in rank.

26 October. Benbow made Captain of the Third Rate HMS *Bonaventure*.

8 November. Benbow appointed Master Attendant of Chatham Dockyard.

12 November. Benbow made Captain of the First Rate HMS *Britannia*. His journey from Third Lieutenant of a Third Rate to Captain of a First Rate is completed in five months without any enemy contact or significant operation of any kind. Nothing is more indicative of his involvement in the Revolution of 1688 than this fast-tracking of his career in 1689.

18 November. HMS *Britannia* docked and found to be rotten.

December. Work is begun on a new dockyard at Plymouth.

1690

March. Benbow applies to Trinity House for a Master's certificate.

14 Benbow appointed Master Attendant of Deptford Dockyard.

2 April. Benbow appointed Master of the First Rate HMS *Royal Sovereign*, Herbert's flagship.

30 June. Battle of Beachy Head. Combined British and Dutch fleet defeated by the French who gain absolute control of the Channel but fail to take advantage. Benbow present on board HMS *Royal Sovereign*.

1691

Spring. Benbow moves to the newly-repaired HMS *Britannia*, serving under Russell.

The campaign season is spent hunting unsuccessfully for Tourville in the Western Approaches.

1692
11 February. Benbow elected to the Younger Brethren of Trinity House.
4 May. Benbow elected to the Elder Brethren of Trinity House, an extraordinarily fast promotion.
June. Trinity House approves proposals for an offshore lighthouse on the Eddystone Rocks off Plymouth.
18-24 May. Battle of Barfleur/La Hougue. French fleet destroyed by English fireships. Benbow not present.
July. Invasion of St. Malo aborted at the last minute because of strategic indecision. Benbow was instrumental in the impressive logistical preparations.

1693
The French navy adopt the *Guerre de Course*, attacking British trade with squadrons of privateers.
17 June. The Smyrna convoy is captured by the French, the British lose 82 merchantmen sunk or captured.
November. Benbow bombards St. Malo, burns the convent and explodes a 300-ton machine vessel in the harbour.

1694
Spring. Benbow cruises off St Malo capturing several prizes.
June. English attack near Brest beaten off with heavy casualties.
July. Benbow bombards Dieppe and Le Havre with great success.
August. Benbow cruising again off St Malo and takes several prizes.
September. Benbow is instrumental in the bombardment of Dunkirk that ends in frustration and failure.
September. Benbow brings his bombardment fleet through sandbanks off Calais but is forced clear by adverse winds.
September. Benbow is granted pay of Rear-Admiral.
December. Mary dies and William commits himself to build a hospital for seamen at Greenwich, one of Mary's favourite schemes. Benbow serves on the Grand Committee and Revenue Sub-Committee to oversee design and construction.

1695

March. Benbow cruises off St Malo, takes several prizes and captures a fort near Granville.

June. Benbow bombards St Malo and Granville with great success.

September. Benbow is requested by name to escort an East India Convoy.

1696

April. Benbow promoted to Rear-Admiral of the Blue. He bombards Calais.

3 May. Benbow discharged from his post as Master Attendant at Deptford.

May. Benbow blockades Dunkirk but Bart escapes and captures a large Dutch convoy. Benbow chases Bart into the Kattegat Sea before being forced home for victuals and repair.

June. Benbow escorts home the Hamburg and Muscovy convoys.

June. Benbow leases Sayes Court.

September. Benbow twice chases squadrons of privateers but with no success as his ships are in such poor condition.

December. Benbow cruises in the western approaches of the Channel to protect British trade, a fundamental shift in the geography of British naval strategy.

1697

May. Benbow cruises in the western approaches and escorts East India Convoy outbound and Virginia convoy inbound.

July. Benbow takes several prizes off Brest and then more off Dunkirk.

10 September. Treaty of Ryswick ends the Nine Year's War. Benbow helps bring troops back from Flanders.

1698

January. Peter the Great arrives in England and sub-lets Sayes Court from Benbow.

May. Benbow petitions the Admiralty to cover the repair costs after Peter's destruction of Sayes Court.

November. The Scots found the Darien colony.

28 November. Benbow escorts Edmund Halley to the Azores on the way to the Caribbean. Benbow goes on to cruise the Caribbean gathering hydrographical, military and political intelligence.

1699

Spring. Rumours arrive that Captain Kidd is sheltering in the Caribbean. Benbow hunts for him unsuccessfully.

June. Benbow heads home via the eastern Seaboard of America. He takes home some, and possibly all, of Captain Kidd's recovered treasure, several of his men and some from Henry Avery's crew.

1700

April. Benbow is prompted to Rear-Admiral of the Red.

July. Benbow is promoted to Vice-Admiral of the Blue.

November. Charles II of Spain dies naming the duc D'Anjou, grandson of Louis XIV of France as his sole heir. His will is contested.

November. With war on the horizon Benbow prepares his fleet for another Caribbean cruise.

1701

October. Benbow cruises off the Azores unsuccessfully for the Spanish flota.

November. Benbow arrives in the Caribbean.

1702

January. Benbow builds a hospital on Jamaica.

8 March. William III dies and Anne, daughter of James II, becomes Queen.

23 April. War is declared against France, which becomes known as the War of the Spanish Succession and lasts for eleven years.

May. Sir John Munden fails to intercept French a convoy bound for Caribbean and is discharged.

18 August. Benbow's last fight.

4 November. Benbow dies.

1703

16 April. Captains Kirkby and Wade are executed in Plymouth. The minutes of their Court Martial are published, the first naval trial ever to be made accessible to the general public.

1705

A defence of Richard Kirkby is published, probably written by his sister.

1708

Benbow's son, John, enjoys some brief fame for surviving a shipwreck and living as a castaway on Madagascar for four years.

1744

The minutes of Kirkby and Wade's trial are published once more in the aftermath of the indecisive battle of Toulon.

1778

The minutes of Kirkby and Wade's trial are published again, this time in the aftermath of the indecisive Battle of Ushant.

1805

Benbow starts to become known as the 'Nelson of his time' in the aftermath of the death of Nelson at the battle of Trafalgar.

1813

The 74-gun HMS *Benbow* is launched at Rotherhithe. Two other warships with his name follow in 1888 and 1913.

1838–1880

Benbow's fame grows amid increased interest in the 'heroic age of sail' as steampower eclipses sail.

1881–2

Robert Louis Stevenson's *Treasure Island* is first serialised as *The Sea Cook* making Benbow's name famous to an entirely new audience.

1967

Ned Sherrin and Caryl Brahms co-author *Benbow Was His Name*, a novel loosely based on his life.

APPENDIX II

Benbow's Warships

If the late seventeenth century is frustrating for its shortage of written sources, it is particularly blessed with images of warships which make that period unique. But whereas the visual record of warships from the eighteenth and nineteenth centuries is characterized by detailed ship plans of increasing complexity as draughtsmen were forced to incorporate things like steam engines, torpedo tubes and electrical wiring, there is simply no equivalent portfolio of technical drawings from the seventeenth century. There is, however, a significant archive of warship portraits made by draughtsmen of extraordinary skill, and these portraits tell us a great deal about the warships of the time and in many instances offer insights into the appearance and even performance of these warships that no technical drawing, however minutely detailed, could ever illuminate. This archive exists largely because of two Dutchmen: Willem van de Velde and his son, also called Willem. They came to England in 1673 to work for Charles II and surveyed a large portion of the English fleet at various times over the following years. Their images are all highly distinctive.

There is also an impressive archive of exquisite ship models from exactly this period. These models provide the three-dimensional details that the drawings cannot, and reveal just how colourful the ships were with their gilded sterns and painted gunports. Because Benbow's career spanned the exact years in which ship modelling and portraiture reached a level of professional skill previously unknown, it is both possible and rewarding to compile a visual appendix of some of the vessels on which he served.

It is important to realize, however, that this appendix is not comprehensive in a number of ways. There are both gaps in our knowledge of

Benbow's naval career, and there are certain ships that do not have a positively identified portrait or model. We know, for example, that Benbow served aboard at least one other ship before he joined his first recorded ship, the *Phoenix*. We also know that, after the Glorious Revolution of 1688, he served aboard another, unknown one before he was made third lieutenant of Herbert's flagship, the *Elizabeth*. Benbow was also highly mobile between 1693 and 1697, when he launched operations against the coast of France, blockaded Dunkirk, escorted convoys in the Atlantic and North Sea and cruised the western approaches. Frequently the ships' administrators had trouble keeping up. We know, for example, that in October 1696 Benbow came aboard the Third Rate *Lancaster*, but we don't know how long he stayed, where he had come from or where he went,[1] and that summer he was on the paybooks of both the *Suffolk* (7 May to 22 September) and the *Norfolk* (23 July to 5 October).[2] For reasons of space those ships on which Benbow spent a very short period, or for which his presence is known but the dates are uncertain, have been omitted. These are: the *York* (two weeks in October/November 1689); *Experiment Galley* (May 1696), whose docking he oversaw at Chatham in the first few weeks of 1690; *Devonshire* (May 1697); *Cornwall* (June 1697); *Lancaster* (an unknown period in 1697); *Torbay* (July 1697); *Newarke* (July 1697); *Centurion* (November 1697).

The portraits and models, moreover, are not always easy to identify. In some instances they are given a title, but in others that title does not exist or the paper has been torn, leaving a tantalizing glimpse of two or perhaps three letters. Nevertheless, our knowledge of shipbuilding and design from the period is sufficiently detailed that, in some cases, we can recognize a ship from her appearance alone, or at least establish her class. In the instances where Benbow's ships cannot be positively identified with a model or image, I have chosen an image from the same or a similar class. In some instances the similarity between ships of the same class was such that they were identical to any but the most critical eye. This appendix, therefore, can be taken as a fair representation of the most significant ships in Benbow's career.

These images reveal a career that directly reflects the most significant strategic shifts in the period. Benbow begins in the late 1670s aboard small, fast ships, perfect for hunting corsairs in foreign waters and then, after 1688, serves aboard increasingly larger ones. By 1690 he is aboard the *Britannia* and then the *Royal Sovereign*, two of the largest ships yet built by English shipwrights, designed to face the mighty battle fleets of Louis XIV – a new and very different threat from the Barbary corsairs. After the defeat of the French at Barfleur in 1692 things change once again and Benbow starts to work on small and nimble ships well suited to coastal operations, exemplified by the *Charles Galley* and the *Kitchen*. There is another change in 1696, towards larger ships such as the *Suffolk* and *Duke*, when he is blockading ports, chasing squadrons of privateers and hoping for fleet battle. The peace of 1697 brings yet another change as Benbow heads towards the Caribbean for a peacetime operation of exploration and discovery, requiring a small ship and yet one large enough to cope with any pirate threat. A year later and with war on the horizon he returns to the Caribbean with a much larger one designed for fleet battle.

Thus the size and type of Benbow's ships together trace the fortunes of England throughout the period. The images are important because they make the point as clearly as anything else – that this was by no means a period of sustained warfare of a single type against a single enemy. Between 1670 and 1702 the Royal Navy was constantly challenged in new ways, and its response was always different, usually appropriate and occasionally effective.

LK – Length of Keel
B – Beam
DH – Depth in hold

Dimensions are feet and inches and are taken from David Lyon's *Sailing Navy List* (1983), Brian Lavery's *Ship of the Line* (1983) and Frank Fox's *Great Ships* (1980).

PHOENIX

---

27 January to 18 April 1678, Master's Mate

A Fourth Rate of forty-two guns, the *Phoenix* was built at Portsmouth in 1671 and survived for only twenty-one years. She was burned near Malaga on 12 April 1692 to prevent capture by the French. Originally built as a Fifth Rate, she was found capable of carrying the armament of a Fourth Rate and was reclassified soon after construction. Note the gunport wreaths around the upper tier, a characteristic of the period. Small and fast, she was an excellent ship for coastal operations against commerce raiders like the Barbary corsairs

The Fourth Rate *Phoenix* by Van de Velde the Younger *c.*1675

Built: Anthony Deane, Portsmouth 1671
LK: 89.0   B: 27.10   DH: 11.2
Tons: 367   Guns: 40
Fate: Burned to avoid capture 1692

RUPERT

30 April 1678 to 13 June 1679, Master's Mate

A far larger ship than the *Phoenix*, the *Rupert* was a Third Rate of sixty-six guns. She was built in Harwich in 1666 by Sir Anthony Deane and with the help of two rebuilds survived until 1769, when she was broken up. Not excessively large, she was an ideal flagship for sustained operations in foreign waters. Benbow still served aboard her as Master's Mate, but as she was Herbert's flagship this was very much a promotion. The painting on the jacket, '*Resolution* in a Gale' by Van de Velde the Younger, is also a fair representation of the *Rupert*. Though larger, the *Resolution* was built in the same yard by the same shipwright and only a year later.

An English Third Rate by Van de Velde the Elder *c.*1673. Probably the *Rupert*

Built: Anthony Deane, Harwich 1666
LK: 119   B: 36.3   DH: 17.1
Tons: 791   Guns: 64
Fate: Wrecked 1703

NONSUCH

15 June 1679 to August 1681, Master

The *Nonsuch* was of a similar size to Benbow's first recorded ship, the *Phoenix*. Built in Portsmouth in 1668, she was armed with forty-two guns. What cannot be seen from this image is that, as an experiment, she was built with the grain of all of her timbers running in the same direction, supposedly to increase her speed. The *Nonsuch* was a very fast ship, but this was generally attributed to the skill of the shipwright, Anthony Deane, and not to her novel construction. Speed was a huge advantage in warfare against the corsairs' vessels, many of which could be rowed. Although the *Nonsuch* was smaller than the *Rupert*, this was a promotion for Benbow as he now served aboard her as Master.

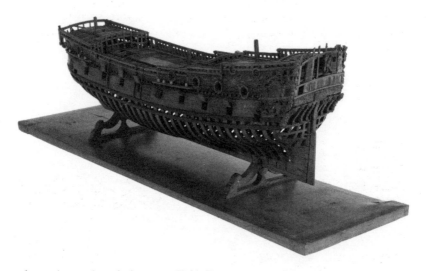

An unidentified 40-gun Fifth Rate *c.*1670 similar to the *Nonsuch*

Built: William Castle, Deptford 1696
LK: 109   B: 34.2   DH: 13.9
Tons: 676   Guns: 50
Fate: Hulk 1740, broken up 1745

ELIZABETH

9 June to 20 Sept 1689, Third Lieutenant

This was the first ship that Benbow served on as a commissioned officer. The *Elizabeth* was a 70-gun Third Rate built in Deptford in 1679 as part of the Thirty Ships programme of 1677. Benbow would serve on three more ships of this class, the *Northumberland* (p.339), the *Suffolk* (p.341) and the *Lenox* (p.343). This is not surprising because, of the thirty ships ordered in 1677, twenty were Third Rates like the *Elizabeth*. It was the first time in history that so many large ships had been built at once. They were all very similar, deliberately standardized more than ever before so that fixtures and fittings could be interchanged in order to reduce cost and ease repair. They were, generally speaking, good ships.

The *Elizabeth* was the largest ship on which Benbow had yet served. Over seven feet longer than the *Rupert*, she was larger by 282 tons. She was also Herbert's flagship, as the *Rupert* had been, and Benbow would have been involved in her repair as Master Attendant at Chatham at the beginning of 1690.

The Third Rate *Elizabeth* by Van de Velde the Elder *c.*1680

Built: William Castle, Deptford 1679
LK: 137.6   B: 40.11 ½   DH: 16.8 ½
Tons: 1108   Guns: 70
Fate: Rebuilt 1704

YORK

---

20 September to 26 October 1689, Captain

The first ship that Benbow commanded, the *York* was the oldest of all those he had served on so far. A 54-gunner built under the Commonwealth in 1654 – only four years after Benbow's birth – she was originally named the *Marston Moor* in celebration of the famous Parliamentarian victory over Prince Rupert. She was renamed in 1660, when Charles II was restored to the throne, along with other ships whose names Charles would find distasteful. The *Naseby*, commemorating the Parliamentarian victory of June 1645, thus became the Royal Charles; the *Worcester*, commemorating the victory of 1651, became the *Dunkirk*; the *Nantwich*, commemorating the victory of 1644, became the *Bredah*. The ships were all hastily redecorated to show the Stuart Royal Arms visible here at the stern. The drawing can be accurately dated because of the inscription on the stern '1674', although she would have appeared slightly different when Benbow commanded her, as in 1688 she had been assigned sixty-two guns whereas she is shown here with her original armament of fifty-four. The *York* was wrecked in the great storm of 1703 on the Shipwash Bank off Harwich.

The Third Rate *York* by Van de Velde the Elder, 1674

Built: by Henry Johnson, Blackwall 1654. Originally named *Marston Moor* to celebrate the decisive Parliamentarian victory of 1644. Renamed *York* at the restoration of Charles II in 1660.

LK: 116   B: 34.6   DH: 14.2   Tons: 734   Guns: 60
Fate: Wrecked 1703

BRITANNIA

---

12 November 1689 to early January 1690, Captain (commission not confirmed owing to ship's rotten state)
13 April 1691 to ?, Second Captain

This was the largest ship on which Benbow ever served, a First Rate of three decks and 104 guns – all but two of which were brass. The *Britannia* was part of the 1677 Thirty Ships programme that produced the Third Rates *Elizabeth* (p.333), *Northumberland* (p.339) and *Suffolk* (p.343) but was the sole First Rate of that programme. Launched in 1682, she spent the next seven years of her life rotting in the River Medway and had to be repaired before she was finally commissioned in March 1691. Even then she was found to be a poor sailer and was re-docked for girdling to improve her stability. She was 1,708 tons burden when Benbow sailed on her in the spring of 1691, 600 tons larger (heavier) than any ship Benbow had ever sailed on. Benbow knew the *Britannia* well. As Master Attendant at Chatham in the winter of 1689–90 he was involved in her docking and the discovery that she was so rotten that she could not be commissioned. It was not until the following year that she was afloat once more, and it was then that Benbow served aboard her as Second Captain.

The First Rate
Britannia by
Van de Velde
the Elder *c.*1685

Built: Phineas Pett, Chatham 1682
LK: 146   B: 47.4   DH: 17.2 ½
Tons: 1739   Guns: 100
Fate: Rebuilt 1719

ROYAL SOVEREIGN

---

2 April 1690 to ?, Master

The *Royal Sovereign* was another First Rate of 100 guns, and the third of Herbert's flagships on which Benbow served. Originally Peter Pett's *Sovereign of the Seas*, built at Woolwich in 1635–7 for Charles I as a magnificent symbol of prestige, by the time Benbow served aboard her she had already been rebuilt twice, in 1660 and 1685. She was burned by accident at Chatham in January 1697. The accident would have profoundly shocked everyone, like Benbow, who was working in the King's yards. This rare bow-view of the *Royal Sovereign* clearly shows the exaggerated tumblehome that was so characteristic of ships of this period. She is shown here lying in ordinary off Gillingham in 1685. Note the magnificent lion figurehead she had received in her great repair of 1685.

The First Rate
Royal Sovereign by
Van de Velde the
Elder *c.*1685

Built: Lee,
Chatham 1685
LK: 135.6
B: 48.4
DH: 19.4
Tons: 1683
Guns: 100
Fate: Burnt by
accident 1697

NORWICH

September 1693 to ?, Captain

Benbow commanded the 1693 bombardment of St Malo from the *Norwich*. A Fourth Rate 48-gunner, she was brand new and had been built at Deptford during the time when Benbow worked there as Master Attendant. He would have known her intimately. Note again how the size of ships has changed to reflect the change in strategy. By now the French battle fleet had been defeated at Barfleur, and Louis, strapped for cash, had changed his naval strategy to commerce-raiding. The English responded, and for the next stage of the war Benbow commanded small, fast or handy craft for coastal operations against France. In this particularly fine model the mainwales have been finished in walnut veneer. The rig is an accurate representation of the period, although it was rebuilt in 1937. Note the characteristic seventeenth-century short mizzen-mast with its lateen yard and the spritsail topmast.

A Navy Board model of a Fourth
Rate *c*.1695 similar to the *Norwich*

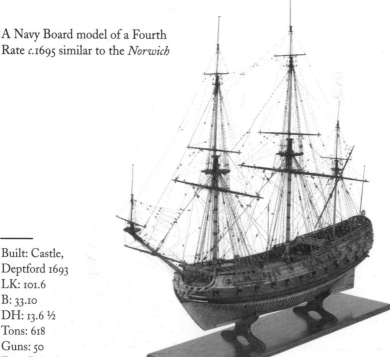

Built: Castle,
Deptford 1693
LK: 101.6
B: 33.10
DH: 13.6 ½
Tons: 618
Guns: 50
Fate: Rebuilt 1718

KITCHEN

September 1694, Captain

During the bombardment campaigns Benbow would have used small ships for the close inshore work of sounding the approaches to his targets, and the one documented example is his use of the *Kitchen* to sound the approaches to Calais in 1694. She was a bomb vessel converted in 1692 from a yacht built in Rotherhithe in 1670. This image shows her before she was converted. Benbow would have known her like this because she was converted at Deptford when he was Master Attendant, and it is likely that he selected her as a suitable ship for conversion.

The Bomb Vessel *Kitchen* by Van de Velde the Younger *c.*1686

Built: Castle, Rotherhithe 1692
LK: 49.6   B: 19.6   DH: 8
Tons: 100   Guns: 8
Fate: Sold 1698

NORTHUMBERLAND

16 June to 9 August 1695, Captain

Benbow conducted the second bombardment of St Malo from the decks of the *Northumberland*, a powerful 70-gun Third Rate, significantly larger than the ship from which he had commanded the first attack, the *Norwich*. Unusually for a Third Rate of the time, she was built in a private yard, Francis Bayley of Bristol. She, like the *York*, was wrecked in the Great Storm of 1703. She was one of twenty similar Third Rates all built in the 1677 building programme. This portrait is of an unidentified member of that class and could be the *Northumberland*. Benbow sailed two other ships of this class, each with more detailed portraits: the *Suffolk* (p.341) and *Elizabeth* (p.333).

A Third Rate of the 1677 programme by Van de Velde the Elder,
possibly the *Northumberland*

Built: Baylie, Bristol 1679
LK: 137   B: 40.4   DH: 17
Tons: 1050 Guns: 70
Fate: Wrecked 1703

CHARLES GALLEY

July 1695, Captain

From the *Northumberland* Benbow moved to the nimble, oar-powered *Charles Galley* to command the inshore squadron for the second St Malo attack. She was one of only two powerful galley-frigates designed for operations against the Barbary corsairs. She had particularly fine lines and was armed with thirty-two guns. The oar ports are clearly visible just above the waterline. This painting is one of three on wood panels that were commissioned by the Woolwich shipwright Phineas Pett, on the personal instructions of Charles II, for the cabin of the royal yacht *Charlotte*, built in 1677.[3] The *Charles Galley* is similar to the *Adventure Galley*, the naval ship that William Kidd commanded in the Indian Ocean when he turned pirate. Benbow also used the similar *Experiment Galley* for his coastal operations in 1696.

The *Charles Galley* by Van de Velde the Younger, 1677

Built: Lawrence (Surveyor), Woolwich, 1693
LK: 124   B: 28.10   DH: 9
Tons: 548 ¼   Guns: 36
Fate: Broken up 1710

SUFFOLK

---

7 May to 22 September 1696, Rear-Admiral of the Blue

For the next phase of the war, which consisted of blockade and cruising in the hope of meeting and engaging Jean Bart's Dunkirk-based squadron of corsairs, Benbow needed a powerful ship but one that could chase and manoeuvre sufficiently well to act as a fleet convoy. He moved to the *Suffolk*, a 70-gun Third Rate launched at Blackwall in 1680. She was part of the same Thirty Ships programme of 1677 that had produced the *Northumberland* (p.339) and the *Elizabeth* (p.333). As is clear from this fine image, they were a beautiful class of ship; their lines lean and graceful and their decoration more appropriate to their size than earlier warship designs. Note how close the lower-deck gunports are to the waterline. The captain has opened a window in his cabin.

A Third Rate of the 1677 programme by Van de Velde the Elder, possibly the *Suffolk* or her sister ship the *Exeter*

Built: Johnson, Blackwall 1680
LK: 138   B: 40.6   DH: 16.9 ½
Tons: 1066 Guns: 70
Fate: Rebuilt 1699

NORFOLK

---

23 July to 5 October 1696, Rear-Admiral of the Blue

In a significant period of overlap in the summer of 1696, Benbow seems to have been aboard the larger *Norfolk* as regularly as he was aboard the *Suffolk*. She was a two-decker of eighty guns, built at a private yard in Southampton. No images of the *Norfolk* survive, but this is a model of the *Boyne*, a ship of almost identical size and built in the same programme. It is one of the finest of all Navy Board models. Note how closely together the gunports are packed on the quarterdeck. This was necessary for the shipwrights to meet the size and armament requirements imposed by politicians. Fine-looking maybe, these ships were a disaster. Placing so many guns at the stern put the hull under far more pressure than it was designed to take, causing the ships to work themselves loose and leak.

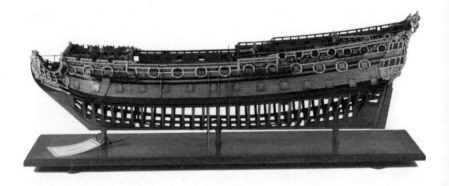

Navy Board Model of the Third Rate *Boyne*, similar to the *Norfolk*

Built: Winter, Southampton 1693
LK: 129.3 ¼   B: 41.6   DH: 17.4
Tons: 1184   Guns: 80
Fate: Rebuilt 1728

LENOX

22 May to 23 June 1697, Rear-Admiral of the Blue

Benbow spent the spring of 1697 in the Atlantic approaches to the Channel, where the navy considered itself safe from privateers. Valuable merchantmen would be escorted from English shores to a point perhaps 100 leagues west of Scilly, where the squadron would remain to meet incoming merchant fleets. During one of several cruises that summer, Benbow spent a month aboard the *Lenox*, a 70-gun Third Rate of the same class as three other ships he had served on: the *Northumberland* (p.339), the *Suffolk* (p.341) and the *Elizabeth* (p.333), all well suited to the challenges of convoy protection. This is most probably of the *Lenox*, a particularly noteworthy ship as she was the first ship to be finished in the Thirty Ships building programme of 1677. She is shown here caught in a sudden gale that has forced the sailors to let go the larboard sheets and tacks of the fore course. This would have allowed the mizzen to push the ship's head into the wind, the safest orientation in a sudden gale.

The Third Rate *Lenox* by Van de Velde the Younger

Built: John Shish, Deptford 1687
LK: 131   B: 39.8   DH: 17
Tons: 1096 Guns: 70
Fate: Rebuilt 1701

DUKE

7 July to 21 July 1697, Rear-Admiral of the Blue

In the summer of 1697 Benbow's hunting grounds shifted from the relatively calm waters of the eastern Channel off Dunkirk to the tumbling and towering seas of the Channel's western approaches. Here he cruised to protect trade and threaten the enemy fleet in Brest – the classic strategy of the Western Squadron that was to become the cornerstone of English naval strategy for more than a century. Needing a powerful and robust ship that could meet any threat from any enemy and hold its own against the Atlantic weather, he chose the *Duke*, a Second Rate of ninety guns, built at Woolwich in 1682. Benbow used the *Duke* as a sort of mother-ship from which he ventured to conduct specific operations. We know, for example, that shortly after arriving on the *Duke* he left her for a raid on Brest aboard the far smaller *Torbay*. The only significant difference between this model and the *Duke* is that the *Duke* had six quarterdeck ports, not the five shown here. Benbow served on several two-decked 80-gunners similar to the *Duke* in the summer of 1697: the *Cornwall*, *Lancaster*, *Torbay* and *Newarke*. (See opposite for dimensions)

A Navy Board model of the Second Rate *Coronation*, almost identical in every way to Benbow's *Duke*

MONMOUTH

28 July to 13 November 1697, Rear-Admiral of the Blue

When Benbow's brief cruise in the western approaches to the Channel ended and he was ordered once more to blockade Dunkirk, he quickly changed ships to the *Monmouth*, an elderly Third Rate of the same class as the *Rupert* (see p.331). A 66-gunner of only 856 tons, she was significantly smaller than the huge *Duke*, with only a little more than half of her tonnage. Small, fast and yet still powerful, she was an ideal ship to restart the hunt for Bart. They never met, however, but Benbow's presence off Dunkirk in the *Monmouth* secured him several prizes

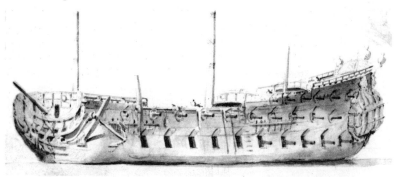

Probably the *Monmouth* by Van de Velde the Younger or Elder

Built: Phineas Pett, Chatham 1667
LK: 118.9   B: 36.10   DH: 15.6
Tons: 856   Guns: 66
Fate: Rebuilt 1700

DUKE
Built: Thomas Sish, Woolwich 1682
LK: 142.6   B: 45.2   DH: 18.9
Tons: 1546   Guns: 90
Fate: Rebuilt 1701 renamed *Prince George*

GLOUCESTER

14 March 1698 to ?, Rear-Admiral of the Blue

Benbow's peacetime commission of 1698–9 to survey unknown waters and hunt pirates in the distant West Indies placed a new requirement on his ships, and he led the Caribbean squadron in the Fourth Rate, 60-gun *Gloucester*. She was small in comparison with some of his most recent commands, but with the main naval powers at peace it was unlikely that she would be forced to lie in the line of battle, though she was powerful enough to overcome any bold pirates. Although small, she was roomy enough to absorb large quantities of stores. She was also relatively new, having been launched in 1695, but the Admiralty's faith in her was misplaced and she leaked badly throughout the cruise. She had been built in a private yard in Bristol that the Admiralty never used again. Such Fourth Rates of the 1691 Twenty-Seven Ships programme are very poorly documented and this model, built in the eighteenth century and with some eighteenth-century characteristics – not the least of which is a steering wheel – is the only known likeness. This is one of only very few models whose construction is known; work began in 1700 and was completed in 1723.

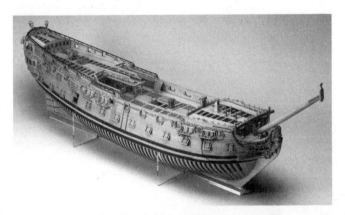

An unidentified model of a Fourth Rate of the mid-1690s, of the same class as the *Gloucester*, shown as outfitted in the early 1700s

Built: Clements, Bristol 1695
LK: 120.4   B: 37.5   DH: 15.8
Tons: 896   Guns: 60
Fate: Harbour service 1706

SAUDADOES PRIZE

Spring 1700, Rear-Admiral of the Blue

The Caribbean in the 1690s wore ships down as quickly as it killed men, and in his hunt for the elusive pirates Benbow was forced to abandon the leaky *Gloucester* in favour of the *Saudadoes Prize*. A 36-gun Fifth Rate, she was French-built and had been captured in September 1692. No image survives of the *Saudadoes* but this is an accurate portrait of another Fifth Rate from the same period, also captured from the French. Not all captured ships were retained for service in the English Navy but French Fifth Rates were excellent ships, direct descendants of the famous Dunkirk frigates of the 1640s – lightly built, fast and appropriately armed for their size. French seamen used many ships of this type as privateers; they were devastatingly effective in this role, and English and Dutch warships were able to catch very few. The *Saudadoes Prize* was therefore a perfect ship for tracking down the elusive pirate captain William Kidd.

The *Play Prize* by Van de Velde the Elder, similar to the *Saudadoes Prize*

Built: France 1692
LK: 86   B: 29   DH: 12.6
Tons: 385   Guns: 36
Fate: Hulked 1702

APPENDIX II

BREDAH

5 June 1701 to 4 November 1702, Rear-Admiral of the Blue and Vice-Admiral of the Blue

When Benbow returned to the Caribbean in 1701 war was very much on the horizon and he took with him a large ship capable of leading a squadron into battle but one that was also of a manageable size for long-distance cruising. The ship he chose was the Third Rate 70-gun *Bredah*, built at Woolwich in 1692. Armed with ten more guns than the *Gloucester*, she was also longer, wider and deeper, a perfect flagship for a foreign station, the 1700s equivalent of the *Rupert* (p.331), which had been Herbert's flagship in the Mediterranean in 1678.

Navy Board model of the Third Rate *Bredah*, 1692

Built:
Lawrence,
Woolwich 1692
LK: 126
B: 40.5
DH: 16.8
Tons: 1094
Guns: 70
Fate: Broken
up 1730

APPENDIX III

Benbow's Songs

This is by no means a comprehensive list of songs about Benbow. In particular, numerous versions of the traditional tune 'The Death of Admiral Benbow' assume the same form though end in slightly different ways. The tradition of Benbow songs continued into the twentieth century. 'The High Barbaree' was composed by Caryl Brahms and Ned Sherrin for their spoof TV play of 1967 *Benbow Was His Name*, and the final song in this appendix appears to have been composed in the late 1970s to accompany a chapter on Benbow in a miscellany of curious tales about the sea.[1]

THE DEATH OF ADMIRAL BENBOW

· Come, all ye seamen bold, lend an ear, lend an ear,
Come all ye seamen bold, lend an ear
'Tis of our Admiral's fame,
Brave Benbow by name,
How he fought on the main you shall hear, you shall hear,
How he fought on the main you shall hear.

Brave Benbow he set sail for to fight, for to fight,
Brave Benbow he set sail for to fight
Brave Benbow he set sail
With a sweet and pleasant gale
But his captains they turned tail in a fright, in a fright,
But his captains they turned tail in a fright.

Says Kirkby unto Wade, 'I will run, I will run',
Says Kirkby unto Wade, 'I will run.
I value not disgrace,
Nor the losing of my place
For my enemies I'll not face with a gun, with a gun,
For my enemies I'll not face with a gun.'

'Twas the *Ruby* and [*Bredah*] fought the French, fought the French,
'Twas the *Ruby* and [*Bredah*] fought the French
For there was ten in all
Poor souls, they fought them all
They valued them not at all, would not flinch, would not flinch
They valued them not at all, would not flinch.

Hard fortune that it was by chain shot, by chain shot,
Hard fortune it was, by chain shot,
Our admiral lost his leg
And of his men did beg,
'Fight on, my British boys; 'tis my lot, 'tis my lot,
Fight on my British boys, 'tis my lot.'

While the surgeon dressed his wounds thus he said, thus he said,
While the surgeon dressed his wounds thus he said
'Let my cradle now in haste
On the quarter-deck be placed,
That mine enemies I may face till I'm dead, till I'm dead,
That mine enemies I may face till I'm dead.'

And there bold Benbow lay, crying 'Boys', crying 'Boys'
And there bold Benbow lay, crying 'Boys,
Let us tack about once more
We'll drive them all on shore
I value not a score, nor their noise, nor their noise,
I value not a score, nor their noise.'

Unsupported thus he fought, nor would run, nor would run
Unsupported thus he fought, nor would run
Till his ship was a mere wreck,
And no man would him back
For the others would not slack to fire a gun, fire a gun
For the others would not slack to fire a gun.

For Jamaica then at last he set sail, he set sail,
For Jamaica then at last he set sail.
Where [Whetstone] he did try
And those cowards that did fly
And from the French in fright turned tail, turned tail,
And from the French in fright turned tail.

And those found most to blame, they were shot, they were shot,
And those found most to blame, they were shot.
Brave Benbow then at last
For grief of what was past,
In a fever died at last, by hard lot, by hard lot
In a fever died at last by hard lot.

ADMIRAL BENBOW (1)

'T was of an Admiral
Called Benbow by his name
He fought on the raging main
You must know
Oh, the ship rocks up and down
And the shots are flying round
The enemy tumbling down
There they lay, there they lay

The ship rocks up and down
And the shots are flying round
The enemy tumbling down
There they lay, there they lay

'T was Reuben and Benbow
Fought the French, fought the French
'T was Reuben and Benbow
Fought the French, fought the French
Down on his old stump he fell
And so loudly he did call
Fight you on, my English lads
'Tis my lot, 'tis my lot

Down on his old stump he fell
And so loudly he did call
Fight you on, my English lads
'Tis my lot, 'tis my lot

When the doctor dressed his wounds
Benbow cried, Benbow cried
When the doctor dressed his wounds
Benbow cried,
Let a bed be fetched in haste
On the quarterdeck be placed
That the enemy I might face
'Til I die, 'til I die

Let a bed be fetched in haste
On the quarterdeck be placed,
That the enemy I might face
'Til I die, 'til I die

On Tuesday morning last
Benbow died, Benbow died
On Tuesday morning last
Benbow died
What a shocking sight to see
When Benbow was carried away
He was carried to Kingston church
There he lay, there he lay

What a shocking sight to see
When Benbow was carried away
He was carried to Kingston church
There he lay, there he lay

ADMIRAL BENBOW (2)

We sailed from Virginia and thence to Fayall
Where we watered our ships and then we weighed all
Full in view on the seas, boys, seven sails we did espy
So we manned our capstern and weighed speedily.

Now the first we come up on was a brigantine sloop
And we asked if the others was as big as they looked
Ah, but turning to windward, as near as we could lie
We saw there were ten men of war cruising by.

We drew up our squadron in very nice line
And so boldly we fought them for full four hours time
But the day being spent, boys, and night a-coming on
We left them alone until early next morn.

Now the very next morning the engagement proved hot
And brave Admiral Benbow received a chance shot
And as he lay wounded to his merry men he did say,
'Take me up in your arms, boys, and carry me away!'

Oh, the guns they did rattle and the bullets did fly,
But brave Admiral Benbow for rout would not cry;
'Take me down to my cabin where there's ease for my smarts,
If my merry men see me, it would sure break their hearts.'

Now, the very next morning at the break of the day
They hoisted their topsails and so bore away;
We bore to Port Royal, where the people flocked much
To see Admiral Benbow buried in Kingston Church.

So come all you brave fellows, wheresoever you have been,
Let us drink a good health to our King and our Queen,
And another good health to the girls that we know,
And a third in remembrance of brave Admiral Benbow.

THE HIGH BARBAREE

The length and breadth of England they toasted Benbow's name
Blow high! Blow low! And so sailed he!
And told again the story that blazoned first his fame
All a'cruisin' down the coast of the High Barbaree!

And look-out in the crow's nest said, 'there's naught upon the lee'
Blow high! Blow low! And so sailed he!
But there's a privateer to windward and she's sailing fast and free
All a'cruisin' down the coast of the High Barbaree!

'Oh Quarter! Oh Quarter!' those pirates smartly said,
Blow high! Blow low! And so sailed he!
But the quarter Benbow gave them was to top them at the head
All a'cruisin' down the coast of the High Barbaree!

When Benbow came to Cadiz he took those heads ashore,
Blow high! Blow low! And so sailed he!
His servant bore them in a sack and Benbow walked before
All a'telling of his triumphs on the High Barbaree!

The officers of Revenue said 'Open up your sack'
Blow high! Blow low! And so sailed he!
He said 'It's salt provisions that will make a tasty snack'
All a'cruisin' down the coast of the High Barbaree!

The Magistrates said 'Open up' and so the bonds fell free,
Blow high! Blow low! And so sailed he!
And thirteen heads came rolling out for all of Spain to see
All a'cruisin' down the coast of the High Barbaree!

Now Benbow is an Admiral and off to try his chance,
Blow high! Blow low! And so sailed he!
God bless the King of England and curse the King of France
And bring back the winds that blew him on the High Barbaree!

JOHN BENBOW

Bill Benbow, the tanner, at Shrewsbury did dwell,
He taught his son Johnny and thrashed him as well;
He 'prenticed him early a butcher to be,
But John loved adventure, and ran off to sea.

So John was a sailor and lived merrily,
A-hunting the Frenchman all over sea,
He caught twelve black pirates a-riding the main,
And had their heads pickled and sold them to Spain.

So more and more famous John Benbow he grew;
They made him a captain, and admiral too;
In battle and tempest for years he was tossed,
yet never a battle he fought but he lost.

His captains were cravens and would not obey;
He swore, and they swore, and Du Casse got away.
A cannon-ball knocked off his leg with a bump –
John merely said '‿' and fought on with the stump.

For he who fights and runs away,
might live to fight another day;
But he who's in battle slain,
will never rise to fight again.

So here's to John Benbow, who loved the salt sea,
Was never a seadog more merry than he.
So gallantly fought he, so roundly he swore,
The like of John Benbow we'll never see more.

APPENDIX IV

Benbow's Fruit Trees

In June 1696 Benbow rented John Evelyn's house in Deptford, Sayes Court, a mansion set in one of the most magnificent and well-documented gardens of the time. It is therefore possible to list some of the trees that Benbow would have enjoyed in his garden during his tenancy. This makes him unique among naval officers, whose home lives, let alone gardens, are usually a closed book.

A prized part of the estate was the 'oval garden', which was replanted in 1684–5 after a winter of particularly severe frosts that even killed Evelyn's beloved tortoise. Twelve named varieties of cherry were planted and more than twenty-one of pear. Between the trees were planted gooseberry and currant bushes, with strawberries in the borders. The cherries were selected to produce fruit from the earliest (May) to very last of the season (July), and the late pear varieties, with careful selection and storage, were designed to produce pears that would last the entire winter. Evelyn was particularly fond of the 'Swanns Egg' pear, shaped like an egg 'of a green colour, thinly covered with brown; its flesh is melting and full of a pleasant juice'. If picked before the first frosts and well stored it would ripen in December. When Benbow leased Sayes Court, more than a decade after this replanting, the garden would have been impressively mature.

When Benbow arrived in June, the 'Duke' and 'Black Heart' cherries would have been ready to press into wine or a cordial to flavour and colour cider, and the 'Vermillion' pear ripening. A month or so later the 'Petite Rousselet' pear would have been ready, one of Evelyn's favourites, with 'the most exquisitely perfum'd Taste'. Many varieties with similar names still exist at the National Fruit Collection at Brogdale but it is unclear how closely they resemble those grown by Evelyn. Nevertheless, it is now possible to grow 'Old Black Heart', 'Archduke', 'Carnation' and 'Caroone' cherries; 'Messier Jean', 'Jargonelle', 'Swans Egg', 'Frangipan' and 'Robin' pears; and the 'Golden Pippin' apple and the 'White Muscadine', now called 'Royal Muscadine' (the Raisin de Champagne).

The named trees in the oval garden relate to Evelyn's plan (see overleaf):[1]

• •

Fruit planted in other places about yr Garden the same day:

Ambret peare 'twixt a Vine & a Fig: west wall of fountaine Garden over against the mount:

Verpoleuse, South-wall of ye Cellar in Fountaine Garden, East end, next ye parsley Vine

Bonne Christienne Sans pepin. West-wall of ye house, fountain Gard: under my bed-chamber:

Chasse-peare, Long wall of the Stable Kitchen-garden:

Parsley Vine, in ye Corer just under my bed-cha[mber]: windo just by ye Kitchin window, Fontaie Gard:

Cherry in the West Comer & end of ye Cellar Wall, in Fountaine Gard

White-Muscadine Cellar Wall South, just under ye Diall:

2 Medlars, in ye Flower & Seede Nursery:

Goose berry of Moore-parke 12 in the Iland ranging wth the long carpet walk.

A large Sort

White Cerrinths & other Cerrinths/ Raspis red & white:} in ye Iland:

This halfe Circle was planted wth Holly 1684.

Bowling-Greene

'Table of Fruit planted in the East & West Triangular grounds 3. Feb. 1684/5 4 new:'

Cherries about ye halfe Circle

357

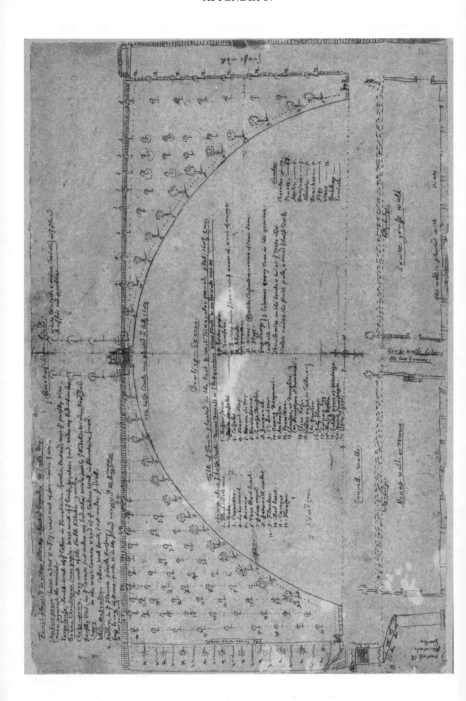

1. Black-Orleanes.
2. Duke.
3. Carnation:
4. Luke Ward.
5. Morocco:
6. True Black-heart:
7. Prince royal:
8. Petworth amber:
9. Flanders:
10. Red heart:
11. Caroone:
12. Flanders:

Peares Dwarfs in ye East-quarter
1. Messier Jean:
2. Petite rousselet:
3. Cassolet:
4. French King:
5. Boeure du Roy:
6. Brutebonne:
7. Grosse Rousslet:
8. Jargonall.
9. St Andrew:
10. Orang Bergamot:
11. Ambrosia:
12. Vermillion:
13. {Lansac, or Dauphine/ or, Frangipan d'Automne}.
14. Elias Rose.
15. {Calliot rosat, or Caillo ou/ de prestre}
16. July flower:
17. Swans egg:
18. Muscq Robin:
19. Golden Peare of Xaintonge:
20. Poire sans pepin:
21. Espine d'yver:

Other Fruit &c on the Walls west &c
Gp. Golden pipin:
A. Damsons:
A. Dwarf fruits I know not ye names of, & out of range:
A. Abricots:
P. Peaches:
V. Vines *White Muscadine: corer of Court door:
F. Figgs:
{Goose-berrys/ &/ Cerrinths} 3 betweene every Tree in the quarters:
Strawberries in the borders twixt ye Trees also.
Violets under the South pale, & round ye halfe Circle

Number
Cherries: - 50
Peares: - 47
Apples: - 5.
Damsons: - 9.
Abricots: - 5
Peaches- 5
Figs- 2
Vines - 12
Gooseberries –
Corrinths –

GLOSSARY

Admiral of the Red, White, Blue: The officer nominally commanding ships of the Red, White or Blue squadron, ranking in seniority in that (descending) order; the rank of Admiral of the Red was created after the Battle of Trafalgar in 1805, the post having been occupied by Admiral of the Fleet. In practice, by the end of the eighteenth century the Admiralty created as many admirals of each rank as it required.

Blue lights: Combustibles used for signalling at night. Also called Bengal light.

Bomb ship: A warship fitted to fire heavy mortars for shore bombardment.

Bow chaser: A long gun fired directly ahead from gunports in a ship's bows.

Careen (v.): To heave a ship down by her masts to expose the bottom for cleaning.

Chasse-marée: A lugger-rigged French coasting vessel.

Companion ladder: Ladders giving access throughout the ship, often with particular emphasis on the ladders by which the officers accessed the quarter deck.

Cutter: 1. A small vessel fore-and-aft rigged on one mast with topmast and bowsprit. 2. A ship's boat designed for sailing, 25ft long in a ship-of-the-line.

False fire: Combustibles packed into a wooden tube and then lit for signalling at night. Similar to a flare. Also see Blue lights.

Fish (v.): To strengthen a damaged spar or mast by lashing spars to it in the manner of splints.

Flyboat: A large flat-bottomed Dutch vessel distinguished by a high stern.

Fother (v.): To stop a leak in a ship's hull by working a sail into a heavy matt using rough yarn, then using water pressure to force the fothered sail into the hole.

Flag-captain: The captain of a flagship.

Forecastle: A deck built over the forward end of the main deck.

Foretopsail: The topsail on the foremast.

Grapeshot: Anti-personnel shot consisting of small shot that scatters on firing.

Grave (v.): To clean a vessel's bottom.

Gundeck: The deck carrying the main battery.

Heave-to: To stop by backing some of the sails.

Hot press: The response to a particularly severe manning crisis, in which numbers of men were of greater concern than their quality. In a hot press, protections against impressment were not valid.

In irons (punishment): The offender's legs were confined by shackles attached to a long iron bar with a padlock at the end.

Jolly boat: A small ship's boat, usually no more than 18ft x 4ft, especially useful in harbour.

Landman/landsman: An unskilled member of the ship's company.

League: Three miles.

Longboat: The largest of the ship's boats, designed for carrying heavy weights.

Lower deck: On a two- or three-decker, the lowest deck carrying the ship's main battery.

Maintopsail: The topsail on the mainmast.

Master: 1. On a warship, the warrant officer responsible for navigation. 2. The commanding officer of a merchant ship.

Master at arms: A petty officer responsible for ship's discipline.

Master's mate: A petty officer assisting the master.

Middle deck: On a three-decker, the deck between the lower deck and the upper deck.

Mizzen mast: The aftermost mast.

The Nore: An anchorage in the mouth of the Thames near the entrance to the River Medway, which led to Chatham naval dockyard.

Ordinary: Ships in reserve.

Orlop (deck): The lowest deck.

Pink: A flat-bottomed cargo ship with a very narrow stern.

Poop: A short deck built over the after end of the quarter deck.

Privateer: A merchant ship licensed by a letter of marque issued by the government to attack shipping of a named enemy nation (or nations).

Progress book: An administrative volume recording the date and cost of a ship's repairs.

Quarterdeck: A deck over the after part of the upper deck.

Quarter gallery: A balcony projecting from the stern and quarter of large ships, accessed via the admiral's or captain's cabin.

Quarter gunner: A rating under the direction of the gunner. One quarter gunner was allocated to every four guns.

Rear-admiral: A flag officer ranking below vice-admiral and admiral.

Receiving ship: A depot used to hold entered or impressed seamen before they were distributed to their ships.

Red-hot shot: Shot which has been heated in a furnace before firing.

Scuttle: A hole cut in the ship's deck or side, generally for ventilation.

Sheet (rope): A rope controlling the clue (bottom corner) of a sail.

Ship of the line: A warship large enough to lie in the line of battle.

Slip (a cable): To cast off; especially to sail without weighing anchor, in which case the anchor cable is let slip and buoyed for later retrieval.

Spithead: An area of the Solent, off Portsmouth.

Step (a mast): To place a ship's mast.

Strike (a mast): To lower a mast.

Studdingsail: A light sail temporarily set outboard of a square sail in light airs.

Taffrail: Bulwark at the after end of the poop or quarterdeck.

Top (of a mast): A platform built at the top of the lower mast.

Upper deck: On a three-decker, the deck above the middle deck.

Van division: The leading division of a fleet or squadron divided into van, centre and rear.

Vice-admiral: A flag officer ranking below admiral and above rear admiral.

Volunteer 1st class: An officer cadet.

Whipstaff: Precursor of the ship's wheel. A long, vertical pole used as a lever to move the tiller.

NOTES

Introduction: Benbow's Book
[1] C. Brahms and N. Sherrin, *Benbow Was His Name*, 204.
[2] CSP America and West Indies 1717–18, 313.

1. Benbow's Bloodline
[1] R. Hutton and W. Reeves, 'Sieges and Fortifications', 219; R. Love, 'Captain John Benbow', 22; H. C. B. Rogers, *Battles and Generals of the Civil Wars*, 198–9.
[2] J. E. Auden, 'Shropshire and the Royalist Conspiracies…', 129–31; J. Heath, *A Chronicle of the Late Intestine War…*, 295.
[3] H. Oxiden to H. Oxiden 27 Jan 1642 quoted in J. S. Morrill, *The Revolt of the Provinces*, 138–9.
[4] Love, 'Captain John Benbow', 22; R. Woof, 'The Personal Expenses of Charles II', 34–6.
[5] B. Donagan, 'War Crime and Treason', 1159.
[6] B. Donagan, 'Varieties of Royalism', 88.
[7] E. Heath-Agnew, *Roundhead to Royalist*, 89.
[8] Heath, *A Chronicle of the Late Intestine War*, 296.
[9] Woof, 'The Personal Expenses of Charles II', 36–8, 40.
[10] M. Atkin, *Worcester: 1651*, 70.
[11] Donagan, 'War Crime and Treason', 1155.
[12] Heath, *A Chronicle of the Late Intestine War*, 296–7; *Mercurius Politicus* no. 66 (4–11 September 1651), 1055; M. Ashley, *The English Civil War*, 175.
[13] *Mercurius Politicus* no. 66, (4–11 September 1651), 1055.
[14] Anon., 'Letter of a Royalist', 338–9.
[15] P. Styles, 'The City of Worcester', 221.
[16] Heath, *A Chronicle of the Late Intestine War*, 297.
[17] Styles, 'The City of Worcester', 220–1.
[18] Atkin, *Worcester: 1651*, 125.
[19] Woof, 'The Personal Expenses of Charles II', 39.
[20] C. Carlton, *Going to the Wars*, 336–7.
[21] J. Campbell, 'Benbow (John)…', 154 (A); Carlton, *Going to the Wars*, 337.
[22] Anon., 'The official record of the proceedings of the court martial', 346.
[23] B. Donagan, 'Prisoners in the English Civil War', 29; Donagan, 'War Crime and

Treason', 1155; T. B. Howell, ed., *A Complete Collection of State Trials*, 294n.

[24] Anon., 'The official record of the proceedings of the court martial', 346–8.

[25] Anon., 'The official record of the proceedings of the court martial', 348–9.

[26] *Mercurius Politicus* no. 66, (4–11 September 1651), 1055.

[27] Campbell, 'Benbow (John)…', 154 n. A; Love, 'Captain John Benbow – Shrewsbury Civil War Hero', 22.

[28] J. K. Laughton, 'Benbow, John (1653–1702)' ODNB (1885).

[29] Anon., *A List of Officers Claiming to the Sixty Thousand Pounds*, 1.

[30] Heath-Agnew, *Roundhead to Royalist*, 90.

[31] BL Egerton Ms 2378, f.29b.

[32] J. Campbell, *Lives of British Admirals*, 334.

[33] Campbell, *Lives of British Admirals*, 332.

[34] W. Benbow, *Brave Benbow*, 23.

[35] G. A. R. Callender and C. J. Britton, 'Fact and Fiction II', 200–19; Campbell, 'Benbow (John)…', 154; Laughton, 'Benbow, John (1653–1702)' ODNB (1885).

[36] R. E. Glass, 'The Image of the Sea Officer in English Literature', 586–7.

[37] Glass, 'The Image of the Sea Officer', 592.

[38] R. D. Merriman, ed., *Queen Anne's Navy*, 310–11.

2. Benbow's Barges

[1] W. Benbow, *Brave Benbow*, 27.

[2] Quoted in S. Inwood, *A History of London*, 238.

[3] Descendants of his daughter Mary have the best of several similar claims that the bodies were exchanged and that Cromwell's undivided body lies in their family vault in Newburgh Park, near Coxwold, in the North Riding of Yorkshire.

[4] Anon., 'Advice from England', 81.

[5] S. R. Smith, 'The London Apprentices as Seventeenth-Century Adolescents', 151–2; T. S. Willan, *River Navigation in England 1600–1750*, 112.

[6] C. Fiennes, *The Journeys of Celia Fiennes*, 11; B. Trinder and N. Cox, eds., *Miners and Mariners of the Severn Gorge: Probate Inventories for Benthall, Broseley, Little Wenlock and Madeley 1660–1764*, 152. I am indebted to Dr Barrie Trinder for his kind help with the Bridegnorth and Shrewsbury Probate Inventories.

[7] William Benbow (1729), Bridgenorth Probate Inventories, LRO.

[8] Fiennes, *The Journeys of Celia Fiennes*, 24, 28, 29, 191.

[9] Fiennes, *The Journeys of Celia Fiennes*, 24, 28 , 29, 191.

[10] T. S. Willan, 'The River Navigation and Trade of the Severn Valley, 1600–1750', 69, 100. There were no towpaths on the Severn until those built 1790–1810 between Shrewsbury and Framilode.

[11] B. Trinder, *Barges and Bargemen*, 67.

[12] Trinder, *Barges and Bargemen*, 67.

[13] A. Warmington, *Civil War*, 9; Willan, 'The River Navigation and Trade', 68.

[14] Willan, *River Navigation in England 1600–1750*, 106.

[15] G. Farr, 'Severn Navigation and the Trow', 68; Trinder, *Barges and Bargemen*, 22; Willan, *River Navigation in England 1600–1750*, 100.

[16] Willan, *River Navigation in England 1600–1750*, 107–9.

[17] CSP Dom 1665–6, 540; TNA: ADM 106/281 f.72; ADM 106/282 f.5. For more on pressing bargemen, see R. Latham and W. Matthews, eds., *The Diary of Samuel Pepys*, 188.

[18] Willan, *River Navigation in England 1600–1750*, 110.

[19] Fiennes, *The Journeys of Celia Fiennes*, 29; Warmington, *Civil War, Interregnum and Restoration in Gloucestershire 1640–1672*, 13.

[20] Willan, 'River Navigation and Trade', 77.

[21] B. Trinder, *The Industrial Archaeology of Shropshire*, 168; M. Wanklyn, 'The Severn Navigation', 36, 44–9.

[22] Anon., 'Advice from England', 81; D. Jones, *A Compleat History*, 496–7, 515–21.

[23] P. Earle, *The Pirate Wars*, 92.

[24] J. D. Davies, *Pepys's Navy*, 119.

3. Benbow's Barbary Coast

[1] I am indebted to Dr Peter Le Fevre for this crucial information that contradicts the established biographies of Benbow. The muster of the *Phoenix* that confirms it is in TNA: ADM 33/112.

[2] TNA: ADM 51/690; 33/95; 33/104; 33/97.

[3] F. Fox, *Great Ships: The Battlefleet of King Charles II*, 151.

[4] H. Teonge, *The Diary of Henry Teonge*, 300.

[5] TNA: ADM 51/690.

[6] A. Bondy, 'The Barbary Regencies', 248 n.8; J. D. Davies, *Pepys's Navy*, 215.

[7] G. Milton, *White Gold*, 9–10; N. A. M. Rodger, *The Safeguard of the Sea*, 384.

[8] J. D. Davies, *Pepys's Navy: Ships, Men and Warfare 1649–1689*, 55, 253; F. E. Dyer, 'The Journal of Grenvill Collins', 206; P. Earle, *Corsairs of Malta and Barbary*, 45; G. A. Kempthorne, 'Sir John Kempthorne and His Sons', 311–14.

[9] G. E. Aylmer, 'Slavery under Charles II', 386; N. Matar, *Britain and Barbary*, 113.

[10] W. Blunt, *Black Sunrise*, 72.

[11] A. G. Jamieson, 'The Occupation of Tangier', 72.

[12] Davies, *Pepys's Navy*, 216.

[13] J. B. Hattendorf, 'Sir George Rooke and Sir Cloudesley Shovell', 47.

[14] S. Hornstein, *The Restoration Navy and English Foreign Trade, 1674–1688*, 131.

[15] G. E. Aylmer, 'Slavery under Charles II: The Mediterranean and Tangier', 386.

[16] R. C. Anderson, *Naval Wars in the Levant*, 61–2; N. Matar, *Britain and Barbary, 1589–1689*, 138–9.

[17] Hornstein, *The Restoration Navy*, 134–6.

[18] Dyer, 'The Journal of Grenvill Collins', 206; Hornstein, *The Restoration Navy*, 68; P. Le Fevre, 'John Tyrell (1646–1692): A Restoration Naval Captain', 151.

[19] 8–17 March 1677/8, TNA: ADM 51/690.

[20] 19–21 Feb 1677/8, TNA: ADM 51/690.

[21] 19–21 March 1677/8, TNA: ADM 51/690; ADM 106/352 f.66; T. Roomcoyle to Adm 29 March 1677/8, ADM 106/338; Log of the *Mary* 19–21 March 1677/8, ADM 51/582.

[22] W. Laird Clowes, *The Royal Navy: A History from the Earliest Times to 1900*, II, 453; P. Le Fevre, 'Arthur Herbert, Earl of Torrington, 1648–1716', 23.

[23] T. Roomcoyle to Adm 29 March 1677/8, TNA: ADM 106/338.

[24] Log of the *Mary* 19–21 March 1677/8, ADM 51/582.

[25] Laird Clowes, *The Royal Navy*, II, 454.

[26] 19–21 Feb 1678, TNA: ADM 51/690; ADM 106/352 f66; T. Roomcoyle to Adm 29 March 1677/8, ADM 106/338; Log of the *Mary* 19–21 March 1677/8, TNA: ADM 51/582.

[27] F. C. Springell, 'Unpublished Drawings of Tangier by Wenceslaus Hollar', 70.

[28] TNA: ADM 33/110.

[29] B. Lavery, *The Ship of the Line*, I, 34.

[30] Laird Clowes, *The Royal Navy*, II, 454.

[31] Thank you to Peter Le Fevre for this.

[32] TNA: ADM 33/110.

[33] J. Glete, *Navies and Nations: Warships, Navies and State Building in Europe and America, 1500–1860*, I, 187, 199.

[34] J. D. Davies, *Gentlemen and Tarpaulins: The Officers and Men of the Restoration Navy*, 26; Davies, *Pepys's Navy*, 90, 101.

[35] Davies, *Gentlemen and Tarpaulins*, 22, 178–87.

[36] Le Fevre, 'Arthur Herbert, Earl of Torrington, 1648–1716', 21.

[37] Davies, *Gentlemen and Tarpaulins*, 187; Le Fevre, 'Arthur Herbert, Earl of Torrington, 1648–1716', 26.

[38] N. A. M. Rodger, *The Command of the Ocean*, 89.

[39] Rodger, *The Command of the Ocean*, 90.

[40] E. M. G. Routh, 'The English at Tangier', 480.

[41] Teonge, *The Diary of Henry Teonge*, 282, 293; F. Wheler to Adm 13 Oct 1680 TNA: ADM 106/352 f.525.

[42] Fox, *Great Ships*, 151; R. Latham and W. Matthews, eds., *The Diary of Samuel Pepys*, IX, 171, 198, 206; J. R. Tanner, ed., *Samuel Pepys's Naval Minutes*, 203.

[43] F. Wheler to Adm 13 Oct 1680, TNA: ADM 106/352 f.525.

[44] Log of the *Nonsuch* June–August 1679, TNA: ADM 51/3923.

[45] H. Cholmley, *A Short Account of the Progress of the Mole at Tangier, from the first beginning of that work*, 1–7; Davies, *Pepys's Navy*, 196; Hornstein, *The Restoration Navy*, 189; E. M. G. Routh, 'The English Occupation of Tangier (1681–1683)', 66.

[46] See for example Rooke to Adm 7 July 1680/1, TNA: ADM 106/352 f.66.

[47] Le Fevre, 'Arthur Herbert, Earl of Torrington, 1648–1716', 25.

[48] Log of the *Nonsuch* August–October 1679, TNA: ADM 51/3923.

[49] Routh, 'The English at Tangier', 470–1.

[50] Routh, 'The English at Tangier', 471; Teonge, *The Diary of Henry Teonge*, 283–4; TNA: ADM 1/5253 ff.2, 18.

[51] Teonge, *The Diary of Henry Teonge*, 270.

[52] R. C. Holmes, 'Sea Fare', 139, 238.

[53] E. M. G. Routh, *Tangier: England's Lost Atlantic Outpost 1661–1684*, 167, 474–80.

[54] Routh, *Tangier: England's Lost Atlantic Outpost 1661–1684*, 167.

55 H. M. McCance, 'Tangier 1680: The Diary of Sir James Halkett', 6.
56 Routh, *Tangier: England's Lost Atlantic Outpost 1661–1684*, 173, 177–8; A. J. Smithers, *The Tangier Campaign*, 109.
57 Quoted in Routh, *Tangier: England's Lost Atlantic Outpost 1661–1684*, 190.
58 Smithers, *The Tangier Campaign: The Birth of the British Army*, 120.
59 Le Fevre, 'Arthur Herbert, Earl of Torrington, 1648–1716', 23–4.
60 J. Childs, *The Army of Charles II*, 150.
61 Jamieson, 'The Occupation of Tangier', 97.
62 Log of the *Nonsuch* July 1680, TNA: ADM 51/3923.

4. Benbow's Court Martial

1 J. Charnock, *Biographia Navalis*, I, 388.
2 W. Laird Clowes, *The Royal Navy: A History from the Earliest Times to 1900*, II, 452–5.
3 Log of the *Adventure* 27–9 March 1681, TNA: ADM 51/11.
4 P. Earle, *Corsairs of Malta and Barbary*, 59; P. Le Fevre, 'Dispute', 314; HMC Finch II, 108.
5 Log of the *Adventure* 27–9 March 1681, TNA: ADM 51/11; Log of the *Callabash* 28–30 March 1681, TNA: ADM 51/163; Le Fevre, 'Dispute', 313.
6 Log of the *Adventure* 27–9 March 1681, TNA: ADM 51/11; Log of the *Nonsuch* 20 March 1681, TNA: ADM 51/3923.
7 Charnock, *Biographia Navalis*, I, 388; Log of the *Adventure* 27–9 March 1681, TNA: ADM 51/11; Log of the *Centurion* 1 April 1681, TNA: ADM 51/440.
8 Log of the *Centurion* 1 April 1681, TNA: ADM 51/440.
9 Log of the *Centurion* 1 April 1681, TNA: ADM 51/440.
10 Quoted in Le Fevre, 'Dispute', 315.
11 Quoted in Le Fevre, 'Dispute', 316.
12 TNA: ADM 1/5253 f.10.
13 TNA: ADM 33/102.
14 TNA: ADM 1/5253 f.12.
15 Le Fevre, 'Dispute', 315.
16 J. D. Davies, *Gentlemen and Tarpaulins: The Officers and Men of the Restoration Navy*, 186.
17 'The Tangier's Lamentation', W. Chappell, ed., *The Roxburghe Ballads*, 474ff.
18 It is likely that there were thirty-four warships in 1676. Sir John Narbrough captured or otherwise handicapped twelve during his tour before Herbert. *The Restoration Navy and English Foreign Trade, 1674–1688*, 146–7.
19 Hornstein, *The Restoration Navy*, 261.
20 P. Le Fevre, 'Arthur Herbert, Earl of Torrington, 1648–1716', 19.
21 John Ehrman quoted in Le Fevre, 'Arthur Herbert, Earl of Torrington, 1648–1716', 19.

5. Benbow's Corsairs' Heads

1 J. D. Davies, *Gentlemen and Tarpaulins: The Officers and Men of the Restoration Navy*, 239–40.

2 Davies, *Gentlemen and Tarpaulins*, 199.

3 F. Wheler to Navy Board 14 Aug 1681, TNA: ADM 106/358.

4 Log of the *Nonsuch* 31 Aug 1681, TNA: ADM 51/3923; ADM 33/102.

5 The ledgers are now held by the Royal Bank of Scotland archives.

6 R. Davis, 'English Foreign Trade, 1660–1700', 80–93; S. Hornstein, *The Restoration Navy and English Foreign Trade, 1674–1688*, 40–1.

7 Hornstein, *The Restoration Navy*, 50.

8 J. Campbell, 'Benbow (John)…' 154; J. Charnock, *Biographia Navalis*, I, 222.

9 Campbell, 'Benbow (John)…' 154–5; J. K. Laughton, 'Benbow, John (1653–1702)' ODNB (1885).

10 J. B. Blakeway and H. Owen, *A History of Shrewsbury*, 392.

11 Campbell, 'Benbow (John)…' 154–5.

12 S. B. A. Willis, *Fighting at Sea in the Eighteenth Century: The Art of Sailing Warfare*, 17, 148–51.

13 Charnock, *Biographia Navalis*, I, 223.

14 J. R. Tanner, ed., *A descriptive catalogue*, III, xxiv and IV, xx–xxii.

15 TNA: ADM 7/75 ff.55, 77.

16 TNA: ADM 7/76 ff.57, 95, 106, 157, 171.

6. Benbow's Revolution

1 He had been Groom of the Bedchamber possibly from as early as 1681. Thanks to Peter Le Fevre for this.

2 P. Le Fevre, 'Arthur Herbert, Earl of Torrington, 1648–1716', 27.

3 D. Davies, 'James II, William of Orange, and the Admirals', 102; J. D. Davies, *Gentlemen and Tarpaulins: The Officers and Men of the Restoration Navy*, 200–2.

4 Davies, *Gentlemen and Tarpaulins*, 192–5.

5 Prince of Orange to Officers and Seamen of the English Fleet 29 Sept 1688, quoted in J. L. Anderson, 'Prince William's Descent', 51 n.13.

6 The Earls of Danby, Shrewsbury and Devonshire, Viscount Lumley, Admiral Edward Russell, Henry Sydney and the Bishop of London, Henry Compton.

7 Davies, *Gentlemen and Tarpaulins*, 206; J. D. Davies, 'Wishart, Sir James (c.1659–1723)' ODNB (2004).

8 I am indebted to Andrew Little for conducting this research.

9 Constantijn Huygens Jr., *Journaal van 21 october 1688 tot 2 september 1696. Eerste Deel* (Utrecht, 1876), 5;
[http://www.dbnl.org/tekst/huyg007jour02_01/huyg007jour02_01_0002.htm]. ('*2 of 3 Engelsche lootzen*').

10 Gilbert Burnet, *Bishop Burnet's History of His Own Time* (1850), I, 499.

11 G. van Alphen, *De Stemming van de Engelschen tegen de Hollanders in Engeland: tijdens de regeering van den Koning-Stadhouder Willem III, 1688–170*, 11 ('*Engelsche loodsen*').

[12] Davies, *Gentlemen and Tarpaulins*, 206.
[13] Anderson, 'Prince William's Descent', 38.
[14] J. Callow, *The Making of King James II*, 104.
[15] Anderson, 'Prince William's Descent', 50 n.10.
[16] Anderson, 'Prince William's Descent', 50 n.5.
[17] W. Benbow, *Brave Benbow*, 40.

7. Benbow's Battle Fleets

[1] TNA: ADM 33/109.
[2] Log of the *Elizabeth* 9–11 June 1689, TNA: ADM 51/4180.
[3] TNA: ADM 36/4717; ADM 52/123.
[4] Benbow to Navy Board 4 October 1689, TNA: ADM 106/386.
[5] TNA: ADM 33/133; ADM 7/655; ADM 2/4 f.379.
[6] J. K. Laughton, 'Benbow, John (1653–1702)' ODNB (1885). No archival sources have confirmed this absolutely. It is, however, certain that his commission for the *Bonaventure* ended on 12 November 1689, exactly the date stipulated by Laughton, and it is more than likely that the rigorous Laughton was correct with the name of his new ship. TNA: ADM 7/655.
[7] F. Fox, *Great Ships: The Battlefleet of King Charles II*, 170.
[8] J. Ehrman, *The Navy in the War of William III 1689–97*, 36–7.
[9] B. Lavery, *The Ship of the Line*, I, 16.
[10] NMM: CHA/L/1–2; TNA: ADM 1/3760 ff.147–9.
[11] BL Harleian Mss 7476 ff.50–2; Add. 70044 f.101; 70035 ff.111, 115, 119; R. D. Merriman, ed., *The Sergison Papers*, 86–7. The wicked devil 'who had never built a ship in his life' was Robert Lee, the master shipwright at Chatham who Hewer loathed. Pepys also slandered Lee with the false claim that he had never built a ship.
[12] TNA: ADM 33/122; ADM 36/3078; ADM 2/180 f.556.
[13] TNA: ADM 106/2908.
[14] Log of the *Royal Sovereign* April 1690, TNA: ADM 51/4320.
[15] Log of the *Royal Sovereign* May–June 1690, TNA: ADM 51/4320.
[16] Log of the *Royal Sovereign* 22 June 1690, TNA: ADM 51/4320.
[17] G. Symcox, *The Crisis of French Seapower*, 99.
[18] Ehrman, *The Navy in the War of William III*, 344; E. H. Jenkins, *A History of the French Navy*, 75.
[19] Torrington to Nottingham 26 June 1690, quoted in Ehrman, *The Navy in the War of William III*, 345.
[20] Lavery, *The Ship of the Line*, 53.
[21] Anon., *An account given by Sir John Ashby…*, 15.
[22] Anon., *An account given by Sir John Ashby…*, 13.
[23] J. R Bruijn, *The Dutch Navy of the Seventeenth and Eighteenth Centuries*, 94.
[24] NMM: HIS/3; SOU/1.
[25] W. Benbow, *Brave Benbow*, 45.
[26] Anon., *An account given by Sir John Ashby…*, 18; Bruijn, *The Dutch Navy*, 139; C.

D. Lee, 'The Battle of Beachy Head: Lord Torrington's Conduct', 270.

[27] Ehrman, *The Navy in the War of William III*, 354. The original is in BL Add 1152A ff.106–8.

[28] Anon., *An account given by Sir John Ashby…*, 17.

[29] P. Le Fevre, 'Arthur Herbert, Earl of Torrington, 1648–1716', 36.

[30] P. Le Fevre, 'Delavall, Sir Ralph (d.1707)' ODNB.

[31] NMM: SOU/1.

[32] J. J. Keevil, *Medicine and the Navy 1200–1900*, II, 174.

[33] Ehrman, *The Navy in the War of William III*, 354 n.5.

[34] G. Symcox, *The Crisis of French Seapower 1688–1697 from the Guerre D'Escadre to the Guerre de Course*, 108.

[35] J. K. Laughton (anonymously), 'The Battle of La Hougue and Maritime War', 463; N. A. M. Rodger, *The Command of the Ocean*, 146.

[36] TNA: ADM 33/134; ADM 2/7 f.407.

[37] Ehrman, *The Navy in the War of William III*, 379–82; Symcox, *The Crisis of French Seapower*, 113.

[38] Laughton, 'The Battle of La Hougue', 468.

[39] See the numerous letters signed by Benbow (initial JB) in TNA: ADM 106/3290. The direct implication made by Aubrey that Benbow was somehow involved in the movement of ships before the battle (see P. Aubrey, *The Defeat of James Stuart's Armada*, 83.) is misleading. The original document to which he refers, UNSC Portland PWA 1091, makes no reference at all to Benbow.

8. Benbow's Dockyard

[1] TNA: ADM 42/5; TNA: ADM 2/4 f.427.

[2] J. D. Davies, *Pepys's Navy: Ships, Men and Warfare 1649–1689*, 91; N. A. M. Rodger, *The Command of the Ocean*, 119–21.

[3] The large number of naval officers who served as MPs in this period are listed in D. W. Hayton, ed., *The House of Commons 1690–1715*, 720.

[4] This was rare, but Benbow was not alone. See J. Ehrman, *The Navy in the War of William III 1689–97*, 107 n.1.

[5] See for example Sir Richard Beach (d. 1692), Sir John Cox (d. 1672), Sir William Jumper (1660–1713), Sir John Kempthorne (d. 1679) and George St Lo (d. 1718). Many thanks to Peter Le Fevre for help with this.

[6] See for example P. K. Crimmin, 'John Jervis, Earl of St Vincent 1735–1823', 344–7.

[7] TNA: ADM 106/485/244.

[8] See for example James Wilson to Adm, TNA: ADM 106/498/156.

[9] TNA: ADM 49/157; NMM Serg MS A 123.

[10] P. MacDougall, *Royal Dockyards*, 79.

[11] J. Haas, *A Management Odyssey: The Royal Dockyards 1714–1914*, 2.

[12] *Navies and Nations: Warships, Navies and State Building in Europe and America, 1500–1860*, I, 220.

[13] TNA: ADM 7/633. Also see ADM 12/36C under Master Attendant.

[14] NMM: ADM A/1764.

[15] See Chapter 7.

[16] NMM: CHA/L/2.

[17] NMM: CHA/L/1.

[18] Deptford Pay Book, TNA: ADM 42/383; ADM 106/496/238.

[19] Ehrman, *The Navy in the War of William III*, 83, 86–7.

[20] B. Dietz, 'Dikes, Dockheads and Gates: English Docks and Sea Power in the Sixteenth and Seventeenth Centuries', 147.

[21] D. A. Baugh, *British Naval Administration*, 264–6; Davies, *Pepys's Navy*, 180–5; MacDougall, *Royal Dockyards*, 60.

[22] Dietz, 'Dikes, Dockheads and Gates', 145.

[23] Not everyone was so in favour of the wet dock. As an isolated stretch of fresh water it easily froze and Pepys was particularly concerned over the risk of fire caused by so many vessels in close proximity. Davies, *Pepys's Navy*, 181; Dietz, 'Dikes, Dockheads and Gates', 146.

[24] Ehrman, *The Navy in the War of William III*, 103–4.

[25] The letter is reproduced in J. B. Hattendorf et al., eds., *British Naval Documents 1204–1960*, 259–60.

[26] Hattendorf et al., eds., *British Naval Documents*, 261.

[27] B. Lavery, *The Ship of the Line*, I, 163. Four of those eight were built at the Royal Dockyard and four at Edward Snelgrove's private yard in Deptford.

[28] Lavery, *The Ship of the Line*, 57.

[29] Davies, *Pepys's Navy*, 185. Also see ADM 36/C under Tobacco.

[30] TNA: ADM 106/2507 n.102.

[31] TNA: ADM 106/2533; ADM 106/2507; ADM 106/3291; P. Le Fevre, 'Re-Creating a Seventeenth Century Sea Officer', 4.

[32] TNA: ADM 106/484 f.15.

[33] Benbow et al. to Adm 12 October 1691, TNA: ADM 106/3290.

[34] Benbow et al. to Adm 2 October 1691, TNA: ADM 106/3290.

[35] Benbow to Adm 17 Feb 1695/6 TNA: ADM 106/3291.

[36] Benbow to Adm 24 Feb 1695 TNA: ADM 106/481.

[37] Benbow to Adm Aug 1694, 29 May 1695, TNA: ADM 106/3291.

[38] Benbow to Adm March–April 1694, TNA: ADM 106/3291.

[39] TNA: ADM 106/484 ff.1, 21, 85; R. Bourne, *Queen Anne's Navy*, 74; Rodger, *The Command of the Ocean*, 190.

[40] Benbow to Adm 25 June 1694, TNA: ADM 106/3291.

[41] CSP America and West Indies 1700, 359.

[42] R. Haddock to T. Willshaw 10 June 1692, R. D. Merriman, ed., *The Sergison Papers*, 36–7.

[43] Benbow to T. Littleton [Treasurer of the Navy] 7 July 1693, H. Southam, 'Vice-Admiral John Benbow (1653–1702)', viii.

[44] Ehrman, *The Navy in the War of William III*, 98.

[45] J. Haas, 'Work and Authority in the Royal Dockyards from the Seventeenth Century to 1870', 419–21.

9. Benbow's Invasion

[1] J. A. Lawson, 'Naval Policy and Public Opinion in the War of the League of Augsburg 1689–1697', 145.

[2] HMC Finch IV, 287.

[3] Anon., 'Extracts from a Commissioner's Note Book', 186.

[4] HMC Finch IV, 287.

[5] P. Aubrey, *The Defeat of James Stuart's Armada*, 136.

[6] Aubrey, *The Defeat of James Stuart's Armada*, 137.

[7] Finch IV, 243–4, 254, 328.

[8] Finch IV, 357.

[9] Finch IV, 257, 299, 315, 406–7.

[10] Finch IV, 287.

[11] Finch IV, 285.

[12] Anon., 'Extracts from a Commissioner's Note Book', 186, 193; Aubrey, *The Defeat of James Stuart's Armada*, 139; Finch IV, 348.

[13] Anon., 'Extracts from a Commissioner's Note Book', 193; J. Ehrman, *The Navy in the War of William III 1689–97*, 140.

[14] *The Manuscripts of the House of Lords 1692–3*, 198–200; HMC Lords 1692–3, 198–200.

[15] Aubrey, *The Defeat of James Stuart's Armada*, 138; HMC Lords 1692–3 200, 238; Finch IV, 318, 341; TNA: ADM 2/29 ff.439, 465.

[16] CSP Dom 1691/2, 345.

[17] Aubrey, *The Defeat of James Stuart's Armada*, 141.

[18] Ehrman, *The Navy in the War of William III*, 407–8.

[19] Anon., 'Extracts from a Commissioner's Note Book', 191.

[20] C. Rose, *England in the 1690s*, 123–4.

10. Benbow's Nail Bomb

[1] J. Glete, *Navies and Nations: Warships, Navies and State Building in Europe and America, 1500–1860*, I, 221–3; G. Symcox, *The Crisis of French Seapower*, 143–5.

[2] J. S. Bromley, *Corsairs and Navies 1660–1760*, 279.

[3] C. L. Grose, 'England and Dunkirk', 2, 26; G. Symcox, *The Crisis of French Seapower 1688–1697 from the Guerre D'Escadre to the Guerre de Course*, 179–185.

[4] Grose, 'England and Dunkirk', 22–5.

[5] Bromley, *Corsairs and Navies 1660–1760*, 280, 284.

[6] N. A. M. Rodger, *The Command of the Ocean*, 158; G. N. Clark, *The Dutch Alliance*, 126; R. P. Crowhurst, 'The Defence of British Trade', 16–19; F. A. Johnston, 'Parliament and the Protection of Trade 1689–1694', 404.

[7] Johnston, 'Parliament and the Protection of Trade', 409.

[8] A. Pearsall, 'The Royal Navy and the Protection of Trade in the Eighteenth Century', 150, 156; Symcox, *The Crisis of French Seapower*, 170.

[9] E. H. Jenkins, *A History of the French Navy*, 89.

[10] For more on this see M. S. Anderson, *War and Society*, 135ff.; J. Black, *A Military Revolution? Military Change and European Society 1550–1800*, 44ff.

[11] C. Ware, *The Bomb Vessel: Shore Bombardment Ships of the Age of Sail*, 10.
[12] S. Martin-Leake, *The Life of Admiral Sir John Leake*, 23 n.2.
[13] HMC Finch IV, 434.
[14] The four largest of 20–7 cwt, one 8-cwt stream anchor and a 4-cwt kedge. A typical First Rate, by contrast, might have as many as nine: five big ones (the smallest maybe 56 cwt and the largest almost 70 cwt), two much smaller stream anchors of about 10 and 20 cwt and two little kedges of commonly 3 and 6 cwt. Thanks to Frank Fox for this.
[15] CSP Dom 1693, 291.
[16] E. W. H. Fyers, 'The Story of the Machine Vessels', 51–5; P. Kirsch, *Fireship*, 192.
[17] Crowhurst, 'The Defence of British Trade', 25.
[18] CSP Dom 1693, 330.
[19] Log of the *Norwich* 17 Nov 1693, TNA: ADM 51/3926.
[20] J. Campbell, 'Benbow (John)…', 155; Fyers, 'The Story of the Machine Vessels', 63; *London Gazette* 2926, 27 Nov 1693, 2.
[21] Log of the *Norwich* 17 Nov 1693, TNA: ADM 51/3926; Fyers, 'The Story of the Machine Vessels', 63–6; Thomas Philips ODNB (2004).
[22] Fyers, 'The Story of the Machine Vessels', 64; N. Luttrell, *A Brief Historical Relation of State Affairs from September 1678 to April 1714*, III, 234.
[23] *London Gazetteer* 26 Nov 1693; Fyers, 'The Story of the Machine Vessels', 64–5.
[24] 29 Dec 1693, TNA: ADM 3/9; ADM 2/385.
[25] TNA: ADM 1/5254 ff.116–17.
[26] Luttrell, *A Brief Historical Relation*, III, 234.
[27] E. S. De Beer, ed., *The Diary of John Evelyn*, 160.
[28] CSP Dom 1693, 424; CSP 1694–5, 356.
[29] Log of the *Norwich* 17 Nov 1693, TNA: ADM 51/3926; Ware, *The Bomb Vessel*, 27–8.
[30] TNA: WO 46/3 f.55; TNA: ADM 3/0.
[31] Ware, *The Bomb Vessel*, 25, 88. Benbow was then Master Attendant at Deptford. For more on his role there, see Chapter 8.
[32] Ware, *The Bomb Vessel*, 14, 90.
[33] TNA: WO 46/3.
[34] Ware, *The Bomb Vessel*, 88; TNA: WO 46/3.

11. Benbow's Bombardments

[1] N. Luttrell, *A Brief Historical Relation of State Affairs from September 1678 to April 1714*, III, 238, 246.
[2] W. Laird Clowes, *The Royal Navy A History from the Earliest Times to 1900*, II, 481 n.2.
[3] Anon., 'Extracts from a Commissioner's Note Book', 202–4; Laird Clowes, *The Royal Navy*, II, 465–6; G. Symcox, *The Crisis of French Seapower*, 152.
[4] CSP Dom 1694, 229.
[5] J. Charnock, *Biographia Navalis*, 124*; CSP Dom 1694, 223.
[6] CSP Dom 1694, 229.

[7] For more on this see M. S. Anderson, *War and Society in Europe of the Old Regime*, 135ff.; J. Black, *A Military Revolution? Military Change and European Society 1550–1800*, 44ff.

[8] E. W. H. Fyers, 'The Story of the Machine Vessels', 69; Laird Clowes, *The Royal Navy*, II, 477.

[9] R. P. Crowhurst, 'The Defence of British Trade 1689–1815', 27.

[10] CSP Dom 1694–5, 229.

[11] Laird Clowes, *The Royal Navy*, II, 477.

[12] CSP Dom 1694–5, 241, 254.

[13] Luttrell, *A Brief Historical Relation*, III, 352.

[14] See for example BL Kings Mss 53, 'Project for surprising Dunkirk harbour c.1695'.

[15] CSP Dom 1694–5, 283.

[16] A. Badin, *Jean Bart*, 127; CSP Dom 1694–5, 283, 290.

[17] CSP Dom 1694–5, 284.

[18] CSP Dom 1694–5, 284; Fyers, 'The Story of the Machine Vessels', 73; J. A. Lawson, 'Naval Policy and Public Opinion in the War of the League of Augsburg 1689–1697', 204.

[19] CSP Dom 1694–5, 284, 304, 305.

[20] Fyers, 'The Story of the Machine Vessels', 75.

[21] CSP Dom 1694–5, 305; Fyers, 'The Story of the Machine Vessels', 75–6; Badin, *Jean Bart*, 127–8.

[22] Fyers, 'The Story of the Machine Vessels', 77.

[23] Fyers, 'The Story of the Machine Vessels', 76.

[24] Berkeley to Shrewsbury 8 Aug 1695, HMC Buccleuch II (1), 212–13.

[25] Fyers, 'The Story of the Machine Vessels', 78.

[26] CSP Dom 1694–5, 240.

[27] C. Ware, *The Bomb Vessel: Shore Bombardment Ships of the Age of Sail*, 16, 84, 90.

[28] CSP Dom 1694–5, 311.

[29] HMC Portland X, 18.

[30] CSP Dom Jul–Dec 1695, 316.

[31] W. Benbow, *Brave Benbow*, 53; Luttrell, *A Brief Historical Relation*, III, 452, 473.

[32] Luttrell, *A Brief Historical Relation*, III, 478; 10 June 1695, TNA: ADM 3/12.

[33] CSP Dom Jul–Dec 1695, 3, 7; CSP Dom 1694–5, 495–6 .

[34] 28 June 1695, TNA: ADM 3/12; ADM 33/180 f.19.

[35] CSP Dom Jul–Dec 1695, 7.

[36] CSP Dom Jul–Dec 1695, 7.

[37] *London Gazette* 22 July 1695, 1–2; BL Add. 21494 ff.33, 93; Log of the *Charles Galley* June–July 1695, TNA: ADM 51/4142; CSP Dom Jul–Dec 1695, 6–8.

[38] CSP Dom Jul–Dec 1695, 26, 27, 31.

[39] CSP Dom Jul–Dec 1695, 25.

[40] CSP Dom Jul–Dec 1695, 49.

[41] CSP Dom Jul–Dec 1695, 15, 51, 57; 12 Sept 1695, TNA: ADM 3/12.

[42] CSP Dom Jul–Dec 1695, 13.

[43] TNA: ADM 2/176 f.119.

[44] TNA: ADM 2/176 f.49.

[45] J. B. Hattendorf et al., eds., *British Naval Documents 1204–1960*, 229.

[46] Benbow, *Brave Benbow*, 58; TNA: ADM 106/494/253.

[47] J. Black, ed., *European Warfare 1453–1815*, 45, 69.

[48] F. Tallett, *War and Society in Early-Modern Europe, 1495–1715*, 244.

[49] HMC Finch IV, 350; N. A. M. Rodger, *The Command of the Ocean*, 156.

[50] H.W. Richmond, *The Navy as an Instrument of Policy: 1558–1727*, 254.

12. Benbow's Convoys

[1] HMC Lords VIII, 58.

[2] R. G. Marsden, ed., *Documents Relating to Law and Custom of the Sea. Vol. 2: 1649–1767*, 220–1; A. Pearsall, 'The Royal Navy and the Protection of Trade in the Eighteenth Century', 149–62.

[3] CSP Dom Jul–Dec 1695, 66; N. Luttrell, *A Brief Historical Relation of State Affairs from September 1678 to April 1714*, IV, 3–5; CSP Dom 1696, 302; TNA: ADM 106/492/377; ADM 106/489/145; ADM 106/493/115; Luttrell, *A Brief Historical Relation*, IV, 116.

[4] Luttrell, *A Brief Historical Relation*, IV, 31, 61; CSP Dom 1697, 166, 174, 206, 228.

[5] CSP Dom 1696, 315, 330, 336.

[6] J. S. Bromley, *Corsairs and Navies 1660–1760*, 62; Luttrell, *A Brief Historical Relation*, IV, 108, 269–70.

[7] Pearsall, 'The Royal Navy and the Protection of Trade in the Eighteenth Century', 152. Also see William Wetstone ODNB (2004).

[8] Bromley, *Corsairs and Navies 1660–1760*, 79. The church of St Eloi is now the location of Jean Bart's tomb, but the original tower has since been separated from the church by a street.

[9] NMM: MRF/153; CSP Dom 1696, 177–9, 227; J. A. Lawson, 'Naval Policy and Public Opinion in the War of the League of Augsburg 1689–1697', 238–9.

[10] Bromley, *Corsairs and Navies 1660–1760*, 81; E. H. Jenkins, *A History of the French Navy*, 90; CSP Dom 1696, 292–3, 299; TNA: ADM 106/482/193.

[11] NMM: MS 80/179.

[12] NMM: MS 80/179.

[13] CSP Dom 1696, 396–7.

[14] CSP Dom 1697, 335, 364.

[15] TNA: ADM 106/488/166.

[16] TNA: ADM 106/482/194; CSP Dom 1697, 335, 364.

[17] TNA: ADM 106/498/262.

[18] TNA: ADM 106/482/96.

[19] Bromley, *Corsairs and Navies 1660–1760*, 60, 80.

[20] CSP Dom 1697, 158; Bromley, *Corsairs and Navies 1660–1760*, 60; TNA: ADM 106/493/118.

[21] CSP Dom 1697, 336.

[22] D. K. Brown, 'The Speed of Sailing Warships 1793–1840', 162.

23 TNA: ADM 106/491/377; E. F. MacPike, ed., *Correspondence and Papers of Edmond Halley*, 106.

24 Bromley, *Corsairs and Navies 1660–1760*, 63.

25 NMM: AGC 1/13; R. Endsor, *The Restoration Warship: The Design, Construction and Career of a Third Rate of Charles II's Navy*, 222.

26 M. Duffy, 'The Establishment of the Western Squadron as the Linchpin of British Naval Strategy', 62–3.

27 Benbow to Adm 9 April 1697, TNA: ADM 106/500.

28 Endsor, *Restoration Warship*, 223; Luttrell, *A Brief Historical Relation*, IV, 25.

29 CSP Dom 1697, 156, 247; Log of the *Torbay* 5 July 1697 ADM 51/4373; Log of the *Monmouth* 27 July 1697, ADM 51/4264.

30 CSP Dom 1697, 440, 441.

13. Benbow's Benevolence

1 W. R. Chaplin, *The Corporation of Trinity House of Deptford Strond from the Year 1660*, 56–64; G. G. Harris, *The Trinity House of Deptford 1514–1660*, 72.

2 GL: MS 30324.

3 Harris, *The Trinity House of Deptford*, 74.

4 GL: MS 300047 f.274; MS 30307.

5 Harris, *The Trinity House of Deptford*, 47.

6 R. Latham and W. Matthews, eds., *The Diary of Samuel Pepys*, IV, 185–7.

7 J. Finglas, *A Sermon preached at Deptford before the Brethren of Trinity House of Deptford Strond: On Trinity Monday, being the day of their annual election of a new master and wardens*.

8 TNA: 1/5253 f.211; ADM 106/483/254.

9 GL: MS 300047 f.289.

10 There are endless examples, but see Hunter to Navy Board 14 Aug 1694, TNA: ADM 106/450; Hunter to Navy Board 30 April 1692 and 3 Feb 1691/2, ADM 106/420. For one with particular relevance to Benbow see TNA: ADM 106/492/377.

11 GL: MS 300047 f.289.

12 GL: MS 300047 f.289.

13 GL: MS 300047 f.289.

14 TNA: ADM 106/495/94, 213.

15 There are some nice images of the Dover proposals in TNA: ADM 1/3584.

16 HMC Lords 1697–9, 213–14; for more on the Aire and Calder Navigation, see L. T. C. Rolt, *Navigable Waterways*, 17–19. and J. Priestley, *Historical Account of the Navigable Rivers, Canals, and Railways of Great Britain…*, 5–18.

17 D. Ogg, *England in the Reign of Charles II*, I, 255.

18 Harris, *The Trinity House of Deptford*, 213.

19 GL: MS 300047 f.285, 288.

20 GL: MS 300047 f.281.

21 GL: MS 300047 f.275.

22 John Fox to Trinity House 23 Jan 1692/3, HMC Finch V, 25.

[23] GL: MS 300047 f.279.

[24] Harris, *The Trinity House of Deptford*, 154.

[25] Harris, *The Trinity House of Deptford*, 167; ADM 2/170 f.296; ADM 106/489/132.

[26] See for example TNA: ADM 106/495/50.

[27] G. G. Harris, ed., *Trinity House of Deptford Transactions 1609–35*, xiii, 160.

[28] GL: MS 300047 f.286.

[29] LRRO: NM 29.

[30] GL: MS 300047 f.292.

[31] N. A. M. Rodger, *The Command of the Ocean*, 206.

[32] GL: MS 300047 f.293.

[33] Rodger, *The Command of the Ocean*, 206–10.

[34] HMC Lords 1693–1695, 390.

[35] J. Ehrman, *The Navy in the War of William III 1689–97*, 131 and n.4.

[36] HMC Lords 1693–1695, 576.

[37] B. R. Leftwich, *The Church and Parish of St. Nicholas, Deptford: The Building and its Associations with the Royal Navy*, 203.

[38] GL: MS 300047 f.285.

[39] GL: MS 300047 f.286; MS 30209.

[40] W. Besant, *The World Went Very Well Then*, 21.

[41] Harris, *The Trinity House of Deptford*, 254. For ransom see Harris, ed., *Trinity House of Deptford Transactions*, 43 n.158.

[42] GL: MS 300047 f.286. The original site of Christ's Hospital was in Newgate, London, and not Horsham, West Sussex, where it is now.

[43] Harris, *The Trinity House of Deptford*, 258.

[44] HMC Finch V, 825.

14. Benbow's Hospital

[1] J. D. Davies, *Pepys's Navy: Ships, Men and Warfare 1649–1689*, 166.

[2] P. Aubrey, *The Defeat of James Stuart's Armada*, 80.

[3] Davies, *Pepys's Navy*, 165.

[4] N. A. M. Rodger, *The Command of the Ocean*, 161.

[5] J. Ehrman, *The Navy in the War of William III 1689–97*, 124.

[6] Davies, *Pepys's Navy*, 166; Ehrman, *The Navy in the War of William III*, 125; R. D. Merriman, ed., *Queen Anne's Navy: Documents Concerning the Administration of the Navy of Queen Anne 1702–14*, 220.

[7] Ehrman, *The Navy in the War of William III*, 126.

[8] J. J. Sutherland Shaw, 'The Hospital Ship 1608–1740', 425.

[9] Sutherland Shaw, 'The Hospital Ship 1608–1740', 422.

[10] Merriman, ed., *Queen Anne's Navy*, 235 and n.1.

[11] Anon., *An Account of the late great victory*, 11; Davies, *Pepys's Navy*, 167.

[12] Ehrman, *The Navy in the War of William III*, 441; Merriman, ed., *Queen Anne's Navy*, 217–18.

[13] Ehrman, *The Navy in the War of William III*, 441–3; P. Newell, *Greenwich Hospital*, 12.

[14] Ehrman, *The Navy in the War of William III*, 444. This was not as random an appointment as it may first appear. He had already served on the commission for the sick and wounded in both the Second and Third Anglo-Dutch Wars (1664–7, 1672–4), an appointment which took up a great deal of his time and energy. He had already proposed a pet project for a seaman's hospital of his own. G. Darley, *John Evelyn: Living for Ingenuity*, xi; P. Newell, *Greenwich Hospital: A Royal Foundation 1692–1983*, 8.

[15] J. Bold, 'Comparable Institutions: The Royal Hospital for Seamen and the Hôtel des Invalides', 136; Ehrman, *The Navy in the War of William III*, 444.

[16] E. S. De Beer, ed., *The Diary of John Evelyn*, 106.

[17] K. Downes, *The Architecture of Wren*, 109.

[18] Bold, 'Comparable Institutions', 137.

[19] Bold, 'Comparable Institutions', 136.

[20] Bold, 'Comparable Institutions', 140.

[21] TNA: ADM 67/1.

[22] TNA: ADM 80/2.

[23] 6 Dec 1696, ADM 106/490/195; A. Forbes, 'Greenwich Hospital Money', 519.

[24] Forbes, 'Greenwich Hospital Money', 519.

[25] TNA: ADM 106/483/232, 246, 281.

[26] TNA: ADM 106/490/195; ADM 106/494/92.

[27] Forbes, 'Greenwich Hospital Money', 519, 526.

[28] TNA: ADM 67/2 f.25; Newell, *Greenwich Hospital*, 18.

[29] TNA: ADM 67/2 f.8, 16, 19, 62; Newell, *Greenwich Hospital*, 20–1.

[30] J. Bold, *Greenwich: An Architectural History of the Royal Hospital for Seamen and the Queen's House*, 108.

[31] J. Summerson, *Architecture in Britain 1530–1830*, 274–5.

[32] Ehrman, *The Navy in the War of William III*, 445; Merriman, ed., *Queen Anne's Navy*, 218–19, 236; Rodger, *The Command of the Ocean*, 195.

[33] Bold, 'Comparable Institutions', 141–4.

[34] Downes, *The Architecture of Wren*, 110.

[35] Summerson, *Architecture in Britain*, 274–5.

[36] W. Besant, *The World Went Very Well Then*, 21.

[37] J. Campbell, 'Benbow (John)…', 156 n.C.

[38] Anon., 'Advice from England', 81.

[39] W. Benbow, *Brave Benbow*, 64.

[40] Sutherland Shaw, 'The Hospital Ship 1608–1740', 425. Also see p. 285.

[41] Newell, *Greenwich Hospital*, 3.

15. Benbow's House

[1] William Wright to Adm 13 June 1696, TNA: ADM 106/498/193.

[2] Surveyor to Adm 18 Aug 1692, TNA: ADM 106/2507.

[3] William Wright to Adm 13 June 1696, TNA: ADM 106/498/193; TNA: ADM 4/383.

[4] J. Haswell, *The Ardent Queen: Margaret of Anjou and the Lancastrian Heritage*, 55.

5 P. Leith-Ross, 'The Garden of John Evelyn at Deptford', 27.

6 Leith-Ross, 'The Garden of John Evelyn at Deptford', 27.

7 G. Darley, *John Evelyn: Living for Ingenuity*, xii; T. O'Malley and J. Wolschke-Bulmahn, eds., *John Evelyn's 'Elysium Britannicum' and European Gardening*, 131.

8 N. Dews, *The History of Deptford in the Counties of Kent and Surrey*, 32.

9 E. S. De Beer, ed., *The Diary of John Evelyn*, 244.

10 P. H. Goodchild, '"No Phantasticall Utopia, but a Reall Place". John Evelyn, John Beale and Backbury Hill, Herefordshire', 106.

11 P. Leith-Ross, 'A Seventeenth-Century Paris Garden', 143, 147, 156; P. J. Tarvis, 'Seventeenth-Century Cedars', 43–4.

12 Leith-Ross, 'The Garden of John Evelyn at Deptford', 147.

13 A. Smith, 'John Evelyn's Manuscript on Bees from Elysium Britannicum', 119; P. Walker and E. Crane, 'The History of Beekeeping in English Gardens', 232, 240–50.

14 Leith-Ross, 'The Garden of John Evelyn at Deptford', 147. For the poem see E. Grosart (ed.) *Abraham Cowley: Complete Works...*, II, 243–58.

15 W. Besant, *The World Went Very Well Then*, 25.

16 Besant, *The World Went Very Well Then*, 18–19.

17 J. Bowle, *John Evelyn and his World: A Biography*, 92.

18 Bowle, *John Evelyn and his World*, 219–20.

19 A. De Jonge, *Fire and Water: A Life of Peter the Great*, 77, 81; L. Hughes, *Peter the Great: A Biography*, 126; O'Malley and Wolschke-Bulmahn, eds., *John Evelyn's 'Elysium Britannicum'*, 153; K. Waliszewski, *Peter the Great*, 122.

20 De Jonge, *Fire and Water*, 82, 87.

21 Hughes, *Peter the Great: A Biography*, 53.

22 A. Cross, *Peter the Great Through British Eyes: Perceptions and Representations of the Tsar Since 1698*, 26; De Jonge, *Fire and Water*, 118; L. Loewenson, 'Some Details of Peter the Great's Stay in England in 1698: Neglected English Material', 434.

23 J. Appleby, 'The Founding of St Petersburg in the Context of the Royal Society's Relationship with Russia', 275; Dews, *The History of Deptford*, 33; Loewenson, 'Some Details of Peter the Great's Stay in England', 432; De Beer, ed., *The Diary of John Evelyn*, V, 284; CSP Dom 1698, 78.

24 Cross, *Peter the Great Through British Eyes*, 33.

25 Appleby, 'The Founding of St Petersburg', 275.

26 L. Loewenson, 'People Peter the Great Met in England. Moses Stringer, Chymist and Physician', 461.

27 De Beer, ed., *The Diary of John Evelyn*, 284 n.5.

28 The fact that Wren was sent to survey Sayes Court further strengthens the case that Benbow and Wren were acquainted, having also worked together on the Greenwich Hospital project.

29 *Notes and Queries* 2nd Ser. I (1856), 365–7; CTP 1607–1702, 158–9; CTB 1697–8, 325, 360.

30 De Beer, ed., *The Diary of John Evelyn*, 290.

31 Dews, *The History of Deptford*, 32–3; M. K. Schuchard, *Restoring the Temple of Vision*, 754. This apocryphal quote is corrupted from Evelyn's *Sylva*. The original, published thirty-two years before Peter's visit, has of course no reference to Peter, but the rest is verbatim, including the reference to 'hedge-breakers'. See J. Evelyn, *Sylva*, 66.

32 Cross, *Peter the Great Through British Eyes*, 25.

33 Dews, *The History of Deptford*, 39–40; B. R. Leftwich, *The Church and Parish of St. Nicholas, Deptford: The Building and its Associations with the Royal Navy*, 197.

16. Benbow's Caribbean

1 TNA: ADM 1/5257, 63, 90, 99, 107.

2 TNA: ADM 1/5257, 113; ADM 1/5260, 233.

3 TNA: ADM 1/5257, 113; ADM 1/5260, 233.

4 NMM: PLA/23.

5 TNA: ADM 1/5260, 231; ADM 1/5262 part II, 174, 207; part III, 370.

6 TNA: ADM 1/5257, 162; ADM 1/5258, 1; ADM 1/5262 part II, 176, 265, 270, 272; part III, 372.

7 TNA: ADM 1/5262 part III, 368.

8 TNA: ADM 1/5261; ADM 1/5262 part II, 169.

9 R. E. Glass, 'Naval Courts Martial in Seventeenth Century England', 58–62.

10 HMC Cowper II, 431.

11 W. G. Bassett, 'English Naval Policy in the Caribbean: 1698–1703', 122.

12 Benbow to Adm 14 Nov 1698, TNA: ADM 106/515.

13 See p. 100.

14 TNA: ADM 1/3584; ADM 2/178 f.485.

15 E. F. MacPike, ed., *Correspondence and Papers of Edmond Halley*, 243.

16 N. Thrower, ed., *The Three Voyages of Edmond Halley in the Paramore*, 36.

17 J. Appleby, 'The Founding of St Petersburg in the Context of the Royal Society's Relationship with Russia', 274; A. Armitage, *Edmond Halley*, 138; A. Cook, 'Halley the Londoner', 171–5.

18 MacPike, ed., *Correspondence and Papers of Edmond Halley*, 105.

19 See for example N. Moses, 'The British Navy in the Caribbean 1689–97', 30.

20 TNA: ADM 33/206 f.10.

21 CSP Dom 1699–1700, 187.

22 CSP America and West Indies 1699, 56, 512; CSP Dom 1699–1700, 284.

23 Benbow to Adm 18 August 1699, TNA: ADM 106/525; CSP Col 1702, 216–17. For more on pressing in the Caribbean in this period, see R. Pares, 'The Manning of the Navy in the West Indies', 41–2.

24 Benbow to Adm. 18 August 1699, TNA: ADM 106/525.

25 C. Nettels, 'British Payments in the American Colonies', 236 n.1.

26 TNA: ADM 2/179 f.92.

27 CSP Col 1700, 18.

28 CSP Col 1699, 401.

29 CSP Col 1699, 492.

30 CSP America and West Indies 1699, 512.

31 CSP America and West Indies 1700, 18.

32 CSP America and West Indies 1699, 512.

33 Benbow to Adm 18 August 1699, TNA: ADM 106/525.

34 Benbow to Adm 8 Jan 1699, TNA: ADM 106/533.

35 TNA: ADM 52/39.

36 This all comes from 'A collection of memorandum & remarks on a voyage to the West Indies on board of his majesties ship *Gloucester* under command of Rear-Admirall Benbow by Robert Thompson master of ye said ship anno domini 1698/9', TNA: ADM 7/833.

37 Benbow knew Peru as the north coast of modern Venezuela and Colombia: the southern coast of the Caribbean Sea.

38 NMM: PLA/23.

39 CSP America and West Indies 1699, 56; NMM: PLA/23.

40 NMM: PLA/23.

41 J. H. Burton, ed., *The Darien Papers: Being a selection of original letters and official documents relating to the establishment of a Colony at Darien by the Company of Scotland trading to Africa and the Indies, 1695–1700*, 102–3.

42 J. Prebble, *The Darien Disaster*, 180; NMM: PLA/23.

43 Prebble, *The Darien Disaster*, 223.

44 NMM: PLA/23.

45 21 June 1699, TNA: ADM 3/13; C. Rose, *England in the 1690s*, 239.

46 NMM: PLA/23.

47 W. H. Bonner, 'Clamors and False Stories – The Reputation of Captain Kidd', 179; R. C. Ritchie, *Captain Kidd and the War against the Pirates*, 2.

48 CSP America and West Indies 1700, 196.

49 G. Brooks, ed., *Trial of Captain Kidd*, 27; Ritchie, *Captain Kidd*, 165.

50 CSP Col 1699, 503; Brooks, ed., *Trial of Captain Kidd*, 27–8; Ritchie, *Captain Kidd*, 165.

51 CSP America and West Indies 1699, 276.

52 Brooks, ed., *Trial of Captain Kidd*, 38.

53 Bonner, 'Clamors and False Stories', 195ff.; D. Cordingly, *Life Among the Pirates: The Romance and Reality*, 222.

54 CSP America and West Indies 1700, 279; TNA: ADM 51/401; TNA: ADM 52/39.

55 Brooks, ed., *Trial of Captain Kidd*, 200–1.

56 Ritchie, *Captain Kidd*, 192–3, 198–9, 230–1; ADM to Privy Council 2 Dec 1699, TNA: ADM 7/335.

57 N. Luttrell, *A Brief Historical Relation of State Affairs from September 1678 to April 1714*, IV, 663.

58 D. Cordingly, 'Avery, Henry (*bap.* 1659–1696?)' ODNB (2004).

59 CSP America and West Indies 1700, 269.

60 CSP America and West Indies 1700, 269, 278–9; Ritchie, *Captain Kidd*, 207.

61 CSP Dom 1700–2, 76–7; T. B. Howell, ed., *A Complete Collection of State Trials*,

XIV, 123–234; Ritchie, *Captain Kidd*, 228.
[62] TNA: ADM 67/3 f. 59, 80, 84, 100, 169; CSP DOM 1700–2, 324.
[63] CSP Col 1701, 13–14, 52.
[64] CSP Col 1701, 52.
[65] CSP Col 1701, 52.
[66] CSP Col 1701, 13–14.
[67] Bassett, 'English Naval Policy in the Caribbean', 123.
[68] W. Benbow, *Brave Benbow*, 79.
[69] CSP America and West Indies 1699, 37.
[70] Burton, ed., *The Darien Papers*, 81–4. He was probably Richard Long. See J. Charnock, *Biographia Navalis*, III, 167, 345.

17. Benbow's Last Fight

[1] Benbow to Adm 2 April 1701; 2 May 1701; 29 May 1701, TNA: ADM 106/541.
[2] TNA: ADM 2/27; J. J. Keevil, *Medicine and the Navy 1200–1900*, II, 253; R. D. Merriman, ed., *The Sergison Papers*, 221.
[3] M. Stringer, *Variety of Surprising Experiments...*, 1–2, 8, 12.
[4] J. Woodward, *The Seaman's Monitor...*
[5] G. Taylor, *The Sea Chaplains: A History of the Chaplains of the Royal Navy*, 118–19.
[6] Benbow to Adm 2 and 5 May 1701; 16 June 1701, TNA: ADM 106/541; ADM 2/181 f.130.
[7] TNA: ADM 2/181 f.173.
[8] See the numerous intelligence reports in TNA: ADM 1/3930.
[9] CSP Dom 1700–2, 407–8.
[10] CSP Dom 1700–2, 392, 403, 429; CSP Col 1701, 494, 590.
[11] J. B. Hattendorf, *England in the War of the Spanish Succession: A Study of the English View and Conduct of Grand Strategy 1702–12*, 57–8; CSP Dom 1700–2, 521–2.
[12] Benbow to Vernon 5 Dec 1701, TNA: SP 42/67/10; CSP Dom 1700–2, 464; CSP Col 1701, 602.
[13] CSP Dom 1700–2, 464, 473; N. A. M. Rodger, *The Command of the Ocean*, 165.
[14] CSP Col 1701, 752–3.
[15] CSP Doc 1702–3, 89, 175–6; Burchett to Newcastle 12 July 1702, TNA: SP 42/6/115.
[16] CSP Dom 1702–3, 175.
[17] Rodger, *The Command of the Ocean*, 165–6.
[18] CSP Dom 1700–2, 473. Benbow had taken Cockbourn's medicine with him on his previous Caribbean tour. TNA: 2/179 f.84.
[19] Keevil, *Medicine and the Navy*, II, 290.
[20] CSP Dom 1702–3, 176. Also see p. 188.
[21] CSP Col 1702, 218; CSP Dom 1702–3, 147.
[22] Benbow to Adm 7 Jan 1702, TNA: ADM 106/553.
[23] Quoted in W. Benbow, *Brave Benbow*, 94.
[24] R. F. Marx, *Port Royal Rediscovered*, 2.
[25] R. Bourne, *Queen Anne's Navy in the West Indies*, 36.

[26] Bourne, *Queen Anne's Navy in the West Indies*, 216.

[27] Benbow to Adm 14 April 1702, TNA: ADM 106/553; CSP DOM 1700–2, 473.

[28] CSP Col 1702, 368.

[29] CSP Dom 1700–2, 431–2.

[30] Rodger, *The Command of the Ocean*, 165.

[31] CSP Dom 1702–3, 92–3. Also see p. 132.

[32] J. B. Hattendorf, 'Benbow's Last Fight', 146.

[33] E. H. Jenkins, *A History of the French Navy*, 95.

[34] He had been this way on his espionage trip of 1699. See Chapter 16.

[35] Hattendorf, 'Benbow's Last Fight', 147.

[36] Hattendorf, 'Benbow's Last Fight', 156.

[37] ADM 1/5263 f.44.

[38] Hattendorf, 'Benbow's Last Fight', 171.

[39] CSP Col 1702, 579–80.

[40] Hattendorf, 'Benbow's Last Fight', 176.

[41] CSP Col 1702.

[42] J. K. Laughton, 'Benbow, John (1653–1702)' ODNB (1885); C. Hunt, ed., *Unpublished Letters from the Collection of John Wild*, 21.

[43] Hattendorf, 'Benbow's Last Fight', 162.

[44] Hattendorf, 'Benbow's Last Fight', 151, 157–8, 162, 173.

[45] Benbow, *Brave Benbow*, 152–4; Hattendorf, 'Benbow's Last Fight', 197.

[46] *Naval Chronicle* 35 (1816), 209.

[47] ADM 1/5263 ff.109, 137.

[48] 5 Jan 1702, ADM 1/4088.

[49] 23 Jan 1703, TNA: PRO, SP 44/209.

[50] TNA: ADM 52/340; N. Luttrell, *A Brief Historical Relation of State Affairs from September 1678 to April 1714*, V, 266. There is some suggestion his body was later removed and he was buried in Deptford. Benbow, *Brave Benbow*, 179.

[51] R. E. Glass, 'Naval Courts Martial in Seventeenth Century England', 58–63.

[52] Hattendorf, 'Benbow's Last Fight', 199.

[53] Thanks to Peter Le Fevre for this.

[54] Hattendorf, 'Benbow's Last Fight', 191–2.

[55] TNA: ADM 1/5263 ff.28, 102.

[56] Hattendorf, 'Benbow's Last Fight', 172.

[57] Hattendorf, 'Benbow's Last Fight', 192.

[58] Hattendorf, 'Benbow's Last Fight', 199.

[59] Hattendorf, 'Benbow's Last Fight', 154.

[60] Hattendorf, 'Benbow's Last Fight', 158, 161.

[61] R. Du Casse, *L'Amiral du Casse*, 257–61; Hattendorf, 'Benbow's Last Fight', 155.

[62] Hattendorf, 'Benbow's Last Fight', 160–1.

[63] M. Duffy, '…All was Hushed Up'.

[64] S. B. A. Willis, *Fighting at Sea in the Eighteenth Century: The Art of Sailing Warfare*, 62.

[65] Hattendorf, 'Benbow's Last Fight', 176.

[66] CSP Dom 1700–02, 229.

[67] W. Laird Clowes, *The Royal Navy: Navy A History from the Earliest Times to 1900*, II, 503.

[68] Bourne, *Queen Anne's Navy in the West Indies*, 15.

[69] Hattendorf, *England in the War of the Spanish Succession*, 209–11; F. O'Gorman, *The Long Eighteenth Century*, 45–6.

[70] Laird Clowes, *The Royal Navy*, II, 501.

[71] J. D. Davies, *Pepys's Navy: Ships, Men and Warfare 1649–1689*, 160–1.

[72] Glass, 'Naval Courts Martial', 59.

[73] See p. [add page ref in present book].

[74] J. Campbell, *Lives of British Admirals*, 331.

[75] R. Park, *Defensive War by Sea*, 123.

[76] Anon. 'Admiral John Benbow', 169.

[77] G. A. R. Callender and C. J. Britton, 'Admiral Benbow Fact and Fiction II', 212.

[78] R. E. Glass, 'The Image of the Sea Officer in English Literature', 586–9; Rodger, *The Command of the Ocean*, 159, 183.

[79] For a good collection of contemporary published trials, see BL 515 L 6.

[80] B. Clarke, *From Grub Street to Fleet Street: An Illustrated History of English Newspapers*, 26.

[81] Clarke, *From Grub Street to Fleet Street*, 9.

[82] Anon., *An Account of the Transaction between Admiral Benbow and Monsieur Du Casse* (1705).

[83] Anon., ed., *The Harleian Miscellany*, 395–401.

[84] A. Lambert, *The Foundations of Naval History: John Knox Laughton, the Royal Navy and the Historical Profession*, 114.

[85] J. Campbell, 'Benbow (John)…' 166.

[86] Anon., 'Admiral John Benbow', 169.

[87] E. Letley, ed., *Treasure Island*, vii–viii.

[88] This list is by no means exhaustive. A. E. Aspinall, *West Indian Tales of Old*; J. Barnett, *Fighting Admirals*; G. A. R. Callender, *Sea Kings of Britain*; E. Giffard, *Deeds of Naval Daring*; B. E. Robinson, ed., *Britain's Sea Kings and Sea Fights*; A. Temple, *Kings of the Quarter Deck*.

[89] H. T. Mason, ed., *Pour encourager les autres: Studies for the Tercentenary of Voltaire's Birth, 1694–1994*.

Epilogue: Benbow's Celebrity

[1] *Admiral Benbow* as Sung by Mr Bannister with Universal Applause at the Royal Theatre. NMM: F4920.

[2] Benbow to Navy Board 7 March 1696, TNA: ADM 106/500.

[3] TNA: ADM 1/5149.

[4] CSP Dom 1694–5, 486.

[5] R. Park, *Defensive War by Sea*, 123.

[6] J. Campbell, *Lives of British Admirals*, 331.

[7] J. Campbell, 'Benbow (John)'…, 157.

8 Anon., 'Advice from England', 81.
9 N. Luttrell, *A Brief Historical Relation of State Affairs from September 1678 to April 1714*, V, 236.
10 J. Haas, 'Work and Authority in the Royal Dockyards from the Seventeenth Century to 1870', 419.
11 For a contemporary opinion, see Anon., 'Advice from England', 81.

Appendix II: Benbow's Warships
1 TNA: ADM 33/206 f.33.
2 TNA: ADM 33/194; ADM 33/197.
3 R. Endsor, 'The Van de Velde Paintings for the Royal Yacht *Charlotte*, 1677', 264–75.

Appendix III: Benbow's Songs
1 J. Canning, ed., *Strange Mysteries From the Sea*, 445–55.

Appendix IV: Benbow's Fruit Trees
1 This list is taken from BL Add. Mss 78628 B.

BIBLIOGRAPHY

Abbreviations:
AL – Admiralty Library, Portsmouth
BL – British Library
CSP Col – Calendar of State Papers Colonial
CSP Dom – Calendar of State Papers Domestic
CTP – Calendar of Treasury Papers
CTB – Calendar of Treasury Books
GL – Guildhall Library
HMC – Historical Manuscripts Commission
LRO – Lichfield Record Office
LRRO – Leicester and Rutland Record Office
NMM – The National Maritime Museum, Greenwich
NRS – Navy Records Society
ODNB – Oxford Dictionary of National Biography
SPCK – Society for the Promotion of Christian Knowledge
TNA – The National Archives
UNSC – University of Nottingham Special Collections

Anderson, J. L. 'Prince William's Descent Upon Devon, 1688: The Environmental Constraints', in *Lisbon as a Port Town: The British Seaman and Other Maritime Themes*, edited by S. Fisher (Exeter, 1988), 37–56.

Anderson, M. S. *War and Society in Europe of the Old Regime* (London, 1988).

Anderson, R. C. *Naval Wars in the Levant 1559–1853* (Liverpool, 1952).

Anon. *An account given by Sir John Ashby, vice-admiral and rear-admiral Rooke to the lords commissioners of the engagement at sea between the English, Dutch and French fleet...* (London, 1691).

———. *An Account of the late great victory, obtained at sea, against the French by Their Majesties fleet, commanded in chief by Admiral Russell, and the Dutch commanded by Admiral Allemond, near the Cape of Barsteur in May, 1692* (London, 1692).

———. 'Admiral John Benbow', *Naval Chronicle* XX (1808), 169–92.

———. 'Letter of a Royalist Giving an Account of the Battle of Worcester', *Chetham Society* 67 (1867), 337–9.

———. *A List of Officers Claiming to the Sixty Thousand Pounds, &c. Granted by His Sacred Majesty for the Relief of His Truly-Loyal and Indigent Party* (London, 1663).

———. 'The official record of the proceedings of the court martial appointed by Oliver Cromwell for the execution of the earl of Derby', *Chetham Society* 67 (1867), 334–57.

———, ed. *The Harleian Miscellany* (London, 1808).

———. 'Advice from England.' *The Present State of Europe or the Historical and Political Mercury...* (1703), 81–4.

———. *Mercurius Politicus* no. 66 (4–11 September 1651), 1055.

Appleby, J. 'The Founding of St Petersburg in the Context of the Royal Society's Relationship with Russia', *Notes and Records of the Royal Society of London* 57, no. 3 (2003), 273–84.

Armitage, A. *Edmond Halley* (London, 1966).

Ashley, M. *The English Civil War: A Concise History* (London, 1974).

Aspinall, A. E. *West Indian Tales of Old* (London, 1912).

Atkin, M. *Worcester: 1651* (Barnsley, 2008).

Aubrey, P. *The Defeat of James Stuart's Armada* (Leicester, 1979).

Auden, J. E. 'Shropshire and the Royalist Conspiracies between the end of the first Civil War and the Restoration', *Transactions of the Shropshire Archaeological and Natural History Society* 10 (1910), 106–32.

Aylmer, G. E. 'Slavery under Charles II: The Mediterranean and Tangier', *English Historical Review* 115, no. 456 (1999), 378–88.

Badin, A. *Jean Bart* (Paris, 1867).

Barnett, J. *Fighting Admirals* (London, 1910).

Bassett, W. G. 'English Naval Policy in the Caribbean: 1698–1703', *Bulletin of the Institute of Historical Research* XI (1933), 122–5.

Baugh, D. A. *British Naval Administration in the Age of Walpole* (Princeton, 1965).

Benbow, W. *Brave Benbow* (Victoria, BC, 1992).

Besant, W. *The World Went Very Well Then* (London, 1891).

Black, J. *A Military Revolution? Military Change and European Society 1550–1800* (London, 1991).

———, ed. *European Warfare 1453–1815* (London, 1999).

Blakeway, J. B. and H. Owen. *A History of Shrewsbury.* Vol. II (London, 1825).

Blunt, W. *Black Sunrise* (London, 1951).

Bold, J. 'Comparable Institutions: The Royal Hospital for Seamen and the Hôtel des Invalides', *Architectural History* 44 (2001), 136–44.

———. *Greenwich: An Architectural History of the Royal Hospital for Seamen and the Queen's House* (New Haven, 2000).

Bondy, A. 'The Barbary Regencies and Corsair Activity in the Mediterranean from the Sixteenth to the Nineteenth Century: From the Community of Origin to Evolutionary Divergence', *Journal of Mediterranean Studies* 12, no. 2 (2002), 241–8.

Bonner, W. H. 'Clamors and False Stories – The Reputation of Captain Kidd', *The New England Quarterly* 17, no. 2 (1944), 179–208.

Bourne, R. *Queen Anne's Navy in the West Indies* (New Haven, 1939).

Bowle, J. *John Evelyn and his World: A Biography* (London, 1981).

Brahms, C., and N. Sherrin. *Benbow Was His Name* (London, 1967).

Bromley, J. S. *Corsairs and Navies 1660–1760* (London, 1987).

Brooks, G., ed. *Trial of Captain Kidd* (Edinburgh and London, 1930).

Brown, D. K. 'The Speed of Sailing Warships 1793–1840', in *Les Empires en Guerre et Paix 1793–1860*, edited by E. Freeman (Vincennes, 1990), 155–94.

Bruijn, J. R. *The Dutch Navy of the Seventeenth and Eighteenth Centuries* (Columbia, SC, 1993).

Burnet, G. *Bishop Burnet's History of His Own Time*, Vol. I (London, 1850).

Burton, J. H., ed. *The Darien Papers: Being a selection of original letters and official documents relating to the establishment of a Colony at Darien by the*

Company of Scotland trading to Africa and the Indies, 1695–1700 (Edinburgh, 1849).

Callender, G. A. R. *Sea Kings of Britain* (London, 1911).

Callender, G. A. R., and C. J. Britton 'Admiral Benbow Fact and Fiction II', *Mariner's Mirror* 30 (1944), no. 4, 200–19.

Callow, J. *The Making of King James II* (London, 2000).

Campbell, J. 'Benbow (John)...', in *Biographia Britannica; or, the lives of the most eminent persons who have flourished in Great Britain and Ireland*, edited by A. Kippis (London, 1778–93), 154–7.

———. *Lives of British Admirals*. 4 vols. Vol. 3 (London, 1779).

Canning, J., ed. *Strange Mysteries from the Sea* (London, 1979).

Carlton, C. *Going to the Wars: The Experience of the British Civil Wars, 1638–51* (London, 1994).

Chaplin, W. R. *The Corporation of Trinity House of Deptford Strond from the Year 1660* (London, 1950).

Chappell, W., ed. *The Roxburghe Ballads*. Vol. V (New York, 1966).

Charnock, J. *Biographia Navalis*. 6 vols. (London, 1794–8).

Childs, J. *The Army of Charles II* (London, 1976).

Cholmley, H. *A Short Account of the Progress of the Mole at Tangier, from the first beginning of that work* (London, 1680).

Clark, G. N. *The Dutch Alliance and the War Against French Trade 1688–97* (Manchester, 1923).

Clarke, B. *From Grub Street to Fleet Street: An Illustrated History of English Newspapers* (London, Ashgate, 2004).

Cook, A. 'Halley the Londoner', *Notes and Records of the Royal Society of London* 47, no. 2 (1993), 163–77.

Cordingly, D. *Life Among the Pirates: The Romance and Reality* (London, 1995).

Crimmin, P. K. 'John Jervis, Earl of St Vincent 1735–1823', in *Precursors of Nelson: British Admirals of the Eighteenth Century*, edited by P. Le Fevre and R. Harding (London, 2000), 325–52.

Cross, A. *Peter the Great Through British Eyes: Perceptions and Representations of the Tsar Since 1698* (Cambridge, 2000).

Crowhurst, R. P. *The Defence of British Trade 1689–1815* (Folkestone, 1977).

Darley, G. *John Evelyn: Living for Ingenuity* (London, 2006).

Davies, D. 'James II, William of Orange, and the Admirals', in *By Force or By Default? The Revolution of 1688–1689*, edited by E. Cruickshanks (Edinburgh, 1989), 82–108.

Davies, J. D. *Gentlemen and Tarpaulins: The Officers and Men of the Restoration Navy* (Oxford, 1991).

———. *Pepys's Navy: Ships, Men and Warfare 1649–1689* (Barnsley, 2008).

Davis, R. 'English Foreign Trade, 1660–1700', in *The Growth of English Overseas Trade in the 17th and 18th Centuries*, edited by W. E. Minchinton (Bungay, 1969), 78–98.

De Beer, E. S. *The Diary of John Evelyn*. Vol. III (Oxford, 1955).

———, ed. *The Diary of John Evelyn*. Vol. V (London, 1959).

De Jonge, A. *Fire and Water: A Life of Peter the Great* (London, 1979).

Dews, N. *The History of Deptford in the Counties of Kent and Surrey* (London, 1971).

Dietz, B. 'Dikes, Dockheads and Gates: English Docks and Sea Power in the Sixteenth and Seventeenth Centuries', *Mariner's Mirror* 88 (2002), no. 2, 144–54.

Donagan, B. 'Prisoners in the English Civil War', *History Today* 41 (1991), 28–41.

———. 'Varieties of Royalism', in *Royalists and Royalism During the English Civil Wars*, edited by J. McElligott and D. L. Smith (Cambridge, 2007), 66–88.

———. 'War Crime and Treason in the English Civil War', *American Historical Review* 99, no. 4 (1994), 1137–66.

Downes, K. *The Architecture of Wren* (London, 1982).

Du Casse, R. *L'Amiral du Casse* (Paris, 1876).

Duffy, M. '...All was Hushed Up: The Hidden Trafalgar', *Mariner's Mirror* 91 (2005), no. 2, 216–40.

———. 'The Establishment of the Western Squadron as the Linchpin of British Naval Strategy', in *Parameters of British Naval Power 1650–1850*, edited by M. Duffy (Exeter, 1992), 60–81.

Dyer, F. E. 'The Journal of Grenvill Collins', *Mariner's Mirror* 14 (1928), no. 3, 197–219.

Earle, P. *Corsairs of Malta and Barbary* (London, 1970).

———. *The Pirate Wars* (London, 2004).

Ehrman, J. *The Navy in the War of William III 1689–97: Its State and Direction* (Cambridge, 1953).

Endsor, R. 'The Van de Velde Paintings for the Royal Yacht *Charlotte*, 1677', *Mariner's Mirror* 94 (2008), no. 3, 264–75.

——. *The Restoration Warship: The Design, Construction and Career of a Third Rate of Charles II's Navy* (London, 2009).

Evelyn, J. *Sylva* (London, 1664).

Farr, G. 'Severn Navigation and the Trow', *Mariner's Mirror* 32 (1946), no. 1, 66–95.

Fiennes, C. *The Journeys of Celia Fiennes*, edited by C. Morris (1947).

Finglas, J. *A Sermon preached at Deptford before the Brethren of Trinity House of Deptford Strond: On Trinity Monday, being the day of their annual election of a new master and wardens* (London, 1695).

Forbes, A. 'Greenwich Hospital Money', *The New England Quarterly* 3, no. 3 (1930), 519–26.

Fox, F. *Great Ships: The Battlefleet of King Charles II* (London, 1980).

Fyers, E. W. H. 'The Story of the Machine Vessels', *Mariner's Mirror* 11 (1925), no. 1, 50–91.

Giffard, E. *Deeds of Naval Daring* (London, 1910).

Glass, R. E. 'The Image of the Sea Officer in English Literature, 1660–1710', *Albion* 26 (1994), 583–99.

——. 'Naval Courts Martial in Seventeenth Century England', in *New Interpretations in Naval History: Selected papers from the twelfth naval history symposium*, edited by W. B. Cogar (Annapolis, 1997), 53–65.

Glete, J. *Navies and Nations: Warships, Navies and State Building in Europe and America, 1500–1860.* Vol. I (Stockholm, 1993).

Goodchild, P. H. '"No Phantasticall Utopia, but a Reall Place". John Evelyn, John Beale and Backbury Hill, Herefordshire', *Garden History* 19, no. 2 (1991), 105–27.

Grose, C. L. 'England and Dunkirk', *The American Historical Review* 39, no. 1 (1933), 1–27.

Grosart, A. B., ed. *Abraham Cowley: The Complete Works in Verse and Prose*, 2 vols. (Olms, 1969).

Haas, J. *A Management Odyssey: The Royal Dockyards 1714–1914* (London, 1994).

————. 'Work and Authority in the Royal Dockyards from the Seventeenth Century to 1870', *Proceedings of the American Philosophical Society* 124, no. 6 (1980), 419–28.

Harris, G. G. *The Trinity House of Deptford 1514–1660* (London, 1969).

————, ed. *Trinity House of Deptford Transactions, 1609–35* (London, 1983).

Haswell, J. *The Ardent Queen: Margaret of Anjou and the Lancastrian Heritage* (London, 1976).

Hattendorf, J. B. 'Sir George Rooke and Sir Cloudesley Shovell, c1650–1709 and 1650–1707', in *Precursors of Nelson: British Admirals of the Eighteenth Century*, edited by P. Le Fevre and R. Harding (London, 2000), 43–78.

————. 'Benbow's Last Fight', in *Naval Miscellany V*, edited by N. A. M. Rodger (Aldershot: NRS Vol. 125, 1984), 143–206.

————. *England in the War of the Spanish Succession: A Study of the English View and Conduct of Grand Strategy 1702–12* (Aldershot: NRS Vol. 125, 1984).

Hattendorf, J. B., R. J. B. Knight, A. W. H. Pearsall, N. A. M. Rodger, and G. Till, eds. *British Naval Documents 1204–1960* (Aldershot: NRS Vol. 131, 1993).

Hayton, D. W., ed. *The House of Commons 1690–1715.* Vol. I (Cambridge, 2002).

Heath-Agnew, E. *Roundhead to Royalist: A Biography of Colonel Birch 1615–1691* (Hereford, 1977).

Heath, J. *A Chronicle of the Late Intestine War in the Three Kingdoms...* (London, 1676).

Holmes, R. C. 'Sea Fare', *Mariner's Mirror* 35 (1949), no. 2, 139–45.

Hornstein, S. *The Restoration Navy and English Foreign Trade, 1674–1688* (Aldershot, 1991).

Howell, T. B., ed. *A Complete Collection of State Trials: and proceedings for high treason and other crimes and misdemeanors from the earliest period to the year 1783.* 34 vols. (London, 1814–28).

Hughes, L. *Peter the Great: A Biography* (London, 2002).

Hunt, C., ed. *Unpublished Letters from the Collection of John Wild* (London, 1930).

Hutton, R., and W. Reeves 'Sieges and Fortifications', in *The Civil Wars: A Military History of England, Scotland, and Ireland 1638–1660*, edited by J. Kenyon, J. Ohlmeyer and J. S. Morrill (Oxford, 1998), 195–233.

Inwood, S. *A History of London* (London, 1998).

Jamieson, A. G. 'The Occupation of Tangier and Its Relation to English Naval Policy in the Mediterranean', MA thesis (Newcastle, 1960).

Jenkins, E. H. *A History of the French Navy* (London, 1973).

Johnston, F. A. 'Parliament and the Protection of Trade, 1689–1694', *Mariner's Mirror* 57 (1971), no. 4, 399–413.

Jones, D. *A Compleat History of Europe for the Year 1702* (London, 1703).

Keevil, J. J. *Medicine and the Navy 1200–1900*. Vol. 2: 1649–1714 (Edinburgh and London, 1958).

Kempthorne, G. A. 'Sir John Kempthorne and His Sons', *Mariner's Mirror* 12 (1926), no. 3, 289–317.

Kirsch, P. *Fireship: The Terror Weapon of the Age of Sail* (Barnsley, 2009).

Laird Clowes, W. *The Royal Navy: A History from the Earliest Times to 1900*, 7 vols. Vol. II (London, 1996).

Lambert, A. *The Foundations of Naval History: John Knox Laughton, the Royal Navy and the Historical Profession* (London, 1998).

Latham, R., and W. Matthews, eds. *The Diary of Samuel Pepys*. 11 vols. (London, 1971–83).

Laughton, J. K. 'Extracts from a Commissioner's Note Book, Annis 1691–4', in *The Naval Miscellany II* (London: NRS Vol. 40, 1912), 137–205.

———. 'Benbow, John (1653–1702)' ODNB (1885).

——— (anonymously). 'The Battle of La Hougue and Maritime War', *Quarterly Review* 176 (1893), 461–89.

Lavery, B. *The Ship of the Line*. Vol. I (London, 1983).

Lawson, J. A. 'Naval Policy and Public Opinion in the War of the League of Augsburg 1689–1697', MA thesis (Leeds, 1952).

Le Fevre, P. 'The Dispute over the Golden Horse of Algiers', *Mariner's Mirror* 73 (1987), no. 3, 313–17.

———. 'John Tyrell (1646–1692): A Restoration Naval Captain', *Mariner's Mirror* 70 (1984), no. 2, 149–60.

———. 'Re-Creating a Seventeenth Century Sea Officer', *Journal for*

Maritime Research, May 2001 (2001).

———. 'Arthur Herbert, Earl of Torrington, 1648–1716', in *Precursors of Nelson: British Admirals of the Eighteenth Century*, edited by P. Le Fevre and R. Harding (London, 2000), 19–42.

Lee, C. D. 'The Battle of Beachy Head: Lord Torrington's Conduct', *Mariner's Mirror* 80 (1994), no. 3, 270–89.

Leftwich, B. R. *The Church and Parish of St. Nicholas, Deptford: The Building and its Associations with the Royal Navy* (London, 1945).

Leith-Ross, P. 'The Garden of John Evelyn at Deptford', *Garden History* 25, no. 2 (1997), 138–52.

———. 'A Seventeenth-Century Paris Garden', *Garden History* 21, no. 2 (1993), 150–7.

Letley, E., ed. *Treasure Island* (Oxford, 1998).

Loewenson, L. 'People Peter the Great Met in England. Moses Stringer, Chymist and Physician', *Slavonic and East European Review* 37, no. 89 (1959), 459–68.

———. 'Some Details of Peter the Great's Stay in England in 1698: Neglected English Material', *Slavonic and East European Review* 40, no. 95 (1962), 431–43.

Love, R. 'Captain John Benbow – Shrewsbury Civil War Hero', *Shropshire Magazine* (1970), 22–3.

Luttrell, N. *A Brief Historical Relation of State Affairs from September 1678 to April 1714*. 6 vols. (Oxford, 1974).

McCance, H. M. 'Tangier 1680: The Diary of Sir James Halkett', *Journal of the Society for Army Historical Research* 1 (1922).

MacDougall, P. *Royal Dockyards* (Newton Abbot, 1982).

MacPike, E. F., ed. *Correspondence and Papers of Edmond Halley* (London, 1937).

The Manuscripts of the House of Lords 1692–3 (London, HMC 14th Report Appendix VI, 1894).

Marsden, R. G., ed. *Documents Relating to Law and Custom of the Sea. Vol. 2: 1649–1767* (London: NRS Vol. 49, 1916).

Martin-Leake, S. *The Life of Admiral Sir John Leake*, edited by G. A. R. Callender. Vol. I (London: NRS Vol. 52, 1920).

Marx, R. F. *Port Royal Rediscovered* (London, 1973).

Mason, H. T., ed. *Pour encourager les autres: Studies for the Tercentenary of Voltaire's Birth, 1694–1994* (Oxford, 1994).

Matar, N. *Britain and Barbary, 1589–1689* (Gainesville, 2005).

Matthews, W., ed. *Charles II's Escape from Worcester: A Collection of Narratives Assembled by Samuel Pepys* (Berkeley, 1966).

Merriman, R. D., ed. *Queen Anne's Navy: Documents Concerning the Administration of the Navy of Queen Anne 1702–14* (London: NRS Vol. 103, 1961).

———, ed. *The Sergison Papers* (London, 1950).

Milton, G. *White Gold* (London, 2004).

Morrill, J. S. *The Revolt of the Provinces: Conservatives and Radicals in the English Civil War* (London, 1980).

Moses, N. 'The British Navy in the Caribbean 1689–1697', *Mariner's Mirror* 52 (1966), no. 1, 13–40.

Nettels, C. 'British Payments in the American Colonies, 1685–1715', *English Historical Review* 48, no. 190 (1933), 229–49.

Newell, P. *Greenwich Hospital: A Royal Foundation 1692–1983* (London, 1984).

O'Gorman, F. *The Long Eighteenth Century: British Political and Social History 1688–1832* (London, 1997).

O'Malley, T., and J. Wolschke-Bulmahn, eds. *John Evelyn's 'Elysium Britannicum' and European Gardening* (Washington DC, 1998).

Ogg, D. *England in the Reign of Charles II*. Vol. 1 (Oxford, 1934).

Pares, R. 'The Manning of the Navy in the West Indies, 1702–63', *Transactions of the Royal Historical Society* 20, 4th series (1937), 31–60.

Park, R. *Defensive War by Sea* (London, 1704).

Pearsall, A. 'The Royal Navy and the Protection of Trade in the Eighteenth Century', in *Guerres et Paix 1660–1815* (Vincennes, 1987), 149–62.

Prebble, J. *The Darien Disaster* (London, 1968).

Priestley, J. *Historical Account of the Navigable Rivers, Canals, and Railways of Great Britain...* (London, 1831).

Richmond, H. W. *The Navy as an Instrument of Policy: 1558–1727* (Cambridge, 1953).

Ritchie, R. C. *Captain Kidd and the War against the Pirates* (Harvard, 1986).

Robinson, B. E., ed. *Britain's Sea Kings and Sea Fights* (London, 1900).

Rodger, N. A. M. *The Command of the Ocean: A Naval History of Britain 1649–1815.* Vol. 2 (London, 2004).

———. *The Safeguard of the Sea: A Naval History of Britain. Vol. 1, 660–1649* (London, 1997).

Rogers, H. C. B. *Battles and Generals of the Civil Wars* (London, 1968).

Rolt, L. T. C. *Navigable Waterways* (London, 1969).

Rose, C. *England in the 1690s* (Oxford, 1999).

Routh, E. M. G. 'The English at Tangier', *English Historical Review* 26, no. 103 (1911), 469–81.

———. 'The English Occupation of Tangier (1661–1683)', *Transactions of the Royal Historical Society* 19 (1905), 61–78.

———. *Tangier: England's Lost Atlantic Outpost 1661–1684* (London, 1912).

Schuchard, M. K. *Restoring the Temple of Vision* (Leiden, 2002).

Smith, A. 'John Evelyn's Manuscript on Bees from Elysium Britannicum', *Bee World*, no. 46 (1965), 116–23.

Smith, S. R. 'The London Apprentices as Seventeenth-Century Adolescents', *Past and Present* 61 (1973), 149–61.

Smithers, A. J. *The Tangier Campaign: The Birth of the British Army* (Stroud, 2003).

Southam, H. 'Vice-Admiral John Benbow (1653–1702)', *Transactions of the Shropshire Archaeological Society* V (1693), vii–viii.

Springell, F. C. 'Unpublished Drawings of Tangier by Wenceslaus Hollar', *The Burlington Magazine* 106, no. 731 (1964), 69–74.

Stringer, M. *Variety of Surprising Experiments…* (London, 1703).

Styles, P. 'The City of Worcester During the Civil Wars, 1640–60', in *The English Civil Wars: Local Aspects*, edited by R. C. Richardson (Stroud, 1997), 187–238.

Summerson, J. *Architecture in Britain 1530–1830* (New Haven, 1993).

Sutherland Shaw, J. J. 'The Hospital Ship 1608–1740', *Mariner's Mirror* 22 (1936), no. 4, 422–6.

Symcox, G. *The Crisis of French Seapower 1688–1697 from the Guerre D'Escadre to the Guerre de Course* (The Hague, 1974).

Tallett, F. *War and Society in Early-Modern Europe, 1495–1715* (London, 1992).

Tanner, J. R., ed. *A descriptive catalogue of the naval manuscripts in the Pepysian library at Magdalene College, Cambridge.* Vol. 3 (London: NRS Vol. 36, 1909).

———, ed. *A descriptive catalogue of the naval manuscripts in the Pepysian library at Magdalene College, Cambridge.* Vol. 4 (London: NRS Vol. 57, 1923).

———, ed. *Samuel Pepys's Naval Minutes* (London: NRS Vol. 60, 1926).

Tarvis, P. J. 'Seventeenth-Century Cedars', *Garden History* 4, no. 2 (1976), 43–6.

Taylor, G. *The Sea Chaplains: A History of the Chaplains of the Royal Navy* (Oxford, 1978).

Temple, A. *Kings of the Quarter Deck* (London, 1905).

Teonge, H. *The Diary of Henry Teonge* (London, 1825).

Thrower, N., ed. *The Three Voyages of Edmond Halley in the Paramore*, Hakluyt Society Series II, no. 156 (London, 1981).

Trinder, B. *Barges and Bargemen: A Social History of the Severn Navigation 1660–1900* (Bodmin, 2005).

———. *The Industrial Archaeology of Shropshire* (Frome, 1996).

Trinder, B., and N. Cox, eds. *Miners and Mariners of the Severn Gorge: Probate Inventories for Benthall, Broseley, Little Wenlock and Madeley 1660–1764* (Trowbridge, 2000).

Van Alphen, G. *De Stemming van de Engelschen tegen de Hollanders in Engeland: tijdens de regeering van den Koning-Stadhouder Willem III, 1688-1702* (Assen, 1938).

Waliszewski, K. *Peter the Great* (London, 1898).

Walker, P., and E. Crane 'The History of Beekeeping in English Gardens', *Garden History* 28, no. 2 (2000), 231–61.

Wanklyn, M. 'The Severn Navigation of the Seventeenth Century: Long-Distance Trade of Shrewsbury Boats', *Midland History* 13 (1988), 34–57.

Ware, C. *The Bomb Vessel: Shore Bombardment Ships of the Age of Sail* (London, 1994).

Warmington, A. *Civil War, Interregnum and Restoration in Gloucestershire*

1640–1672 (Woodbridge, 1997).

Willan, T. S. 'The River Navigation and Trade of the Severn Valley, 1600–1750', *Economic History Review* 8, no. 1 (1937), 68–79.

——. *River Navigation in England 1600–1750* (Oxford, 1936).

Willis, S. B. A. *Fighting at Sea in the Eighteenth Century: The Art of Sailing Warfare* (Woodbridge, 2008).

Woodward, J. *The Seaman's Monitor...* (London, 1705).

Woof, R. 'The Personal Expenses of Charles II in the City of Worcester', *Transactions of the Royal Historical Society* 1 (1872), 34–53.

Young, P., ed. *The Royal Martyrs: A facsimile reprint from the original in the author's collection* (London, 1983).

INDEX

Clerk of the Ropeyard 121
Clerk of the Survey 121, 127
Coale, Thomas 204
Cochrane, Thomas 83, 228
Cockburn, Dr 213, 284
Colbert 48
Collingwood, Cuthbert 228
Collins, Grenville 194
Columbus, Christopher 20
Commonwealth 23–5
Congreve, William
  Love for Love 18
Constable, Captain John 295, 300,
  301
Cook, James 20, 30, 228, 255
Cornwall 328
Cornwallis, Lord 153
Coronation 113
corsairs *see* Barbary corsairs/pirates
courts martial 251, 253
Cowley, Abraham 235
Cromwell, Oliver xxvii, xxix, 3, 6, 7–8,
  23, 24, 26, 32, 148
Cromwell, Richard xxix, 245
Crow, Benjamin 180–1
Cutts, John 280

Daily Courant 306
D'Anjou, Duc of 279
Darien colony 259, 264–5, 266, 269
Dartmouth, Admiral Lord 88
Dauphin Royal 107
De Ruyter, Admiral Michiel 20
De Say, Geoffrey 231
Deane, Sir Anthony 37–8, 46, 53, 130,
  194
'Death of Admiral Benbow, The' 349,
  350–1
Defiance 284, 290, 291, 298, 301
Delavall, Admiral Ralph 104, 119, 302
Den Briel 90, 95
Deptford 212
Deptford Dockyard 114, 124–8, 193,
  229–30, 235
  becomes central warehouse for Royal
  Navy 125–6

Benbow as Master Attendant at 124,
  130–2
building of new warships 129
comparison with Chatham 124
focusing on smaller warships 124, 125
location 125, 126
Master Attendant post 127
officers' houses and facilities 229–30
officers' pay 127
reputation of 126–7
wet dock 126
working conditions 130–1
Deptford Ketch 37
Derby, Earl of 6, 10–11, 12
Derwenter, Earl of 221
desertion 251–2
Devonshire 328
Dieppe
  bombardment raid on (1694) 164–5
diseases, suffered by sailors 212
Dolphin 265
Drake, Francis 20, 227
Dreadful 172
du Casse, Rear-Admiral Jean 286, 287,
  294, 301, 317
Duchess 102
Duke 329, 344, *344*
Dummer, Edward 151
Dunkirk (ship) 334
Dunkirk 142–3, 148, 152, 153, 179
  blockading of (1696) 183, 341
  raid on (1694) 166–8
  raid on (1696) 175
Dutch Wars 17, 24, 25, 31, 47

East India Company 181, 221
Eddystone lighthouse 200–2
Eldridge, John 272
Elizabeth 99, 333, *333*, 335
Elliot, Stephen 301
English Civil War xxviii–xxix, 3–10, 16,
  24, 313
Evans, David 272
Evelyn, John xxx, 158, 176, 211, 216, 236
  A Character of England 236
  and damage caused to Sayes Court